(Re)Framing College Access
by and with Communities of Color

SUNY series, Critical Race Studies in Education

Derrick R. Brooms, editor

(Re)Framing College Access by and with Communities of Color

Our Knowledge, Our Process, Our Choice

Edited by

CHRYSTAL A. GEORGE MWANGI AND
YEDALIS RUÍZ SANTANA

Foreword by

JUDY MARQUEZ KIYAMA

SUNY
PRESS

Cover art by Kaleighia Green

Published by State University of New York Press, Albany

© 2025 State University of New York

All rights reserved

Printed in the United States of America

Links to third-party websites are provided as a convenience and for informational purposes only. They do not constitute an endorsement or an approval of any of the products, services, or opinions of the organization, companies, or individuals. SUNY Press bears no responsibility for the accuracy, legality, or content of a URL, the external website, or for that of subsequent websites.

EU GPSR Authorised Representative:
Logos Europe, 9 rue Nicolas Poussin, 17000, La Rochelle, France
contact@logoseurope.eu

For information, contact State University of New York Press, Albany, NY
www.sunypress.edu

Library of Congress Cataloging-in-Publication Data

Names: Mwangi, Chrystal A. George, editor. | Ruíz Santana, Yedalis A.,
    1976– editor.
Title: (Re)framing college access by and with communities of color : Our knowledge,
    our process, our choice / edited by Chrystal A. George Mwangi and Yedalis A. Ruíz
    Santana ; foreword by Judy Marquez Kiyama.
Description: Albany : State University of New York Press, [2025] | Series:
    SUNY series: Critical Race Studies in Education / Derrick R. Brooms,
    editor | Includes bibliographical references and index.
Identifiers: LCCN 2024042769 | ISBN 9798855801941 (hardcover : alk. paper) |
    ISBN 9798855801958 (ebook) | ISBN 9798855801934 (pbk. : alk. paper)
Subjects: LCSH: College choice—United States. | Universities and colleges—
    United States—Admission. | Minorities—Education (Higher)—United States. | People
    with social disabilities—Education (Higher)—United States. | College costs—
    United States. | College attendance—Social aspects—United States. | Educational
    attainment—United States. | Educational equalization—United States.
Classification: LCC LB2350.5 O87 2025 | DDC 378.1/61080973—dc23/eng/20241106
LC record available at https://lccn.loc.gov/2024042769

To my father, Gilbert, for modeling that college was possible, and to my mother, Annunciata, for making sure college was a reality for me. And to Alex, my husband, for providing the foundation that empowered access to my PhD journey. I wouldn't have any of these degrees without my family.

—Chrystal

Le dedico este libro a la niña que aspiro y logró cuando le dijeron que no era posible.

To my mother, Carmen Julia Santana, and my father, Rubén Ruíz, who believed in my strength to persevere, loved and cared for me, and gave me my culture y mi lengua Puertorriqueña.

And to my beautiful partner of 25 years, Cristina: You bore witness to my journey and I wouldn't be here today without you.

—Yedalis

Contents

Foreword

JUDY MARQUEZ KIYAMA

"How did you learn about college?" "Who or what first introduced you to the idea of college?" I have had the privilege of teaching a graduate-level, higher education course on the topic of College Access multiple times during my career as a professor. I've posed some iteration of these two questions to open the course each time. Likewise, I've used them in workshops with other faculty and staff, particularly when introducing the theoretical and pedagogical concept of funds of knowledge (Gonzalez, et al., 2005; Moll, et al., 1992). The questions are inspired by my own very first doctoral course that I took with Dr. Jenny Lee (University of Arizona) on the topic of college access over 20 years ago! She posed similar questions to our class, and I continue to use them because they open up a space for conversation and community building that is informed by students' home, cultural, community, and historical knowledges and experiences. What emerges are beautifully rich introductions that illustrate students' educational journeys, the important role parents, families, friends, and mentors played, linguistic capital (Yosso, 2005), and yes, sometimes the more challenging experiences that demonstrate how students have navigated long-standing structural and systemic barriers.

When I began reading through Chrystal and Yedalis' beautifully edited book, *(Re)Framing College Access by and with Communities of Color: Our Knowledge, Our Process, Our Choice*, I quickly realized they, along with all of the chapter authors, have gifted us with a collection of culturally affirming and rich responses to the questions posed earlier, to the college access journeys of communities of Color. Writing this foreword was an honored invitation to witness the theoretically, culturally, and community-engaged (re)telling of foundational college access knowledge. This collection of authors pushes us to clearly see that "foundation knowledge" *is* our community, home, and cultural knowledge. I encourage readers to pay as much attention to the journey and praxis narratives as they would to the statistics, previous literature, and theories. For it is precisely our journey and praxis narratives that prepare us for this work, that guide our research and practice, and serve as a centering purpose for how we engage in and (re)shape educational spaces.

Just as Chrystal and Yedalis describe their collaborations as a process of "co-creating community with students of Color" (p. 00), this assemblage of chapters is also a co-creation of community with and for and by scholars of Color. Again, I encourage readers to move with intention into this community space of co-creation, and as you do, hold your own college access stories, journeys, and cultural knowledge at the center. Find the connections among the narratives and literature offered here, sit with the questions that may emerge as points of divergence, and recognize that the students in your classes and programs, particularly those from minoritized backgrounds and communities of Color, hold a wealth of knowledge that will help us to continue to shape the study and practice of college access.

In addition to being conceptually and culturally rich, this book is also very useful across P-20 practice. I especially appreciate the reflection questions offered at the end of each chapter. The questions are not only useful for researchers, scholars, and practitioners, but also for students and their communities. I encourage readers to incorporate the reflection questions into pedagogical practice as I am confident that in doing so, even more types of knowledges will emerge. This brings me back to funds of knowledge, commonly defined as "historically-accumulated and culturally-developed bodies of knowledge and skills essential for household or individual functioning and well-being" (Moll et al., 1992). The concept of funds of knowledge has served as a conceptual and pedagogical grounding for me since I began my own doctoral program. As such, when I read each chapter and the reflection questions posed throughout, I hear and feel funds of knowledge. And so, I end with a thank you, an immense and overflowing note of gratitude, to the late Dr. Luis Moll, whose work on funds of knowledge changed how I approach the work of college access, how I engage with families and communities, and how I understand and value my own cultural knowledges. His mentorship is everlasting. And I offer a thank you to Chrystal and Yedalis for continuing the work, and to each of the chapter authors for building on his legacy.

References

Gonzalez, N., Moll, L. C., & Amanti, C. (Eds.). (2005). *Funds of knowledge: Theorizing practices in households, communities, and classrooms.* Erlbaum.

Moll, L. C., Amanti, C., Neff, D., & Gonzalez, N. (1992). Funds of knowledge for teaching: Using a qualitative approach to connect homes and classrooms. *Theory Into Practice, 31*(2), 132–141.

Yosso, T. J. (2005). Whose culture has capital? A critical race theory discussion of community cultural wealth. *Race Ethnicity and Education, 8*(1), 69–91. DOI: 10.1080/1361332052000341006

Acknowledgments

Thank you, Yedalis, for your colleagueship that has turned into friendship—you are an amazing thinker, writer, and scholar. I am so grateful to have taken this journey with you—we did it! And thank you to each of the contributors of this edited volume—I am in awe of each of your chapters. Much gratitude to Amanda Corso, who supported editing and formatting of this book as a research assistant. And to each of the research participants and co-researchers who participated in the studies within this volume, thank you for sharing your stories and experiences with us.

Thank you, Jason Irizarry, for inviting me to your youth participatory action research project and partnership years ago—it was the catalyst for this book project. Thank you, Korina Jocson and Antonio Martinez (may he rest in power), for your early partnership in the project. All of the appreciation in the world to my friend and collaborator Keisha Green—you are truly a phenomenal scholar who modeled to me what work with youth of Color can look like in schools; through our work together at Dean Tech, you forever changed the way I do research and I am so grateful. Thank you, Genie Bettencourt and Daniel Morales, for your work as graduate assistants—y'all kept the train on the tracks! And thank you to the Our Literate Lives Matter students who challenged me, learned with me, grew with me, and taught me so much.

I am so appreciative of Dana Altshuler for opening the door to my collaboration with the ethnic studies program and being such a supporter in the development of the UCAP college access after school program. You are an outstanding educator. Thank you to former UCAP students who entrusted us with supporting your college access journey—you are the muse for this book. And many thanks the Student Bridges Agency and UMass Amherst graduate students who helped to facilitate UCAP over the years. Thank you to former graduate assistants on the project, Joel Arce, Ashley Carpenter, and Kat Stephens-Peace for helping us sustain the program. And thank you to Joseph Krupczynski and Ellen Correa with Community Engagement and Service Learning at UMass Amherst for providing me with a fellowship opportunity to focus on UCAP.

Muchas gracias to Alberto Cabrera for my first exposure to college access and choice on a scholarly level. From taking your classes to working with you as a teaching assistant to being a guest lecturer in your classes, I began to think about this topic based on the foundation you set. And thank you to Sharon Fries-Britt for encouraging me to be innovative in my dissertation work on college access. And I express major appreciation to the college admissions and financial aid office staff at my alma mater, Rollins College, who supported my access journey as a student and later hired me for my first job out of college as an admissions counselor—y'all started it all!

Thank you to #FOCC2014—Nancy Acevedo, Cameron Beatty, Ginny Boss, Brian Burt, Marcela Cuellar, Amalia Dache, Gina Garcia, Juan Garibay, Siduri Haslerig, Jennifer Johnson, Vijay Kanagala, Darris Mmeans, Keon McGuire, Rosie Perez, Lissa Ramirez-Stapleton, Awilda Rodriguez, Mahauganee Shaw, Michael Steven Williams, and Christina Yao—you are my scholar family! And much thanks to the Scholar Mamas—Leslie Gonzales, Kimberly Griffin, Rosie Perez, OiYan Poon, and Bridget Turner Kelly—you remind me that we are not only professional educators but are also our children's first teachers.

And I can't thank my family enough, especially Alex Mwangi, Stokely Mwangi, Blyden Mwangi, Annunciata George, Gilbert George, Jane Wairimu Peters, Ed Peters, Jackie Mwangi, Nancy Pinder, Cyril Nedd, Ralda Nedd and all of my amazing aunts, uncles, and cousins. You've seen me access and obtain three degrees—and it goes without question that your unwavering love, support, and belief in me has gotten me to the finish line each time. Thank you to Derrick Brooms for the opportunity to be in community with the other amazing books in the SUNY series, Critical Race Studies in Education, and to Rebecca Colesworthy for your guidance throughout the publishing process.

—Chrystal

I love books. It was in books that I discovered my love for learning and where I found narratives of the people who inspired me to pursue higher education. Having access to community narratives in books, research, and in community-based advocacy at an early stage of my professional journey taught me how to recognize and counter the dominant deficit perspectives that exist about people of Color. Thank you to the contributors to this book. I am very humbled that my journey and work is being published among yours. I am very grateful that our collective will contribute to uplifting community narratives.

I want to express my gratitude to my first professional colleagues, my supervisors, co-workers, and the youth in the community-based organizations in Hartford, Connecticut, who were already centering and uplifting community voices and valuing diverse cultural representations and practices through community action and research. Thank you for your commitment to bridging access to health and education for our community. Thank you for welcoming me into your organizations and to the work. It was in this setting that I honed in on my interests and where I found the encouragement to pursue higher education. I am very grateful to the mentors that recognized my curiosity and hunger for learning and who provided me with opportunities to grow and expand my mind through creativity within safe and welcoming spaces. Two notable places that were fundamental in my development during my youth are Real Art Ways and the Hartford Public Library. More specifically, Will K. Wilkins, thank you for your mentorship and for being my champion.

I express my gratitude to Dr. Jason G. Irizarry, who was the chair of my dissertation committee and has been an inspiration, mentor, and friend since. You motivated me to take a strong step forward as Doctora Yedalis Ruíz Santana. I am grateful for the opportunity to teach and conduct humanizing critical research with you. I thank the Aspirantes Puertorriqueñas and their families who graciously welcomed me into their lives and who so openly shared their important narratives with me while I was conducting my research. Thank you to the faculty at the University of Massachusetts Amherst for teaching me and for inviting me to join you as your colleague. I am grateful to all of my students who engaged with me in mutual learning, upheld criticality, and joined me outside the gates of the university for community-engaged work. Thank you to the Student Bridges Agency. You are true leaders of access and equity work. I learned so much from you and with you. I am grateful to Caring Health Center (CHC). It was at a community health center that my family sought refuge and support when we first arrived from the Island. I am very proud to be a current member of the talented and devoted team of workers at

CHC. Thank you, Tania M. Barber, president and CEO, for recruiting me to join you on your long-standing vision to uplift our community and for embracing my scholarship and my narrative. Let us continue on this beautiful journey together.

And, Chrystal, thank you for *seeing* me. Thank you for valuing my voice and elevating my criticality and my scholarship. I am incredibly honored that you invited me to join you as your co-leader for this project. I can't wait to continue building and learning with you. I have found a true comrade in this work!

—Yedalis

Introduction

CHRYSTAL A. GEORGE MWANGI AND
YEDALIS RUÍZ SANTANA

College access within the United States in the 21st century reflects several gains given that the rate at which recent high school graduates enroll is significantly higher now than it was in any decade of the previous century and continues to increase (Hussar et al., 2020). Yet, this indicator can be deceiving as people of Color (POC) remain inequitably stratified in the pursuit of access to higher education and college enrollment rates continue to differ substantially by student race and ethnicity (Kim et al., 2024). For example, since 2011, the college enrollment rate for white students immediately after high school has been higher than the rate for Black students in every year (Hussar et al., 2020). Furthermore, at most colleges and universities, the share of students of Color enrolling still does not reach parity with their presence in the US general population (Baker et al., 2018). Black, Indigenous, Latinx, and Pacific Islander students are also less likely than their white peers to apply to selective colleges that they are academically qualified to attend (i.e., undermatching) (Carnevale et al., 2018; Kim et al., 2024) and are more likely to have a gap between the cost of college and the financial resources available to them (i.e., unmet need) (Vargas & Dancy, 2023). Despite these racial equity gaps, in 2023 the US Supreme Court ended consideration of race in the college admissions process by abolishing Affirmative Action policy. As higher education institutions shift their focus away from access toward a more singular emphasis on student success, they are silencing the possibilities of POC who never enter a college pathway or who pursue a college pathway that does not set them up for college retention and completion (Gándara & Rutherford, 2020).

Disparities in college access persist despite numerous research studies, theories, and frameworks that have been developed to help understand the college-going pathways of students in the US educational system. Much of extant college access literature is founded upon comprehensive models of college choice, which integrate human capital and sociological perspectives to explain how students gain access to college. Yet, these models of college choice are not sufficient for understanding diverse students' college-going process because they do not account for structural inequities and racism, unequal access to information about college, diverse pathways to college, or the capacity and activated navigational strategies of students of Color and their communities (Acevedo-Gil, 2017; Bettencourt et al., 2022; Cox, 2016).

Often touted as foundational, college access and choice frameworks can have limited relevance for POC because of how they are situated within a broader sociohistorical context. For example, US society has had a history of devaluing the ways of knowing of POC that originates from settler colonialism and transatlantic slavery in which Indigenous and African cultures, knowledges, and people were labeled as backward, barbaric, and not wholly human (Tuck & Yang, 2012; Williams et al., 2021). Erasure of these ways of knowing occurred through force, religious indoctrination, and formal education (Child & Klopotek, 2014). The practice of upholding white eurocentric ways of knowing continued through waves of immigration in which the expectation was for immigrants to strip themselves of their home cultures and to assimilate into an American "melting pot," a practice affirmed and reinforced via the US education system (Skerrett, 2008; Valenzuela, 2019). Today, these racist and oppressive values have been systemically ingrained into the ways in which educational research, practice, and policy function (Zuberi & Bonilla-Silva, 2008).

As researchers and policymakers search for education solutions, they often fail to meaningfully engage those most directly impacted by changes in policy and practice—namely, students, families, and local communities of Color (Bettencourt et al., 2020; Irizarry, 2011; Morales et al., 2017). The overwhelming majority of school improvement initiatives are upstream, and created without meaningful input or participation from those they intend to serve (Bettencourt et al., 2020; Irizarry, 2011). Yet, by 2060, more than half of all Americans will be POC (Vespa et al., 2020). Given this context, we argue that improving access to college will require frameworks that are developed by people of Color and with people of Color at the center because we have navigated, advocated for, and mitigated systemic barriers for generations, and these models should be shared and scaled.

Purpose of the Book

The aim of our book is to present college access and choice work written by scholars of Color that is grounded in youth- and community-centered, culturally sustaining, participatory, and critical race approaches. Our definition of *scholars* moves within and beyond the walls of academia to include college students, high school students, education practitioners, community members, and faculty who have contributed. Thus, the community of scholars of Color represented within these pages aligns with a critical race theorization of education (Ladson-Billings & Tate, 1995) that recognizes and uplifts the lived experiences and epistemologies of POC and the relevance of our lives to scholarship, particularly as current and former students of Color who have or are navigating college access.

The goals of this book are threefold: (1) To amplify POC research and knowledge to transform and redefine "foundational" college access and choice scholarship that is applicable to the experiences of POC; (2) to offer college access frameworks, models, and theorizing developed by scholars of Color alongside communities of Color; and (3) to present strategies for applying the frameworks to educational practices that more effectively reflect the processes and pathways of college aspirants of Color. We reject a deficit-informed approach to research and knowledge production, and instead embrace the diverse assets that communities of Color bring to and share forward in their college-going process, while interrogating the inequitable structures that create barriers. In doing so, we aim to give readers an understanding of the ways in which structural oppression, systemic racism, and institutionalized power are undertheorized in many college access frameworks to the detriment of students of Color.

We intentionally choose the racial term *people of Color* throughout this book (unless discussing a single racially minoritized group). We define people of Color as those marked via racialization as nonwhite persons. For example, in the United States today, this can be inclusive of African American, Asian, Asian American, biracial, Black, Latinx/Hispanic, multiracial, Native American, and Pacific Islander persons. We say "in the United States today" because racial formation and racial categories are constructed within societal sociohistorical contexts and evolve over time

(Omi & Winant, 1994). We acknowledge the heterogeneity within each of these groups and associated categorizations to represent the ever-evolving intersectional gender, geographic, and political history of racial/ethnic populations. For this reason, we selected *Latinx/Hispanic* as two terms used to describe Latino/a, Latine, Latinx, and Hispanic communities. We recognize and acknowledge that a major critique of the term *people of Color* is that placing all nonwhite racial groups together under one umbrella can essentialize racial identity and racialization. This is not our intention. We do not believe that all racial groups experience racism and its effects in the same ways or proportionally, particularly when it comes to college going. It is our intention to demonstrate the nuanced and distinct ways in which students and their communities are experiencing college access and choice. Our choice to use the term *people of Color* is grounded in our assertion (and demonstrated in this book) that there are commonalities of experiences and coalitional opportunities for nonwhite people in the United States given the centrality of the 21st-century racial project in US politics, culture, social ordering, and organization of reality (Omi & Winant, 1994; Vidal-Ortiz, 2008). This term also allows for individuals to identify as people of Color while simultaneously holding other identity markers central to their experience (e.g., ethnicity, nativity, gender, sexuality, religion).

This book provides critical analyses of the ways in which college aspirants of Color have been represented in college access research and offers new knowledge and frameworks that can inform educational prac- tices and further embolden the knowledge bearing that communities of Color bring to the process of gaining access to college. The chapters engage in empirical analyses of data as well as conceptual analyses of existing literature and theory. We offer education researchers, practitioners, and policymakers considerations for better supporting students of Color through awareness of their college access experiences, needs, challenges, and successes. Across each of the chapters in this book, authors integrate a critical approach to the process of accessing college that considers the macrostructural educational inequities that students of Color face in their lived experiences and conceptually in research.

Situating Our Access Journeys as Knowledge Production

Each of the contributors to this book has a passion for equity and access within communities of Color that is connected to their own experiences.

Thus, throughout the chapters, authors share their own journeys and praxis as an additional form of knowledge production and theorizing on college access. As editors, we begin with our individual journeys that eventually merged into a collaborative one leading to the development of this volume.

YEDALIS'S JOURNEY

I am a Puertorriqueñx born on the island of Puerto Rico. After a decade of circulatory migration between Puerto Rico, New York City, and Hartford, Connecticut, my family settled in Hartford, home to the fifth largest concentration of Puerto Ricans in any city outside of the Island. Throughout many moves from basements of family members to Section 8 apartments, I was surrounded by my father's beloved *trovador* music and an abundance of nutrient-rich root vegetables, fruits, and stews shared among my large, extended family. Simultaneously, gunshots and break-ins penetrated our heavily barricaded doors amid the surge of gang violence that proliferated in the city. My family, like so many others, came to the United States in search of opportunities. On the Island, we lived off the land and were never confronted with the concept of being poor. Once in the states, we were met with hardship and negative stereotypes; I became the language and culture broker for my parents as we navigated welfare and food stamp systems to secure a stable home life. Perplexed by the negative reaction to our sophisticated and beautiful Spanish language, I became an avid student of the English language. Within two quarters, I went from having been placed in the Spanish-language reading group (considered "remedial" simply by being in Spanish only) to being in the advanced placement English reading group. My family in Puerto Rico referred to our move as *la mudanza pa'ya fuera* (the move to the far-off place) and would say *estudia pa' que nos saque de apuro* (study so that you can get us out of the pinch). Unfortunately, accessing high-quality education in an economically challenged district at a high school lacking resources with high teacher attrition rates wasn't as straightforward as simply being a dedicated, hard-working, intellectually curious and capable student.

I knew early in life that I loved to learn. Among my earliest and fondest memories was receiving a dictionary from my aunt, which I read daily to learn new words, and my cousin gave me a microscope that I used to investigate the world around me. From movies to music with my father, I would repeat phrases to learn culturally relevant conversation and memorize lyrics as a way to learn pronunciation. When I was able to ride the public bus alone—around age 12—I scheduled daily visits to the public library and can still picture the librarian selecting books for us to read together aloud. It didn't take long for me to develop enough confidence to independently peruse the books of the youth section aisle by aisle. I took advantage of other free educational programs, including a computer technology course provided by the local insurance company where we were called the "up-and-coming geeks" amid the emerging technology explosion of our time. I was accepted to the Classical Magnet program. Philosophy, Greek plays, and comedy written by playwrights like Aristophanes nurtured my creative mind and I found myself lost in a world of literature. This was my first exposure to developing an intellectual identity. Despite my self-directed efforts and passion for reading and learning and several caring and inspirational teachers along the way that helped to sustain me against the many barriers, I received a subpar public school education and zero college messaging or guidance. In fact, my school counselor discouraged me from college, stating that I'd be better off getting a job immediately after high school.

And so I sought employment opportunities that would advance my learning. After graduating high school, I worked in community-based organizations on educational advocacy and participatory research with majority POC youth and adult communities. I developed invaluable skills in qualitative and quantitative methods and research design. I presented at national conferences and developed leadership and administration skills. Simultaneously, I enrolled as a nonmatriculated student at a local community college and took courses in psychology and education. It was my supervisor, a PhD in medical anthropology and leader of a community research institute, who suggested that I apply to college. She said to me, "You already do the college thing! Go out there and get credit for it!" I applied to Mount Holyoke College (MHC) and in January 2005 I was accepted full-time as a Frances Perkins Scholar (nontraditional-age adult learner). I uprooted my life as I knew it and moved to Massachusetts to earn my bachelor's degree—an academic milestone that felt more like a dream I hadn't believed would ever be accessible. In 2008, I graduated Phi Beta Kappa with a bachelor of arts in psychology and education and with department honors. I went on to earn a master's degree in educational policy and a PhD in higher education from the University of Massachusetts Amherst. I've received awards honoring my teaching excellence and was named the 2021 Mary Lion recipient—an award to an MHC alumna for sustained life and career achievements based in humane values.

My lived experience and career inform my assumptions about college going. I believe minoritized students of all ages should have equitable access to accurate and informative resources about college going and an opportunity to fulfill their educational aspirations. I believe that economic mobility is accessible with increased education and that, without advanced education, it is almost impossible to break the cycle of poverty. I've worked in academia as faculty and in student affairs' access and equity bridge programs for over a decade and am currently focused on increasing access to higher education and workforce development opportunities in community-based settings for first generation and POC, and reducing disparities among minoritized communities who have been historically underrepresented. In my professional roles and as the co-editor of this book, I am joined by a community of scholars and practitioners of color who are actively redefining the access pathway to college.

CHRYSTAL'S JOURNEY

As a Black woman with a West Indian heritage, I often say that I went through the academy and I work in the academy, but I am not of the academy. I grew up in a home where we lived paycheck to paycheck, and despite how many hours those in my family worked, it was a constant struggle to make ends meet. But despite the financial challenges, my family always supported my love for school because school is where I thrived.

My mother also understood that some schools had better resources than the ones I was zoned to in my neighborhood, and so she would use the address of a co-worker who lived in a "better" neighborhood so that I could go to that zoned elementary school instead of my own. Each morning my mother and I would get up extra early so that she could drive me to that fancy neighborhood where I'd be dropped off before any other kids got there and wait on the corner for the school bus. I was always praying that the other, mostly white, kids who eventually arrived at the bus stop wouldn't ask which house was mine.

I quickly learned that the school I went to had fancy computers and music classes and more teachers and nicer playgrounds and a host of other resources compared to the school that the kids in my real neighborhood went to—Black and Brown kids like me who also deserved to get the very best at school. I am forever grateful to my mother for her foresight and sacrifice. I quickly learned that for someone like me, you had to be the smartest—both book smart and street smart—in order to beat the system that was not created with me in mind. I strove to get the best grades, do all the extra credit assignments, tried to never miss a day of school, and got as involved as I could (given my family's limited financial resources) in extracurricular activities. I worked twice as hard and I got pretty far by traditional standards—getting tracked into a gifted and talented program and later accepted into an International Baccalaureate program for high school (with additional busing to schools far away from my real neighborhood). And when I graduated academically in the top 20 of a class of over 800 students my senior year of high school, the financial aid and scholarships I received allowed me to go to a small private, liberal arts college for free and even included enough funding for my textbooks.

However, despite achieving the ultimate in college access, there was so much I had to give up along the way—authentic relationships with kids in my neighborhood who saw me as an outsider; authentic relationships with kids I went to school with because I never felt I could be honest with them about where I lived, and so I pretended that I was financially well-off like they were to feel like I fit in; authentic relationships with family members who I felt did not understand what I was going through as a student academically and socially.

Like in my K–12 education, I did well academically in college. I knew how to "do" school at that point. But at this small liberal arts college comprised of mostly wealthy white students, I didn't feel like I truly fit in yet another space. However, one space in which I found acceptance was the admissions office where I had a job as a work-study student. I loved the staff there, and when I graduated they offered me a job as an admissions counselor and director of multicultural recruitment. Through this position, I traveled around the United States visiting high schools and working with students and their families on how to apply to college. It was through these travels that I was widely exposed to the systemic inequities present in the education system and how even the most talented and dedicated students at underresourced schools were often positioned to be less competitive college applicants than their peers at schools our admissions office considered elite. These students were frequently low income, first generation to college, immigrants, and/or students of Color. It was in working with these students, who in many ways reflected my own background, which finally led me to ask questions about educational equity, access, success, minoritized communities, social justice, and diversity in higher education. Over time, I went back to school for my master's and PhD in higher education in order to build the scholarly knowledge and research skills needed to answer those questions, and that would ultimately lead to the position I hold as a faculty member.

It was not until graduate school and in my work as a professor that I learned the language and frameworks that would carry me to the co-development of this book. I had to engage in a process of *un*learning the ways in which I have been told by dominant society what educational opportunities and barriers mean. Then, I had to move toward *re*learning for myself the possibilities and limitations of what higher education can offer in order to engage in the research and praxis that reimagines college access in the ways that are presented throughout this book.

WHERE WE CONVERGED

As Chrystal began to study higher education in her early faculty career, she pursued a community-engaged project with other faculty of Color at UMass Amherst alongside the Holyoke Public School district (HPS). In 2015, she co-taught an 11th grade Pre-AP English Language Arts class in Holyoke with another faculty member, Dr. Keisha Green, that they called Our Literate Lives Matter. The course was themed around the application of critical consciousness and a social justice lens to the education system, and educational and professional pathways after high school. They both worked with the students in the course to develop a youth participatory action research (YPAR) project. They continued to work with this group of students into their 12th-grade year and through their graduation from high school. Chrystal was later able to partner with the HPS high school's Ethnic Studies program to develop an after-school college preparation initiative (UCAP) with two chapter contributors, Dr. Ashley Carpenter and Joel Arce, specifically working with high school students beyond college preparation skills and knowledge to learn about the educational inequities existing in college access and strategize for greater college accessibility in their community.

Yedalis was a doctoral candidate in the same department and was engaged in a similar project within the same district. In the spring of 2015, Yedalis was invited to join her advisor and dissertation chair, Dr. Jason Irizarry, to co-teach a Puerto Rican history course, Project CACI-QUE (Creating Authentic Counternarratives to Improve the Quality of Urban Education), that was part of the same research collaborative initiative that Chrystal was engaged in. Despite the predominant Puerto Rican presence in the city and school district, no such course has ever been offered and Puerto Rican culture and values were largely invisible in the school. Yedalis extended her work through her dissertation—a yearlong ethnographic study embedded in the larger YPAR collaborative project. After Yedalis earned her PhD, she continued her work on access as director of the Student Bridges Agency at UMass. Student Bridges is an organization with a mission to increase college access and success for underrepresented students on the university campus and in neighboring communities of Color. In this role, Yedalis taught community engagement and education courses focused on the critical analysis of access, equity, and college choice. She worked collaboratively with undergraduate and graduate students in co-creating access programs with high school students within underrepresented communities as a way to increase access to resources and create bridges of representation and mentorship.

Our partnership began in 2017 when Chrystal collaborated with the HPS Ethnic Studies program to develop the after-school college preparation program for their high school students. The collaboration was expanded to include the UMass Student Bridges Agency that Yedalis was directing and graduate students within the UMass College of Education. Chrystal and Yedalis, along with College of Education graduate students and Student Bridges undergraduate students, facilitated programs with HPS Ethnic Studies 10th–12th graders each year.

Our programs offered access to information about college admissions and financial aid while building community and mentor relationships between high school students and teachers, UMass undergraduate, graduate students, staff, and faculty. Through our work together, we recognized our shared worldview about the knowledge that is generated by the lived experience of students of Color and the opportunity to scaffold mentorship (e.g., high school peers to each other, undergraduate students to high school students, graduate students to both, and us as faculty and staff to all of them as well as our learning from students). We were able to co-create community with students of Color that moved beyond just talking about college access or supporting students in their college access journeys.

We began a journey together of recognizing that *our knowledge* as POC is critical to navigating college access. As a community we affirmed in one another that going to college was *our process* and, despite the many barriers and what we have been told to believe, there were still ways to support one another to make it *our choice*. Ultimately, we recognized the need to amplify the critical knowledge that exists among us and use it to create new frameworks, theories, and practices.

Significance of the Book

The knowledge and theories of communities of Color need to be situated and valued within an academic platform to uphold the integrity of diverse forms of knowledge and experiences (Aguilar-Smith & Flores, 2020; Johnson et al., 2018). Equally important is the need to interrogate the inequitable structures that create barriers to college going and to directly impact and transform—both in scholarship and representation—the field of higher education and the academy. This book aims to accurately capture the diverse assets that communities of Color bring to the college-going process.

Tuck and McKenzie contend in education scholarship, "Many researchers and communities have turned to participatory forms of research that, rather than research 'on' or 'for,' entail research 'with' and 'by' " (2015, p. 118); yet, broadly speaking, college access and choice scholarship still engage epistemological and methodological approaches that center on the researcher's expertise and agenda. Alternatively, as scholars of Color working with and within our communities, we are committed to "research as responsibility, answerable and obligated to the very persons and communities being engaged" (Dillard, 2006, p. 5). As part of that commitment, we write this book to and for POC, including, but not limited to, teachers and staff of Color in K–12 schools, staff of Color working in precollege and college access programs, executive leadership and scholar practitioners of Color working in community-based organizations, students of Color and their families navigating the education system, and faculty and researchers of Color.

We also recognize the importance of using academic tools to present the diverse assets that communities of Color bring to and share forward in their college-going process, while interrogating the inequitable structures that create barriers. This empirical representation and validation of our experiences reflects bell hooks' (1989) concept of "talking back": "Moving from silence into speech is for the oppressed, the colonized, the exploited, and those who stand and struggle side by side; a gesture of defiance that heals, that makes new life and new growth possible. It is that act of speech, of 'talking back,' that is no mere gesture of empty words, [it] is the expression of our movement from object to subject—the liberated voice" (p. 9). It is our goal that our book "talks back" to deficit-oriented and race-neutral college access and choice frameworks as well as to dominant structures within academia and broader society. We offer the book as a space where people of Color can come and read about their diverse experiences and knowledges as valued and instrumental in a path toward improved college access and equity.

Our Assumptions and Request to Readers

As POC authors of this book, we have all intentionally come together to create a collective of voices to disrupt deficit-based college access and choice scholarship by presenting various examples of critical, POC-centered, and community-engaged frameworks and research approaches. We challenge models of college going that perpetually underrepresent the knowledge, experiences, and expertise of POC communities as they navigate access to college. Each chapter offers college access and choice constructs, frameworks, and ways of knowing developed with and alongside POC communities. We seek to deconstruct the boundaries of college access and choice scholarship. We affirm approaches that embrace and bridge boundaries across communities. We believe that using research approaches without the practice of critical analysis and acknowledgment of the absence of POC representation and experiences restricts the ability to disrupt oppressive structures that POC communities encounter.

We ask each reader to engage in this book with an intentional and reflexive approach. Be purposeful as you navigate through the chapters. Our book will provide multiple opportunities for you to expand on college access and choice theories centering the lived experiences of POC communities. We invite you to challenge yourself and your peers to (re) frame notions of college access and choice by centering POC communities and community-focused principles. Each chapter will present you with a selection of reflection questions carefully crafted by each of the authors to elicit thought and encourage you to become agents of change. It is our responsibility as students, scholars, educators, education practitioners, activists, researchers, policymakers, religious leaders, and community members to better understand what keeps POC communities from actualizing their aspirations and to effectively support their access to higher education. It is equally critical to understand the factors that drive POC communities and to legitimize their knowledge within the academy so that their voices and lived experiences are *seen* within the literature. This book is one step on that journey.

Organization of the Book

This book moves through 11 chapters, each with the goal of complicating, nuancing, (re)framing, and amplifying the college access journeys of POC. In chapter 1, George Mwangi and Ruíz Santana lay groundwork for subsequent chapters by discussing the assumptions and values undergirding the collective of scholarship presented. In this chapter, we amplify and show gratitude to scholars of Color who have provided relevant ways to understand the college access and choice of students of Color. The chapter concludes with considerations for conceptualizing college access, readiness, and choice as a means of grounding key terms that will be used throughout this book. The remainder of the book is organized around three themes or framings: (1) Youth-Centered Framings, (2) Community-Grown Framings, and (3) Culture- and Family-Oriented Framings. We do not consider these themes to be mutually exclusive but instead use them to draw synergies across the bodies of work represented as well as to serve as a constant reminder of the origins of the knowledge shared.

Chapters 2 through 4 are grouped within the theme of youth-centered framings, which reflect the voices and knowledge of youth of Color navigating college going. Chapter 2 engages the experiences of high school students participating in an after-school college access program, which was coordinated in partnership with a high school ethnic studies program and local university faculty, staff, and students of Color. Arce and Carpenter share the concept of critically conscious college knowledge, which is grounded in an ethnic studies lens that grew out of students' understanding of college going, perceptions of their schooling conditions, and skill building for college entry while also challenging educational inequities that exist in college access. In chapter 3, Luu acknowledges the costs that refugee students experience through posttraumatic stress and presents intergenerational posttraumatic transformation (IPT) as an alternative framework to elucidate the college access experiences of youth from refugee backgrounds. He demonstrates the influential role that intergenerational ties and familial narratives of flight and resettlement provide as sources of motivation, inspiration, and aspiration for refugee students of Color to pursue higher education. Similarly, in chapter 4, Ruíz Santana continues to frame how youth of Color process their educational journeys by sharing a reframework of the concept of resilience from the collective narratives of Puertorriqueña students as they formed their college-going identities. Pushing back on the commonly touted strength of resilience, she highlights a counterstory framed as "removing la cascara" (removing the callus) to demonstrate the cost of being resilient due to chronic exposure to barriers as they navigate the college choice process.

Chapters 5 through 8 are organized as community-grown framings, each highlighting the knowledge creation of people of Color working within schools, community organizations, student organizations, and higher education institutions. Chapter 5 connects to the theme of partnership and community engagement in POC access by emphasizing "When Impossible Becomes Possible." In this chapter, Barber describes an initiative birthed from the pain points of seeing low-income POC stuck in poverty and struggling to make ends meet, a context she also experienced. She describes her fight to champion a learning institute at a health center that is dedicated to engaging community in education and career development opportunities while simultaneously centering a mission-driven equity framework of community consumer-led models of care. In chapter 6, Carey deploys his experience as a student, and later as an urban high school teacher and education researcher, to deeply humanize and crystalize college-going realities through personalized accounts of challenges and opportunities. He explores how approaches that draw from community assets and critical and developmental theories can help education stakeholders build interventions that better confront the challenges facing Black and Latino boys. In chapter 7, Morton focuses on breaking white supremacist cycles of oppression through lessons she has learned as a college administrator working with students of Color to navigate first-generation warfare—what she describes as the unspoken racist and political systems that wear on the mental, spiritual, emotional, physical, and financial well-being of first-generation, low-income students of Color as they seek access to college and the workforce. Chapter 8 focuses on the Student Bridges Agency, an organization comprised of undergraduate and graduate students who have worked toward increasing access, retention, and success for historically marginalized students on the campus of a predominately white institution and in neighboring communities. Told from the perspective of former Student Bridges student-staff of Color, Correa and Ruiz, the chapter frames the building of collaborative partnerships with campus departments, local schools, and community organizations in improving POC college access.

Chapters 9 through 11 reflect framings that are grounded in the cultures and family knowledge of POC. Acevedo continues the emphasis on POC ways of knowing in chapter 9 by using the *college conocimiento* framework to illustrate how Latinx students negotiate the centering of their financial and emotional well-being, both as individuals and as part of a family unit, while simultaneously being driven by the potential future benefits of earning a college degree. In chapter 10, Yellow Bird, Tachine, and Cabrera center Indigenous ways of knowing by sharing how college choice is conceptualized by Native students as *family building*. Using Indigenous methodology, the authors demonstrate how family, culture, and place frame the ways Native students view college choice. George Mwangi continues a focus on family in chapter 11 by sharing the experiences of (re)constructing college choice alongside Black African immigrant families living in the United States. Using a baobab tree as metaphor, the families placed family, community engagement, and culture at the center of college going and as protective elements against the structural challenges faced during the process.

Each of the chapters inform the conclusion chapter, which shares strategies for applying the constructs and frameworks presented throughout the book to educational practices that more effectively reflect the college-going processes and pathways of POC. The chapter offers an agenda for research that continues to build from the work shared by chapter contributors. Finally, we share a "love letter" to POC college aspirants that provides possibilities for using the frameworks and concepts described in this book to support their college-going journeys.

Critical Reflection
(Adapted from Course SRCVLRNG 293,
Learning through Community Engagement)

As a reflection exercise, we invite you to reflect on your life experiences thus far and how these experiences are connected to where you are today:

1. Begin by reflecting on your family history: trace back three generations of your family (or as far back as you know—going back one or two generations is also okay) and consider your family's relationship to education. How did this history inform your ideas about access to education? How does your family history relate to your life story?

2. Then turn to your life and consider your own education. Provide a *context*:

a. What type of school did you attend (public or private) for elementary, middle, and high school?

b. Where was your school? Was it in your neighborhood or did you have to travel to school?

c. What was the demographic makeup of your school? Class size? What were the assumptions made about college access for you and other students at your school(s)?

d. What educational experiences did you have outside of schools (youth programs, sports, travel, etc.)? How did those experiences affect your understanding of college access?

3. Underscore some of the *key events* in your life that reveal something about your educational development. How did your social identities, both privileged and marginalized, relate to these events? When thinking about key events, consider questions such as:

a. How did the key event(s) make you feel?

b. What did you do about the key event(s) and how you felt?

c. How did the key event(s) affect your access to education and learning?

d. Were you hindered by this key event(s)? Did the key event(s) help you to be more motivated?

4. *Make meaning* of your story:

a. How has what you have reflected on thus far informed your ideas about and your access to education?

b. How did your schools (and other opportunities and key events) impact your college access and success?

c. How did these experiences that you have reflected on influence your current goals and priorities?

References

Acevedo-Gil, N. (2017). College-*conocimiento*: Toward an interdisciplinary college choice framework for Latinx students. *Race Ethnicity and Education, 20*(6), 829–850. https://doi.org/10.1080/13613324.2017.1343294

Aguilar-Smith, S., & Flores, A. (2020). Intergenerational lessons to and from higher education educators of color. *About Campus, 25*(2), 20–23. https://doi.org/10.1177/1086482220913023

Baker, R., Klasik, D., & Reardon, S. F. (2018). Race and stratification in college enrollment over time. *AERA Open, 4*(1), 1–28. https://doi.org/10.1177%2F2332858417751896

Bettencourt, G. M., George Mwangi, C. A., Green, K., & Morales, D. (2020). High school–university collaborations for Latinx student success: Navigating the political reality. *Journal of Higher Education Outreach and Engagement, 24*(1), 17–34.

Bettencourt, G. M., George Mwangi, C. A., Green, K., & Morales, D. (2022). But do I need a college degree? College-going perceptions of students enrolled in a career and technical high school. *Innovative Higher Education, 47,* 453–470. https://doi.org/10.1007/s10755-021-09585-3

Carnevale, A. P., Van Der Werf, M., Quinn, M. C., Strohl, J., & Repnikov, D. (2018). *Our separate & unequal public colleges: How public colleges reinforce white racial privilege and marginalize Black and Latino students.* Georgetown University Center on Education and the Workforce. https://cew.georgetown.edu/cew-reports/sustates/

Child, B. J., & Klopotek, B. (Eds.) (2014). *Indian subjects: Hemispheric perspectives on the history of Indigenous education.* School for Advanced Research Press.

Cox, R. D. (2016). Complicating conditions: Obstacles and interruptions to low-income students' college "choices." *Journal of Higher Education, 87*(1), 1–26. https://doi.org/10.1080/00221546.2016.11777392

Dillard, C. B. (2006). *On spiritual strivings: Transforming an African American woman's academic life.* State University of New York Press.

Gándara, D., & Rutherford, A. (2020). Completion at the expense of access? The relationship between performance-funding policies and access to public 4-year universities. *Educational Researcher, 49*(5), 321–334. https://doi.org/10.3102/0013189X20927386

hooks, b. (1989). *Talking back: Thinking feminist, thinking Black.* South End Press.

Hussar, B., Zhang, J., Hein, S., Wang, K., Roberts, A., Cui, J., Smith, M., Bullock Mann, F., Barmer, A., & Dilig, R. (2020). *The condition of education 2020* (NCES 2020-144). US Department of Education. National Center for Education Statistics.

Irizarry, J. G. (2011). *The Latinization of U.S. schools: Successful teaching and learning in shifting cultural contexts.* Paradigm.

Johnson, J. M., Jones, G. M., George Mwangi, C. A., & Garcia, G. A. (2018). Resisting, rejecting, and redefining the professoriate: Faculty of Color in higher education. *Urban Review, 50*(4), 630–647. https://doi.org/10.1007/s11256-018-0459-8

Kim, J. H., Soler, M. C., Zhao, Z., & Swirsky, E. (2024). *Race and ethnicity in higher education: 2024 status report.* American Council on Education. https://www.equityinhighered.org

Ladson-Billings, G., & Tate, W. F. (1995). Toward a critical race theory of education. *Teachers College Record, 97*(1), 47–68. https://doi-org.mutex.gmu.edu/10.1177/016146819509700010

Morales, D., Bettencourt, G., Green, K., & George Mwangi, C. A. (2017). "I want to know about everything that's happening in the world": Enhancing critical awareness through youth participatory action research with Latinx youth. *Educational Forum, 81*(4), 404–417. https://doi.org./10.1080/00131725.2017.1350236

Omi, M., & Winant, H. (1994). *Racial formations in the United States: From the 1960s to the 1990s.* Routledge.

Skerrett, A. (2008). Racializing educational change: Melting pot and mosaic influences on educational policy and practice. *Journal of Educational Change, 9,* 261–280. https://doi.org/10.1007/s10833-008-9071-0

Tuck, E., & McKenzie, M. (2015). *Place in research: Theory, methodology, and methods.* Routledge.

Tuck, E., & Yang, K. W. (2012) Decolonization is not a metaphor. *Decolonization: Indigeneity, Education & Society 1*(1),1–40.

Valenzuela, A. (2019). The struggle to decolonize official knowledge in Texas' state curriculum: Side-stepping the colonial matrix of power. *Equity & Excellence in Education, 52*(2–3), 197–215. https://doi.org/10.1080/10665684.2019.1649609

Vargas, M., & Dancy, K. (2023, August 16). *College affordability still out of reach for students with lowest incomes, students of Color.* Institute for Higher Education Policy. https://www.ihep.org/college-affordability-still-out-of-reach-for-students-with-lowest-incomes-students-of-color/

Vespa, J., Medina, L., & Armstrong, D. M. (2020). *Demographic turning points for the United States: Population projections for 2020 to 2060.* US Census Bureau. https://www.census.gov/content/dam/Census/library/publications/2020/demo/p25-1144.pdf

Vidal-Ortiz, S. (2008). People of Color. In R. T. Schaefer (Ed.), *Encyclopedia of race, ethnicity, and society* (vol. 2, pp. 1037–1039). Sage.

Williams, B. C., Squire, D. D., & Tuitt, F. A. (Eds.). (2021). *Plantation politics and campus rebellions: Power, diversity, and the emancipatory struggle in higher education.* State University of New York Press.

Zuberi, T., & Bonilla-Silva, E. (Eds.) (2008). *White logic, white methods: Racism and Methodology.* Rowman & Littlefield.

Chapter 1

A POC-Centered (Re)Framing of College Access and Choice

Chrystal A. George Mwangi and
Yedalis Ruíz Santana

Let's begin by setting the stage for our reader. We expect that you will notice the style, format, language, and approach in this book are different from other academic texts. These differences are intentional and, by design, we aim to engage the reader in a process of learning, reflection, self-care, and action. Some of the differences you may notice include the representation of scholars and community practitioners as equal contributors to knowledge-making and to radical shifts in addressing college choice and access. You may notice all of the editors and authors are persons of Color. We intentionally have created an anthology of scholarship entirely led by authors of Color to demonstrate (a) this is possible; (b) we exist; (c) our scholarship and practice are already in progress; (d) we are not seeking to modify long-standing inadequate models to include us because we have our own approaches, programs, initiatives, scholarship, and practice; and (e) efforts to present a collective of scholarship by a group of authors of Color are needed to advance the overall representation of our voices in the broader body of literature. Each author writes from their authentic voice and lived experience, including their personal, professional, and academic experience as well as their faith, cultural, and creative identities and lenses. We celebrate the uniqueness of each author's language, style, and messaging. We ask that you do the same and consider what it would mean if, in your own scholarship and practice, you actively worked to incorporate knowledge from academics and community as co-contributors, co-creators, and co-actors as we have modeled here.

Finally, we acknowledge there are real tensions in college access work. Addressing access barriers to higher education will not eliminate those tensions. Rather, our hope is that it will provide a range of lenses through which to better understand the tensions, the reasons why they exist, and how to activate through scholarship and practice a collective responsibility to address them. Take into consideration, for example, the complexity facing students and communities of Color as they consider if and how to pursue opportunities into higher education, particularly into predominantly white institutions (PWIs). Young and adult students of Color will confront racism operating in an institution and system that has systematically excluded them and those before them. They will not see their names or faces in the majority of the scholarship they are required to learn. They will frequently be the one, the only one, in any given classroom, committee, student group, or event. They may face financial burdens and fear.

Unlike the experience of many white students who have developed generational wealth of college going (e.g., their older siblings, parents, aunts, uncles, grandparents, and in some cases great-grandparents have a college degree), many students of Color are first-generation college students (Serna & Woulfe, 2017). Parallel and intersecting with this truth is that generational wealth (e.g., a financial safety net) follows a similar pattern. Therefore, while college degrees and training certifications are expensive for all students, the cost and burden of that expense is experienced differently by students of Color and their families (Serna & Woulfe, 2017). Students of Color also frequently face physical, emotional, and cultural distancing from their families. Where not having access to college has become a defining truth in some communities, having the opportunity to obtain a college degree can feel and is often felt like an abandonment of one's family and ancestors—akin to survivors' guilt (Covarrubias et al., 2021). This tension is a reality for many students of Color and impacts their day-to-day experience of support, relatability, and sense of belonging (George Mwangi, 2019). Scholars and practitioners of Color have brought these and other critical tensions into focus in college choice and access literature. We aim to build on that growing body of knowledge with the contributions herein.

Unlearning and Relearning College Access and Choice

Unlearning and relearning how we write about college access and choice with and for communities and students of Color is necessary because the approach so far of trying to fit our experiences into models and frameworks not created with us in mind has been ineffective and perpetuates structural racism. The contributors of Color in this book clearly illustrate how college access and choice are not just concepts or a framework to learn from or use in policies and scholarship. Rather it is lived experience and it is embodied among communities of Color. For many first-generation college aspirants, it is hope, aspiration, dreams not just for themselves but for the entire family. While aspirations abound, college access is also an imagined place—something to envision but still infrequently achieved. The concept of "being the one" and perhaps the only one in an entire family and the collective responsibility of "getting out" of poverty and seeking opportunities as illustrated in Ruíz Santana's chapter, Morton's chapter, and Carey's chapter is both a powerful motivator for college aspirants as well as a substantial burden to carry.

College access and choice need to be *re*framed to include the multiple true experiences of communities of Color. The works contained in this book are not just for us to "learn" about how communities of Color experience accessing college in order to create alternative programs for communities, but rather each chapter helps us to interrogate and acknowledge the chronically outdated higher education system wherein nonconformity with college access and choice based on traditional models continues to disproportionately and systematically exclude those students who are minoritized. Why does higher education continue to expect that communities of Color will do whatever it takes, piece together resources that are not fully accessible or sufficient, and be grateful for "whatever they can get"? This expectation for communities of Color to operate from a position of resourcefulness and resilience is a product of the structural racism and exclusion that has resulted in higher education disparities. Communities of Color often have to conform and contort their rich cultural identities in order to fit into models that do not engage the experiences of college aspirants and learners of Color (George Mwangi, 2018).

As scholar-practitioners of Color, we often navigate in a liminal space between where we were/came from and "arriving" at this point of academic prestige when one becomes a *true* scholar. It does not always feel like we can just *be* our authentically *true* selves. We have shared stories of feeling like an impostor or the experience of being questioned, despite the fact that our advanced preparation and high performance often led us to substantially outperform others in order to be recognized. As scholar-practitioners of Color, we are whole when we are able to integrate our scholarship with our lived, community experiences. More than "representation," the idea of making it, of belonging, and of excelling is one that we have to continue to imagine for ourselves, even once we are in college and beyond.

A Letter of Gratitude to Scholars of Color

This component of the chapter centers on research conducted by previous scholars of Color as a means of creating a specific foundation and centering of college access and choice scholarship. We include works that were solo-authored or first-authored by scholars of Color. Additionally, we included scholarship published up to 2013 to ensure we included a strong quantity of scholarship that also has had at least a decade of impact on the field at the time of writing this chapter. It is our reimagining of a literature review as we write in a voice *to* these scholars of Color as a form of grounding this book in a spirit of gratitude to the many who have researched, practiced, and supported college access within communities of Color with an ethos of care and criticality. It is because of you that we believed we could develop this book and build from the work that you created.

We thank you for introducing us to relevant frameworks for understanding the college access of communities of Color and applying them in your scholarship. While we read critiques of early econometric and status attainment models for their focus on the experiences of white male college-going students and knew that they could not be sufficient in explaining the process for communities of Color, we were often left with the question of "What lenses should we be using?" You introduced us to theories, models, and frameworks that were often outside of the education field and innovatively brought them into our field in order to move the needle in how the college-going experiences of communities of Color were grounded and understood. We are also grateful to the scholars who were groundbreaking in developing their own frameworks when existing ones did not suffice.

Although we know that we will inevitably miss some scholars and/ or works, we hope that our intent in celebrating and thanking you is apparent—we view your work as the foundational and formative pieces to understanding college access and choice that scholars working with communities of Color should ground themselves within into the future.

Thank You for Showing Us How to Call Out Racism in College Access and Choice

We are grateful to the scholars who in the 1990s and early 2000s used critical race theory (CRT) to ground us in the knowledge that racism and white supremacy are embedded within our education system via admissions processes, education policies like affirmative action, academic tracking practices, standardized testing, and beyond, which are maintained through systems of power resulting in and reifying racial marginalization (Ladson-Billings & Tate, 1995; Solórzano, 1997; Solórzano & Delgado Bernal, 2001). Critical race theory was first developed during the 1970s by activists and legal scholars who centered race, racism, and power in the US legal system (Crenshaw, 1988; Matsuda et al., 1993). Central to CRT is that racism is more than individual prejudice and bigotry; rather, it is a central and endemic feature of US society that masks racial inequity as natural (Tate, 1997).

As it extends to education, Solórzano and Yosso (2002b) define CRT as "a framework or set of basic insights, perspectives, methods, and pedagogy that seeks to identify, analyze, and transform those structural and cultural aspects of education that maintain subordinate and dominant racial positions in and out of the classroom" (p. 25). Thank you, Dr. Daniel Solórzano (1997) and colleagues (Solórzano & Delgado Bernal, 2001; Solórzano & Villalpando, 1998; Solórzano & Yosso, 2001, 2002a, 2002b), for gifting us with a strong foundation for using CRT to analyze how race and racism act as inequitable determinants in college access (and attainment) for students of Color. Your work illustrates the cumulative effects of racially inequitable schooling conditions and resources experienced in K–12 for pathways into and through higher education.

Thank You for Centering Our Voices and Our Stories

We learned from scholars of Color that counterstories could be a powerful vehicle for resisting majoritarian narratives regarding who is "worthy" of going to college—stories that are central to our understanding of college access and choice, particularly for first-generation, low-income students of Color. Thank you, Dr. Michelle Knight and colleagues (2004), for counterstorying college access by discounting master narratives that families of working-class Black and Brown youth are disengaged from their children's college pathways. Instead, you reinforced to us that these families play an integral role in the college-going process and in navigating systems of oppression involved in that process.

We appreciate your work, Dr. Ifeoma Amah (2012), for looking at the experiences of Black students who had been labeled "non–high performing" and/or "non–college bound" and counterstorying their high school experiences to demonstrate the ways in which they showed commitment to college-going pathways. You helped us see the structural factors impacting any academic disengagement or pushing out they experienced, and the value of targeted student support services, such as Gaining Early Awareness and Readiness for Undergraduate Programs (GEAR UP) and the Educational Opportunity Program (EOP), that address the inequities in their college choice process. The outcomes of counterstorying in this research connect to another core tenet of CRT in its critiques of liberalism and meritocracy to reject color evasiveness, notions of a postracial society, and the belief that individual failure or success is driven by ability (Bell, 2009; Crenshaw, 1988; Delgado & Stefancic, 2000; McCoy & Rodricks, 2015).

Thank You for Naming the Master's Tools

We honor the work of scholars who have situated the racialized and racist impact of law and public policy on postsecondary pathways for POC, including Dr. Tara Yosso and colleagues' (2004) analysis of the debate on affirmative action within legal trials using historical foreshadowing and an unpacking of majoritarian narratives and rationales regarding affirmative action. We also appreciate Drs. Robert Teranishi and Kamilah Briscoe's (2008) application of CRT to California's Proposition 209 to analyze Black students' college aspirations as a racialized phenomenon. Rather than focus on the institutional impact of color-evasive policy change, you made empirically visible the ways that Californian Black youth interpret postsecondary opportunities as more limited, their confidence as applicants weakened, and their sense of belonging in highly selective institutions challenged after affirmative action was eradicated in California. We are grateful for the work of Drs. Elena Bernal, Alberto Cabrera, and Patrick Terenzini (2000) for demonstrating through their analysis of National Center of Education Statistics (NCES) data that race-conscious affirmative action matters for improving POC college access and a class-based affirmative action policy would disproportionality benefit low-income white students. Dr. Alberto Cabrera, your work has also further strengthened the important truth that race and class, while often related, cannot be conflated in higher education research (Cabrera & La Nasa, 2000). We thank Dr. Shaun Harper and colleagues (2009), who also took a policy focus to analyze the historical progression and regression of education policy related to college access and equity for African Americans, ultimately concluding, "Consistent attacks on affirmative action; funding inequities for public institutions that annually offer college opportunity to more than a quarter million African American students; the implementation of policy initiatives that distract HBCUs from their original missions; and infrequent policy analyses will continually manufacture insufficient access and equity barriers for those who could ultimately benefit from college participation" (p. 410). This college access scholarship foregrounds how law and public policy have been used as tools for racial subordination that align benefits and privileges with whiteness and the protection of whiteness, only shifting with the presence of interest convergence that occurs when the dominant white culture tolerates advances for racial justice to suit its personal interest.

Thank You for Your Intersectional and Antiessentialist Lens

Critical race theory has provided scholars a vehicle to unpack intersectionality (the multiple, interlocking systems of oppression) faced by students of Color as well as nuance the experiences of these students given that their racial minoritization is not homogenous. We thank Dr. Robert Teranishi (2002) for his use of CRT to debunk the Asian "model minority" myth within college access and demonstrate the barriers to opportunities keenly felt by Filipino students, a point further taken up by Dr. Tracy Lachica Buenavista (2010) who used CRT to illustrate how the intersectional oppressions via race, class, and immigration status for these students creates barriers to access via racist academic tracking and historical and contemporary colonial relations between the United States and the Philippines.

We also appreciate your work, Drs. Kimberly Griffin and Walter Allen (2006) for demonstrating that while not all students of Color attend underresourced high schools, systemic racism creates a context in which all experience racialized challenges impacting their access to college. This includes Black high achievers at highly resourced and predominantly white high schools who have more school-based supports in college choice available, but who experience a racially hostile school climate preventing them from fully utilizing those resources (e.g., gatekeeping of college preparatory coursework due to staff stereotypes about Black students' intellectual capacity). Conversely, students at an underresourced and predominantly Black high school may receive high levels of encouragement and validation from their teachers and counselors for college but not have access to tangible resources and information to support their choice process. Thank you for amplifying how, in both school environments, Black students are persistent in their pursuit of college going, which in your study was also heavily influenced by having high-achieving peer groups who supported their goals and aspirations.

Your work provides us with empirical support for an antiessentialist approach to college access and choice as well as a need to disaggregate data for students of Color in order to ensure that their multiple marginalizations are seen and their nuanced needs are met throughout the process.

Thank You for Amplifying Our Assets, Our Networks, and Our Knowledge

Critical race theory was used to later inform the powerful construct of cultural wealth defined as the unique forms of cultural capital, accumulated resources, and assets that students of Color develop and utilize in spaces of marginality within educational institutions (Villalpando & Solórzano, 2005; Yosso & Solórzano, 2005). Cultural wealth moved college access scholarship away from merely seeing what students of Color bring to the college-going process from a deficit perspective. It also rejected white middle-class norms as the gold standard of culture. We are forever grateful for Dr. Tara Yosso's (2005) conceptualization of cultural wealth for communities, or community cultural wealth (CCW). CCW is nurtured through six forms of capital that are assets often going unrecognized in dominant culture: aspirational, linguistic, familial, social, navigational, and resistance. Each tenet of the CCW model is linked together and defined by the experiences of communities of Color:

Aspirational capital refers to the ability to maintain hopes and dreams for the future, even in the face of real and perceived barriers. *Linguistic capital* includes the intellectual and social skill attained through communication experiences in more than one language and/or style. *Familial capital* refers to those cultural knowledges nurtured among *familia* (kin) that carry a sense of community history, memory, and cultural intuition. *Social capital* can be understood as networks of people and community resources. *Navigational capital* refers to skills of maneuvering through social institutions. *Resistant capital* refers to those knowledges and skills fostered through oppositional behavior that challenges inequalities. (Yosso, 2005, pp. 79–80)

Scholars of Color have used CCW to amplify the knowledge, experiences, and resources of students of Color and we have turned to their scholarship time and time again to confirm that CCW must be integrated and validated in the learning environment and college-going process. We thank Dr. Uma Jayakumar and colleagues (2013) for applying CCW to the experiences of Black students in a college outreach program and demonstrating that "even in resource-rich high school environments, college preparation rarely leverages community cultural wealth and transformative resistance to address oppressive schooling conditions and to facilitate college pathways for Black youth" (p. 568). You countered their oppressive environment with a liberatory college-going culture model that supports the CCW of Black students and places cultural integrity and critical consciousness as central to schooling processes. Your model fosters transformative resistance among students in order to encourage their successful matriculation to college through a lens of consciousness that challenges social reproduction.

We admire how Dr. Erica Yamamura and colleagues (2010) engaged CCW and Chicana feminist theory to conceptualize a new hybrid framework of borderland cultural wealth (BCW) in your study of Latina/o college readiness in the South Texas border region and the assets these students bring. BCW is defined as "cultural assets present in this region that when cultivated and tapped into effectively can improve college preparation and access" (p. 126), which you described as being grounded in collective responsibility, recognizing the importance of starting early and multiple pathways to college, acknowledging intergroup diversity, and supporting family and community engagement. Dr. Melissa Martinez (2012) similarly investigated the experiences of South Texas border youth, focusing on their community context and community cultural wealth in the college choice process. You found that Mexican American students rely heavily on nonfamilial and community members (e.g., church, neighbors) in their process, but also that resistant and aspirational capital were essential in resisting stereotypes about themselves, their cultures, and the reputations of the institutions in which they were planning to enroll. Thank you for this work.

We have turned to the work of Dr. Daniel Liou and colleagues (2009), who showed us that information networks are not only essential for students of Color seeking access to college, but that teachers and counselors do harm when they do not see the value and assets, or cultural wealth, that students bring, thus, not deeming these students worthy of college access information. In your earlier work with Dr. Robert Cooper (Cooper & Liou, 2007) you discuss a term, *high stakes information*, defined as leading "students to understand the school culture, policies, and practices in ways they can access, embrace, and develop a strong academic self-identity" (p. 44), which is often part of the hidden curriculum. In later combining this concept with CCW, you were able to empirically demonstrate the critical nature of these students out of school networks, knowledge, and cultural wealth that will help bridge school and home/ community for the goal of college going (Liou et al., 2009). In the same vein of uplifting and making visible the networks of students of Color, Drs. Patricia Pérez and Patricia McDonough's (2008) application of CCW's social capital alongside chain migration demonstrated Latina and Latino students' social networks are wide ranging beyond parents (e.g., extended family, acquaintances), but that parents were also essential as a positive source of support. You demonstrated that the dominant narrative that parents/family limit the college endeavors of Latino/a students is false and that their families facilitated trusting relationships with individuals who could also support their children.

Thank You for Valuing Our Families and Communities

We further saw the focus on families of Color with the introduction of funds of knowledge to the college access and choice space. *Funds of knowledge* is an anthropological concept defined as "historically accumulated and culturally developed bodies of knowledge and skills essential for household or individual functioning and well-being" (Moll et al., 1992, p. 133). Funds of knowledge focus on factors including a household's labor history, social interactions, educational experiences, language use, and daily activities (Rios-Aguilar, 2010). It was first used to describe how working-class Mexican immigrant families utilize their social networks, labor skills, and knowledge about goods and services to enhance their well-being and transmit funds to their children (Vélez-Ibáñez & Greenberg, 1992). Children are directly and indirectly exposed to funds of knowledge, which are found both within households and within the cluster networks of the community where children live and socialize (Vélez-Ibáñez & Greenberg, 1992). We are grateful that the concept of funds of knowledge was adapted by education researchers Dr. Luis Moll and colleagues (1992) to acknowledge that students' homes and communities "contain rich cultural and cognitive resources" that can be connected and integrated into the school environment.

Thank you, Dr. Judy Kiyama (2010), for applying funds of knowledge to understand the college aspirations and ideologies of Mexican American families, which were developed via college artifacts, academic cultural symbols, and social networks. We also appreciate your later demonstration of how Mexican American families transfer funds of knowledge to their children via *consejos*, life lessons, reciprocal services, and family business engagement (Kiyama, 2011). And thank you Dr. Cecilia Rios-Aguilar (2010) for calling on educational institutions to use Latinx students' funds of knowledge to amplify their academic and nonacademic success and demonstrating that these outcomes are indeed significantly associated with components of funds of knowledge.

While most higher education research incorporates parental characteristics (e.g., parental level of education) or suggests that parental involvement is critical in students' college outcomes, we appreciate Rios-Aguilar and Kiyama's (2012) critique that this does not reflect the diverse ways in which families influence students of Color, nor is it inclusive of the diverse family configurations present in households (e.g., extended family, fictive kin), which can also impact students' outcomes. You helped us to see how the notion of funds of knowledge reframes the role of family in higher education through a focus on families as the unit of analysis.

Scholars of Color have continuously worked to extend understanding of how family and community impact college access for students of Color. There are so many examples of how you have made visible the breadth and depth of our networks that education scholars and practitioners have historically refused to acknowledge. Thank you to Dr. Miguel Ceja (2006) for focusing on college-going older siblings who created college-going traditions and expectations in their households for their younger Chicana siblings. Thank you Dr. Kenneth González and colleagues (2003), Dr. Nicole Holland (2010), Dr. Judy Kiyama (2011), Drs. Patrica Pérez and Patricia McDonough (2008), and Drs. Marisela Rosas and Florence Hamrick (2002) for emphasizing extended family, including grandparents, cousins, aunts, and uncles in addition to the nuclear family. We learned from you Dr. Holland (2010) that family members and same-generation peer role models who had gone to college provide "concrete blueprints" for how to attain access just by setting an example of going to college themselves, showing the impact of representation and disproving stereotypes for students of Color. Then, in 2011, you came back to show us the role of peer influence in the college aspirations and planning of African American students specifically. We are grateful for Dr. Melissa Martinez's (2012) and Dr. Reddick and colleagues' (2011) concentration on students' local communities and community members' support for college going, which can include members and leaders of religious organizations, community leaders, local college outreach program staff, peers, friends, and neighbors. Alongside this focus on the communal and collective in the college choice process, thank you Dr. Martinez (2013) for later applying the concept of *familismo*, "the tendency to hold the wants and needs of family in higher regard than one's own" (p. 22), in your study of Latino/a high school students' college choice process. You demonstrated the strong sense of *familismo* among these students whether that be opting to stay closer to home due to familial bonds or going to college to better the lives of not just themselves but also their families. We were informed by each of you on how college-going family and community members could help with college applications, financial aid forms, preparation for admissions interviews, and share personal stories as a form of college knowledge; and even those who had not attended or completed college can still play a major role in students' college-going process through encouragement (Ceja, 2006; González et al., 2003; Kiyama, 2011; Martinez, 2012; Pérez & McDonough, 2008; Reddick et al., 2011). We appreciate that you all did not dismiss or create a deficit orientation around the parents in students' lives but were seeking to demonstrate the culturally sustaining support roles that other family and community members can also play, which could otherwise be overlooked with a sole focus on parents.

Thank You for Making Our Choices Visible across Diverse Institutional Types

We thank the scholars who focused on institutional diversity in the college choice process, particularly given that it is more likely for students of Color to attend open access institutions, for-profit institutions, and minority-serving institutions as compared to their white peers. This includes Drs. Leticia Oseguera and Maria Malagon (2011) who focused on Latina/o student enrollment in for-profit colleges and universities, finding that students choosing these institutions were more likely to have fewer high school resources supporting their college choice process and preparing them academically.

We learned from Drs. Kassie Freeman and Gail Thomas (2002), who highlighted the reasons that Black students choose historically Black colleges and universities (HBCUs), both historically and in contemporary times. You showed us that regardless of time period, financial support and cost of college were main drivers of students' decisions of whether to attend an HBCU. Your work elucidates that Black students who attended predominantly white high schools were more likely to select an HBCU than students at predominantly Black high schools because they were seeking a Black cultural connection in college that they had not otherwise had in their high school experience. And we were reminded of the benefit of HBCUs by Dr. Walter Allen and colleagues (2007) in your explanation that HBCUs are more likely to enroll low-income and first-generation students who have been academically underserved in US K–12 education and support their success, well-being, and economic mobility.

Within the Hispanic-serving institution (HSI) context, we appreciate Drs. Anne-Marie Núñez and Alex Bowers's (2011) research showing us that having Hispanic teachers and peers of Color increased the likelihood of enrollment in 2-year and 4-year HSIs. Thank you for also showing the ways that 2-year HSIs can be clear gateways to a bachelor's degree for students of Color. Your results show that high schools that were more likely to send students to 2-year HSIs were in states like California and Texas that have strong 4-year transfer agreements, providing the option for these students to eventually pursue a bachelor's degree (2011). And it was important to see students of Color enrolling at 2-year HSIs being more likely to aspire to attend 4-year institutions than their peers at non-HSI community colleges, despite demographic characteristics often perceived as restrictive or risk factors to their college success (Núñez, Johnelle Sparks, & Hernández, 2011).

Thank You For (Re)Imagining Our Framing of College Access and Choice

Thank you Dr. Sylvia Hurtado and colleagues (1997) for your study examining the predisposition and application behavior of students from different ethnic/racial groups. Not only did you outline differences across race/ethnicity in the college choice process, but you found that existing choice models might not adequately address the process of ethnic/racial groups, particularly because they do not account for factors such as racial inequalities that exist (Hurtado et al., 1997). Thus, we thank the scholars who developed their own frameworks when they found existing ones to be inadequate in describing and explaining the college access and choice of students of Color.

Thank you to Dr. Kassie Freeman for your research on race as a factor in college choice for African Americans (1999) and your model of predetermination (2005). Your qualitative study analyzed how African American high school students engaged the "predisposition" stage of college choice—a stage when students begin to formulate a desire and plan to go to college—and considered factors impacting predisposition, including the influence of family and kinship, economic issues, culture, gender, school characteristics (e.g., curriculum, resources). We appreciate how you argued that for African American youth, predisposition is filtered by communal culture alongside school and individual factors, thus offering a "model of predetermination" as an extension of an existing framework and a culturally informed revision. You acknowledged how the dominant culture of individualism within schools often clashes with the cultural beliefs of Black families and how the underresourced schools that Black urban youth attend constrain their support for college going. Thus, aspirations for college are not enough on their own to translate into college enrollment and instead cultural support is needed alongside aspirations and ability as "the interpretation of any findings absent an understanding of a group's culture is analogous to attaching wings to a turtle and then being perplexed as to why the turtle cannot fly" (p. 111). The first phase of college choice becomes "predetermination," rather than predisposition, because many of the factors impacting the process are environmental constraints beyond the students' control, complicating our understanding of what choice means. Your conceptualization has opened doors for other scholars to build upon. This includes your work, Dr. Crystal Gafford Muhammad (2008), which operationalized Freeman's framework to further demonstrate that the college search process of African American students is heavily connected to cultural support networks and their perceptions of school counselors.

We appreciate the work of Drs. Michael Herndon and Joan Hirt (2004), who proposed a model of family involvement that spans precollege to college completion for Black students. Specifically, your model considers the involvement factors that affect students' motivation to attend college as well as persist and complete their degree through three stages of family involvement: precollege influences, early college influences, and late college influences. Precollege influences include family influence, macro-perspectives on race, and motivating factors that encourage college enrollment. Early college influences incorporate negotiating a new environment, sense of community with other Black individuals on campus, and spiritual support. Late college influences include both family expectations for a return on investment and the importance of being served by role models and being a role model to others. Your model humanizes the educational pathways of students who do not live siloed processes but instead bring their whole selves to each point in their educational trajectory whether in K–12 or college. You showed us that we must also recognize that families and communities of Color do not stop their engagement with students once they transition to higher education. Instead of the dominant white norms in the United States, which emphasize adolescent autonomy in transitioning from high school to college (Jenkins, 2013), you amplified how populations of Color often emphasize collectivism and familial interdependence into adulthood and are more likely to define family by including extended family, fictive kin, and local community networks. This was essential in moving away from how family is traditionally delimited in higher education research and the college choice process solely as parents or nuclear family.

Thank you to all of the scholars of Color who provided a foundation and space to question, critique, and (re)imagine college access and choice within our communities. Your work revised how POC were viewed within these processes by contextualizing our complex challenges, assets, and lived experiences. You circulated knowledge that could better inform praxis and policy by challenging dominant pejorative narratives about communities of Color, while also naming the structural barriers and institutionalized racism impacting college access inequitably. Within this book, we seek to build upon your foundation and knowledge sharing, which we are forever grateful for and in solidarity with.

Considerations for College Access, Choice, and Readiness

Our book is not meant to refute or reject the research and framing of nonscholars of Color or research based on samples exclusive of POC. Instead, it is meant to (re)center and (re)anchor the ways in which we frame and understand college access and choice within communities of Color. We do not propose a singular way of defining the concepts of college access, college choice, and college readiness because doing so runs counter to our purpose of expanding and diversifying our understanding of these constructs. However, we offer considerations for how these concepts are constructed as informed by the literature discussed herein and the subsequent chapters in this book.

COLLEGE ACCESS

We move away from constructing college access as an opportunity or privilege given the harm and violence that is often experienced by POC within higher education institutions. Instead, given the role a higher education degree plays in economic and social positioning, we consider college access a right that is due communities of Color. To reinforce this consideration, we turn to Ladson-Billings's discussion of education debt when we consider the concept of college access:

> I am arguing that our focus on the achievement gap is akin to a focus on the budget deficit, but what is actually happening to African American and Latina/o students is really more like the national debt. . . . I am arguing that the historical, economic, sociopolitical, and moral decisions and policies that characterize our society have created an education debt. . . . Taken together, the historic, economic, sociopolitical, and moral debt that we have amassed toward Black, Brown, Yellow, and Red children seems insurmountable, and attempts at addressing it seem futile. Indeed, it appears like a task for Sisyphus. But

as legal scholar Derrick Bell (1994) indicated, just because
something is impossible does not mean it is not worth doing.
(Ladson-Billings, 2009, pp. 5, 9)

If we come from the standpoint of education debt, then we place the onus
of access to college on us all, but particularly on the structures that have
reinforced inequity in order to "make it right." This includes public policy
and policymakers, K–12 schools and college preparation efforts, colleges
and universities particularly within the realm of admission, and broader
society. We do not expect the systems and structures built to reinforce
racial stratification and racist norming to automatically pursue equity in
access as their obligation and responsibility, but we must call for and hold
them accountable, nonetheless.

COLLEGE CHOICE

We recognize that there are race-based inequities in the possibilities of
what choice can be in college going. Yet, we claim the choice-making of
POC because although our choices are often constrained and sought to
be confined in a racist society, our humanity as POC must not be denied
and our choice-making is part of our humanity. Given this context, in
considering college choice we focus less on a stage-based process and,
instead, center on how choice is rendered (im)possible for students of
Color and what we can draw from, amplify, and strengthen (i.e., our
assets, our knowledge) in college going as POC.

COLLEGE READINESS

We consider college readiness as knowledge and skills that include academic preparedness but extend far beyond this singular factor. While
academic preparedness is important, it cannot be made proxy for college
readiness and will only set up students of Color to fail when it is. We
know that students of Color must also be ready to navigate the racialization and racism that is embedded within higher education institutions.
Thus, in our consideration of college readiness, we draw from Freire's
critical consciousness, which is also taken up in chapter 2 by Arce and
Carpenter. Freire (1970/2000) described critical consciousness as a state
of awareness enabling individuals to perceive economic, political, and
social oppression, and to use that understanding to act against oppressive

forces and oppressors. We consider the ways in which students of Color can be prepared intellectually, academically, emotionally, mentally, socially, and culturally so that they can be ready to move into, through, and out of higher education spaces whole. While some of this preparation for readiness will happen in their K–12 schools, we also consider the ways it happens in their homes and communities, and how that preparation can also be reinforced in the school space.

Critical Reflection

We express our gratitude to you as a reader for engaging in this chapter and encourage you to consider those that have positively impacted your journey by reflecting on these critical questions:

1. What or who informs how you have come to understand college access, choice, and readiness? In what ways is your understanding of college access, choice, and readiness in connection or in tension with what we have suggested in this chapter?

2. To whom might you address your "letter of gratitude" in terms of individuals who have strongly and positively influenced your own thinking about college access and choice?

References

Allen, W. R., Jewell, J. O., Griffin, K. A., & Wolf, D. S. S. (2007). Historically Black colleges and universities: Honoring the past, engaging the present, touching the future. *Journal of Negro Education, 76*(3), 263–280.

Amah, I. A. (2012). Beyond the GPA: Counter-narratives of non-high performing African American students. *International Review of Qualitative Research, 5*(2), 225–250. https://doi.org/10.1525/irqr.2012.5.2.225

Bell, D. (2009). Who's afraid of critical race theory? In E. Taylor, D. Gillborn, & G. Ladson-Billings (Eds.), *Foundations of critical race theory in education* (pp. 37–50). Routledge.

Bernal, E. M., Cabrera, A. F., & Terenzini, P. T. (2000). The relationship between race and socioeconomic status (SES): Implications for institutional research and admissions policies. *American Association of Community Colleges: Removing Vestiges*, 6–19.

Buenavista, T. L. (2010). Issues affecting U.S. Filipino student access to postsecondary education: A critical race theory perspective. *Journal of Education for Students Placed at Risk, 15*(1–2), 114–126. https://doi.org/10.1080/10824661003635093

Cabrera, A. F., & La Nasa, S. M. (2000). *Understanding the college choice of disadvantaged students: New Directions for Institutional Research. Number 107.* Jossey-Bass.

Ceja, M. (2006). Understanding the role of parents and siblings as information sources in the college choice process of Chicana students. *Journal of College Student Development, 47*(1), 87–104. https://www.doi.org/10.1353/csd.2006.0003

Cooper, R., & Liou, D. D. (2007). The structure and culture of information pathways: Rethinking opportunity to learn in urban high schools. *High School Journal 91*, 43–56. https://doi.org/10.1353/hsj.2007.0020

Covarrubias, R., De Lima, F., Landa, I., Valle, I., & Hernandez Flores, W. (2021). Facets of family achievement guilt for low-income, Latinx and Asian first-generation students. *Cultural Diversity and Ethnic Minority Psychology, 27*(4), 696–704. https://doi.org/10.1037/cdp0000418

Cox, R. D. (2016). Complicating conditions: Obstacles and interruptions to low-income students' college "choices." *Journal of Higher Education, 87*(1), 1–26. https://doi.org/10.1080/00221546.2016.11777392

Crenshaw, K. (1988). Race, reform and retrenchment: Transformation and legitimation in antidiscrimination law. *Harvard Law Review, 101*(7), 1331. https://doi.org/10.2307/1341398

Delgado, R., & Stefancic, J. (2000). *Critical race theory: The cutting edge.* Temple University Press.

Freeman, K. (1999). The race factor in African Americans' college choice. *Urban Education, 34*(1), 4–25. https://doi.org/10.1177/0042085999341002

Freeman, K. (2005). *African Americans and college choice.* State University of New York Press.

Freeman, K., & Thomas, G. E. (2002). Black colleges and college choice: Characteristics of students who choose HBCUs. *Review of Higher Education, 25*(3), 349–358. https://doi.org/10.1353/rhe.2002.0011

Freire, P. (1970/2000). *Pedagogy of the oppressed* (30th Anniversary ed.). Bloomsbury.

George Mwangi, C. A. (2018). "It's different here": Complicating concepts of college knowledge and first generation through an immigrant lens. *Teachers College Record, 120*(11), 1–36.

George Mwangi, C. A. (2019). Navigating two worlds: Exploring home-school dissonance in the college going process of immigrant families. *Harvard Educational Review, 89*(3), 448–472. https://doi.org/10.17763/1943-5045-89.3.448

González, K. P., Stone, C., & Jovel, J. (2003). Examining the role of social capital in access to college for Latinas: Toward a college opportunity framework.

Journal of Hispanics in Higher Education, 2(2), 146–171. https://doi.org/
10.1177/1538192702250620

Griffin, K., & Allen, W. (2006). Mo'money, mo'problems? High-achieving Black
high school students' experiences with resources, racial climate, and resilience. *Journal of Negro Education*, 478–494.

Harper, S. R., Patton, L. D., & Wooden, O. S. (2009). Access and equity for African
American students in higher education: A critical race historical analysis
of policy efforts. *Journal of Higher Education, 80*(4), 389–414. https://doi.
org/10.1080/00221546.2009.11779022

Herndon, M. K., & Hirt, J. B. (2004). Black students and their families: What
leads to success in college. *Journal of Black Studies, 34*(4), 489–513. https://
www.doi.org/10.1177/0021934703258762

Holland, N. E. (2010). Postsecondary education preparation of traditionally underrepresented college students: A social capital perspective. *Journal of Diversity
in Higher Education, 3*(2), 111–125. https://doi.org/10.1037/a0019249

Hurtado, S., Inkelas, K. K., Briggs, C., & Rhee, B. (1997). Differences in college
access and choice among racial/ethnic groups: Identifying continuing barriers. *Research in Higher Education, 38*(1) 43–76. https://doi.org/10.1023/
A:1024948728792

Jayakumar, U. M., Vue, R., & Allen, W. R. (2013). Pathways to college for young
Black scholars: A community cultural wealth perspective. *Harvard Educational
Review, 83*(4), 551–579. https://doi.org/10.17763/haer.83.4.4k1mq00162433l28

Jenkins, T. S. (Ed). (2013). *Family, community, and higher education*. Routledge.

Kiyama, J. M. (2010). College aspirations and limitations: The role of educational ideologies and funds of knowledge in Mexican American families. *American Educational Research Journal, 47*(2), 330–356. https://doi.
org/10.3102/0002831209357468

Kiyama, J. (2011). Family lessons and funds of knowledge: College-going paths in
Mexican American families. *Journal of Latinos & Education, 10*(1), 23–42.
https://doi.org/10.1080/15348431.2011.531656

Knight, M. G., Norton, N. E., Bentley, C. C., & Dixon, I. R. (2004). The power
of Black and Latina/o counterstories: Urban families and college-going
processes. *Anthropology & Education Quarterly, 35*(1), 99–120. https://doi.
org/10.1525/aeq.2004.35.1.99

Ladson-Billings, G., & Tate, W. F. (1995). Toward a critical race theory of education. *Teachers College Record, 97*(1), 47–68. https://doi-org.mutex.gmu.
edu.1177/ 01614681950970010

Liou, D. D., Antrop-González, R., & Cooper, R. (2009). Unveiling the promise of
community cultural wealth to sustaining Latina/o students' college-going
information networks. *Educational Studies, 45*(6), 534–555. https://doi.
org/10.1080/00131940903311347

Martinez, M. A. (2012). Wealth, stereotypes, and issues of prestige: The college
choice experience of Mexican American students within a community

context. *Journal of Hispanic Higher Education, 11*(1), 67–81. https://doi. org/10.1177/1538192711428992

Martinez, M. A. (2013). (Re)considering the role familismo plays in Latina/o high school students' college choices. *High School Journal, 97*(1), 21–40.

Matsuda, M. J., Lawrence, C. R., Delgado, R. & Crenshaw, K. W. (1993). *Words that wound: Critical race theory assaultive speech, and the First Amendment.* Westview Press.

McCoy, D., & Rodricks, D. (2015). Critical race theory in higher education: 20 years of theoretical and research innovations. *ASHE Higher Education Report, 41*(3), 1–117.

Moll, L. C., Amanti, C., Neff, D., & Gonzalez, N. (1992). Funds of knowledge for teaching: Using a qualitative approach to connect homes and classrooms. *Theory into Practice, 31*(2), 132–141. https://doi.org/10.1080/00405849209543 534

Muhammad, C. G. (2008). African American students and college choice: A consideration of the role of school counselors. *NASSP Bulletin, 92*(2), 81–94. https://doi.org/10.1177/0192636508320989

Núñez, A. M., & Bowers, A. J. (2011). Exploring what leads high school students to enroll in Hispanic-serving institutions: A multilevel analysis. *American Educational Research Journal, 48*(6), 1286–1313. https://doi. org/10.3102/0002831211408061

Núñez, A. M., Johnelle Sparks, P., & Hernández, E. A. (2011). Latino access to community colleges and Hispanic-serving institutions: A national study. *Journal of Hispanic Higher Education, 10*(1), 18–40. https://doi. org/10.1177/1538192710391801

Oseguera, L., & Malagon, M. C. (2011). For-profit colleges and universities and the Latina/o students who enroll in them. *Journal of Hispanic Higher Education, 10*(1), 66–91. https://doi.org/10.1177/1538192710392040

Pérez, P. A., & McDonough, P. M. (2008). Understanding Latina and Latino college choice: A social capital and chain migration analysis. *Journal of Hispanic Higher Education, 7*(3), 249–265. https://doi.org/10.1177/1538192708317620

Reddick, R. J., Welton, A. D., Alsandor, D. J., Denyszyn, J. L., & Platt, C. S. (2011). Stories of success: High minority, high poverty public school graduate narratives on accessing higher education. *Journal of Advanced Academics, 22*(4), 594–618. https://doi.org/10.1177/1932202X11414133

Rios-Aguilar, C. (2010). Measuring funds of knowledge: Contributions to Latina/o students' academic and non-academic outcomes. *Teachers College Record, 112*(8), 2209–2257. https://doi.org/10.1177/016146811011200805

Rios-Aguilar, C., & Kiyama, J. M. (2012). Funds of knowledge: An approach to studying Latina(o) students' transition to college. *Journal of Latinos and Education, 11*(1), 2–16. https://doi.org/10.1080/15348431.2012.631430

Rosas, M., & Hamrick, F. A. (2002). Postsecondary enrollment and academic decision making: Family influences on women college students of Mexican descent. *Equity and Excellence in Education, 35*(1), 59–69. https://doi.org/10.1080/713845240

Serna, G. R., & Woulfe, R. (2017). Social reproduction and college access: Current evidence, context, and potential alternatives. *Critical Questions in Education, 8*(1), 1–16.

Solórzano, D. G. (1997). Images and words that wound: Critical race theory, racial stereotyping, and teacher education. *Teacher Education Quarterly, 24*(3), 5–19.

Solórzano, D. G., & Delgado Bernal, D. (2001). Examining transformational resistance through a critical race and Latcrit theory framework: Chicana and Chicano students in an urban context. *Urban Education, 36*(3), 308–342. https://doi.org/10.1177/0042085901363002

Solórzano, D., & Villalpando, O. (1998). Critical race theory, marginality, and the experience of minority students in higher education. In C. Torres & T. Mitchell (Eds.), *Emerging issues in the sociology of education: comparative perspectives* (pp. 211–224). State University of New York Press.

Solórzano, D., & Yosso, T. (2001). Critical race and Latcrit theory and method: Counterstorytelling Chicana and Chicano graduate school experiences. *International Journal of Qualitative Studies in Education, 14*, 471–495. https://doi.org/10.1080/09518390110063365

Solórzano, D., & Yosso, T. (2002a). A critical race counterstory of affirmative action in higher education. *Equity & Excellence in Education, 35*, 155–168. https://doi.org/10.1080/713845284

Solórzano, D., & Yosso, T. (2002b). Critical race methodology: Counterstorytelling as an analytical framework for education research. *Qualitative Inquiry, 8*(1), 23–44. https://doi.org/10.1177/107780040200800103

Tate, W. F. (1997). Critical race theory and education: History, theory and implications. *Review of Research in Education, 22*(1), 195–247. https://doi.org/10.3102/0091732X022001195

Teranishi, R. T. (2002). Asian Pacific Americans and critical race theory: An examination of school racial climate. *Equity & Excellence in Education, 35*, 144–154. https://doi.org/10.1080/713845281

Teranishi, R. T., & Briscoe, K. (2008). Contextualizing race: African American college choice in an evolving affirmative action era. *Journal of Negro Education, 77*(1), 15–26.

Vélez-Ibáñez, C., & Greenberg, J. (1992). Formation and transformation of funds of knowledge among U.S.-Mexican households. *Anthropology & Education Quarterly, 23*(4), 313–335. https://doi.org/10.1525/aeq.1992.23.4.05x1582v

Villalpando, O., & Solórzano, D. G. (2005). The role of culture in college preparation programs: A review of the research literature. In W. G. Tierney, Z. B. Corwin, & J. E. Colyar (Eds.), *Preparing for college: Nine elements of effective outreach* (pp. 13–28). State University of New York Press.

Yamamura, E. K., Martinez, M. A., & Saenz, V. B. (2010). Moving beyond high school expectations: Examining stakeholders' responsibility for increasing Latina/o students' college readiness. *High School Journal, 93*(3), 126–148.

Yosso, T. J. (2005). Whose culture has capital? A critical race theory discussion of community cultural wealth. *Race Ethnicity and Education, 8*(1), 69–91. https://doi.org/10.1080/1361332052000341006

Yosso, T. J., Parker, L., Solórzano, D. G., & Lynn, M. (2004). From Jim Crow to affirmative action and back again: A critical race discussion of racialized rationales and access to higher education. *Review of Research in Education, 28*, 1–25. https://doi.org/10.3102/0091732X028001001

Yosso, T., & Solórzano, D. (2005). Conceptualizing a critical race theory in sociology. In M. Romero & E. Margolis (Eds.), *Blackwell companion to social inequalities* (pp. 117–146). Blackwell.

Part I

Youth-Centered Framings

"Why college?" SOC brainstorm session. Whiteboard notes from a UCAP after-school college access program activity in which high school students of Color brainstormed whether and why they should go to college, who might assist them in getting to college, and who controls choice in going to college. The following chapters in this section similarly center how youth of Color framed college access and choice. *Source*: Photo by the editors.

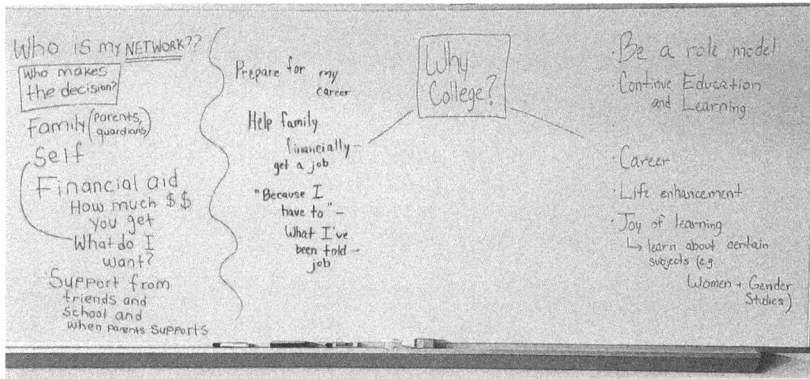

Chapter 2

Critically Conscious College Knowledge

Critiquing Notions of College Readiness through an Ethnic Studies Lens

Joel A. Arce and Ashley Carpenter

As students enrolling in college become more representative of global identities (Markey et al., 2023), institutional and systemic barriers (i.e., anti-DEI/anti-CRT legislation, repeal of affirmative action) can impact the successful matriculation, retention, and graduation rates for minoritized students (Johnson, 2019). Unfortunately, educational disparities persist despite numerous research studies and theories developed to help understand the college-going pathways of students in the United States (Hines et al., 2021). However, in the past decade, new scholarship has emerged to meet the increasing need to support students to become college ready. According to Conley (2007), college readiness is defined as students' ability to complete entry-level coursework without needing remediation, and their comprehension of the social norms of a postsecondary institution. Similar to George Mwangi and Ruíz Santana's discussions in chapter 1, we acknowledge the importance of going beyond this one-dimensional framing of college access and readiness by lifting up asset-based lenses (see Yosso, 2005). This (re)framing considers students' cultural identities to be a valuable and essential part of their learning process that is reinforced through the cultural resources they acquire from their communities and families. Through this, we recognize that the current dominant models of college access and readiness primarily rely on essentialized and deficit notions of minoritized students[1] rather than building on their varying cultural assets to strengthen their college pathways (Liou & Rojas, 2020). As envisioned in chapter 1, we seek to push the work of unlearning and relearning college access and readiness through a holistic model that outlines educational policies, measurements, and practices that meet the needs of students as they transition into postsecondary education.

This chapter introduces a *critically conscious college knowledge* (C³K) framework that guides college access and readiness programming and policies to be more culturally sustaining for minoritized students. The C³K framework emerged from a semester-long pilot, after-school college access program (UCAP) with high school students who had the opportunity to engage and learn alongside a class of graduate students studying college access inequities. In addition to building a learning exchange opportunity for students, UCAP was unique in that it consisted of high school students who had either taken or were taking an ethnic studies course at the time of the program. Student participants' prior knowledge and engagement with ethnic studies material enriched the UCAP discussions and participation throughout the sessions.

Unlike traditional conceptualizations of college knowledge, a C³K framework engages students in critical reflection and discussions about educational injustices. By engaging students in these conversations during their college-going process, practitioners and scholars can foster a wide range of learning opportunities to hone college-level critical thinking skills and develop nuanced understandings of the potential postsecondary experiences that await them after high school. Dominant college access and readiness models typically frame intervention and programming to supplement existing unjust educational experiences and structures for students. However, instead of merely supplementing students' experiences, engaging a C³K framework would directly address these inhibitive experiences that are reinforced in and out of schools and other educational contexts.

In more recent scholarship, many scholars have relied on social and cultural capital theories to outline renewed ways to measure readiness and develop interventions and strategies (Almeida, 2015; Bryan et al., 2019). However, these research frameworks and methods typically relegate culturally responsive college access programming to an approach that views youth as students with deficit gaps and does not seek to transform the systemic injustices built into the college-going process for minoritized students. In contrast, other scholars have grounded their research using a variety of critical, community-engaged, and culturally sustaining frameworks such as critical race theory and community cultural wealth to gain insight into the unique factors, contextual experiences, and relationships that might impact the postsecondary trajectories of underrepresented students (Acevedo, 2020; Castro, 2013; Liou et al., 2009; Liou & Rojas, 2020; Welton & Martinez, 2014). We argue it is not enough for these college access programs to exist: they must have intentional approaches considering the macrostructural inequities that minoritized students face in their school and community contexts (Castro, 2013; Kolluri & Tierney, 2020).

The following sections offer some of our experiences and backgrounds as researcher-practitioners. We discuss how our identities impacted our entry and engagement with UCAP. In addition to providing this context, we detail our experiences and takeaways through dialogue with existing scholarship about college access and ethnic studies. We then unpack and describe our proposed C³K framework, concluding with implications and reflection questions for practitioners and researchers.

Researcher Positionality and UCAP Context

As researcher-practitioners, our intersecting identities informed our work throughout this project. Similar to the positionalities and commitments of community-oriented *nepantlera* educators (Acevedo, 2020; see also chapter 9 in this volume), we were working with UCAP students as university-based facilitators of Color within an "education borderlands" where deficit ideology was prevalent, but there existed pockets of critical educators trying to build college-going pathways for minoritized students. Our school research site reflects a common phenomenon in which students of Color are *systemically* pushed into de facto segregated, underresourced schools with high concentrations of student poverty, which is conducive to conditions that cause traditional academic underperformance (Reardon et al., 2022). Furthermore, at the time of the project, we were doctoral students attending a land-grant predominantly white institution (PWI), which often was not reflective of our cultural identities or structured to support our community-oriented educational pursuits. Nevertheless, we were driven by a commitment and desire to work within a school community in which we saw ourselves within our students, and our students saw themselves in us.

Building on a prior relationship with a local district ethnic studies program, we found a place to carry out our social justice commitments and fulfill a stated need by the ethnic studies program director for college access programming. With the support of our faculty mentor, Dr. Chrystal George Mwangi, we envisioned a semester-long high school college access program that would happen in tandem with a graduate course that focused on issues of college access and inequity. As facilitators, we recognized that the 12-student UCAP cohort had some background in ethnic studies coursework and was already critically engaged in sociohistorical material and inquiry about power, oppression, and resistance at micro- and macrolevels. Therefore, we scaffolded a series of biweekly workshops that complemented students' experiences in ethnic studies classrooms through structured dialogue with graduate students about college access and readiness. The UCAP meeting location alternated between the UCAP students' high school and the research team's university. Eleven of the 12 UCAP students were students of Color, reflecting the high school's demographics—primarily Latinx, low income, and first generation.

Throughout UCAP, we examined students' perceptions and aspirations around the admissions process while supporting them in developing college-going identities (Brown, 2024; Gutierrez-Serrano, 2023) through structured workshops with information and discussion activities on traditional college knowledge and C³K. From our standpoint, educational attainment can serve as a potential pathway for minoritized youth to access dominant forms of social capital that can lead to shifts in generational material realities. That said, we constantly reflected on the importance of a framework that would allow students to authentically complicate dominant notions of college access, while recognizing that we are two college-educated scholars with professional experience in higher education who went through a pipeline that often reinforces inequities. In that vein, it is necessary to be transparent about our personal narratives surrounding college access and how it complicates our scholarly analysis and engagement with students. Following are our stories on what brought us to this work.

Ashley's Story

Growing up in a suburb of Chicago, my parents were adamant about showcasing Black culture within my home. It was evident in the shows we watched, the music we listened to, the books they read to me, and our conversations. These moments shaped my intellectual thoughts and experiences with Blackness and Black identity. And most notably, Black women educators were prominent in the foreground, shaping these thoughts. My mother was my first teacher, in particular. I enjoyed seeing my mother, an eighth-grade math and science teacher in Chicago, teach Black and Brown kids new concepts about everything from ecosystems to trigonometry. Even though I was much younger than the older students my mother taught, I was amazed by their engagement and interest. I often saw students hang out with my mom during their lunch period as she sat grading in her small and hot classroom. She constantly overextended herself to ensure students were learning, a trait she brought into our household. She would often bring her lesson plans home with entertaining experiments. Some of my best memories are working on projects for the elementary school science fair, where I had some advantages and often placed in the contests. As a young child, I saw her teach students with such tough love and, arguably, I utilize similar tactics as a professor now. There has always been a sense of joy in seeing Black women teaching students who looked like me.

However, even though I could see Black educators teaching Black and Brown students, that was not indicative of my individual learning experiences. Though I had Black educators outside the classroom—inside the classroom space, I was often the only Black student or person of Color. As my parents afforded me the opportunities to attend schools with significant resources, including participation in multiple extracurricular activities, I still felt that I did not belong or was a part of these communities. While I experienced privilege in some of my academic and social spaces, no financial capital could insulate me from the marginalization and microaggressions I felt from white teachers and peers. The culture I received from my Black educators in my personal life was missing from my academic life. These tokenized, racialized, and discriminatory experiences within these white academic spaces reshaped how I construct my vision and work within academia. In particular, I am intentional in the classroom in seeing women of Color's invisibility. In social, political, and academic discussions—including policies and research—the term *women and minorities* is regularly used to ignore the overlaps between the two. Therefore, within this chapter, as a Black woman, I advocate for the deliberate embodiment of students' cultures as a strategy for success.

Joel's Story

Prior to returning to graduate school, my professional experiences as a classroom teacher in the Bronx and a college access counselor working for a nonprofit greatly informed my perspective on college access and admissions. However, reflecting on my own educational narrative, as a first-generation Latino college student from a working-class background, in recent years has nuanced the ways I engage with research and has reshaped how I understand academic achievement and success. I attended New York City public schools that were externally and internally defined by academic tracking, criminalization tactics, multiple forms of violence, overcrowding, low graduation rates, and low teacher expectations.

In high school, I completed my first three years without any access or structured learning opportunities about college knowledge. Moreover, as I look back to my senior year, it is abundantly clear that the two main college advising office staff were stretched thin as they balanced a teaching load and a senior class of more than 700 students. In spite of this, about a month into my senior year, a peer told me about a free college access program housed within a nearby community center that was offering SAT classes and college application support to students from public high schools in Queens, New York. It was in this unadvertised, word-of-mouth, college access program that I obtained traditional college knowledge and learned about the financial aid at my disposal.

Today, I consider myself to be one of the fortunate few in my high school graduating class to learn about the different aspects of the college admissions process because of how I happened to hear about a free program a couple subway stops away from where I lived. It is an example of how low-income students of Color who attend schools that underserve them are systematically denied access to information networks that could help them see higher education as a viable option after high school. My transition into college also spotlighted how schools with predominantly low-income student of Color populations undervalue and underdevelop students' sociopolitical identities and critical thinking skills. Despite my strong grades and sense of academic identity, I often felt unprepared and uninformed when I encountered college coursework that asked me to critically engage in conversations about power, identity, and resistance. To an extent, I struggled my way through parts of college and began to see the gaps in my schooling experiences. These moments of reflection inspired my path to become an educator and an eventual researcher in the field of critical education.

Dominant Notions and Practices of College Access and Readiness

Today, most schools remain stubbornly reliant on "white, middle-class, monolingual, and monocultural norms of educational achievement" (Paris & Alim, 2014, p. 95), as evidenced in widely used noncritical curricula and standardized assessments that are devoid of engagement with POC home knowledges and histories, and higher-order, problem-posing thinking (Au, 2023; Chapman et al., 2020; Ladson-Billings, 2014). Furthermore, mainstream discourse on the achievement gap implicitly attributes student failure to individuals' inability to adapt to the academic rigor of schooling. This dominant discourse often ignores how formal educational achievement hinges on narrowed white-centric standards and rote forms of learning. It also ignores how schools are beholden to neoliberal accountability measures that create sterile learning environments and offer no incentive for educators to broaden the experiences of their students (Au, 2023; Ladson-Billings, 2014). These practices reveal the inconspicuous ways schools adopt deficit thinking (Valencia, 2010; see also Luu's chapter 3) in the present day by dressing it up in narratives about rigor and accountability while ignoring how the culture, knowledge, and analytical frameworks of POC are rooted in intellectually rich traditions that merit academic engagement.

Moreover, deficit-thinking models are pervasive in the day-to-day realities of schools and discussions about college access programming. Paris and Alim (2014) argue, "For too long, scholarship on 'access' and 'equity' has centered implicitly or explicitly around the question of how to get working-class students of [C]olor to speak and write more like middle-class [w]hite ones" (p. 87). Additionally, college access programming rarely emphasizes nontraditional indicators of college readiness, such as racial and critical literacy skills (de los Ríos et al., 2015) and critical leadership praxis, which is grounded in a commitment to social justice (Tintiangco-Cubales et al., 2015). Instead, college access programs usually focus on preparedness to perform on high-stakes college entrance exams, submitting tailored application materials, and occasionally helping students understand financial aid (not necessarily building financial literacy) and on-campus resources and structures.

UCAP Student Experiences and Perceptions of College Access and Readiness

Throughout the after-school sessions, UCAP participants shared experiences and expressed frustrations with learning environments and school staff that reflected deficit thinking. Although the students' ethnic studies background provided them with language to name the injustices that persist in their high school and other settings, the experiential knowledge they shared and peer dialogue about differential treatment and access spoke for itself. During one session, when facilitators unpacked the connections between race, socioeconomic status, employment earning power, and postsecondary degree attainment, students were asked to make sense of the low enrollment rates of their graduating peers (particularly peers of Color) to the larger local 4-year university. While they could not speak to the racialized recruitment and admissions practices that contribute to such patterns, UCAP participants identified numerous school practices and dominant school discourse about low-income students of Color.

For example, students pointed to biased advising practices that led to predominantly white student enrollment in AP classes in a school that is approximately 80% students of Color. One student shared, "What I hear a lot in this school is how people say—[students of Color] don't try . . . normally [students] are just like—oh when I graduate, I'm gonna go to [the community college]. It's too much [money] to go anywhere else." In an after-school session earlier in the semester, UCAP participants indicated that most of their peers did not know of the many 4-year institutions in the region and tended to only speak about the local community college regarding postsecondary education plans. We emphasized throughout the program that enrolling in the local community college should not be seen as an indicator of inferiority or poor choices. In fact, one of the high school student alumni attending the local 4-year university, who sat on a Q&A panel we organized, shared his story of an alternative pathway that helped him strengthen his academic identity in community college before entering the university. At the same time, we were also well aware of the persistent issue of college "undermatching" in communities of Color that funnels students into postsecondary institutions that might not be an appropriate academic fit and might be reflective of low academic expectations (Naranjo, 2016).

When the group reflected on their peers' low matriculation rates to 4-year colleges, a student poignantly said, "Maybe [students] feel like [college] is not the place for them. Because [school staff] made it feel like high school isn't the place for them just because of the way they're always pushed out. Because kids of Color come with that preconceived notion of—they don't care, they don't try. So that teachers put them to the side . . . so maybe [students] feel like they can't fit in college." School staff's lower expectations of students reflect a common theme in the literature. In other sessions, other students described these messages as "discouraging" and challenging to break free from when "you make a mistake, and people stereotype you as a bad student even if you change and want to do better." Another high school alum on the Q&A panel also discussed the stigma of being a student at their school. He mentioned how some people at the university negatively view their high school and often look down on their educational experience, which generates self-doubt.

In addition to the more explicit deficit-oriented schooling experiences, UCAP participants offered insight into how their high school framed and approached college readiness, grounded in college access models that lack relevance to minoritized students. During a discussion about how their peers think about postsecondary plans, some UCAP participants shared that college was not the focus at the high school in the past, so now teachers and staff were "trying to force it onto students." This shift in school messaging was likely due to the district's turnaround plan, created two years prior, to outline measurable academic outcomes for the state. One UCAP participant expressed frustration with how the high school structured its academies[2] and "annoyingly" asked students to frequently fill out career interest forms in ninth grade with little guidance and limited choices. In schools that attempt to build a college-going culture, particularly with minoritized students, Kolluri and Tierney (2020) suggest moving away from rational choice theory and toward a model of cultural integrity. Their proposed shift underscores the importance of aligning college readiness to students' cultural identities, sociocultural realities, and lived experiences through "leverage points" such as assessment, curriculum, and bridge programming. Kolluri and Tierney (2020) argue, "Providing enhanced information to guide students toward making rational choices is important, but students are not automatons for whom informational data inputs necessarily lead to predictable outcomes. Rather, they are steeped in cultural and social contexts that bound their rationality, willpower, and self-interest" (p. 90). The career interest forms and recently created academy structure at the UCAP students' high school reflect a rational choice theory model that fails to take into account their lived realities. On the other hand, ethnic studies coursework and pedagogy could serve as a leverage point to enact cultural integrity within the high school's college-going culture. However, while the district had recently allowed the ethnic studies program to expand into the high school, this type of learning was not widespread in the school nor fully embraced by non–ethnic studies staff.

Regarding explicit conversations and guidance around college knowledge and readiness, the recent push for college at the high school did not translate into tangible advising and programming experiences for many students before our after-school program. One of the UCAP participants said at one point, "This is the first time I've actually talked about college, and I'm already a junior." During another session in which UCAP participants, alongside graduate students, brainstormed ways their peers can be better supported with college readiness, another student shared, "I don't even know who my advisor is." In this moment, UCAP participants began to share other experiences, including another junior who said she learned about a college tour field trip from her friend after it happened—"I didn't even know about it; I didn't even get a paper for it . . . where did you even get the paper and why is it first come, first serve. What fairness is that?" These statements illustrate a school leaving many students outside of a vital information network that can put them on a pathway to college.

When students get left out of essential information networks about college readiness, they might rely on dominant notions of college access and academic success that are very individualized. At different points in the program, many UCAP participants repeated common mantras steeped in modern-day meritocracy ideologies (Generett & Olson, 2020). They sometimes spoke or wrote on worksheets about grit and perseverance as a way to overcome barriers to college. Similarly, when UCAP participants were preparing to create a video guide to give their peers vital college knowledge that was lacking in their school, their brainstorming worksheets included some pointed warnings: "pick good friends," "don't slack," and "get ready for the [state exam] (Review! Review! Review!)." Although we encouraged UCAP students to build strong academic identities and a passion for learning, a narrowed "work-harder" mentality can sometimes be detrimental to students if their school structures make it challenging to reap the benefits of hard work.

Finally, another dominant notion that many UCAP students upheld was the limited perception of college as a way to make money and have individualized success. Throughout the after-school sessions and in the peer video guide, most students spoke about their desire to "get a good job." Early on in the program, when facilitators asked, "Why college?" one student responded, "I'm gonna be honest. The only reason why I feel like I have to go to college is because I have to. I feel like that's the only way to have a good life . . . The more degrees you get, the more likely you are to have a better job." During the high school student alumni panel, one alum said he chose the 4-year university "mostly because of the name, the clout that it carries. I truly believe that you need the swagger to go wherever you're gonna go." In unpacking these responses from UCAP participants and alums, it is important to consider their positionalities to put their responses in context. As students from low-income backgrounds, this potential change in their material realities cannot be dismissed. A couple of students paired their "get a good job" responses with the desire to help their family financially. That said, it is important to note that many students were not initially talking about the community-oriented benefits and possibilities of going to college. Rather than seeing college as both an individual and collective endeavor in generating social and economic change (grounded in the ethnic studies tradition), many UCAP students were relying on a narrowed understanding of the purpose of college that they were socialized to accept.

The Struggle for and Relevancy of Ethnic Studies

The ethnic studies program at our research site is part of a broader movement for ethnic studies in K–12 public schools that was rekindled in 2010 with the outlawing of the Mexican American studies program in the Tucson Unified School District (Buenavista, 2016). We also recognize the rich history of ethnic studies as a transdisciplinary field of study and praxis (Cammarota, 2016; Tintiangco-Cubales et al., 2015) that emerged from the demands and successes of student-activists, community organizers, cultural workers, and critical educators of the 1960s. Broadly conceptualized, ethnic studies is a direct response to the (violent) historical erasures and deficit-oriented narratives of racially minoritized peoples in the United States and abroad (Sleeter & Zavala, 2020). Moreover, while many educational spaces that teach ethnic studies center an analysis of race and racism, the field also engages in a macroanalysis of power to both unpack the ways different systems of oppression intersect to produce social hierarchies and to understand how social movements seek to enact alternative ways of being (Cuauhtin, 2019; Sleeter & Zavala, 2020).

In the context of higher education, the expansion of ethnic studies throughout the last five decades has contributed to a robust and diverse critical network of activists, community organizers, cultural workers, and educators—a network reflective of the sociopolitical contexts of the 21st century. While some would argue the reformed academic policies and programs that resulted from the efforts of student-activists from more than 50 years ago fall short of the counterhegemonic education and praxis they originally envisioned (Okihiro, 2016), the legacies of their activism are substantive nonetheless. On college campuses, ethnic studies has influenced student life and culture. Thus, students of Color can explore different ways of being in college and discover a variety of pathways to community-engaged praxis, whether they take ethnic studies coursework or not.

At the secondary school level, ethnic studies both meets and transcends traditional standards and notions of college preparatory classwork by centering a curriculum on critical conversations about the histories and cultures of minoritized peoples, systems of oppression, and resistance efforts, as well as a community-responsive pedagogy (Sleeter & Zavala, 2020; Tintiangco-Cubales & Duncan-Andrade, 2021). Chapman et al. (2020) present ethnic studies as a way to not only "disrupt and displace the curriculum as the property of whiteness in K–12 education" (p. 8) but also to guide students to be "knowledgeable agents of change to develop their academic skills to problematize issues of race and racism" (p. 9). This "necessary pairing" of academic outcomes and critical consciousness, as presented by Chapman et al. (2020), illustrates how K–12 ethnic studies can make learning relevant and support students to navigate and critique a "culture of power" (Delpit, 2006), preparing them for college and postsecondary life.

In terms of pedagogy, ethnic studies classrooms at the secondary level emphasize praxis as a way for students to recognize the value of their own experiential and cultural knowledge as well as a way to develop critical consciousness, self-efficacy, and a robust academic identity (Cammarota, 2016; Duncan-Andrade & Morrell, 2008; Tintiangco-Cubales et al., 2015). Drawing on the work of Freire (1970/2000), ethnic studies scholars describe praxis as a cyclical, collective learning process in which students (and educators) reflect on a problem in the community, create an action plan to address the problem, and evaluate the impact of the collective action

(Duncan-Andrade & Morrell, 2008). Often, youth participatory action research (YPAR) projects are embedded into the ethnic studies curriculum to enact praxis and provide students with learning opportunities that are culturally relevant and engage in academic skill building that prepares them for college, career, and civic life after high school (de los Ríos et al., 2015; Tintiangco-Cubales et al., 2015). Furthermore, when YPAR is done through an authentically caring approach and critical lens, it can help students reorient their relationships with their communities through research skill building (Duncan-Andrade & Morrell, 2008). By engaging in community asset-based praxis, students can develop a collective investment in their peers' success and in preserving and advancing cultural knowledge (Tintiangco-Cubales & Duncan-Andrade, 2021). Students who critically reflect on their own social and material lives and the social and material realities of their families and communities are better prepared to be agents of change and interrupt dominant narratives and inequities that hamper individual and community transformation.

The Transformative Potential of Ethnic Studies for College Readiness

In the same spirit of the UCAP participants' ethnic studies courses, as facilitators, we intentionally drew on significant themes and principles of ethnic studies for our workshop sessions. To disrupt traditional learning spaces for high school students, we engaged UCAP participants in a learning exchange that put them in dialogue with graduate students who were also critically reflecting on college access. As a result of this structured learning experience, UCAP participants could discuss issues of college knowledge and access with graduate students across various sessions, including co-facilitated small group presentations. For example, UCAP participants watched a presentation explaining the development of "conscious college factsheets and maps" meant to help prospective college students gauge "institutional fit" by identifying campus spaces and resources that reflect the traditions of culturally sustaining pedagogy and ethnic studies. This learning exchange allowed UCAP participants to peer into a window of possible academic experiences that affirm critical and multicultural identities.

In addition, UCAP prioritized student-centered learning by allowing participants to engage in knowledge production (not just college knowledge consumption) through critical reflection activities, dialogue with near-peer undergraduates who had attended the same high school, and co-presentations at a regional academic conference. Alongside this student-centered learning, the facilitators explicitly crafted workshops to build on their learning in ethnic studies classes. For example, an entire session was dedicated to teaching and collectively unpacking statistics spotlighting the disproportionately adverse outcomes of education for minoritized students. These discussions revealed that critical consciousness is not linear and that students and educators are constantly unlearning. In one instance, a student displayed frustration with his peer's outlook on college access. After taking some time to digest statistics about disparities in college access, the following exchange occurred:

> STUDENT NO. 1: As long as I succeed in my own life, I'm happy.
>
> STUDENT NO. 2 [*arms folded*]: Jesus! Fuck everyone else?
>
> STUDENT NO. 1: Exactly.
>
> STUDENT NO. 2: No, not exactly!

This contentious yet brief exchange during a session illustrated the different stages of critical consciousness facilitators might encounter in any given college access program, even when students have been exposed to ethnic studies material. While the first student's comment was grounded in an individualistic "beat-the-odds" mentality, the second student had adopted a community-oriented response to social injustices that encouraged us to think beyond individualism. Overall, UCAP illustrated that we, as facilitators and students, could engage in difficult conversations that challenge one another while still being supportive—demonstrating another principle of ethnic studies pedagogy.

Despite this moment of disagreement, the UCAP participants collectively reached a point in the program where they felt it was necessary to disrupt their high school's long-standing pattern of college misinformation that influenced low matriculation and retention rates. Romero (2014) reminds us of the potential of "the praxis-based process of constructing a counter-story that can be used as a tool of emancipation" (p. 17). Throughout UCAP, in true praxis form, participants uncovered the deficit narratives and structural limits to their peers accessing college opportunities, including traditional college knowledge. They developed a plan to pass down their newfound college knowledge to their peers through an educational video guide because, as one participant indicated, "some people are lost in [high school] and don't know what to do [for college applications and admissions]." Under this praxis model, the potential student-led shift in their peers gaining college knowledge to make informed decisions about their high school experiences reflects a counterstory. In another example of counterstorytelling, during a visit to the local 4-year university, one UCAP participant said, "I am going to come here. No matter what . . . *and I am going to bring all my people with me.*" This notion of "lifting as we climb" is integral to developing critical consciousness by collaborating with community members and passing on knowledge.

The counterstorytelling and narratives UCAP participants discussed within sessions contextualized the structural realities that impact their ability to thrive in institutions traditionally designed to be exclusionary. For example, responding to a prompt in the UCAP-produced video guide, one student said, "I want to beat the stereotype that I won't amount to anything in life"—a testament to the collective students' desire to reject the deficit thinking that has dictated their schooling experiences and demonstrate a change in their collective sense of agency and power.

A Critically Conscious College Knowledge (C³K) Framework

While we understand the profound impact of sharing traditional college knowledge with minoritized students, limiting college readiness to this approach can be antithetical to a broader project for educational justice. Recent studies have explored the downside of ignoring the noncognitive variables of college readiness and the potentially harmful psychological effects of intensive college-going school cultures on minoritized students (Martinez et al., 2020). This kind of college access model tends to reinforce many of the dehumanizing experiences minoritized students face in their classrooms because it is void of authentic, critical caring (Antrop-González & De Jesús, 2006; Bonanno et al., 2023) and lacks attention to socioemotional well-being. College access and readiness are often relegated to a prescriptive process through which students passively consume and retain college knowledge to compensate for perceived deficits, replicating a banking model approach to learning (Freire, 1970/2000). This model generally limits college access to an individualized, achievement-focused endeavor. Furthermore, it does not explicitly engage students in learning that asks them to reflect on how pipelining structures and admissions processes sometimes reify racist educational standards and social stratification.

Therefore, we propose a C^3K framework (see figure 2.1) that draws on scholarship from ethnic studies and culturally sustaining pedagogies (Paris & Alim, 2014; Tintiangco-Cubales & Duncan-Andrade, 2021) and that challenges students to both navigate and critique the culture of power (Chapman et al., 2020; Delpit, 2006).

As Paris and Alim (2014) remind us, "As a result of continuing demographic change toward a majority multilingual society of [C]olor . . . multilingualism and multiculturalism are increasingly linked to access and power in U.S. and global contexts" (p. 87). Building on this premise, the dynamic intergenerational cultural and linguistic practices within minoritized communities deserve to be uplifted and recognized as

Figure 2.1. Critically conscious college knowledge (C^3K) framework. *Source*: Created by the author.

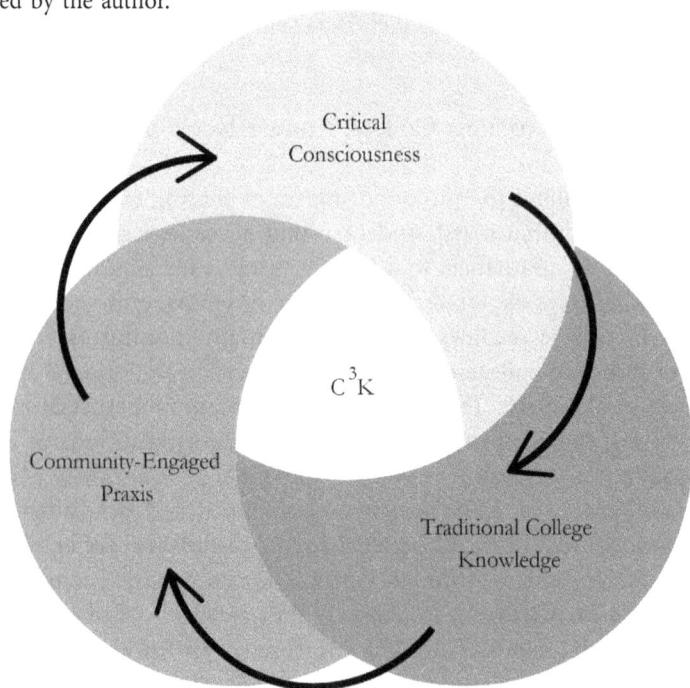

powerful tools of critical engagement in sociopolitical institutions beyond K–12 schools.

In recent years, the movement for ethnic studies in K–12 schools has fostered opportunities for practitioners and researchers to utilize and embed this proposed C³K framework in academic spaces like college access programs. C³K allows students to experience a learning environment that affirms their critical academic and cultural identities—in high school and beyond. Although job security and social mobility are undeniably important factors driving many students to pursue higher education (McArthur & Ashwin, 2020), C³K can offer students an opportunity to expand upon preconceived notions about the purpose and implications of going to college. At its core, critical consciousness encourages students to consider how their individual lives are inextricably tied to larger overarching social systems and the experiences of people in broader communities. Moreover, in describing how community-responsive pedagogy informs the broader goals of ethnic studies, Tintiangco-Cubales and Duncan-Andrade (2021) emphasize teaching and learning experiences that can support an "individual child's growth in the interest of community actualization and cultural perpetuity, rather than just individual achievement" (p. 12). C³K similarly encourages students to look at college access and education from a community-centered perspective and not solely as an individualized beneficial experience.

College readiness programming that utilizes a C³K framework also centers on praxis, a central component of ethnic studies. The learning that students experience through praxis can provide them valuable insight and tools to better understand and challenge the sociopolitical contexts surrounding college readiness and access in their local and broader communities. Without the critical lens and opportunity to collectively reflect on persistent school problems, such as low or disproportionate rates of college matriculation, minoritized students might perceive this pattern as a reflection of poor individual peer choices rather than systemic and institutionalized barriers (Scott et al., 2014; Welton & Martinez, 2014). While praxis can be enacted through other means, we look to Scott et al.'s (2014) study on a YPAR-based college access program as additional context for outlining C³K. As student participants in the study grappled with the tensions between their internalized investment in meritocracy and their newfound critical consciousness, these scholars saw YPAR projects as a way for high school students to gain college-level academic skills and to use research to spotlight and address inequities in local-national college pipeline structures. Moreover, they recognized the contradictions in a college access program that aimed to raise critical consciousness yet support students as they navigated an inherently unjust meritocratic system in which higher education plays a role. Scott et al. (2014) identify themselves "as critical pedagogues who recognize the dual nature of [higher education]," but they "also hope that [students'] emerging consciousness will have longer-term impacts on the structures of higher education itself" (p. 142). We similarly recognize these contradictions and believe in the transformative potential of critically conscious students to become change agents who disrupt the status quo.

Cammarota (2016) argues that when praxis is intentionally coupled with an understanding of systems of oppression, students can undergo internal and external transformations that embody critical consciousness. Through a praxis of critical consciousness, students not only come to recognize the way socioeconomic structures produce injustices, but they also gain a personal and collective sense of civic efficacy and seek ways to change their social environments (Cammarota, 2016). A C³K framework embraces praxis so that students can reflect on their (mis)conceptions about college access, which may contribute to dominant views of the postsecondary trajectories of their peers.

Moving C³K Forward

College access programs must diligently provide meaningful, holistic exposure and engagement for minoritized students. Traditional and dominant college access and readiness models focus on noncritical, neoliberal academic coursework and admissions material preparation and, more recently, on fostering noncognitive skill development among students. However, these intervention practices often replicate some of the same dehumanizing conditions and practices pervasive in schools and ignore students' cultural identities and experiences within broader socioeconomic structures.

Through our own experiences as scholars of Color and researcher-practitioners, we recognize how deficit narratives permeate the lives of minoritized students, which can affect their internalized understandings of the purpose of college and their postsecondary prospects and trajectories. Moreover, unequal access to consistent and well-developed information networks reinforces harmful messaging around who should go to college and what kind of college readiness experience is appropriate for students, depending on their racial identities and socioeconomic status. Therefore, we also see the urgency and impactful role of educators who can leverage their access to institutional resources in ways that align with a critical research agenda that disrupts an unjust higher education pipeline.

An abundance of scholarship outlines how educators and policymakers can support minoritized students as they navigate the college-going process (see Ballysingh et al., 2021; Carey, 2019). However, C³K represents a shift in how we should frame college readiness and access, and it rejects the deficit-thinking models embedded in the K–12 educational system. C³K encourages students to collectively reflect on and critique the unequal pathways to higher education and consider the possibilities for counternarratives and counterpathways that challenge dominant perceptions around the academic abilities of their peers—who often get stigmatized as not smart enough or not financially positioned to experience college. Critical education spaces, such as ethnic studies, can help us reimagine traditional academic achievement and success indicators and promote a collective vision for social justice and community change. Furthermore, ethnic studies has implications for secondary schools, students' critical consciousness development, and access to higher education. Critical consciousness *is* college readiness in that such a lens can help students academically excel in college classrooms (across different disciplines), navigate contentious educational spaces, and grow into agents of change on college campuses. At the center of C³K, this lens paves the way for potentially transformative experiences for individual students and the people in their surrounding communities.

Our partnership with an ethnic studies program was integral to developing UCAP and implementing a C³K framework. In addition to sharpening their critical literacy and thinking, ethnic studies courses prepared UCAP students to engage in thoughtful discussions about the intersections of race, class, college access, and campus culture. Rather than solely building networks for minoritized students to access college, ethnic studies challenges us to rethink college admissions and access (see Pulido, 2006, for more historical analysis) so that critical forms of learning and academic identity development are honored and recognized as valuable to the college campus experience. UCAP illustrates how C³K can support the development of minoritized students' college-going identities while fostering a space where students can strengthen and apply their critical consciousness to the college-going process and their eventual campus experiences.

Critical Reflection

1. When developing a college access program, consider whether there are critical education spaces (e.g., an ethnic studies program) in the high school where students can engage in critical consciousness development and praxis. How might those spaces align and complement a college access program that utilizes a C³K framework?

2. What reflective activities would you incorporate into a college access program to support students grappling with deficit-oriented messaging and internalized beliefs centered around meritocracy?

3. When planning a college access program that utilizes a C³K framework, what learning outcomes and assessments might students engage with that can impact their local (school) community and demonstrate a stronger sense of self-efficacy?

Notes

1. Use of the term *minoritized students* in this chapter refers to students who are of Color, low income, and first generation.

2. As part of the district's redesign plan, the high school rolled out a phased model for students to select one of four theme-based academies, which were presumed to motivate students to learn through personalized learning pathways within each academy. Similar to academy models in other school districts, the four academies are meant to prepare students for college or career options through specific learning trajectories and exposure to postsecondary fields.

References

Acevedo, N. (2020). *Nepantleras* building bridges toward college readiness: Latina/o/x educators fostering equity in an urban high school. *Education Sciences, 10*(4), 88. https://doi.org/doi:10.3390/educsci10040088

Almeida, D. J. (2015). College readiness and low-income youth: The role of social capital in acquiring college knowledge. In W. G. Tierney & J. C. Duncheon

(Eds.), *The problem of college readiness* (pp. 89–113). State University of New York Press.

Antrop-González, R., & De Jesús, A. (2006). Toward a theory of critical care in urban small school reform: Examining structures and pedagogies of caring in two Latino community-based schools. *International Journal of Qualitative Studies in Education, 9*(4), 409–433. https://doi.org/10.1080/09518390600773148

Au, W. (2023). Unequal by design: High-stakes testing and the standardization of inequality (2nd ed.). New York: Routledge.

Ballysingh, T. A., Rangel, V. S., Gonell, E. A., & Sáenz, V. B. (2021). Mechanisms of matriculation: School counseling resources and college going for Latino men. *Professional School Counseling, 25*. https://doi.org/10.1177/2156759X211040033

Bonanno, S. L., Walls, J., Lavigne, A. L., & Washburn, K. (2023). Theorizing a culturally and linguistically sustaining school leadership: Exploring the intersections of cultural sustenance and care. *Journal of School Leadership, 33*(3), 241–268. https://doi.org/10.1177/10526846221133985

Brown, C. S., Usher, E. L., Coleman, C., & Han, J. (2024). Perceptions of discrimination predict retention of college students of color: Connections with school belonging and ethnic identity. *Journal of College Student Retention: Research, Theory & Practice, 26*(1), 240–258. https://doi-org.proxy006.nclive.org/10.1177/15210251211070560

Bryan, J., Griffin, D., Henry, L., & Gilfillan, B. (2019). Building culturally relevant school-family-community partnerships that promote college readiness and access. In *Fundamentals of College Admission Counseling* (5th ed.) (pp. 467–488). NACAC.

Buenavista, T. L. (2016). Introduction: The making of a movement—Ethnic studies in a K–12 context. In D. M. Sandoval, A. J. Ratcliff, T. L. Buenavista, & J. R. Marín (Eds.), *"White" washing American education: The new culture wars in ethnic studies, vol. 1: K–12 education* (pp. vii–xxvii). Praeger.

Cammarota, J. (2016). The praxis of ethnic studies: Transforming second sight into critical consciousness. *Race Ethnicity and Education, 19*(2), 233–251. http://dx.doi.org/10.1080/13613324.2015.1041486

Carey, R. L. (2019). Am I smart enough? Will I make friends? And can I even afford it? Exploring the college-going dilemmas of Black and Latino adolescent boys. *American Journal of Education, 125*(3), 381–415. https://doi.org/10.1086/702740

Castro, E. L. (2013). Racialized readiness for college and career: Toward an equity-grounded social science of intervention programming. *Community College Review, 41*(4), 292–310. https://doi.org/10.1177/0091552113504291

Chapman, T. K., Jones, M., Stephens, R., Lopez, D., Rogers, K. D., & Crawford, J. (2020). A necessary pairing: Using academic outcomes and critical consciousness to dismantle curriculum as the property of whiteness in K–12 ethnic studies. *Equity & Excellence in Education, 53*(4), 569–582. https://doi.org/10.1080/10665684.2020.1791767

Conley, D. T. (2007). *Redefining college readiness.* Educational Policy Improvement Center.

Cuauhtin, R. T. (2019). The ethnic studies framework: A holistic overview. In R. T. Cuauhtin, M. Zavala, C. Sleeter, & W. Au (Eds.), *Rethinking ethnic studies* (pp. 65–79). Rethinking Schools.

de los Ríos, C. V., López, J., & Morrell, E. (2015). Toward a critical pedagogy of race: Ethnic studies and literacies of power in high school classrooms. *Race and Social Problems, 7*(1), 84–96. https://doi.org/10.1007/s12552-014-9142-1

Delpit, L. (2006). *Other people's children: Cultural conflict in the classroom.* New Press.

Duncan-Andrade, J. M. R., & Morrell, E. (2008). *The art of critical pedagogy: Possibilities for moving from theory to practice in urban schools.* Peter Lang.

Freire, P. (1970/2000). *Pedagogy of the oppressed* (30th Anniversary ed.). Bloomsbury.

Generett, G. G., & Olson, A. M. (2020). The stories we tell: How merit narratives undermine success for urban youth. *Urban Education, 55*(3), 394–423. https://doi.org/10.1177/0042085918817342

Gutierrez-Serrano, G., Romo, L. F., & Chagolla, D. (2023). Latina first-generation college students' motivation to persist: An attribution theory and self-determination theory perspective. *Journal of Latinos and Education, 22*(5), 2164–2177. https://doi-org.proxy006.nclive.org/10.1080/15348431.2022.2096611

Hines, E. M., Mayes, R. D., Hines, M. R., Henderson, J. A., Golden, M. N., Singleton, P., Cintron, D. W., Wathen, B.-J., Wright, C. G., Vega, D., & Slack, T. (2021). "You are going to school": Exploring the precollege experiences of first-year Black males in Higher Education. *Professional School Counseling, 25*(1). https://doi.org/10.1177/2156759X211040044

Johnson, A. M. (2019). "I can turn it on when I need to": Pre-college integration, culture, and peer academic engagement among Black and Latino/a engineering students. *Sociology of Education, 92*(1), 1–20. https://doi.org/10.1177/0038040718817064

Kolluri, S., & Tierney, W. G. (2020). Understanding college readiness: The limitations of information and the possibilities of cultural integrity. *Educational Forum, 84*(1), 80–93. https://doi.org/10.1080/00131725.2020.1672003

Ladson-Billings, G. (2014). Culturally relevant pedagogy 2.0: A.k.a. the remix. *Harvard Educational Review, 84*(1), 74–84. https://doi.org/10.17763/haer.84.1.p2rj131485484751

Liou, D. D., Antrop-González, R., & Cooper, R. (2009). Unveiling the promise of community cultural wealth to sustaining Latina/o students' college-going information networks. *Educational Studies, 45*(6), 534–555. https://doi.org/10.1080/00131940903311347

Liou, D. D., & Rojas, L. (2020). The significance of the racial contract in teachers' college expectancies for students of color. *Race Ethnicity and Education, 23*(5), 712–731. https://doi.org/10.1080/13613324.2018.1511529

Martinez, M. A., Lewis, K., & Marquez, J. (2020). College ready at a cost: Underrepresented students overwhelmed, scared, increasingly stressed, and coping. *Education and Urban Society, 52*(5), 734–758. https://doi.org/10.1177/0013124519887713

Markey, K., Graham, M. M., Tuohy, D., McCarthy, J., O'Donnell, C., Hennessy, T., Fahy, A., & O'Brien, B. (2023). Navigating learning and teaching in expanding culturally diverse higher education settings. *Higher Education Pedagogies, 8*(1), 2165527.

McArthur, J., & Ashwin, P. (2020). Introduction. In J. McArthur & P. Ashwin (Eds.), *Locating social justice in higher education research* (pp. 1–20) Bloomsbury Academic.

Naranjo, M. M. (2016). *Roadblocks to a 4-year university: Understanding college undermatch and college choice process of first-generation, low-income high school Latina/o students* [Doctoral dissertation, Claremont Graduate University and San Diego State University]. ProQuest.

Okihiro, G. Y. (2016). *Third World studies: Theorizing liberation.* Duke University Press.

Paris, D., & Alim, H. S. (2014). What are we seeking to sustain through culturally sustaining pedagogy? A loving critique forward. *Harvard Educational Review, 84*(1), 85–100. https://doi.org/10.17763/haer.84.1.982l873k2ht16m77

Pulido, L. (2006). *Black, brown, yellow, and left: Radical activism in Los Angeles.* University of California Press.

Reardon, S. F., Weathers, E. S., Fahle, E. M., Jang, H., & Kalogrides, D. (2022). *Is separate still unequal? New evidence on school segregation and racial academic achievement gaps* (Working Paper No. 19-06). Stanford Center for Education Policy Analysis.

Romero, A. (2014). Critically compassionate intellectualism: The pedagogy of barriorganic intellectualism. In J. Cammarota & A. Romero (Eds.), *Raza studies: The public option for educational revolution* (pp. 14–39). University of Arizona Press.

Scott, M. A., Pyne, K. B., & Means, D. R. (2014). Approaching praxis: YPAR as critical pedagogical process in a college access program. *High School Journal, 98*(2), 138–157.

Sleeter, C., & Zavala, M. (2020). *Transformative ethnic studies in schools: Curriculum, pedagogy, and research.* Teachers College Press.

Tintiangco-Cubales, A., & Duncan-Andrade, J. (2021). Chapter 2: Still fighting for ethnic studies—The origins, practices, and potential of community responsive pedagogy. *Teachers College Record, 123*(13). https://doi.org/10.1177/016146812112301303

Tintiangco-Cubales, A., Kohli, R., Sacramento, J., Henning, N., Agarwal-Rangnath, R., & Sleeter, C. (2015). Toward an ethnic studies pedagogy: Implications for K–12 schools from the research. *Urban Review, 47*(1), 104–125. https://doi.org/10.1007/s11256-014-0280-y

Valencia, R. R. (2010). *Dismantling contemporary deficit thinking: Educational thought and practice*. Routledge.

Welton, A. D., & Martinez, M. A. (2014). Coloring the college pathway: A more culturally responsive approach to college readiness and access for students of color in secondary schools. *Urban Review, 46*, 197–223. https://doi.org/10.1007/s11256-013-0252-7

Yosso, T. J. (2005). Whose culture has capital? A critical race theory discussion of community cultural wealth. *Race Ethnicity and Education, 8*(1), 69–91, https://doi.org/10.1080/1361332052000341006

Chapter 3

Intergenerational Posttraumatic Transformation

Reframing College Access for Students
from Refugee Backgrounds

DIEP H. LUU

One in every 74 people on Earth has been forced to flee their home due to conflict or persecution (United Nations High Commissioner for Refugees [UNHCR], 2024). By mid-2023, there were nearly 110 million people in the world who had been forcibly displaced from their homes, and among them, 36.4 million had refugee status, with an estimated 40% under the age of 18 (UNHCR, 2024). Since the US Congress passed the Refugee Act of 1980, over 3.6 million refugees have been resettled in the United States (Refugee Processing Center, 2024). Forty-seven states and the District of Columbia received refugees for resettlement in the fiscal year 2023 (UNHCR USA, 2023).

Students from refugee backgrounds are not monolithic. These students' experiences are diverse in their country of origin, preflight experience, flight experience, and resettlement. The top countries of origin that resettled globally in 2022 were Syrian Arab Republic, Ukraine, and Afghanistan (UNHCR, 2024). In the United States, the top three countries of origin for refugees in 2022 were the Democratic Republic of the Congo, Syria, Afghanistan, and Myanmar (UNHCR USA, 2023). Of the 60,014 refugees who resettled in the United States in the fiscal year 2023, 41% were from Africa, 34% from the Near East and South Asia, 5% from Europe, 10% from East Asia, and 10% from Latin America and the Caribbean.

The educational starting points for students from refugee backgrounds are widely divergent because of their experiences prior to their resettlement countries and are "dependent on the person's previous environments, education, occupations and skills, and whether these are transferable, adjustable or obsolete in the next context" (Suleman & Whiteford, 2013, p. 207). One way to help refugees achieve social and economic mobility in the United States is to increase refugee access to postsecondary education (i.e., colleges, universities, and technical/vocational training). Increased access to higher education for students from refugee backgrounds benefits the individuals, their families, and the US society.

Even though postsecondary education is seen as the most effective vehicle for economic participation and entering the 21st-century workforce (Ma et al., 2016), most higher education systems in the world, including the United States, are not prepared to absorb and support a high number of students from refugee backgrounds. Worldwide, only 7% of eligible refugees have access to postsecondary education, compared to 42% of nonrefugee global youth (UNHCR, 2024). Between 2015 and 2019, only 3% of adult refugees in the United States was working on a bachelor's degree and only 3.1% on an associate degree (Office of Refugee Resettlement, 2023). Keeping in mind that 42% of the refugee population in the United States comprises children under the age of 18 (Office of Immigration Statistics, 2024) and given the low educational attainment rate of students from refugee backgrounds, promoting educational access among students from refugee backgrounds and understanding their experiences in accessing higher education in the United States is critical.

The lack of attention to students from refugee backgrounds in higher education literature and policy in the United States deems invisible a set of experiences that are unique to students from refugee backgrounds and confounds them with those of other immigrants and other underrepresented or marginalized groups (Luu & Blanco, 2019). By grouping them together, researchers assume that the experiences of refugees, immigrants, and other underrepresented groups are the same even though refugee communities are diverse and not all are POC. As a result, the unique needs and challenges of students from refugee backgrounds remain unacknowledged.

An Antideficit Perspective for Refugee College Students

One of the challenges that students from refugee backgrounds face most saliently is posttraumatic stress disorder (PTSD) (McBrien, 2005; Thabet et al., 2004) and interrupted education (Sinclair, 2001), which stem from the experience of displacement and resettlement. Posttraumatic stress disorder is a chronic mental health condition that develops in some people who have experienced or witnessed a terrifying or dangerous event; symptoms include flashbacks, nightmares, avoidance, severe anxiety, and having angry outbursts (National Institute of Mental Health, 2022). Research has yet to study how PTSD and other experiences that are unique to refugees impact their access to higher education in the United States. Posttraumatic stress disorder among refugee populations is well documented in the literature (Sirin & Rogers-Sirin, 2015; Thabet et al., 2004). During flight from the home country, refugees may witness horrible acts of violence. These experiences can range from sexual violence to witnessing the killing of their own family members, to living in unsanitary conditions in refugee camps (Kline & Mone, 2003; Thabet et al., 2004). Children and youth living in refugee camps do not get the adequate education needed to keep up with their age level (Dryden-Peterson, 2016; Sinclair, 2001). As a result of these events and interrupted education, refugees can experience psychological harm such as PTSD and lower educational performance (Allwood et al., 2002). Previous research has documented that children of refugees can experience indirect trauma passed down from their parents and families also known as transgenerational trauma (Kwan, 2019). However, the small proportion of refugees that enters higher education constitutes one of the most resilient student populations and merits further study.

In this chapter, I use an asset-based approach to provide a counter-narrative to the pervasive deficit perspective in the literature. Traditionally, the educational performance of students of Color has been viewed from a deficit perspective. For example, the following assumptions about communities of Color are frequently held: (a) they do not value education, (b) they lack the motivation to learn, or (c) they have cognitive deficiencies that hinder academic achievement (Valencia, 1997). This deficit approach blames the students, perpetuates the status quo, and leaves negative assumptions unquestioned (Villalpando & Solórzano, 2005).

Understanding the college access and transitions of refugee populations requires shifting perspectives from a deficit- to an asset-oriented lens or a cultural wealth paradigm (Garcia & Guerra, 2004; Villalpando & Solórzano, 2005). As noted in chapter 1, community cultural wealth (CCW) is defined as "an array of knowledge, skills, abilities and contacts possessed and utilized by communities of Color to survive and resist macro and micro-forms of oppression" (Yosso, 2005, p. 77). The CCW model is grounded on critical race theory (CRT), which (a) acknowledges the centrality of racism in the oppression and inequality experienced by POC in the United States, (b) challenges the dominant white, middle-class ideology and values as the gold standard in US society, and (c) validates and honors POC's experiences and knowledge (Solórzano & Villalpando, 1998). Adapted from Oliver and Shapiro's (1995) research on income and wealth gaps between Black and white populations, Yosso's (2005) community cultural wealth model identified six forms of capital that communities of Color possess: (1) aspirational, (2) navigational, (3) social, (4) linguistic, (5) familial, and (6) resistant capital.

The cultural wealth paradigm has been applied to research on the educational experiences of students of Color (e.g., Kwan, 2019; Valencia, 1997, Villalpando & Solórzano, 2005), but it could be applied to refugee populations as well because many of them are POC. Furthermore, refugees often experience marginalization, racialization, and/or xenophobia, which makes the CCW a relevant framework for their experiences. Regardless of race and ethnicity, refugees resettling in the United States still face some degree of cultural differences compared to their home countries.

Like research about students of Color that found teachers' and administrators' perception of language competency and parents' education levels were areas of deficit (e.g., Block et al., 2014; Valencia & Black, 2002), studies also focus on the fact that many students from refugee backgrounds are English-language learners and their parents do not have college degrees from the United States or at all. Rather than solely focusing on English-language skills and parents' education level as deficits, a cultural wealth perspective also acknowledges the evidence that suggests that families from refugee backgrounds value education and that their cultural values are assets to their educational experiences. To be effective, educational systems need to acknowledge the cultural assets that communities—refugees, communities of Color—have to offer (Villalpando & Solórzano, 2005).

Students from refugee backgrounds are not only absent as a student population in higher education research, they are also largely absent from US policy documents (Luu & Blanco, 2019). In response to this invisibility, it is important to pay attention to the stories of students from refugee backgrounds. These stories, like all narratives, exist at the individual level but are also a reflection of society as a whole (Gubrium & Holstein, 2009). They can educate about contemporary events related to displacement and educational disparity. Educated students from refugee backgrounds will not only have a better chance to contribute to a globalized labor market that demands credentials beyond secondary education, but they also will likely obtain better outcomes for themselves, their families, and their communities (Ma et al., 2016). After all, seeking a better life is a common reason refugees resettle in the United States or other host countries.

Posttraumatic Growth

The existing literature on PTSD among students from refugee backgrounds is focused primarily on the effect of PTSD on learning in K–12 education (e.g., Sirin & Rogers-Sirin, 2015; Thabet et al., 2004), but the psychological well-being of students from refugee backgrounds has not been examined extensively in the context of college access and transition. For refugee populations, the trauma associated with displacement can be transmitted across generations, which is known as transgenerational trauma (Kwan, 2019). Despite the negative effects of trauma, posttraumatic growth (PTG) could occur from trauma (Calhoun & Tedeschi, 2014). Tedeschi and Calhoun (2004) defined PTG as "the experience of positive change that occurs as a result of the struggle with highly challenging life crises" (p. 1). Calhoun and Tedeschi's (2014) PTG model postulated that a person experiences a "seismic event" that could lead to distress, posttraumatic growth, narrative development, and wisdom (p. 8). The seismic events for the participants in my study were associated with being from refugee backgrounds, including fleeing war and oppressive government, living in a refugee camp, and resettling in the United States.

Growth is defined as "changes in the perception of self, changes in the experience of relationships with others, and changes in one's general philosophy of life" (Calhoun & Tedeschi, 2014, p. 5). The PTG model posited that challenges experienced from a seismic event could lead to cognitive engagement that resulted in preparedness and resilience (Calhoun & Tedeschi, 2014). There are caveats about posttraumatic growth: (a) focus on growth should not come with a sacrifice of empathy for the pain and suffering of trauma survivors, (b) growth can occur in the absence of trauma, (c) PTG does not suggest life crises, loss, and trauma are good, and (d) PTG is not universal and inevitable (Tedeschi & Calhoun, 2004). Although the posttraumatic growth model originated in the field of psychology, I have adapted the model to higher education given its focus on the positive aspects of the struggle with trauma, which is compatible with the antideficit, asset, and cultural wealth approach of my research.

My Journey as a Refugee Scholar-Practitioner

My interest in studying access to US postsecondary education for students from refugee backgrounds stems from my personal and professional experiences. My family and I are refugees. The Vietnam War has had a huge impact on millions, including my family and me, who immigrated to the United States as a result of the its humanitarian resettlement program for former reeducation camp detainees and their immediate family members. My father's involvement in the war—on the South Vietnam side—and reeducation camp experience were the catalysts for moving our family to the United States, in hopes of providing a better future for his children and escaping political persecution by the communist government. Additionally, I came from a low-income family, and I was the first person in my family to graduate from college even though I am the third sibling. My educational attainment is very different than my three siblings: my oldest brother never attended college; my younger sister graduated from a private, for-profit art university with a lot of student debt; and my older sister dropped out of college after a decade of enrollment in a community college and local state university. My father graduated from high school in Vietnam, and my mother only has a grade-school education.

I am passionate about studying college access among students from refugee backgrounds because it makes me think about my siblings and other minoritized students who are not getting the support they need to make informed decisions about where to attend college. Researching the experiences of students from refugee backgrounds, many of whom are low-income, first-generation college students of Color, is an emotion-laden topic because it is a part of my identity. It can be heartbreaking to hear participants discuss their hardships and their family background. I am also aware that not all participants' stories are heartbreaking. Some stories are uplifting or a mixture of both heartbreaking and uplifting.

I identify with college students from refugee backgrounds based on my personal and professional background. I can relate to the different rates of language acquisition and role reversal between parents and children. While my first language is Vietnamese, my siblings and I learned English a lot quicker than my parents. We had to help our parents translate important medical and school documents, and I had to translate for my parents during parent-teacher conferences in school. I was glad to help my parents, but it was still frustrating to deal with something that was beyond my age and knowledge, particularly technical terms and phrases (e.g., bank routing number, marital and residency status) that require certain cultural capital to know. Despite these challenges, I developed a deeper bond with my family because we needed each other to overcome life adversities together. I also learned to be self-reliant, take charge of my situation, ask for help, and advocate for myself and my family. At the end of the day, family was the constant aspect I had during the many transitions I experienced in my life. I worked hard in school to excel academically not only for my future self but also for my family. That dedication to my future self and family has paid off today in terms of earning a terminal degree, having a successful career, no longer living in poverty, and being able to elevate my family's financial situation.

College Access and the Intergenerational Family Bond

Seeking to overcome the deficit approach that characterizes much of the literature on refugees in higher education, my study (Luu, 2021) explored how students from refugee backgrounds describe the role of community cultural wealth (Yosso, 2005) in their movement into and through their university experience. I analyzed the educational journey of five students from refugee backgrounds in the Greater Boston area. The participants' countries of origin included Egypt (Mary), Eritrea (Lula), Japan/Togo (Charlotte), and Vietnam (Valentina and Hue Han) (all pseudonyms). I followed a narrative inquiry approach and relied on semistructured interviews and participants' personal statements for university application. I spent some time at the beginning of the first interview to build rapport by sharing a brief story about my refugee and educational background before conducting the first in-depth interview. Sharing my story first modeled vulnerability and openness to share, which the students appreciated and reciprocated. I also benefited from sharing my story because it was cathartic and an opportunity to reflect on my own personal and educational journey.

For underrepresented student populations (e.g., low income, first generation, and students of Color), the lack of parental or family involvement in education settings is well documented in the literature (Cabrera & La Nasa, 2001; González et al., 2003; McBrien, 2005). The traditional view of this lack of involvement has been that the students' parents and other family members do not value education or care about their children's academic achievement (Block et al., 2014). However, the findings of my research support other studies on minoritized student populations revealing that minoritized students and their families do care and value education highly (González et al., 2003; Portes & Rumbaut, 2001). Four of the five participants in my study were from lower-income households and their parents worked long hours to support their families. Most of the parents learned to speak English, but not fluently, and all their family members lacked knowledge about the US educational system. As a result, some of the students had to take care of their younger siblings, as Lula and Valentina shared in their narratives: "At the age of nine, I started taking care of my siblings" (Lula); or they helped younger siblings with schoolwork, such as in Hue Han's and Charlotte's narratives: "I think that educationally [my parents] relied on me like a role model, [to] help my brother with school and things like that, and things they couldn't do" (Hue Han). While this role reversal was consistent with other studies on students from refugee and immigrant backgrounds (Fuligni & Fuligni, 2007; Trickett & Jones, 2007), the students in my study either were glad to help their families or later came to understand that their familial struggles were not their parents' fault.

As students and parents in my study experienced different rates of English-language acquisition and acculturation, they also experienced some family tensions related to communication challenges and disagreements on cultural values and norms (Portes & Rumbaut, 2001). Although the students in my research experienced some family tensions and wished that their parents could have helped them navigate the college admission process, the students' strong ties with their families motivated them to seek resources that would be helpful to their college access, such as asking teachers to help with their college personal statements. One of the participants, Valentina, said, "Because there wasn't a lot [of resources] at my high school, so in order for me to get the things that I eventually got, I had to look for them and go after and take initiative." This experience is also similar to other first-generation college students (Richards, 2020).

However, students from refugee backgrounds have a nuanced experience because they turned to their family's histories and stories of displacement as refugees for inspiration and as reminders of their strength and how far their families had come. One of the participants, Hue Han, attributed her academic success to not forgetting her roots and having strong feelings for what she is doing: "I don't lose sight of what I'm here for, and I'm really grateful for it. And it makes me really determined to chase that goal because I wanna make my family proud. And I know how much they gave up for me to be here."

Compared to their families' lives and struggles in their countries of origin, their current struggles in the United States, while challenging, did not feel impossible to overcome. For example, Mary was motivated to do well in school and pursue a college degree because of the sacrifices Mary's mother made for her daughters: "Honestly, it's my mom. Seeing that she's worked so hard for my sister and I. It just makes me want to succeed and be better for her sake because honestly, I know that if it wasn't for her, I wouldn't be here now. I wouldn't be in college. I wouldn't be in the United States at all. I wouldn't have graduated high school." I would further argue that the strong family connections and a strong sense of familial obligation to make their family—especially their parents—feel proud more than made up for the families' perceived lack of knowledge about college. If it were the other way around, where the family had college knowledge but did not experience any hardships, the students might not have been as motivated and determined to attend college. That is because these students might feel too comfortable in their lives and lose touch with their family histories, and as a result, they might take things, such as higher education, for granted. Simply put, familial motivation is an important factor that promotes academic achievement (George Mwangi et al., 2017; George Mwangi et al., 2020; Nicholas et al., 2008).

Despite the obstacles just discussed, there were other ways that the students' parents supported them. Emotional support and encouragement were two forms of support mentioned by the participants, which is also consistent with other studies on racially minoritized student populations (Cabrera & La Nasa, 2001; González et al., 2003). For example, Lula thought that the emotional support from home was the most important form of support for her:

It can get so stressful and so hard . . . So, having a person to talk to so I could get all my feelings out was really helpful . . . I would go and complain to my mom. And she was that person to calm me down and say, "No, it's okay." And one of my biggest fears was disappointing her. And when she was like, "That's okay." That sort of made me feel better. It made me feel like, "It's okay, I can do better next time. I'll do better next time." For me, she's my motivation because she has sacrificed so much for me. I'm always afraid of disappointing her. So, talking to her and saying, "Oh, I got a bad grade" and she said, "Nah, it's okay. Do better next time." That gave me the reassurance that I needed. So, I would say that was the most helpful support.

Feeling emotionally connected to and encouraged by her mother, Lula was motivated by a strong desire to succeed and make her mother proud.

Moreover, there was a cultural nuance for three of the participants (Hue Han, Valentina, and Charlotte) who have parents from Vietnamese and Japanese cultures that do not express emotions openly. For these parents, actions spoke louder than words; their ways of expressing their love and support for their children were through actions, such as cooking, cleaning, and driving the students to places (e.g., an SAT testing site). This support was different, but no less valuable than what the participants observed among the parents from their white middle or upper-middle-class peers, such as paying for private tutoring lessons or attending parent-teacher conferences (McBrien, 2005; Trickett & Jones, 2007). Hence, these alternative forms of familial support must be acknowledged and promoted in different settings when supporting students from refugee backgrounds and other minoritized student populations.

The students in my research and their family members were connected through their shared family histories, particularly the trauma associated with displacement. Not all the students experienced this trauma directly. Some participants, like Hue Han and Charlotte who were born in the United States, experienced it through the stories they heard from their parents or other family members. These strong familial connections were necessary for the students in my study to not forget their roots and stay grounded and committed to their schoolwork. Therefore, participants were able to put their struggles in perspective and find strength in the affective support they received from their families. Kwan (2019) labeled this shared experience around trauma within refugee families as *affective capital*, or the ability to tap into affects of gratitude, motivation, inspiration, and awe, which not only connect families but also act as an impetus for educational aspirations and success.

Similar to the students from refugee backgrounds in Kwan's (2019) study, the participants in my study developed an appreciation of their parents' sacrifices and felt deeply connected to their family culture and refugee history. The participants often credited their families for being the reason why they worked as hard as they did in school and why they aspired to attend college and make their parents and other family members proud. All five participants felt that they owed their parents for making sacrifices for their families to have better lives in the United States. For example, one of the participants, Charlotte, noted, "I always knew I wanted to go to college because I wanted to be successful and have a stable life in the future to give back to my dad and mom." Tapping into family bonds or *affective capital* impacted the students' *aspirational capital*, or "the ability to maintain hopes and dreams for the future, even in the face of real and perceived barriers" (Yosso, 2005, p. 78), which in turn motivated them to pursue higher education to have a better life and repay their family and community for their support and sacrifices (Shapiro, 2018).

Intergenerational Posttraumatic Transformation

My research confirmed several factors cited in the literature that can impact students from refugee backgrounds' college access and transition into higher education. These factors included the intersection of poverty and educational aspiration (Stevenson & Willott, 2007), the importance of language acquisition (Naidoo et al., 2018), the impact of trauma associated with displacement (Sirin & Rogers-Sirin, 2015), interrupted education and uncertainty of immigration status (Custodio & O'Loughlin, 2017), lack of parental involvement in school settings (Rah et al., 2009), role reversal with parents (Trickett & Jones, 2007), and having to cope with discrimination, racism, and xenophobia (Dryden-Peterson, 2015). Traditionally, these obstacles and challenges were viewed from a deficit perspective, which blamed minoritized students, including students from refugee backgrounds, for their lack of educational success and cultural capital from a western, white, and upper-class perspective (Villalpando & Solórzano, 2005). However, my research revealed that while students from refugee backgrounds experienced multiple transitions and hardships in their lives, they persisted and succeeded academically.

Even though the findings mirrored factors found in the literature, I took an antideficit interpretation of the participants' experiences. An antideficit approach does not mean letting institutions "off the hook" for providing support to address students' needs and trauma. On the contrary, an antideficit approach can hold institutions *more* accountable by not allowing K–12 schools or universities to blame students and families for their troubles but to acknowledge their assets and fill in with support where there are gaps in knowledge and skills.

The participants in my research overcame the challenges and obstacles that stemmed from their refugee backgrounds and persevered in the pursuit of their educational aspirations. For students from refugee backgrounds, the trauma associated with displacement can be felt across generations, also known as transgenerational trauma (Kwan, 2019), as one of my participants described:

> My parents were born and raised in Vietnam. My dad was one of the boat people who left after the war . . . My grandparents, on my father's side and my great-grandparents from my mother's side, left China after also another war. And they resettled in Vietnam and had their children there . . . So that's something that I think about a lot. It's just a big part of our history . . . But we have a lot of history of relocation and refugees in our family. And on my mother's side, my great-grandfather, I also hear stories of him being young and seeing war and seeing Japanese soldiers in China and children being killed. And it's very traumatizing, very, very difficult. (Hue Han)

A deficit perspective would associate trauma with poor mental health and attribute students' lack of success to trauma (Garcia & Guerra, 2004). From an antideficit perspective, I argue that adversity and trauma could conversely lead to personal growth and life transformation (see figure 3.1).

Figure 3.1 shows that different forms of cultural wealth (Yosso, 2005) contribute to successful college access, transition, and persistence among students from refugee backgrounds, which could lead to life-changing transformation across generations, known here as *intergenerational posttraumatic transformation* (IPT). Despite the multiple life transitions, poverty, racism, and other hardships, students tapped into various forms of capital (i.e., community cultural wealth, affective capital, and agentic capital) that gave them the strength, motivation, and determination to enter college and move through college successfully. Agentic capital is a new form of capital that I identified in my research. *Agentic capital* refers to having self-agency that students from refugee backgrounds harnessed from taking on role reversal with their parents (Trickett & Jones, 2007), taking initiative, seeking resources, and being responsible and self-sufficient. For example,

Figure 3.1. Intergenerational posttraumatic transformation (IPT). Students from refugee backgrounds can achieve life-changing transformation as a result of leveraging CCW, affective capital, and agentic capital to successfully enter and move through higher education. *Source*: Created by the author.

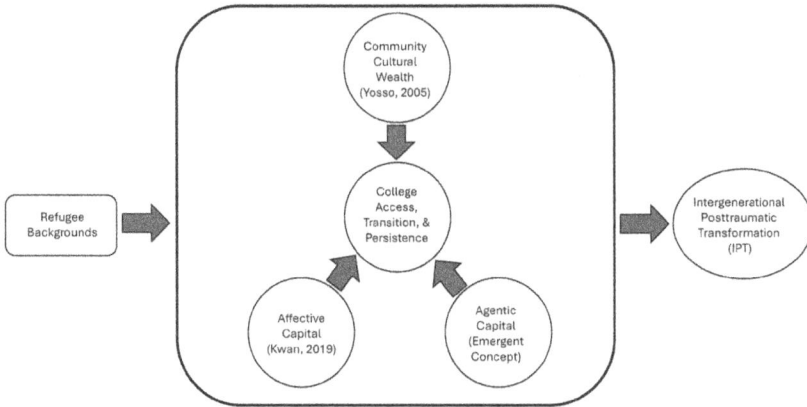

Valentina said, "[Coming from a refugee background] kind of made me claw my way to get opportunities. I clawed my way to get opportunities that weren't carved out for me." This means that being resourceful and a self-advocate was necessary to pursue her dreams and achieve her goals because opportunities were not handed to her.

The results of coping with intergenerational trauma and overcoming intergenerational obstacles could lead to life-changing transformation not only for the students but also for their families, known here as *intergenerational posttraumatic transformation* (IPT), which is adapted from Calhoun and Tedeschi's (2014) comprehensive model of *posttraumatic growth* (PTG). The PTG model posited that challenges experienced from a seismic event could lead to cognitive engagement that resulted in preparedness and resilience (Calhoun & Tedeschi, 2014). For example, Lula believed that being a refugee had taught her to prepare for the future because, "if there are challenges that you face tomorrow, you can easily handle them . . . And it's best that you're in a good position to handle it instead of being in a bad position where it's just going to make your life difficult."

Intergenerational posttraumatic transformation is the experience of positive change that occurs as a result of transgenerational trauma associated with displacement. The IPT concept I am proposing posits that students from refugee backgrounds either experience trauma directly from flight or indirectly through their family history of displacement and that transgenerational trauma could result in life-changing transformation for both the student and their families. Because of the students' and their families' hardships and obstacles, they saw higher education as a way to break the cycle of poverty and transform their and their families' lives. The seismic events that stemmed from participants' refugee backgrounds changed their perspectives on the world and of themselves and gave them a sense of appreciation for the opportunities that they have and the people in their lives. Lula described having this global perspective:

> Coming to the United States and living here, you can get really lost and all the things that you don't have, especially I feel like in this country there is a lot of . . . inequalities based on your race or your gender or your sexuality. So, you can get caught up in all the things that you don't have instead of sort of appreciating what you do have . . . I now have clothes that I can fit [in]. And I have many clothes, many options. I also have many options when it comes to shoes . . . I don't have to go out to get water . . . There was only one location to get water, to get clean water [in the refugee camp]. And sometimes the water isn't running. And you would see a line of people waiting. Sometimes there is only one faucet running . . .

Having a global perspective helped the participants in "appreciating the little things that often in the United States, you take for granted" (Lula) and to "not lose their roots and lose their background because how important it is and how strong it is" (Hue Han). The participants realized that their backgrounds were assets that they could tap into as a source of inspiration to persevere. When they think about their parents' sacrifices and family history of displacement, they are reminded to take full advantage of all of the opportunities, including higher education, available to them in the United States. The participants in my study leveraged their capital, including community cultural wealth, affective capital, and agentic capital, to not only successfully enter college but also to transition through their first year in college and beyond.

This transformation, however, does not mean that the participants did not struggle and experience challenges along the way. Participants struggled socially and academically, but they worked hard by spending a lot of time on their academics and were focused and determined by staying grounded in their roots and taking advantage of the opportunities available in the United States that their families did not have in their countries of origin. The people and resources that helped these students along the way were also critical to their success. For example, Charlotte attributed the success of her college admission process to a college information session that her friend invited her to attend, which was organized by the Institute of East African Councils. Valentina's "saving grace" was an external college preparatory program that recruited students from her high school and other underresourced high schools: "I knew academically that [my] school was not going to support me, so luckily, I joined a college-prep program called 'SEO Scholars.' They recruited students from freshman year. It's a big time commitment. You commit three Saturdays a month from 8:30 am to 4:30 pm to do extra prep classes and stuff like that. So, that was my space of being with people who wanted to go to college in the end as well." I argue that intergenerational posttraumatic transformation is a form of resistance, along with embracing their languages and cultures of origin, that the students from refugee backgrounds demonstrated in my research. The participants' journeys of "self-acceptance" and "self-discovery" also have a lasting impact on their "passion for fighting for what's right, fighting for justice" and to "always stand up for what's right, even if it's really hard to do." Lula said, "Being able to share [my] story and educate people on [my refugee experience], I think that for me it's really powerful, and it has helped me connect with people. But also, I call people out when they're saying something that isn't right." These students defied the odds of moving in and moving through college given that approximately 7% of global students from refugee backgrounds are in higher education (UNHCR, 2024).

Nonetheless, trauma must not be romanticized. Although these students are empowered by their trauma instead of being victims of it, this triumph does not mean that the trauma still has not caused some form of harm in their lives and made things more difficult than for some of their peers:

> [Your refugee] background is a strength, not a weakness, not letting anyone else make them feel any other way. And then also knowing that [you] probably worked a lot harder than some of the people who are [in college]. We'll have to continue working harder and that's not fair, but it just shows how strong

[we] are. Because you are coming from a disadvantaged place, but you're like pulling yourself up really, really hard to get to [college]. I've got to work twice as hard as some other people to get to the same place. (Hue Han)

Moreover, from an antideficit perspective, not all students from refugee backgrounds should have to climb so many mountains to achieve the kind of success illustrated in my study, because not all of them have the necessary resources and support in their lives. That reality does not make those refugee students any less worthy of achieving success, but rather reflects an inequitable society. To promote a more equitable society and education system, the next section discusses implications of leveraging IPT to provide students from refugee backgrounds better opportunities and supports to successfully access and move through college, which could be transferable to other minoritized populations as well.

Leveraging IPT to Promote College Access among Students from Refugee Backgrounds

Intentional development and implementation of effective policy and institutional practices are crucial to support students from refugee backgrounds because their educational successes should not be left to chance. Because family and intergenerational histories are important sources of motivation and inspiration for students from refugee backgrounds, institutional agents should acknowledge their families and family histories as assets, not as deficits. Students from refugee backgrounds often relied on institutional agents like school staff (Baker et al., 2018) to help them navigate the college application process. Therefore, it is important that school guidance counselors and teachers conduct their duties in ways that are culturally sensitive and responsive in their work with students from refugee backgrounds (Lemke & Nickerson, 2020).

It is important that institutional agents, like school counselors and college advisors, schoolteachers and college professors, and school and college administrators, practice a trauma-informed approach (Lemke & Nickerson, 2020). Trauma-informed educational practice is a burgeoning concept in the literature (Champine et al., 2019; Oehme et al., 2019). A trauma-informed approach involves "integrating understanding of trauma throughout a program, organization, or system to enhance the quality, effectiveness, and delivery of services provided to individuals and groups" (Champine et al., 2019, p. 418). In higher education, for instance, discussions of trauma-informed practice have become frequent in response to the COVID-19 pandemic (Griffin, 2020). However, this awareness must continue as larger numbers of postsecondary students have experienced some form of trauma.

A trauma-informed approach is compatible with and complementary to asset-based support. As illustrated in the narratives, trauma is particularly pervasive in families from refugee backgrounds given the history of displacement. Students from refugee backgrounds experienced trauma in different ways, either directly, like Lula, who fled with her family to an Ethiopian refugee camp, or indirectly, like Hue Han, who was born in the United States but was deeply affected by her family history of displacement over multiple generations. A trauma-based approach in educational settings would empower students through building positive relationships and create a safe space for students to process their past trauma (Gutierrez & Gutierrez, 2019). For example, Mary's teacher dismissed her two traumatic life events when he said her father's death and moving to the United States were irrelevant topics for her college personal statement because, in the teacher's view, a lot of people experience those events. A trauma-informed approach would acknowledge the importance of these events in Mary's life and encourage her to process her traumatic experiences through writing and otherwise, whether or not that discussion is included in the final version of a college personal statement. As Mary expressed in my study, having her experiences and feelings dismissed altogether added to her trauma.

Encouraging students from refugee backgrounds to process their trauma is important because the participants' and their families' trauma associated with displacement was not discussed at home. Valentina's and Charlotte's fathers were silent about their flight experiences, so these students learned to not bring up the topic at home because it is sensitive. Even when Valentina asked her father about his refugee experience, he remained silent or got agitated so she learned to stay quiet. Valentina openly discussed her father's alcoholism, which she attributed to her father's flight experience. This experience in and of itself can be traumatic, or it signals the presence of unprocessed intergenerational trauma. Therefore, institutional agents (Baker et al., 2018) at both K–12 and postsecondary education levels would benefit from using a trauma-informed approach when supporting students from refugee backgrounds (Lemke & Nickerson,

2020). To promote college access among students from refugee backgrounds, institutional agents can help these students tap into their intergenerational family histories as a strategy for collective healing and affirmation. For example, when working with students from refugee backgrounds in the classroom or a one-on-one setting, model vulnerability by sharing your family history and encourage students to share their family stories and validate their experiences as strengths rather than deficits. For me, sharing my refugee story and family history was a powerful way to do just that with my participants.

I conclude this chapter with some advice to students from refugee backgrounds and their families: I want you to know that you are not alone. While the struggles associated with your family history of displacement are real, you are also capable, strong, courageous, resourceful, and resilient. Embrace who you are and be proud of your refugee background, language, and culture. Stay grounded in your family roots and continue to work hard to create a better life for yourself and your family. Growth and transformation can occur when you capitalize on your assets (e.g., family, language, aspiration), which are already in front of you, so do not let others tell you otherwise.

Critical Reflection

1. How might education institutions (K–12, higher education) be more proactive in identifying and acknowledging students from refugee backgrounds? In what ways could education institutions include students from refugee backgrounds in their diversity, equity, and inclusion initiatives and programming?

2. How might education institutions support students from refugee backgrounds to access higher education?

3. How can postsecondary education institutions incorporate antideficit and trauma-informed approaches in their admission policies and practices? How might a trauma-informed approach improve other areas across campus, for instance like academic advising, teaching, pedagogy and curriculum, and student support services?

4. How might the concept of intergenerational posttraumatic transformation be applied beyond students from refugee backgrounds to support students of Color and other minoritized student populations?

References

Allwood, M. A., Bell-Dolan, D., & Husain, S. A. (2002). Children's trauma and adjustment reactions to violent and nonviolent war experiences. *Journal of the American Academy of Child & Adolescent Psychiatry, 41*(4), 450–457. https://doi.org/10.1097/00004583-200204000-00018

Baker, S., Ramsay, G., Irwin, E., & Miles, L. (2018). "Hot," "cold" and "warm" supports: Towards theorizing where refugee students go for assistance at university. *Teaching in Higher Education, 23*(1), 1–16. https://doi.org/10.10 80/13562517.2017.1332028

Block, K., Cross, S., Riggs, E., & Gibbs, L. (2014). Supporting schools to create an inclusive environment for refugee students. *International Journal of Inclusive Education, 18*(12), 1337–1355.

Cabrera, A. F., & La Nasa, S. M. (2001). On the path to college: Three critical tasks facing America's disadvantaged. *Research in Higher Education, 42*(2), 119–149. https://doi.org/10.1023/A:1026520002362

Calhoun, L. G., & Tedeschi, R. G. (Eds.). (2014). *Handbook of posttraumatic growth: Research and practice.* Routledge.

Champine, R. B., Lang, J. M., Nelson, A. M., Hanson, R. F., & Tebes, J. K. (2019). Systems measures of a trauma-informed approach: A systematic review. *American Journal of Community Psychology, 64*(3–4), 418–437. https://doi. org/10.1002/ajcp.12388

Custodio, B., & O'Loughlin, J. B. (2017). *Students with interrupted formal education: Bridging where they are and what they need.* Corwin.

Dryden-Peterson, S. (2015). *The educational experiences of refugee children in countries of first asylum.* Migration Policy Institute.

Dryden-Peterson, S. (2016). Refugee education: The crossroads of globalization. *Educational Researcher, 45*(9), 473–482.

Fuligni, A. J., & Fuligni, A. S. (2007). Immigrant families and the educational development of their children. In J. E. Lansford, K. Deater-Deckard, & M. H. Bornstein (Eds.), *Immigrant families in contemporary society* (pp. 231–249). Guilford Press.

Garcia, S. B., & Guerra, P. L. (2004). Deconstructing deficit thinking: Working with educators to create more equitable learning environments. *Education and Urban Society, 36*(2), 150–168. https://doi.org/10.1177/0013124503261322

George Mwangi, C. A., Daoud, N., English, S., & Griffin, K. A. (2017). "Me and my family": Ethnic differences and familial influences on academic motivations of Black collegians. *Journal of Negro Education, 86*(4), 479–493.

George Mwangi, C. A., Malcolm, M., & Thelamour, B. (2020). Our college degree: Familial engagement in the lives of diverse Black collegians. *Race Ethnicity and Education, 26*(7), 872–891. https://doi.org/10.1080/13613324.2020.184 2347

González, K. P., Stone, C., & Jovel, J. (2003). Examining the role of social capital in access to college for Latinas: Toward a college opportunity framework. *Journal of Hispanics in Higher Education, 2*(2), 146–171. https://doi.org/ 10.1177/1538192702250620

Griffin, G. (2020). Defining trauma and a trauma-informed COVID-19 response. *Psychological Trauma: Theory, Research, Practice, and Policy, 12*(S1), S279– S280. https://doi.org/10.1037/tra0000828

Gubrium, J. F., & Holstein, J. A. (2009). *Analyzing narrative reality*. Sage.

Gutierrez, D., & Gutierrez, A. (2019). Developing a trauma-informed lens in the college classroom and empowering students through building positive relationships. *Contemporary Issues in Education Research, 12*(1), 11–18. https://doi.org/10.19030/cier.v12i1.10258

Kline, P. M., & Mone, E. (2003). Coping with war: Three strategies employed by adolescent citizens of Sierra Leone. *Child and Adolescent Social Work Journal, 20*(5), 321–333. https://doi.org/10.1023/A:1026091712028

Kwan, Y. Y. (2019). Providing asset-based support for Asian American refugees: Interrogating transgenerational trauma, resistance, and affective capital. *New Directions for Higher Education, 2019*(186), 37–47. https://doi.org/10.1002/ he.20322

Lemke, M., & Nickerson, A. (2020). Educating refugee and hurricane displaced youth in troubled times: Countering the politics of fear through culturally responsive and trauma-informed schooling. *Children's Geographies, 18*(5), 529–543. https://doi.org/10.1080/14733285.2020.1740650

Luu, D. H. (2021). *Exploring the role of community cultural wealth in college access and transition: A narrative inquiry of students from refugee backgrounds* (Publication No. 2197) [Doctoral dissertation, University of Massachusetts Amherst]. ScholarWorks@UMass Amherst.

Luu, D. H., & Blanco, G. L. (2019). Exploring US federal policy discourse on refugee access to post-secondary education. *Higher Education Policy*. https:// doi.org/10.1057/s41307-019-00144-2

Ma, J., Matea, P., & Welch, M. (2016). *Education pays 2016: The benefits of higher education for individuals and society. Trends in higher education series*. The College Board.

McBrien, J. L. (2005). Educational needs and barriers for refugee students in the United States: A review of the literature. *Review of Educational Research, 75*(3), 329–364. https://doi.org/10.3102/00346543075003329

Naidoo, L., Wilkinson, J., Adoniou, M., & Langat, K. (2018). *Refugee background students transitioning into higher education: Navigating complex spaces.* Springer.

National Institute of Mental Health. (2022). *Post-traumatic stress disorder.* Retrieved March 5, 2023, from: https://www.nimh.nih.gov/health/topics/post-traumatic-stress-disorder-ptsd

Nicholas, T., Stepick, A., & Dutton Stepick, C. (2008). "Here's your diploma, mom!" Family obligation and multiple pathways to success. *Annals of the American Academy of Political and Social Science, 620*(1), 237–252.

Oehme, K., Perko, A., Clark, J., Ray, E. C., Arpan, L., & Bradley, L. (2019). A trauma-informed approach to building college students' resilience. *Journal of Evidence-Based Social Work, 16*(1), 93–107. https://doi.org/10.1080/237 61407.2018.1533503

Office of Immigration Statistics. (2024, December 2). *Yearbook of immigrant statistics.* https://www.dhs.gov/ohss/topics/immigration/yearbook

Office of Refugee Resettlement. (2023, November 14). *Office of Refugee Resettlement annual report to Congress fiscal year 2020.* https://www.acf.hhs.gov/orr/report/office-refugee-resettlement-annual-report-congress-2020

Oliver, M., & Shapiro, T. (1995). *Black wealth/white wealth.* University of California Press.

Portes, A., & Rumbaut, R. G. (2001). *Legacies: The story of the immigrant second generation.*

Rah, Y., Choi, S., & Nguyễn, T. S. T. (2009). Building bridges between refugee parents and schools. *International Journal of Leadership in Education, 12*(4), 347–365. https://doi.org/10.1080/13603120802609867

Refugee Processing Center. (2024). *Summary of refugee admissions as of 30-April-2024.* US Department of State, Bureau of Population, Refugees, and Migration. https://view.officeapps.live.com/op/view.aspx?src=https%3A%2F%2Fwww.wrapsnet.org%2Fdocuments%2FPRM%2520Refugee%2520Admissions%2520Report%2520as%2520of%252030%2520Apr%25202024.xlsx&wdOrigin=BROWSE LINK

Richards, B. N. (2020). Help-seeking behaviors as cultural capital: Cultural guides and the transition from high school to college among low-income first generation students. *Social Problems.* https://doi.org/10.1093/socpro/spaa023

Shapiro, S. (2018). Familial capital, narratives of agency, and the college transition process for refugee-background youth. *Equity & Excellence in Education, 51*(3–4), 332–346. https://doi.org/10.1080/10665684.2018.1546151

Sinclair, M. (2001). Education in emergencies. In J. Crisp, C. Talbot, & D. B. Cipollone (Eds.), *Learning for a future: Refugee education in developing countries* (pp. 1–84). United Nations Publications.

Sirin, S. R., & Rogers-Sirin, L. (2015). *The educational and mental health needs of Syrian refugee children.* Migration Policy Institute.

Solórzano, D., & Villalpando, O. (1998). Critical race theory, marginality, and the experience of minority students in higher education. In C. Torres &

T. Mitchell (Eds.), *Emerging issues in the sociology of education: Comparative perspectives* (pp. 211–224). State University of New York Press.

Stevenson, J., & Willott, J. (2007). The aspiration and access to higher education of teenage refugees in the UK. *Compare: A Journal of Comparative Education, 37*(5), 671–687. https://doi.org/10.1080/03057920701582624

Suleman, A., & Whiteford, G. E. (2013). Understanding occupational transitions in forced migration: The importance of life skills in early refugee resettlement. *Journal of Occupational Science, 20*(2), 201–210. https://doi.org/10.1080/14427591.2012.755908

Tedeschi, R. G., & Calhoun, L. G. (2004). Posttraumatic growth: Conceptual foundations and empirical evidence. *Psychological Inquiry, 15*(1), 1–18. https://doi.org/10.1207/s15327965pli1501_01

Thabet, A. A. M., Abed, Y., & Vostanis, P. (2004). Comorbidity of PTSD and depression among refugee children during war conflict. *Journal of Child Psychology and Psychiatry, 45*(3), 533–542. https://doi.org/10.1111/j.1469-7610.2004.00243.x

Trickett, E. J., & Jones, C. J. (2007). Adolescent culture brokering and family functioning: A study of families from Vietnam. *Cultural Diversity and Ethnic Minority Psychology, 13*(2), 143. https://doi.org/10.1037/1099-9809.13.2.143

United Nations High Commissioner for Refugees. (2023). *Figures at a glance.* Retrieved May 19, 2024: from https://www.unhcr.org/about-unhcr/who-we-are/figures-glance

United Nations High Commissioner for Refugees. (2024). *Higher education and skills.* Retrieved May 19, 2024, from: https://www.unhcr.org/us/what-we-do/build-better-futures/education/higher-education-and-skills

United Nations High Commissioner for Refugees USA. (2023). *Refugee resettlement facts.* Retrieved May 19, 2024, from: https://www.unhcr.org/us/media/refugee-resettlement-facts

Valencia, R. R. (Ed.) (1997). *The evolution of deficit thinking: Educational thought and practice.* Falmer Press.

Valencia, R. R., & Black, M. S. (2002). "Mexican Americans don't value education!" On the basis of the myth, mythmaking, and debunking. *Journal of Latinos and Education, 1*(2), 81–103. https://doi.org/10.1207/S1532771XJLE0102_2

Villalpando, O., & Solórzano, D. G. (2005). The role of culture in college preparation programs: A review of the research literature. In W. G. Tierney, Z. B. Corwin, & J. E. Colyar (Eds.), *Preparing for college: Nine elements of effective outreach* (pp. 13–28). State University of New York Press.

Yosso, T. J. (2005). Whose culture has capital? A critical race theory discussion of community cultural wealth. *Race Ethnicity and Education, 8*(1), 69–91, https://doi.org/10.1080/1361332052000341006

Chapter 4

"Removing *la cascara*"

The Cost of Being Resilient among Puertorriqueña College Aspirants

Yedalis Ruíz Santana

One afternoon, after our last interview, Yazmín and I walked back from the library where we had finished a productive two-hour meeting to plan the rest of her schedule for her senior year in anticipation of her transition to college.[1] As we went down a flight of stairs into the second-floor hallway, she slowed her gait and took in a deep breath, so deep that it seemed to reverberate against the lockers. I turned to acknowledge her and, with a mournful gaze, she signaled with a gesture to stop. She sank into the brick wall and told me she had something important to share with me. She appeared discouraged, as if something negative had suddenly triggered her emotionally. I became concerned and was not sure what had just happened since we had such a good connection in our meeting. We had collaboratively made an agreement that she was going to continue to work hard in all her classes and seek guidance and support from a group of mentors we identified together. We also created a timeline to ensure she could meet the requirements toward her college-going plans. It included strategies for her to stay on top of the deadlines of her work and her college applications. We were pumped about her plan.

After our meeting, Yazmín enthusiastically suggested we start regular "mentoring meetings" where we could invite other Puerto Rican students to join in the conversations. She explained that meeting with me was the first time she had ever met regularly with an adult in the school to talk about her aspirations for going to college. She was already at the school for three years when we initiated our work together. But at that moment, I could tell that something was troubling her. She disclosed that what she was about to tell me was not directed at me, but rather that she had been triggered by the positive affirmation and motivation she had received from our meeting. She explained that despite feeling motivated and encouraged, she could not get herself to truly believe that she could be successful academically and that one day she could earn a college degree. With tears in her eyes she said, "Even though I have tried and tried to do well in school, and you are encouraging me to do the best I can and I focus myself to do the right thing, it still feels impossible to get ahead. This place isn't created for us to do good and to be successful. People say, do your best, learn to play the game, fight and don't give up. But, ay, miss, why bother playing a game that is rigged for us?" After a moment of silence, we embraced with a hug. She cried and I found myself without a response. Yazmín was speaking her truth and, in doing so, she was speaking the reality of many Puerto Rican students at the high school. Yazmín believed that the odds were already against her. The concept of "the game being rigged" as she explained is evidence of her keen awareness and critical understanding of the impact of oppression on her experiences in school—day in and day out. It should be a major concern that the students we want and need to support, whom we encourage to do well in school, and whose aspirations to go to college could be actualized if given the opportunity and the sustainable resources needed for a successful academic process, are the same students who feel like they do not have a chance.

This narrative, while common, lacks a more nuanced analysis of Latinas' experiences while engaged in the college choice process. Even when Latina high school students aspire to earn a bachelor's degree and are positioned to enter postsecondary education, they experience barriers that can affect their participation in higher education.

The Strength in a Name: Aspirante

The notion of Aspirante serves as a powerful label for the young Puertorrriequeña students highlighted in this chapter, who were young people enrolled in a study about their culture and aspirations for attending an institution of higher education. I borrowed the term *Aspirante* (aspirant) from Dr. Antonia Pantoja, a leading figure in the Puerto Rican struggle for educational equity (Centro de Estudios Puertorriqueños, 2007). Pantoja was a pioneer in working toward a culturally relevant model of educational equity for Puerto Ricans in the United States. In 1961, Pantoja founded ASPIRA, an organization dedicated to investing in Latinx youth. This organization, now a legacy among Puerto Rican and Latinx communities, calls its participants Aspirantes. As such, the notion of Aspirante serves as a powerful label for the Puertorriqueñas highlighted in this chapter who welcomed me into a critical analysis of their aspirations for attending an institution of higher education. In this chapter, I share a *re*framework of the concept of resilience that emerged from a critical ethnographic study that I conducted informed by the collective narratives of Aspirantes Puertorriqueñas as they formed their college-going identities.

"Removing *la cascara*": Why Does This Matter?

While the reframing of the concept of resilience emerged from a research study, the context is intrinsically connected to who I am professionally and personally. It matters to acknowledge the impact of having to be resilient throughout one's life. I remember the time I walked into my dissertation defense. I experienced a deep fear and a resurgence of the all-too-familiar impostorism came over me. I sought out the support of my dissertation chair, who was himself Puerto Rican. He was an incredible source of inspiration for me during my process. My dissertation chair did not hesitate nor did he question what I was experiencing. He instead affirmed my process, acknowledged my strengths and assets, and encouraged me to lean into my identity as a Puertorriqueña and as educated. We called this process the moment when I needed to "remove *la cascara*" (removing the callus).

For years, I realized I had moved through each educational setting with strength from resilience. And even though my aspirations at that point had been fulfilled and I had surpassed my expectations, I still felt the impact. To this day, I can feel the impact of the racism and oppression that I felt as I was moving through the systems of education. Even when I had achieved the incredible milestone of earning a PhD, I still felt oppressed and like I didn't belong. By removing the cascara, I am describing a process of "bearing it all" after removing the callus created from a life of having to have a resilient identity. And so I trusted in the process and I started to remove it and even though it was painful and exposed, it was the time to heal and to try to experience myself as Dr.

Yedalis Ruíz Santana. Therefore, my work as a researcher, a scholar, and a practitioner will always be tied to my personal journey.

Examined through a LatCrit theoretical and analytical lens, the lives and experiences of the Aspirantes Puertorriqueñas in this chapter were plagued by limited access to opportunities and inadequate resources and information about college going. Using LatCrit theory, I centered their college-going identity formation process by addressing factors beyond race alone to include the racialization of their language, cultural values, migration, socioeconomic status, and transgenerational experiential knowledge (Delgado & Stefancic, 2012; Irizarry, 2011; Rolón-Dow, 2007) to better understand the school-based barriers that the students confronted while continuing to summon self-directed agency to sustain their hopes and aspirations to attend college. The LatCrit lenses of race, racism, and intersectionality; of challenging the dominant ideology; and of experiential knowledge were instrumental to disentangle the racialized mistreatment, active withholding of college-promoting academic opportunities, and unacceptably subpar college preparatory guidance and resources the Aspirantes experienced.

Resilience in academic research is defined as having the capacity to survive with challenges and adversity while having the ability to achieve academic success (York et al., 2015). The Aspirantes were indeed resilient and have had to conquer and sidestep many obstacles in their educational trajectory. And they were also exhausted, frustrated, and remained unsure of how to actually reach their educational goals. We cannot expect students to rely on their ability to continue to navigate through murky waters based on the fact that they can because they are resilient. We are placing an additional burden of achieving a higher education degree squarely on their shoulders with little to no institutional support or even awareness of the struggles they are fighting to make small and slow advancements. It seems caution is warranted when resilience and survival are equated with capital as it can disguise the students' experience of struggling to get a foothold while dodging institutional and structural barriers as something innately heroic about their ability to succeed despite disparities.

Quienes Somos (About Us): The Aspirantes

The five Aspirantes in this study all self-identified as Puertorriqueñas with aspirations to attend college and were enrolled in Knight High School (pseudonym), located in the medium-sized Esperanza City (pseudonym) in western Massachusetts. The city is comprised of a majority Hispanic/Latinx residents. Knight High School was and remains under state receivership. Each of the Aspirantes were enrolled in a Puerto Rican History and Education course facilitated by the research team who had developed a strong community engagement partnership with the school. The Aspirantes included Luz, Yadira, Yazmín, Melody, and Damaris.

Luz was born in Cayey, Puerto Rico, where she remembers collecting eggs from the chickens in the mornings at her *abuelos'* farms. She moved early on to Esperanza City and speaks more English than Spanish. An "A" student who had plans to enroll in AP courses, she described her educational experience within the context of moving from a neighborhood rife with violence, "stabbings and assault," to one with deep community connection and a sense of security.

Yadira was born in Esperanza City. As a preemie, she began life fighting for survival. Her frequent hospitalizations served as an early inspiration for her aspiration to become a nurse. As the one her family hoped to be the "first" to attend college, her parents frequently emphasized college as a way to do "something good for ourselves and for the family." She lived with "worry and fear," hearing gunshots in her neighborhood, and she balanced this reality with her family's message to not end up on welfare and to "do it on my own."

Yazmín began by describing herself as someone who "has always loved learning different things . . . my father influenced me about my education and everything." She dreamt of being a singer and voice actress and excitedly shared that she heard you can study acting in college. Peers would jest that she lived in the white neighborhood where all of the houses are, and she further contextualized that hers is "this big project of apartments" surrounded by nothing but houses.

Melody self-identified with her middle child status of "having to do the right thing." Her favorite pastimes were reading books and watching musicals and she affirmed she is not a partier. She said confidently, "I don't let the peer pressure get to me." She had aspirations to be a nurse practitioner or a teacher but stated, "I don't think I can be a doctor." Having grown up in Esperanza City she loved that everyone knew each other, sharing a common theme of "Oh you know my cousin!" In describing her educational aspirations, she reflected on her parents who dealt with dropping out of high school and having to leave college after a year due to cost.

Damaris was born in Guayama, Puerto Rico, and moved back and forth from Puerto Rico to Esperanza City. She grounded herself in her "huge family" and being a longtime cheerleader. Her aspiration to begin her career as a nurse "and then go further" stemmed from her mom's dream to be a nurse. Her mom became a certified nursing assistant (CNA), and Damaris was inspired by the opportunity to communicate and work with people. She described Esperanza City as "not the worst" and likes living near the mountains where everyone knows each other and the people are good.

Countering Dominant Narratives

In discussing the perceptions of being a Puertorriqueña student at the high school, the Aspirantes described how they were impacted by disparities and limitations every day during the school day. They shared that getting up each day to go to school motivated them to learn and engage, like being a good student was like fighting a battle. They expressed frustration because they knew that the perception of who they were was not of being an excellent student and a college aspirant even though they were. In response to this lived experience, Yazmín created a counterstory to the dominant narrative about the Puerto Ricans in the school.

The concept of college going for Yazmín and for other Aspirantes had been influenced by a consciousness of educational inequity. Even though participants identified as being college aspirants, they also identified as being the inheritors of a history of racism and disparities in the US educational system. In my first interview with Yazmín, she shared her philosophy about the education system in the city. I was struck by the criticality of her statement. She observed: "This is an urban city but people of Color are the ones that mostly endure the struggles and the hard times and since the whites don't have all that oppression, the support is not there. That is something that holds a barrier. They don't understand the situation. Society makes that barrier and the oppression puts us in that spot. This is how I think about my education" (Yazmín, First Interview). It has been well established that historically quality education and resources have been unequally distributed in the United States (Oakes et al., 2003). Yazmín, Melody, Damaris, Yadira, and Luz were students in a district where the disproportionate distribution of educational resources had impacted their entire community. They expressed feeling the burden of what it meant to be a student in Esperanza City and from a school that was taken over by the state. Despite their aspirations for college, they were aware that they did not have access to critical resources to ensure they are well prepared for college. Thus, this awareness also created fear among participants.

Having aspirations for college also generated worry that participants described as fear. They feared the possibility of failing to fulfill the goal of going to college for themselves and for their families. Their goals were linked to the hopes that their parents had for their futures. For example, Luz explained that even though she was motivated to go to college by her parents, she also feared that she would not be able to make it into college based on the anticipated barriers related to the lack of college preparatory resources available to her. She said: "I want to go [to college] and I feel like I have to go. I don't want to struggle. I don't want my parents to struggle. I feel that college is a way to prevent it. But I am scared that I don't have what it takes to make it there." However, the fear served to motivate participants to forge ahead in their plans toward their college-going goal. Melody was aware of the limited resources that her school district offered and felt tentative about her preparedness. She also felt fear about her ability to gain admission into college. However, she explained that, despite the barriers, she found motivation to find a way. In a class discussion on hopes and fears about college, Melody, who was usually fairly shy in the spotlight, shared the following with the group: "Not a lot of women who are Puerto Rican or of Color have the opportunity to go to college because the schools that they are in don't prepare them well. That happened to my mother and I want to be one of those people that do go to college and succeed. I am scared that I don't know what I don't know but because of that, I am going to try my best" (Melody, Hopes and Fears about College Class Discussion). Melody's hands were shaking as she held her palms together and shared her statement with the class. From across the room, Yadira nodded her head in agreement and raised her hand immediately after Melody finished talking. Yadira bellowed, "I know what you are talking about girl!" "I feel you!" Yadira said emphatically: "You don't know how much I worry about my future. I want to do good and I work hard and get good grades, but when I find out that what I am doing is not good enough, that scares me. But I feel what you are saying, Melody. I work even harder to make the point that I can even though I am from the projects of Esperanza City" (Yadira, Hopes and Fears about College Class Discussion).

I was struck by both students' contributions. Each was often shy and less frequently shared their ideas outwardly, let alone with such intention and emphasis. Their statements indicated a clear consciousness of their reality as aspiring to go to college, knowing that their educational experiences have lacked potentially critical opportunities and resources, and while maintaining their passion and drive to be the one to attend college, they also held a transgenerational fear that these obstacles could ultimately keep them from achieving their goal. As high school juniors, having faced the navigational and opportunity barriers they have, the students articulated their positionality and were deeply reflexive and aware of its complexity.

Using the LatCrit analytic lens, there are several critical points worth noting. The Aspirantes shared that their college-going aspirations stemmed directly from their sense of responsibility to realize their parents' unfulfilled aspirations. Yosso's (2005) community cultural wealth (CCW) framework was developed using a critical race theory (CRT) framework and identifies six forms of capital, including aspirational capital. As illustrated by the experiences of the Aspirantes, aspirational capital is "the ability to sustain high aspirations" even in the face of significant barriers (Yosso & Garcia, 2007, p. 169). Yazmín referred to her father's aspiration to become a pilot and Damaris to her mother's aspiration to become a nurse. Both were unable to achieve their aspirations. This legacy of having aspirations and being faced with the possibility or the reality of not being able to actualize them is the experiential knowledge of their parents shared to motivate the Aspirantes toward their own college-going goals. However, the Aspirantes also indicated that they were not sure or did not know how they would achieve their aspirations because they too—like their parents 20 years prior—were facing having inadequate preparation and resources for college.

The participants revealed the long-lasting structural and systemic barriers that have limited Puerto Rican college going for generations. Additionally, the experiential knowledge that was shared by parents and lived by the participants was coupled with a keen awareness and consciousness of the limitations and inequities. As framed by LatCrit, this is an example of the "race consciousness" and "insider knowledge" (Irizarry & Raible, 2014) among Puerto Ricans that motivates them to challenge the dominant ideology and structures. This was illustrated by the Aspirantes' commitment and conviction that they will realize their goal and their parents' goal for them to attend college. While they were conscious of the lack of preparation they had been provided and were aware of the fact that they did not know how they were going to accomplish their goal, even despite the fear that these conditions incited, the participants were committed to transforming their families' narrative about college going with the ultimate goal of making their parents proud. Yadira exclaimed: "I work even harder to make the point that I can [go to college] even though I am from the projects of Esperanza City." Akin to the "critical consciousness" described in Irizarry and Raible (2014), the transferred aspiration of college going from their parents served as deep motivation for participants in this study, along with an acute awareness of their potential limitations based on the educational circumstances they had experienced that translated into fear. They harnessed both the motivation and the fear and remained deeply committed to achieving their own aspirations for college-going despite the vast unknown associated with their goal.

Opportunity Gaps

Having spent a year teaching and conducting research in the high school, on numerous occasions I witnessed passive and active racism by teachers directed at Puerto Rican students. There were teachers that used discriminatory practices in their classrooms that often targeted Puerto Rican students, which led to a hostile learning environment. During the year of the study, I witnessed teachers tell Puerto Rican students directly that there was no hope for them in their classroom. These teachers had superficial understanding of the students' background and experiences, they articulated having no interest in Puerto Rican students' educational experiences in and out of the school. I witnessed the cultural disconnection between teachers and Puerto Rican students. For example, in a hallway full of predominantly Puerto Rican students, I witnessed two teachers publicly addressing two Puerto Rican students who had apparently left their classroom while class was still in session. They called out to them and said, "We don't care if you leave and if you fail the class, we will still get paid." I took that opportunity to engage with one of the teachers. She explained: "*These students* come from Puerto Rico in the middle of the year, they lack the motivation to learn English and to work hard academically to get good grades. They have no hope" (Field Notes, Teachers in the Hallway, emphasis original). She further explained that she was tired of trying to communicate with students from Puerto Rico when it was clear to her that there was a language barrier and a cultural disconnection and what she perceived to be a disinterest in learning. She said with frustration: "They don't want to be here and so they don't do the work. That is very frustrating and we can't help all of them" (Field Notes, Teachers in the Hallway). There is no doubt that teachers' efforts to bridge the gaps that students may need in their educational transitions may be at times taxing and possibly frustrating largely due to the systems-level resource deficits including an absence of proper professional training in areas like cultural humility and bridging culturally appropriate learning environments. It saddened me to bear witness to the experiences that the Aspirantes had shared with me. It was true that students' cultural and educational experiences were being misunderstood and at times devalued at Knight High School.

The intersectional racism was also evident in teachers' active withholding of college-promoting academic opportunities that the high-achieving Aspirantes Puertorriqueñas were both qualified for and had set goals to achieve. The Aspirantes reported multiple accounts of not being allowed to take advanced placement courses, incidents of negative mischaracterization, and misplaced punishment by the teachers. There was also evidence of intersectional racism toward Puerto Ricans among students. The Aspirantes reported that students had developed the term *linguis* to use in a derogatory way to describe newly arriving Puerto Rican students who were either monolingual Spanish-speakers or who had heavy Spanish accents. The racism created a divisive environment and, to avoid being targeted, longer-residing Puerto Ricans would clarify they were *not* a *lingui* to distance themselves from those who were perceived as newly arrived.

Pervasive intersectional racism as evidenced in this study can have major implications for Aspirantes Puertorriqueñas' college-going identity formation and process. The Aspirantes frequently reported "fear" and "worry" about the impact of being withheld college-bound opportunities or the lasting effects that being mischaracterized might have on their ability to get into college.

The narratives from the Aspirantes helped to spotlight an overt mischaracterization of Puerto Rican students. At the time of my work there, Knight High School was working to increase partnerships with local universities to promote the development of college access bridge programs. However, the environmental context was challenged by being under state receivership, experiencing frequent turnover of superintendents and principals, and being required to focus on performance benchmarks. There is a dire need for antiracism and cultural humility training among teachers and guidance counselors to actively address the racialized targeting and withholding of resources from Puerto Rican students and other students of Color. The broader community in Esperanza City had voiced serious concern about the state of the public school system. I attended several Town Hall meetings focused on the current state of Latino education in Esperanza City. A parent couple that I met shared their experience of the process with me stating, "Estamos aquí perdiendo tiempo" (We are wasting time here).

Community Cultural Wealth and the Narrowing Opportunity Structure

The culture of higher education is rooted in a history of discrimination (Levine & Nidiffer, 1996) and practices that perpetuate inequitable access to college resources for marginalized and minoritized groups (Contreras, 2011). Too often, Latinx students are at a disadvantage because they are unable to find adequate and culturally relevant transitional tools that will help them navigate the college identity formation and choice process. To address these differences and ameliorate the barriers that students experience in their transitions, we need frameworks that respond to students' needs as they navigate through the process by bridging information gaps and translating the cultural practices and value from both institutional and individual-based capital. Additionally, the role of family as well as other aspects of their social identities need to be recognized as meaningful influences in the process.

Building on Dr. Luu's description of community cultural wealth (Yosso, 2005) in chapter 3, several forms of capital served as facilitators or barriers to Aspirantes' educational processes as they cautiously navigated conflicting identities of race, class, and gender during their college choice process. Aspirantes used aspirational, linguistic, familial, social, navigational, and resistant capital (Yosso, 2005). Each of the forms of capital used by each of them, though tied to an element of pride when considering the families' efforts to seek a better life, were not catalyzing the students' goals. Even though, according to the literature, each form of capital is an asset, there was a lack of congruence between the Aspirantes' sources of capital and the capital that is valued in the process of college choice. For example, their sources of capital were not transformed into access to college preparatory academic programming and resources—an example of cultural capital (Bourdieu, 1986; McDonough, 1997). The Aspirantes described having to constantly push against stereotypes and barriers and to sidestep obstacles during their educational experiences while their narratives still reflected their use of CCW.

El Embudo de College Choice

Equipped with their developing college-going identity, the Aspirantes confronted challenging conditions during the college choice process. *El Embudo de College Choice* (The Funnel of College Choice, see figure 4.1) illustrates how the college choice model manifested in the lives of the Aspirantes and how their process is better illustrated as funneling through a series of barriers. The Aspirantes anticipated that the process of college choice would be difficult to navigate and they were determined to do their best to find a way through the process. Informed by the Aspirantes' process, *El Embudo* includes three conditions (though not limited to these) that students needed to reconcile as they engaged in their college choice process. These three conditions are *Context Matters*, *Buscando una Aguja en un Pajar*, and the *Illusion of Choice*, offering critical insight into a different pathway from that proposed in a prior model's linear stages of predisposition, search, and choice (Hossler & Gallagher, 1987). The conditions that constitute *El Embudo* illustrated how the Aspirantes, based on their positionality, explained having to constantly work against stereotypes and to sidestep obstacles. It is no surprise that the Aspirantes felt lost and discouraged (not disinterested and unmotivated) in the college-going process. The following is a discussion of the three conditions within *El Embudo de College Choice*.

CONTEXT MATTERS IN PREDISPOSITION

In my work with the Aspirantes Puertorriqueñas, I learned that each of them had developed a college-going identity that was responsive and had adapted to the challenging conditions of their context by activating their capital related to their community cultural wealth (Yosso, 2005). Context mattered in their college choice process. They had not received guidance about what college going is and how it occurs. They had not visited any colleges or universities. In fact, the local area colleges and universities in the surrounding area, of which there are quite a few, had not visited or recruited students from Knight High School.

Figure 4.1. *El Embudo de* [the funnel of] *College Choice. Source:* Created by the author.

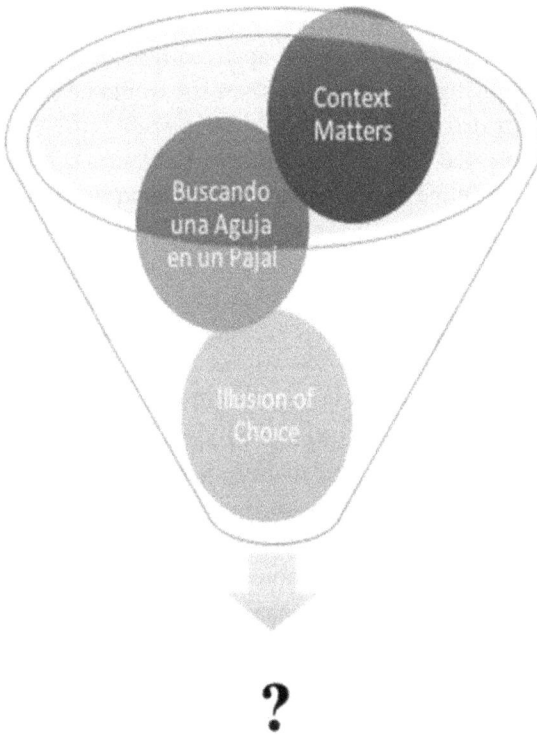

The Search for Una Aguja en Un Pajar

For the Aspirantes, college going and the college choice process were only notions/imaginations and they did not have concrete examples and were not provided tools, resources or opportunities to engage in the actual steps of the college choice process. The "search for una aguja en un pajar (a needle in a haystack)" is symbolic of the Aspirantes' college choice process. Without a college going culture in place or a formal process of engaging the Aspirantes, the Aspirantes reported alternative steps they had to take to prepare for the college choice process on their own. Melody, who found support in the GEAR UP program, shared disappointment that the program was cut for the fall when she needed it the most. She shared that she was hopeful the program would resume again in the spring but it was never reinstated due to a limited school budget. The Aspirantes shared their frustration of having to "jump through hoops" and of having to "figure it all out as [they] go." For example, they did not know what they needed to do in order to prepare for the career they wanted. They were always trying to piece together college information. One Aspirante shared with me that she felt that it would be best to just apply to the community college that everyone was applying to because she knew she would be accepted. Without having been provided any information about possible colleges or about how to search for potential colleges, none of the Aspirantes conducted a formal college search and none had a strategy for a search process.

ILLUSION OF CHOICE

As is stated in the literature, open access policies at community colleges provide educational access to minoritized groups and are well regarded among supporters of open access policy (Goldrick-Rab, 2010). However, in my engagement with the Aspirantes, I also witnessed how community colleges engage students in the management of ambition in a process that is believed to deter students from college aspirations and outcomes associated with a 4-year college opportunity (Brint & Karabel, 1989, p. 225; Pincus, 1974). Instead of "Choice," their aspirations are controlled and tempered through the management of ambition (Brint & Karabel, 1989) so that instead they experience an illusion of choice.

Moving from no choices to one choice is not a *choice set* for college and is inadequate for students who aspire to go to college. When asked about the colleges they had visited, the Aspirantes could only recount two local community colleges in the area. Those two community colleges were proximate to the high school, as were two other 4-year colleges and, just several miles away, three other higher education institutions. None of these institutions reached out to the student population at Knight High School for recruitment or distribution of college-going resources.

Institutions of higher education use college choice models to inform their recruitment practices and to reach prospective students who are participating in the college choice process. It is a symbiotic relationship, of sorts, in which *choice* is meant to ultimately reflect the best fit both for the student and for the institution. However, the Aspirantes had no access to the schools that they aspired to attend. They were planning to apply to colleges and universities that they had never visited and had only gathered basic information from general internet searches. As scholars and practitioners, this warrants critical reflection and a united consideration of how to counter the Aspirantes' recent accounts of the long-standing notion put forth by Clark in 1980 when he described the institutional process of redirecting students with low academic skills but who had aspirations to transfer to 4-year colleges to remain in 2-year college as "cooling out"—a method intentionally utilized to keep people from advancing. It seemed like the Aspirantes were receiving messages that their only options would be to attend community college. While community college is an essential part of the higher education spectrum of opportunities, a college choice process including only two local community colleges is incomplete. For example, two Aspirantes who were pursuing a career in nursing knew only about one program within one community college in the area despite there being many nursing programs in the region.

Researchers have examined important factors that impact and inform Latinxs in their college choice process. They have found that they depend considerably on their families, friends, and trustworthy school representatives for information. The "chain migration contacts" (Perez & McDonough, 2008) was coined to illustrate how Latinx students rely the most on their extended family members for information about college and make their choices to attend college based on where the people they know had attended (Jun & Colyar, 2002; McDonough, 1997; McDonough & Calderone, 2006; Perez & McDonough, 2008). Similarly, other scholars propose that student college expectations and aspirations are constructed through their relationships and interactions with important people in their lives, and as such are considered "institutional agents" (McDonough, 1997; McDonough & Calderone, 2006) and agents of support (Sapp et al., 2016). Though consistent with the narratives of the Aspirantes, current seminal frameworks illustrate the responsibility of the college choice process being with the individual and do not consider institutional accountability. We have a crisis of historic and persistent racial/ethnic access to higher education disparities and higher education as an institution needs to assume institutional responsibility for best practices that can bridge and yield access to quality education and provide resources for a successful college choice process that is culturally responsive and sustaining for students like the Aspirantes in this study.

The Complexity of College "Choice" for Aspirantes Puertorriqueñas

The concept of college choice in higher education assumes that in order to successfully participate in the college choice process, a student must be able to share in the values espoused within the academic community and thus be aware of the markers and symbols that are a part of that culture. For example, minoritized students, like the Aspirantes in this study, whose educational experiences were affected by conditions of an underresourced school district, have limited to no access to the resources that more affluent students acquire during their educational experiences from an early age (Tierney et al., 2005; Tinto, 1987, p. 87). The college choice process for each Aspirante did not map onto the existing traditional models of college choice. Each Aspirante was "the first" in their family who was navigating the process of college choice, primarily on their own and with a primary intention to break the cycle of poverty. Furthermore, even though they all felt fear of failing, they were determined to find their way through their process of college choice. A sustainable model for a college choice process and access initiative between higher education and schools would include university-supported programmatic partnerships to provide resources, education, and research about the specific and required steps to successfully attend college and to expose college aspirants to the widest range of local and national programs aligned with their goals. It would engage students in college positive messaging, education about the college choice process, and would document the narratives of college aspirants who are largely excluded from current theoretical frameworks for college choice process. These narratives will unmask the true navigational strategies of the Aspirantes and can inform more representative frameworks to create culturally relevant policy for outreach, engagement, and retention of Puerto Rican Aspirantes and other minoritized student groups of Color who are chronically marginalized in college. Only then will the college choice process yield the outcome it is intended to achieve among Aspirantes Puertorriqueñas.

What Can You Do?

First, the educational institutions—both secondary and higher education—must involve the families, including their values, strengths, and capacity to support and shape students' college-going aspirations. Each Aspirante reported that their aspiration to go to college stemmed from their parents' well-established college positive messaging from an early age at home even when their parents were not able to attend college themselves. By involving the students' parents and family-based social networks, the educational institutions can create opportunities to demystify the college-going process because—while supportive of the goals—they too are frequently uninformed about the process. Therefore, the students and their families would be better able to make informed decisions based on true and accurate information rather than the process remaining an imagined and hoped for but otherwise unknown and often unrealized goal. I must admit, however, that I confronted a double-edged sword with the implications of these recommendations. On the one hand, engaging the parents and families is essential based on the meaning-making that students' have about the origin and overall purpose for pursuing higher education, namely to be "the one" to catapult the family forward both economically and socially. On the other hand, if the students—and by extension their families—are approaching college going with community cultural wealth (Yosso, 2005), a source of capital that is often undervalued, there is a fundamental chasm between how they are arriving at the goal to attend college and the actual expectations from higher education to become independent for individual advancement.

Therefore, to rectify this misalignment in how traditional and existing college-going frameworks situate Aspirantes frequently without family engagement, there is a need to *re*frame and center families' cultural capital in culturally sustaining ways throughout the college choice process. An example of this approach is spotlighted by Dr. George Mwangi in chapter 11. This in turn would also introduce the families to their children's context and help them to understand the complexity of navigating between two distinct and often disconnected worlds of home and school and the sophisticated code-switching practices and strategies their children have had to master.

Furthermore, bridging access from the university should include representation from several important sectors of the institution. The undergraduate student population should be included to provide mentorship opportunities and access to Aspirantes to truly know rather than imagine the lived experiences and requirements of a first-generation college student of Color. The collaboration should also include academic affairs, student affairs, and admissions to provide comprehensive information about the college application, admission process, and college learning experience. This collaborative higher education leadership should provide wrap-around college choice process education and resources and actively seek to recruit and engage Puerto Rican Aspirantes shifting the burden of the college choice process from the individual students disproportionately impacted by higher education disparities to the higher education institution. Currently, university efforts to engage Puerto Rican Aspirantes and other first-generation students of Color are fragmented with little to no sustainable funding since most are grant funded, creating inconsistent and transient programs that students cannot count on being available when they need them. As a result, there is not an opportunity in the current structure to scaffold on the learning, both institutional and individual. However, there are campus initiatives to increase student diversity. This is an opportunity to institutionalize a sustainable funding stream to support this college choice and access collaborative bridging initiative. The schools where Puerto Rican Aspirantes and other similar students are completing secondary education are struggling. Being under state receivership, for example, illustrates the gravity of school environments and they are unable to provide the support and resources needed to increase college access and choice. Therefore, if higher education institutions aim to increase student diversity and, specifically, if higher education institutions aim to engage the fastest growing population in the United States, it is incumbent on the universities to take action.

During the time of my research study, for example, I witnessed such faculty engendered opportunities to connect with Puerto Rican students and other first-generation students of Color and prioritize building partnerships and long-term mentorship despite the absence of any corresponding gains in their tenure-track process. Simultaneous to the need to engage the families, we must engage our first-generation teachers, community scholar-practitioners, and faculty of Color who are likely success stories among their families and communities and whose achievements are frequently the definition of resistant capital. Like the Aspirantes, they seek to support, and for many of them, having been an Aspirante facing similar barriers at one point, their commitment to this work is in addition to the fundamental requirements of their institutions. In other words, they continue to have to work more than their counterparts in order to fulfill their commitment to a similar promise of being "the one" to help their family (i.e., community) to advance. These professionals are knowledgeable, both firsthand and through their research and partnerships, concerning the educational inequities and are unified in their acknowledgment and commitment to address the disparity, making them collaborative agents of change with the Aspirantes.

Finally, researchers and practitioners should continue exploring what a collective- and family-oriented approach to the college-going process may look like so that college aspirants can maintain their cultural identity and values and uphold their family responsibilities within the context of being a college student. If we aim to provide a holistic experience to the Aspirantes, it requires applying in-depth understanding of the family values and incorporating them into the approach for college going. Additionally, parents and extended families of collegegoers should be engaged in the college preparatory process to educate families about the potential for college-related experiences like living further from the family and among a diverse array of cultures. Families should be connected with the higher education student affairs leaders and practitioners who address access and engagement to cultural groups and resources on campus so that parents and families understand the opportunity for sustaining community and cultural values even if/while living at a distance or becoming integrated into a college-going culture.

Critical Consideration

There is a paucity of research about Puerto Rican people's educational experiences and their aspirations to attend college. I embarked on this research process committed to using my platform as a researcher to conduct humanistic research (Paris & Winn, 2014) and with a goal to address both a gap in the existing literature and to inform research, practice, and policy aimed at increasing access to higher education for Puertorriqueñx students, Latinxs, and communities of Color in general. Puerto Rican students in the United States most often experience an educational system fraught with inequities and curricula that marginalizes and dehumanizes their experiences on a daily basis (Irizarry, 2011; Nieto, 2000; Solís-Jordan, 1994; Valenzuela, 1999). Systematically, the educational system is structured to underserve Latinx students in the United States. They should not have to tolerate these conditions. For at least seventy years, efforts to address educational inequities among Puerto Rican communities have been underway (Centro de Estudios Puertorriqueños, 2007). How many students have gone through high school and were told they would not amount to anything, that they are better off getting a job, they are not college material, or have been handed incomplete information about college? When will there be an acknowledgment that we are failing our Puerto Rican student communities?

A shift from models that focus on individual resilience as sources of capital to ones that focus on institutional competence of how best to engage and sustain resilient learners is warranted. The current community cultural wealth model frames students' of Color assets and highlights strengths acquired in various home, community, and cultural domains. This model offers an important shift from deficit-based to asset-based perceptions of how students of Color approach and navigate their educational trajectories. It also builds on the resilience of the student and is structured so that resilience, developed in response to the chronic barriers students of Color often face, is often heralded as the driver of the student's potential success. However, the Aspirantes highlighted that though they were indeed resilient and have had to conquer and sidestep many obstacles along the way, they were also exhausted, frustrated, and remained unsure of how to actually attain their educational aspirations.

Consider that for each of the forms of capital proposed in CCW, there is a counterstory that demonstrates that capital is acquired in response to institutional-level oppression and discrimination. Therefore, when highlighting these forms of capital as assets, it is equally important to acknowledge the counterstory, to understand their origin, and to consider how institutional-level responsibility and competence is required so as not to misinterpret student resilience as simply a source of inner strength but rather as an acquired response to structural and systemic barriers. How can we relieve the individual burden faced by students of Color? How can we support students of Color so that their achievement does not have to be a sign of succeeding against all odds? Though beyond the scope of this chapter, it is important to recognize that for every one student of Color who is resilient and navigating against obstacles to reach her aspirations, there are many more who have not been able to activate their community cultural wealth and, thus, an even broader question is: How do we support the activation of students of Color, not just those who have independently launched themselves onto the long and arduous path of seeking higher education?

This chapter demonstrates that we must take responsibility for the fact that institutional structures are creating oppressive conditions for students of Color, specifically those who come from underrepresented backgrounds. By shifting the focus away from deficits in order to highlight student strengths, in essence we allow the source of actual student deficits (e.g., lack of access to early academic preparation, limited access to college preparation information and materials, lack of exposure to guidance and role models, and chronic exposure to poverty)—namely institutional-level disparities—to remain unburdened by the need to identify a means for providing equitable opportunities and supports by which students of Color can achieve their academic goals without having to resist and survive but rather through the ability to embrace and progress.

After concluding the study, I continued to volunteer at Knight High School and joined efforts with several faculty and community stakeholders to develop a college access and positive messaging program at Knight High School. The Aspirantes endured a system that underestimated their academic potential. However, the findings conveyed participant narratives of aspiration, resistance, and transformation related to the process of developing the concept and identity of college going. Damaris, Luz, Yadira, Yazmín, and Melody have actualized their aspirations and continue to activate their agency, eyes wide open, fueled by their internal resources of cultural pride, committed to being representatives for their families and communities in educational attainment and justice.

Critical Reflection

Consider the following critical points of inquiry:

1. How could you complicate the concept of resilience as it relates to the historical impact that it has had on our student communities of Color? Is it ethical to "facilitate student survival and nurture resistance" when we have data that reveals that there is a cost to their survival and resistance? How can we complicate resilience in our scholarship and practice? What systemic and structural changes are needed to shift the expectation and glorification of students' of Color resilience to expecting policy and institutional-level reframing, culturally sustaining support, and equitable resource distribution for college choice and access?

2. How can we support and foster student aspirations while also supporting them as they bridge the deficits that have been imposed upon them via systemic and institutional oppression? How can we hold ourselves and our colleagues accountable to reject the deficit perspectives and rather redirect our students of Color to expand their expectations and offer opportunities to grow and develop in a humanizing and affirming way?

3. How can we mitigate fear and create a humanizing educational environment that offers trust so that our student communities of Color can truly engage and love the experiences of learning?

Note

1. All participant names are pseudonyms.

References

Bourdieu, P. (1986). The forms of capital. In J. G. Richardson (ed.), *Handbook of theory and research for the sociology of education* (pp. 241–258). Greenwood Press.

Brint, S. G., Karabel, J. (1989). *The diverted dream: Community colleges and the promise of educational opportunity in America, 1900–1985.* Oxford University Press.

Centro de Estudios Puertorriqueños. (2007, April 16). Guide to the Antonia Pantoja Papers 1922–2002. Retrieved from: https://centropr.hunter.cuny.edu/sites/default/files/faids/pdf/Pantoja%2C%20Antonia%20Oct%202014.pdf

Clark, B. R. (1980). The "cooling out" function revisited. *New Directions for Community Colleges, 1980*(32), 15–31.

Contreras, F. (2011). *Achieving equity for Latino students: Expanding the pathway to higher education through public policy.* Teachers College Press.

Delgado, R., & Stefancic, J. (2012). *Critical race theory: An introduction.* New York University Press.

Goldrick-Rab, S. (2010). Challenges and opportunities for improving community college student success. *Review of Educational Research, 80*(3), 437–469. https://doi.org/10.3102/0034654310370163

Hossler, D., & Gallagher, K. S. (1987). Studying student college choice: A three-phase model and the implications for policymakers. *College and University 2*, 207–221.

Irizarry, J. G. (2011). *The Latinization of U.S. schools: Successful teaching and learning in shifting cultural contexts.* Paradigm.

Irizarry, J. G., & Raible, J. (2014). "A hidden part of me": Latino/a students, silencing, and the epidermalization of inferiority. *Equity & Excellence in Education, 47*(4), 430–444. https://doi.org/10.1080/10665684.2014.958970

Jun, A., & Colyar, J. (2002). Parental guidance suggested: Family in college programs. In W. Tierney & L. Hagedorn (Eds.), *Increasing access to college:*

Extending opportunity for all students (pp. 195–216). State University of New York Press.

Levine, A., & Nidiffer, J. (1996). *Beating the odds: How the poor get to college.* Jossey-Bass.

McDonough, P. M. (1997). *Choosing colleges: How social class and schools structure opportunity.* State University of New York Press.

McDonough, P. M., & Calderone, S. (2006). The meaning of money: Perceptual differences between college counselors and low-income families about college costs and financial aid. *American Behavioral Scientist, 49*(12), 1703–1718. https://doi.org/10.1177/0002764206289140

Nieto, S. (Ed.). (2000). *Puerto Rican students in U.S. schools.* Erlbaum.

Oakes, J., Rogers, J., Lipton, M., & Morrell, E. (2003). The social construction of college access: Confronting the technical, cultural, and political barriers to low-income students of color. In W. G. Tierney & L. S. Hagedorn (Eds.), *Increasing access to college: Extending possibilities for all students* (pp. 105–121). State University of New York Press.

Paris, D., & Winn, M. T. (2014). *Humanizing research: Decolonizing qualitative inquiry with youth and communities.* Sage.

Perez, P. A., & McDonough, P. M. (2008). Understanding Latina and Latino college choice: A social capital and chain migration analysis. *Journal of Hispanic Higher Education, 7*(3), 249–265. https://doi.org/10.1177/1538192708317 620

Pincus, F. (1974). Tracking in community colleges. *Critical Sociology, 4*(3), 17–35.

Rolón-Dow, R. (2007). Passing time: An exploration of school engagement among Puerto Rican girls. *Urban Review, 39*(3), 349–372. https://doi.org/10.1007/ s11256-007-0063-9

Sapp, V. T., Marquez Kyama, J., & Dache-Gerbino, A. (2016). Against all odds: Latinas activate agency to secure access to college. *NASPA Journal about Women in Higher Education, 9*(1), 39–55. https://doi.org/10.1080/1940788 2.2015.1111243

Solís-Jordan, J. (1994). *Public school reform in Puerto Rico.* Greenwood Press.

Tierney, W. G., Corwin, Z. B., & Colyar, J. E. (Eds.) (2005). *Preparing for college: Nine elements of effective outreach.* State University of New York Press.

Tinto, V. (1987). *Leaving college: Rethinking the causes and cures for student attrition.* University of Chicago Press.

Valenzuela, A. (1999). *Subtractive schooling: Issues of caring in education of US-Mexican youth.* State University of New York Press.

York, T., Gibson, C., & Rankin, S. (2015). Defining and measuring academic success. *Practical Assessment, Research, and Evaluation 20*(1), 5.

Yosso, T. J. (2005). Whose culture has capital? A critical race theory discussion of community cultural wealth. *Race Ethnicity and Education, 8*(1), 69–91. https://doi.org/10.1080/1361332052000341006

Yosso, T. J., & Garcia, D. (2007). "This is no slum!" A critical race theory analysis of community cultural wealth in culture clash's Chavez Ravine. *Aztlán: A Journal of Chicano Studies, 32*(1), 145–179.

Part II

Community-Grown Framings

Asset-based community assessment map. High school students of Color in Springfield, Massachusetts, created a map of their community during a college access program. They were asked to draw the places and spaces they viewed as assets and with pride as a counter to the deficit narrative their community often receives. The following chapters in this section are written by scholars of Color working within their communities as organization leaders, former teachers, student advisors, and advocates and activists. *Source*: Photo by the editors.

Chapter 5

When Impossible Becomes Possible!

A Critical Access Model That Centers Equity in Community Health

Tania M. Barber

Are you a product of your environment? Do you feel defined by where you come from or where you live? Has anyone ever said to you that you would never be able to achieve your aspirations and dreams? Or, has anyone ever said to you that it would be impossible for you to improve your life's circumstances? If you've answered yes to any of these questions, please continue reading. These questions may resonate for some, particularly for communities of Color.

When referencing communities of Color, I am referring to individuals who are not white. I am referring to Black people, Indigenous people, Asian people, Latinx people; not monolithic, these groups uniquely hold racial and cultural identities that are often compared to white people as though the white group were the model from which all other groups should be based. Throughout, I will use the terms *you* and *we* to refer to those of us who either have been subjected to oppression or who are defining our vision of a future together by working to dismantle oppression.

In this chapter, I build on my knowledge and career of 27 years at Caring Health Center (CHC) where I started as an entry-level switchboard operator, and today I am in my 11th year as president and CEO. In this capacity, I grew the organization from an operating budget of $13 million to $40 million, meeting numerous critical milestones for healthcare reform and innovation. I will share a model birthed from the pain points of seeing communities of Color stuck in poverty and struggling to make ends meet. I will share my journey as I fought to champion the creation of an access model, the recently CHC board–approved Tania M. Barber Learning Institute, to critically address the needs of the community of Color that CHC serves. Dedicated to engaging the community in entry-level opportunities for learning while earning and to providing career development opportunities, the model centers equity in community health while simultaneously advancing the mission-driven equity framework of federally qualified community health centers (FQHCs).

Caring Health Center, an FQHC located in Springfield, Massachusetts, has a rich and vibrant diversity within its community of employees and the patients it serves. We serve patients in over 39 languages. In 1976, a group of Springfield residents recognized the need for a community health center to meet the increasing health and social needs of city residents. They organized a coalition, called the Springfield South End Community Health Center Development Corporation (SSECHCD), to petition for accessible and affordable primary health care in Springfield's South End neighborhood. Their federal application for funding to support a Section 330 Community Health Center was approved in 1980, but the funds for this initiative were whisked away by budget cuts and priority shifts before the project could begin. Sixteen years later, the commissioner of the Springfield Department of Health and Human Services received the original proposal and established a 40-member citywide task force to revise and resubmit the application for a Section 330 Community Health Center. In 1993, the teamwork of service providers, community members, and state agencies paid off when the United States Public Health Service approved the city's request for funds. Upon receiving this award, in 1995 the Springfield Southwest Community Health Center was born. Many years later it was decided the name was too long, prompting a community naming competition. Springfield residents entered a naming competition for a grand prize of $1,000 to rename the organization. There was a tie resulting in two residents splitting 50% of the winning prize. Two residents thought the name Caring Health Center was fitting based on demonstrated concern for the well-being of its patients and community.

The value proposition at Caring Health Center is that we are all unique in each of our individual self-identities, race, culture, ethnic background, religious practices, and customs. Our employees and patients are Black, African American, Hispanic/Latinx, Vietnamese, Ukrainian, Somali, Arabic speaking, Nepali speaking, Iraqi, Bhutanese, and Afghani, to name just a few. Our patient and employee communities experience the day-to-day impact of significant social inequities such as unemployment, barriers to educational access, food and housing insecurity. Unemployment in Springfield typically runs somewhat higher than the statewide rate (US Bureau of Labor Statistics, 2022). For example, 6.4% of Springfield's residents were unemployed in August 2021, as compared to 5% of all Massachusetts residents (US Bureau of Labor Statistics, 2022). As defined by the US Department of Agriculture (USDA), food insecurity refers to a situation in which a person lacks adequate food to lead a fully active life (Feeding America, 2020). High housing costs and associated housing insecurity represent a significant barrier for residents of greater Springfield. According to the US Department of Housing and Urban Development (HUD User, n.d.), a person is "housing cost burdened" when 30% or more of their income is absorbed by housing costs—at which point it becomes increasingly difficult to pay for other necessities such as food, clothing, or medical care. When assessed by this standard, Springfield residents are seriously impacted by housing insecurity, with 46% of Springfield residents being identified as housing cost burdened. All of these adverse social determinants of health exacerbate the challenges to living healthy lives in one form or another. Racial and ethnic disparities are strong factors in rates of poor health outcomes within communities of Color. All can be directly attributed and linked to lack of resources such as education, ultimately impacting one's ability to obtain employment, adding to stress and the potential of homelessness and/or poor health (Feeding America, 2020; HUD, n.d.; US Census Bureau, 2019).

For instance, in Springfield, 26.9% of all residents live at or below the federal poverty limit, as compared to 12.3% of Massachusetts residents (US Census Bureau, 2019). Hispanic and African American individuals in Springfield confront levels of poverty that are higher than comparable groups locally and statewide. For example, 28.0% of Springfield's Hispanic residents live in poverty, as compared to 19.9% of the city's white residents, and 17.2% of Hispanic residents of Massachusetts (US Census Bureau, 2019). Twenty-nine percent of Springfield's African American residents live in poverty, as compared to 21.2% of African American residents of Massachusetts (US Census Bureau, 2019). Several neighborhoods in the city, including the Metro Center, Mason Square, and South End neighborhoods, where large populations of CHC patients live, have been designated as racially/ethnically concentrated areas of poverty (R/ECAPs) by the US Department of Housing and Urban Development (HUD) (Pioneer Valley Planning Commission, 2020). R/ECAPs are defined as areas where a majority of residents are persons of color, and where at least 40% of residents live at or below the federal poverty limit. In Springfield, 46,604 residents live in the city's HUD-designated R/ECAPs. As a member of this community for 55 years, I have had to navigate the same system that systemically undermines opportunities for success in communities of Color.

Transforming Dishonorable Labels and Shifting Accountability

The concept of *access* for the communities I serve encompasses a historic navigational complexity that needs to be interrogated more deeply in order to disrupt the perpetuated disparity that exists. Communities of Color are navigating and securing opportunities for themselves every day. I skillfully negotiated opportunities in my journey toward professional stability. However, every step of the way I used strategies to get around the deficit perspectives that were constantly being imposed on me and the lack of opportunities that existed for me. An experience that negatively impacted me, and that I can see impacting my community, is the experience of negative labeling. I called these negative labels *dishonorable labels* to reflect the notion of shame, blame, and disgrace that the words carry as they are used to negatively characterize individuals.

Communities of Color have been assigned dishonorable labels from their inceptions that do not reflect or highlight our accomplishments and achievements, especially given the inequitable circumstances we have to fight against to pursue achievement. The dishonorable labels are masked in society's everyday language, as they have become situational identifiers but carry connotations that are negative and at times detrimental to growth and development. The labels are masked, portraying a common theme in medicine and public health of individual-level blame for poor outcomes. Yet, these labels are used to characterize who we are and not what our environment has imposed upon us as people of Color. Too often, we are labeled with descriptors such as *underserved, vulnerable, at risk, marginalized,* or *disenfranchised* as an expression or identifier of who we are. These labels are also used to define us, communities of Color, as a monolithic group, dismissing our intersectional identities and diverse experiences and our many successes and contributions to society. They are also not a manifestation of who we are, but rather they are a result of institutional and systemic oppression that has negatively impacted our communities of Color. When we label someone as an *at-risk, underserved, vulnerable, disenfranchised, marginalized* individual, without contextualizing the origin of the disparity, we inadvertently impose the burden on the individual. At times it feels like we, as People of Color, have internalized and embodied these labels as our truth and the terms have been bestowed upon us as a badge we have to wear as part of our narrative. A badge of honor is worn with pride, respect, support, and honor. These dishonorable labels, however, remain negative and, in fact, represent stigmatization and deficit perspectives that in turn are embodied as trauma and pain in the individuals who are dishonorably labeled throughout their life trajectory. Academic and community-engaged scholars in the field have addressed related concepts that center the misplaced individual-level burden of racism and oppression on people of Color. Dishonorable labels expand this body of work and actively name the impact of commonly used terms whose negative impact has gone unacknowledged (Hernández & Villodas, 2020; Irizarry & Raible, 2014; Solórzano et al., 2000).

Words have power! As I became an adult, I learned that names not only carry meaning but also carry power, and what one gives energy or credence to . . . well . . . it becomes you, as if it was your truth. Let me expound. My life as a leader intersects with two positionalities. I am not only a president/CEO of a nonprofit organization, but I am also an ordained pastor. I am the founder of a nonprofit church, Living Water Global Ministries. Living my life based on biblical principles and teach-ings, and having studied theology for many years, my brain often crosses over into scripture as a resource for reference. I have long navigated two parallel universes: one in public health in my career at Caring Health Center; one as a pastor. For years, I have kept those two worlds separate. However, more recently, community-engaged initiatives have recognized the capacity and importance of considering faith and spirituality within public health settings. As such, I am cognizant and remain aware of the distinct frameworks and lenses that are informed by each, public health and religion, and I chose to operate with them both as integrated com-ponents of who I am as a leader and innovator. For anyone who does not share one or either of these frameworks, my message is independent of any specific faith or practice. My message is that we, as a people and as a community, are impacted deeply by how we are described over the course of a lifetime.

Hence, the power of words. In Proverbs 18:21, the scripture says, "life and death are in the power of the tongue" (King James Bible, 2017/1769). In essence, it is like one can believe the negative connotation and then become it. The best example I can provide is found in the Bible in 1 Chronicles 4:10 (King James Bible, 2017/1769). It is characterized by a person whose mother named (labeled) him Jabez, a name that in Hebrew means "he makes sorrowful, because she birthed him in sorrow." However, Jabez did not want his identity to be shaped by a label that was stigmatizing and he cried out for this not to be his case. Jabez wanted, instead, to prosper and have favor in all that he set out to do.

The impact of negative labeling is very prevalent among my community as we experience the impact of living with limited resources. When a person is called or identified as "poor," day in and day out, they can internalize the impact of the negative stereotypes associated with being poor. Being poor can feel demoralizing and shameful and can be associated with the notion that the values of the poor perpetuate poverty. Though a contested notion, *the culture of poverty* is a concept that continues to influence how people who experience poverty are treated and characterized (Gorski, 2008). There needs to be a shift in perspective so that we can acknowledge the structural factors that in fact shape and influence the reproduction of poverty and thus cause social inequality.

In order to challenge deficit perspectives, we must examine the impact that dishonorable labels have on community experiences. We need to critically analyze how we are characterizing our communities of Color and consider how we are labeling our communities of Color. Society has beautifully commodified stereotypical labels that are now normalized and sadly embodied by communities of Color. Unfortunately, the internalization of negative stereotypes and the perpetual deficit perspective are conditions that communities of Color are struggling against. These conditions are present within institutions such as health care, social services, education, and within the workplace. These negative perceptions create false notions of culture and practices among the dominant groups about communities of Color (Hernández & Villodas, 2020; Irizarry & Raible, 2014; Solórzano et al., 2000). Therefore, as a community, we must not let this become our permanent position and disposition. We have to activate from within our communities to counter the negative and deficit narratives and demand accountability from the institutions that perpetuate these inequities.

Thus, rather than owning these conditions and allowing the negative labels to be placed upon us, we can seek accountability from those who assigned them to us in the first place. We need to counter the narrative by not downplaying what is actually happening and disrupting the vicious cycle of stigmatization. Living under the stereotypes of these labels is traumatic for communities of Color and the systems that created and perpetuate them also traumatize. Communities of Color have embodied the negative impact of this type of inequity and are made to relive consistent trauma and hurt every day. We must redirect the narrative, and demand accountability from the institutions and the dominant privileged groups that perpetuate and uphold systems of oppression, social injustice, social trauma, social deprivation, social disparities, systemic racism, and the generational hurt that our communities of Color have had to endure. While, indeed, acts of oppression can be and are reified within communities of Color as well (e.g., anti-Blackness among communities of Color), it is imperative that this is understood also within the systemic lens of whiteness and white supremist framing that communities of Color are operating under and within (Haynes, 2023; 2017; Bonilla-Silva, 1997).

Figure 5.1 illustrates a nonexhaustive list of terms commonly used to characterize low-income populations of Color in the United States. These terms are often used to emphasize population needs related to disparities. This approach of using individual-level terms to characterize a group removes the more accurate descriptions of the "why" behind the disparities. As a woman of Color from the community we serve, my reaction to this default set of dishonorable labels is to state boldly, "Stop calling me that!" In contrast, I present the alternate words and phrases I use to more specifically and accurately name the systems-level oppression and structural inequities that contribute to the disparities and to shift the accountability "upstream" to policies, laws, and other governing forces. Additionally, drawing from Dr. Yedalis Ruíz Santana's scholarship and practices on access and equity in her role at CHC, we have taken this shift in language a step further to more accurately describe the populations we serve using asset- and strengths-based language that represents the rich and dynamic set of collective experiences and capacities among them (see Ruíz Santana, chapter 4 in this volume).

Why call me "at risk" rather than a person of high priority? Why call me "disenfranchised" when, based on the US Constitution, I have the same rights and privileges that white society has and continues to take from me? The root word for *dis* in disenfranchise means "apart/

Figure 5.1. "Stop calling me that!" From dishonorable labels to systemic account-ability. *Source*: Created by the author.

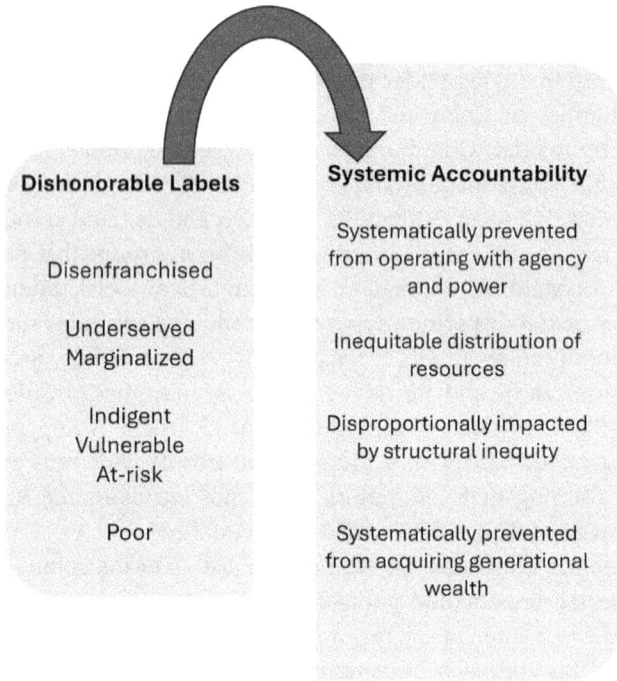

Dishonorable Labels

Disenfranchised

Underserved
Marginalized

Indigent
Vulnerable
At-risk

Poor

Systemic Accountability

Systematically prevented from operating with agency and power

Inequitable distribution of resources

Disproportionally impacted by structural inequity

Systematically prevented from acquiring generational wealth

separate," which reminds me of segregation. It is not the desire of people of Color to be separate or segregated from the same opportunities as others. People of Color are being labeled and identified by the names that society continues to plague them with through the systemic creation of bondage. Calling me "underserved" makes me think of being beneath, below, subservient, oppressed; yet you, society, are those trying to keep me down! Why are we, people of Color, still being oppressed, when slavery was abolished years ago in the Thirteenth Constitutional Amendment in 1865? Yet here we are today. As referenced in Deuteronomy 28:13, "I am the head and not the tail, I am above and not beneath"; therefore, why call me "underserved"? Why? Because society continues to mask bondage and access through other subtle forms, whether covertly or overtly. Why call me "vulnerable" when you set the vicious snares of injustices to hurt and harm me? Society, you place me in this situation and now call me helpless! Why are you calling me "marginalized" when *I'm* not limiting myself to the resources and access, *you are*? I am of central importance, not marginal. I am not a deficit, I have plenty of profit margin gain! "Stop calling me that!"

Challenging the Deficit Perspectives and Reconstructing Access

As a woman of Color, I was born into a structural system of institutionalized oppression. I grew up on welfare, a public financial assistance program that provides just enough resources for families to rub two pennies or nickels together—barely enough to make ends meet, but not nearly enough to help build capital wealth. Although this system is supposedly created to assist families in need, it can also imprison them in poverty and thoughts of *im*possibilities. This system has created an incentive for individuals to remain on welfare forever and makes people financially fragile rather than agile. There is not a system in place that links the welfare assistance program to employers willing to offer on-the-job training with an emphasis to encourage becoming self-sufficient. Most communities of Color do not have an inheritance to leave to their children and are impacted by the generational-racial wealth gap (Marmot, 2005).

My cultural wealth was quite different from that of my white counterparts because I was part of a system structured to keep me and my family to what felt like the hamster wheel of life. It was an ongoing plight and, like the hamster, we kept running in place on the same wheel believing it was going somewhere. Yet, we remained in the same place and got no further than where and when we started because "the wheel" was structured purposely to keep us running but with no finish line. Similarly, the vicious cycle of barriers is built and maintained, creating an arduous path for those who are being marginalized to achieve their aspirations and their dreams. It is very difficult to find a way to get off the wheel that has been set up to keep one there with no destination in sight. The continued upstream struggles of inequities and systemic challenges that plague communities of Color are perpetuated by institutional systems and they keep people bound to poverty, leading to the downstream effects of never being able to rise up and achieve their goals.

Formal education or postsecondary schooling was not a topic of conversation in my household. In fact, it was considered "the white thing to do, not the right thing to do." The education that was valued was beyond traditional schooling and it stemmed from the rich and critical wisdom that we had gained through our lived experiences. This type of education is a sophisticated type of knowledge and the skills gained are relevant to our historical journeys and continue to be at the center of our lives. However, it can (and should) enhance traditional education as one navigates and secures opportunities. My lived experiences made me resilient; it was the learned experiences from a life of oppression and barriers that provided me with the stamina, the hunger, and the thirst to want something different in life other than the deck of cards that was handed to me. I had what seemed and felt to me like the "losing hand," however, I played that same hand to win! Even when my internal GPS navigational system was faulty and hard to navigate, I had aspirational capital, an ability to hope despite barriers (Yosso, 2005). The same intentionality that I navigated with past these obstacles is the same intentionality I used to create opportunities.

Too often, the resources that are readily available and accessible to white people are not available in communities of Color. Using myself as an example, like many Black African American families, I did not have a plethora of funds sitting in a bank account or generational wealth to depend on as a safety net. My family instead experienced the impact of the significant wealth gap that my community endures. Thus, when I decided to return to pursue higher education, neither my family nor I had the financial means to afford the cost. I had no other choice but to incur a significant amount of student loan debt, which took well over 10 years to pay off. In contrast, my friend, Lisa, who is white with a middle-class background, did not incur student loan debt. She instead had her entire postsecondary schooling paid in full by her parents, including her undergraduate and graduate degrees. Lisa experienced the benefit of generational wealth. The difference between her and my experience with accessing higher education illustrates so clearly the racial wealth divide that is so prominent for communities of Color. This type of disparity and gap leads to vulnerability for communities like mine who aspire to do more and seek opportunities to become educated in order to achieve upward mobility. Yet, still, communities of Color end up with increased debt that negatively impacts many aspects of their lives, positioning them at a greater distance from achieving their aspirational goals. Additionally, other barriers complicate access such as the inability to secure and build a credit history, which prohibits them from obtaining other life necessities such as a vehicle, a home, and academic opportunities (Serna & Woulfe, 2017).

Today, the average white family has roughly 10 times the amount of wealth as the average Black family, and white college graduates have over seven times more wealth than Black college graduates (Perry et al., 2021). Students of Color are disproportionately taking on more debt to finance their education than their white counterparts. This reality continues to reinforce the racial wealth gap. Additionally, the pressure to work hard toward securing and identifying opportunities for accessing education is also insurmountable and disproportionately felt and experienced by people of Color. Getting a higher education certification, certificate, diploma, degree, or training is a necessity that many are still not able to achieve. Even our first and only Black president, Barack Obama, confirmed this chronic crisis as stated following in his 2009 national address. Obama (2009) stated: "No matter what you want to do with your life, I guarantee that you'll need an education to do it." However, what may seem like an easy decision to return to school to obtain a postsecondary education is not as accessible as one may think, at least not for communities of Color. These communities experience an ongoing plight.

When Impossible Becomes Possible

My aspirational and navigational capital (Yosso, 2005) provided me with the skills and knowledge to lift myself from being the switchboard operator to becoming the president/CEO at Caring Health Center. In 2001, my desire to address systematic barriers affecting BIPOC, immigrant, and refugee communities in Springfield, Massachusetts, was born. While there was not a formal workforce development model at Caring Health Center when I began working at the organization, I had mentors who saw my potential and noticed my aspirational capital (Yosso, 2005). These mentors were the former presidents and CEOs. The first predecessor not only encouraged me to return to school but informed me of the company's tuition reimbursement program for undergraduate education. I was excited about the door of opportunity that was opening, and I was determined to walk through it, as I was always told when opportunity knocks, you answer. The tuition reimbursement program helped with some of the incurred debt but did not alleviate the burden of expensive fees on my family. When the former CEO left the organization, it was as if he passed the mentorship baton to his successor, who carried it forward by nurturing and developing me. She afforded me the time to pursue graduate studies while I worked and mentored me through my academic journey. As I continued to develop and worked toward obtaining a master of business administration degree, she promoted me to an executive-level position. These two mentors believed in me and allowed me to activate my assets and my cultural wealth capital (Yosso, 2005; Yosso & Garcia, 2007). They acknowledged and honored my expertise, including that acquired prior to my academic training that I developed through my lived experience, and provided me with access to actualize my aspirations. Furthermore, and even more importantly, I believed in myself. Through this process, I was able to counter the self-limited thinking and deficit perspective forced upon me. It is important to note that my predecessors saw the capacity in me, but I too had to see it within me and was willing and motivated to cultivate the gift within.

Being a teenage mother, domestic violence survivor, and growing up supported by the government welfare system in a single-parent home, I overcame becoming a product of my environment despite the many dishonorable labels used to define the groups from which I grew up and was identified as being a member in my community. In my own trajectory, I resisted the systemic poverty mindset and the structural barriers in which I was born. At the age of 38 I remember writing in my steno notebook on a yellow piece of paper, "By the time I am 45 years old I will graduate with a master of business degree." With these words, I charted my course, which was a 7-year challenge. During this time, I worked full-time along with the duties of a full-time mother and wife; I never veered off course. At the exact age of 45, I graduated with a master of business degree in entrepreneurial thinking and innovative practice from Bay Path University. This degree added to my bachelor's degree in organizational management from the University Without Walls at UMASS Amherst. Rising from the government system, I progressed from switchboard operator to assistant front office supervisor, front office operations manager, chief operations officer, vice president of operations, and now, for the past decade, to president/CEO of a multi-million-dollar agency, leading over 300 employees. I also launched my own business. I am the founder and pastor of Living Water Global Ministries and founder of EST.HER, LLC, and Touch Healing Encounter—TOUCH: Transformation Offers Undeniable Complete Healing. I am a John Maxwell independent certified coach, speaker, and trainer.

It gave me great joy to see my children at my graduation. I became the example of breaking down the walls of poverty, or as I call it "the generational curse." When you consider the meaning of the root word *gene* one might think it will be inherited as part of the DNA from one family line to the next family line, as this is "rational" reasoning. Combined together you get "gene-rational." It is with the same logic that one might have thought the generational curse of poverty would have been passed or transferred along from me to my children. However, the generational woe of poverty stopped with me; the curse/transfer of poverty infliction upon me and my immediate family ended with me. My daughter followed in my footsteps, graduating with a master of public health degree, and my sons have very good positions at their full-time jobs while working on entrepreneurial business plans for their future to become self-employed business owners. I am proud of my children. The vicious cycle and the generational curse ended with me! My passion is to add value and impact to the lives of those who have been and are *being* disenfranchised (those who have had their rights and privileges taken from them) or who are dealing with similar struggles of limiting beliefs and doubts that stem from this structural cycle of inequity.

A Call to Action: The Learning Institute

In 2001, I initiated my vision to address systematic barriers affecting BIPOC, immigrant, and refugee communities in Springfield, Massachusetts. During my career development at Caring Health Center, I knew that my commitment would be to continue to hire from the community, as my predecessors had done, in order to respond to workforce shortages and disparities like racial wealth gaps and barriers to educational access. I then took it a step further by not just hiring from the community but also by providing necessary tools to help people go further in their careers and by transforming opportunities for careers and professional development among those disproportionately impacted by educational and workforce opportunity gaps. For more than two decades at CHC, I have been committed to "lifting others up." This vision was completely informed by my lived experiences and my unwavering commitment to never leave my community behind. The Learning Institute is the actualization of my long-standing vision to build into practice the transformative power of creating career opportunities through on-the-job learning for community members who would otherwise have few to no career prospects.

As exemplified earlier in the chapter, equity is at the heart of our institutional mission and our innovation initiatives stem from an equity approach. The newly launched Learning Institute has been a part of the fabric of the CHC's mission-driven commitment to hire from the community served and to promote from within as a way to expand representation of entry-level community members in clinical and public health workforce and career opportunities. CHC has been committed to having a staff that mirrors the patients in order to serve a global patient population with culturally and linguistically appropriate services (CLAS). This approach is in direct response to the national disparities in higher education, and to health care workforce shortages. Therefore, it has been our motivation to create entry points in health care employment that incorporate learning and advancement that are responsive to the needs and entry points of communities of Color who are constantly being minoritized and made to lag behind those who are the beneficiaries of privilege and self-identify as part of a majority or dominant group. Because of a lack of equitable prioritization and privilege, communities of Color are disproportionately impacted by structural inequities in accessing and obtaining advanced training, education, or professional opportunities. Creating an in-house strategy for professional development and support has been key to the successful recruitment and retention of CHC employees.

In the summer of 2021, I hired Dr. Yedalis Ruíz Santana as a consultant to conduct a feasibility study to increase understanding of the mechanisms by which a Learning Institute could be beneficial to the workforce community at Caring Health Center (CHC) and the patients it serves. By design, Dr. Ruíz Santana's research was conducted with a participatory consulting approach that centered CHC's collective staff knowledge and lived experiences as guiding frameworks to inform the way that CHC can form, reshape, and nurture its workforce career advancement identities within an environment where learning would be designed to be equitable, culturally responsive, and sustaining. In her research, Dr. Ruíz Santana highlighted the following five guiding and emerging themes from the literature (Ruíz, 2021). First, since at least 1999, community health centers have been "unrecognized" partners in health professions education (Cooksey et al., 1999). Second, the majority of workforce development, workforce pipeline, or health professions workforce training programs are focused on provider-level staff, thus, creating an access gap for entry-level opportunities (Colwell & Kelley, 2021). Third, the resources to support targeted workforce development and quality healthcare, specifically for the frontline workforce, is emerging (Brewer et al., 2020; Custodio et al., 2009). Fourth, the FQHC setting is facing increasing challenges with job satisfaction related to burnout and other factors (Wakefield, 2021). Fifth, training and workforce programs within FQHCs were linked to quality care and retention rate of employees (Durham & Town, 2020). In addition to the findings from the literature, Dr. Ruíz Santana's stakeholder interviews indicated a desire for the CHC Learning Institute to provide a centralized space from which workforce and career development would be valued and materialized through actionable frameworks centered on access and equity within a setting where learning occurs while earning. Specifically, the Learning Institute was described as an initiative that should nurture and sustain a strong workforce and emphasized each of the themes identified in the literature, including and particularly the approach as "Caring." Dr. Ruíz Santana presented the feasibility study findings to CHC's 51% consumer-led board of directors and they unanimously approved the proposal for the development and implementation of the Learning Institute. As I imagined, my vision of the benefits that a Learning Institute would yield proved positive and fruitful. Overall, Dr. Ruíz Santana's findings indicated that a Learning Institute would address a critical gap in workforce development specifically geared toward hiring directly from the community served to right long-standing structural inequities and provide entry opportunities where none currently exist. This model was identified as needed, and that it would greatly contribute to the development of a mission-aligned work environment that is focused on growth and retention and committed to the learning and development of the employee community.

As a demonstration of institutional commitment to the concept of equity through workforce learning and development, I then hired Dr. Ruíz Santana as the executive director of the Learning Institute as well as the chief access and equity officer to lead in the development of an agencywide workforce equity model. My vision included the centralization and sustainability of a workforce learning model. I provided guidance and dedicated institutional resources toward the development of a department within the health center that we named the Office for Access and Equity.

My interest in retaining Dr. Ruíz Santana as an executive leader at the center was very intentional. She herself is a representation of what it means to succeed against access barriers and make possible what seemed impossible. Dr. Ruíz Santana, as she shares the introduction to this volume,

obtained her bachelor's and master's degrees and her PhD as a Puertorriqueña first-generation college graduate. She pursued a nontraditional
educational trajectory and focused her work and research on the critical
analysis of access and equity in education for communities of Color. I
wanted her to lead in the continued development and implementation of
the vision of the Learning Institute. Dr. Ruíz Santana and I will continue
to be collaborative partners with the aim to build a scalable and culturally
responsive model of education and professional training that supports
"learning while you earn" built on the mission of "lifting others up."

A FQHC Workforce Equity Model

The newly launched CHC Office for Access and Equity and Learning
Institute is the institutionalization of my vision to invest in the center's
employees through opportunities for growth, development, and advancement within the organization (Ruíz et al., 2023; 2024). CHC has been
committed to this notion for over two decades. Like myself, many of
the leadership, to include C-Suite, began in frontline and/or entry-level
positions. Through CHC's commitment to professional development and
advancement opportunities they have successfully earned certification and
postsecondary degrees while working full-time. Based on the evidence
from within our own workforce, these two factors may be important contributors to the length of service to the organization and therefore serve
as guideposts for the return on such investments in the community and
their professional and educational trajectory within community health care.

Our federally qualified community health center (FQHC) workforce
equity model aims to put into practice a broad set of workforce development opportunities and support informed by a lens focused on equity
through learning (Ruíz et al., 2023; 2024). Our intention is to interrupt
a cycle of institutional inequity that limits access to career opportunities
and development for our communities of Color. This model is specifically
for CHC's workforce community centered on careers within FQHCs. The
commitment is to address workforce growth and employment disparities in
low-income, first-generation communities of Color. Our model will address
access to careers in community health and will prioritize the strengths
and assets of our community frequently acquired through lived experience
and linked to aspirations rather than the deficit approach more common
to traditional recruitment and hiring practices that exclude candidates

based on demonstration of prior achieved academic and professional successes. Our workforce equity model will offer our community access opportunities to develop entry-level credentials through learning (training) while earning (working) and with no other cost to the individual beyond their aspirations and commitment. It engages our employees in holistic career development coaching and training from the frontline through the executive team. It offers a range of learning opportunities that meet staff where they are based on their needs to address workforce disparities and to reduce turnover, thereby contributing to the in-house return on investment and demonstrating scalability.

Under my leadership, Dr. Ruíz Santana and her team have institutionalized the Learning Institute's mission, values, and aims and the theoretical frameworks from which all programming and curricula are being co-created and are becoming accessible to CHC employees and external stakeholders. The workforce equity model offers sustainable resources to support staff to be successful in their jobs and does it in a way that's developmental and "caring." It creates a pipeline of opportunity and access to jobs within CHC for community members who are impacted by systemic oppression and racism. Our workforce equity model is informed by the community cultural wealth framework (Yosso, 2005), which centers the strengths and talents that our community brings with them and provides pathways for current and future employees to develop their skills *and* have access to a sustaining, satisfying, upwardly mobile career in community health care.

Tania M. Barber Learning Institute: "Lifting Others Up"

In March 2023, the Caring Health Center Board of Directors approved the naming and dedication of the Learning Institute as the *Tania M. Barber Learning Institute* in honor of my commitment to build into practice the transformative power of creating career opportunities through on-the-job learning in community health care for communities of Color. The mission and values of the Tania M. Barber Learning Institute are as follows:

Mission

To serve as a leader in access and equity in FQHCs through a "lifting others up" framework for training, education, career development, and research founded on a commitment to caring.

AIMS

- To respond to an opportunity gap in the workforce among diverse community members with entry-level skills by offering culturally responsive and sustaining careers in health care;

- To maximize training and capacity that correspond with job satisfaction, retention, and career development/advancement;

- To improve health center delivery of value-based quality care to its patient population, including clinical quality, cost containment, and operational efficiency.

VALUES

- We are committed to providing the FQHC workforce with equitable opportunities to develop and sustain thriving, satisfying, and upwardly mobile careers in community health care.

- We are committed to providing holistic learning and career development grounded in community cultural wealth and a caring approach that fosters a professional commitment to FQHCs dedicated to quality care and health equity.

- We work to dismantle the systems in our society designed to maintain, perpetuate, and reproduce inequities that have created an education debt and racial wealth gap.

APPROACH

Our tagline is "lifting others up" because we are committed to the history of a community that is rich in assets and strengths. The Learning Institute centers "caring" to acknowledge that the act of caring is a critical resource that our community provides for one another. Our approach to caring is holistic and utilizes our own community-based social capital to build and sustain our collective growth. The Learning Institute at Caring Health Center will foster this development among its workforce community, who are themselves from groups that have and continue to be marginalized—treated as less than and insignificant as noted by the dishonorable labels—and who are members of the community served. We will honor their wisdom while fostering their professional and educational development on the job. The Learning Institute will be very instrumental to the promotion of agency and healing from the effects of oppression for our community, which is a critical and missing component of traditional workforce development and access models. In collaboration, Dr. Ruíz Santana, her team, and myself are motivated to address these inequities for communities of Color in western Massachusetts and expect to scale the model beyond this region, making it accessible to other FQHCs and other community-based and community-engaged institutions and sectors. As the president and CEO, I have been able to realize my vision and am incredibly dedicated to see this grow. This 23-year dream went from a vision to a reality. The Tania M. Barber Learning Institute is a critical access model that centers equity in community health.

A Message to Readers of Color

I believe everyone has seeds of greatness inside them. However, I believe that your potential deserves to be watered and nurtured in order to sprout up and blossom. *You* are worth investing in and you are valuable, but if you are unable to see the value in your own worth, you will make little to no effort needed to grow your potential. I encourage you to cultivate the dreams inside you so that you can also become the next president/CEO or whatever your heart's desire is for your future. Consider challenging self-limiting beliefs and dishonorable labels so that you don't become a product of your environment if it is not one that promotes your growth. An experience that I had, and that is a source for my own inspiration and motivation, is a relationship that I developed with one of my plants. I was given a beautiful plant as a housewarming gift 17 years ago. The plant came in this little black and white cow-shaped planter. For more than a decade, I nourished the plant faithfully, watering it once a week as required. I made sure it received enough sunlight and also provided enough shade to keep it in balance. However, I never changed its soil or changed the little black and white cow-shaped pot that it came in. The design of the pot was beautiful and besides I thought it would take away from the originality of the gift. I never once considered I was stunting and stifling the ability for the plant to grow and blossom into a much larger, healthier plant. The plant remained alive, but it never grew beyond the capacity of the pot due to its restricting environment. No matter how much water, sunlight, and shade I provided, the plant would never become bigger than the pot (environment) it was in. The plant remained the same size as its environment, small. I had stunted and inhibited its growth for 17 years, until one day, after years of seeing no growth, I decided to change its environment. I purchased a large pot and new soil. I repotted the plant. Watering as required in its new home, eventually the plant grew very large because it was transported into a growth environment.

Each of us is a gift from God. And like this plant, there are systemic limitations that have been created intentionally restricting the ability for our growth. However, when opportunity knocks, it is our responsibility to not focus on yesterday's problem, but rather focus on today's solutions. Search for the resources to change the environment and act today. Use your own community cultural wealth (Yosso, 2005). Use your own navigational capital, and use your community's social capital. Don't wait 17 years for someone to assist you, if it's in your control. Make a change in your environment through action now because what we do now controls who we become and where we end up in the future. Don't become a product of your environment—captive to the systems of limitations, intentionally creating systems of belief that you were meant to remain small.

While pursuing the vision of the Learning Institute, because it had taken years before others could see what I saw, it kept being denied by the powers that be who were authorized to approve the concept. I never gave up; instead I persevered. Each time I presented the idea for a vote to move forward, I kept getting a "NO" vote! I also recall being told by a consultant who was helping with CHC's 3-year strategic plan, "If I were you, I would let that idea go." Well, I thank God for who He has designed me to be, and that is one who perseveres, never giving up and turning my "no" into a "yes"! After several attempts the Learning Institute was not approved. Nonetheless, as unorthodox as it was, I continued pursuing, operating in *faith*, raising upward of $50,000 at the time, believing it would come to pass. I was securing money for something that did not exist in the natural eye or in the verbal approval, trusting that it would manifest itself, through believing the following scripture, "Write the vision, and make it plain upon tables, that he may run that readeth it. For the vision is yet for an appointed time, but at the end shall speak and not lie: though it tarry, wait for it; because it will surely come, it will not tarry" (King James Bible, 2017/1769, Habakkuk 2:2–3). I wrote the vision and waited for the appointed time. I have secured, as of today, more than a million dollars in funding through workforce grants for the now-approved Tania M. Barber Learning Institute. The construction of the site is almost complete. What an exciting journey. The resistance was turned up several times and although it did not feel good, I increased the cadence as it was the stamina needed to continue forging ahead, not giving up on the vision that would address inequities within our community and workforce challenges. It was my desire to pay it forward, the opportunities afforded to me.

Thus, I held on to my dream, driven by the hope of helping to lift others up. I received confirmation and affirmation. While shopping at a home store, hidden in the back behind other items, I found a piece of art similar to another piece of artwork that sits on my desk. Both pieces of art inspire the concept of lifting others up. These artworks reaffirmed this vision and led to the development of the CHC Learning Institute logo (see figure 5.2).

Immediately, when I found this second piece of art, the thought that came to mind was, "Once you make it to the top, hold the ladder to help others up!" This is the true art of a leader, that we become the rungs on the ladder helping others climb higher. Hold on to your dream! Many people don't see the possibilities that God put in them . . . "With man this is impossible, but with God all things are possible" (King James Bible, 2017/1769, Matthew 19:26). I intentionally decided to integrate CHC's heart logo design as a strategic way of increasing CHC's brand. The heart enforces

Figure 5.2. The Tania M. Barber Learning Institute logo, Caring Health Center, 2023. *Source*: Caring Health Center Tania M. Barber Learning Institute Logo. Used with permission.

connection between the Learning Institute and Caring Health Center. The books are purposely placed at an angle with an upward slant symbolizing "lifting others up" through education, while at the same time addressing upstream disparities of educational inequities, which leads to poor health outcomes. The people are community members, a collaborative effort and commitment to "lifting others up." As we know, our community is fraught with experiencing the impact of systematic oppression and limited access to equitable opportunities.

Critical Reflection

1. What opinions have you formed against others who have not had the opportunities of obtaining postsecondary education? What labels have you assigned to people of Color?

2. How can you help remove the stigmatization of labeling? How do you create words that do not have a negative connotation?

3. What solutions can you come up with for the problems outlined in this chapter? How can you magnify the assets rather than the deficits in people? How can you be the rung of a ladder to help others go higher? How can you help shape the possibilities for others when all they see are impossibilities?

References

Bonilla-Silva, E. (1997). Rethinking racism: Toward a structural interpretation. *American Sociological Review, 62*(3), 465–480. https://doi.org/10.2307/2657316

Brewer, L. C., Fortuna, K. L., Jones, C., Walker, R., Hayes, S. N., Patten, C. A., & Cooper, L. A. (2020). Back to the future: Achieving health equity through health informatics and digital health. *Journal of Medical Internet Research mHealth and uHealth, 8*(1), e14512. https://doi.org/10.2196/14512

Colwell, A., & Kelley, E. (2021). Developing the FQHC workforce pipeline: A look at how one primary care association is reaching students in their state. *Journal of Health Care for the Poor and Underserved, 32*(3), xi–xiii. https://doi.org/10.1353/hpu.2021.0111

Cooksey, J. A., Kaur, K., Matters, M. D., Simone, B., Chun, E., & Hoekstra, A. (1999). Community health centers: Unrecognized partners in health professions education. *Journal of Health Care for the Poor and Underserved, 10*(3), 349–361. https://doi.org/10.1353/hpu.2010.0551

Custodio, R., Gard, A. M., & Graham, G. (2009). Health information technology: Addressing health disparity by improving quality, increasing access, and developing workforce. *Journal of Health Care for the Poor and Underserved, 20*(2), 301–307. https://doi.org/10.1353/hpu.0.0142

Durham, M. L., & Town, E. (2020). Interprofessional student quality improvement project in a federally qualified health center. *Journal of Nursing Education, 59*(10), 585–588. https://doi.org/10.3928/01484834-20200921-09

Feeding America. (2020). *Map the meal gap.* https://map.feedingamerica.org/

Gorski, P. (2008). The myth of the culture of poverty. *Education and Learning, 65*(7): 32–36.

Haynes, C. (2017). Dismantling the white supremacy embedded in our classrooms: White faculty in pursuit of more equitable educational outcomes for racially minoritized students. *International Journal on Teaching and Learning in Higher Education, 29*(1), 87–107.

Haynes, C. (2023). The susceptibility of teaching to white interests: A theoretical explanation of the influence of racial consciousness on the behaviors of white faculty in the classroom. *Journal of Diversity in Higher Education, 16*(1), 97–108. https://doi.org/10.1037/dhe0000256

Hernández, R. J., & Villodas, M. T. (2020). Overcoming racial battle fatigue: The associations between racial microaggressions, coping, and mental health among Chicana/o and Latina/o college students. *Cultural Diversity & Ethnic Minority Psychology, 26*(3), 399–411. https://doi.org/10.1037/cdp0000306

HUD User. (n.d.). *Rental burdens: Rethinking affordability measures.* Office of Policy and Development and Research. https://www.huduser.gov/portal/pdredge/pdr_edge_ featd_article_092214.html

Irizarry, J. G., & Raible, J. (2014). "A hidden part of me": Latino/a students, silencing, and the epidermalization of inferiority. *Equity & Excellence in Education, 47*(4), 430–444. https://doi.org/10.1080/10665684.2014.958970

King James Bible. (2017/1769). King James Bible Online. https://www.kingjames-bibleonline.org/

Marmot, M. (2005). Social determinants of health inequalities. *Lancet, 365*(9464), 1099–1104.

The Obama White House. (2009, September 8). *President Obama's message for America's students* [Video]. YouTube. https://www.youtube.com/watch?v=8ZZ6GrzWkw0&t=2s

Perry, A. M., Steinbaum M., & Romer, C. (2021). *Student loans, the racial wealth divide, and why we need full student debt cancellation.* Brookings. https://

www.brookings.edu/research/student-loans-the-racial-wealth-divide-and-why-we-need-full-student-debt-cancellation/.

Pioneer Valley Planning Commission. (2020, April). *Analysis of impediments to fair housing choice for the municipalities of Springfield, Holyoke, Chicopee and Westfield.* Pioneer Valley Planning Commission, the Massachusetts Fair Housing Center, University of Massachusetts Donahue Institute. https://www.pvpc.org/sites/default/files/files/ FourcityAIReport_Draft%20for%20 Springfield%20posting.pdf

Ruíz, Y. (2021). *Learning Institute feasibility study final report.* Caring Health Center.

Ruíz, Y., Barber, T. M., & DeBari, J. (2023). *A FQHC workforce equity model and learning in action!* MassLeague of Community Health Centers Community Health Institute.

Ruíz, Y., Barber, T. M., & DeBari, J. (2024). *Bridging the access barrier: An FQHC-led equity and learning model.* MassLeague of Community Health Centers Community.

Serna, G. R., & Woulfe, R. (2017). Social reproduction and college access: Current evidence, context, and potential alternatives. *Critical Questions in Education, 8*(1), 1–16.

Solórzano, D. G., Ceja, M., & Yosso, T. (2000). Critical race theory, racial microaggressions, and campus racial climate: The experiences of African American college students. *Journal of Negro Education, 69*(1–2), 60–73.

US Bureau of Labor Statistics. (2022). *Monthly labor review.* US Bureau of Labor Statistics. https://www.bls.gov/opub/mlr/2022/home.htm

US Census Bureau. (2019). *American community survey, poverty status in the past 12 months* (S1701) [Dataset]. https://data.census.gov/table?q=poverty&t=-Poverty&g=010XXE0US _010XXG0US_010XX00US&tid=ACSST5Y2021. S1701&hidePreview=true

Wakefield, M. (2021). Federally qualified health centers and related primary care workforce issues. *Journal of the American Medical Association, 325*(12), 1145–1146. https://doi.org/10.1001/jama.2021.1964

Yosso, T. J. (2005). Whose culture has capital? A critical race theory discussion of community cultural wealth. *Race Ethnicity and Education, 8*(1), 69–91, https://doi.org/10.1080/1361332052000341006

Yosso, T. J., & Garcia, D. (2007). "This is no slum!" A critical race theory analysis of community cultural wealth in culture clash's Chavez Ravine. *Aztlán: A Journal of Chicano Studies, 32*(1), 145–179.

Chapter 6

Widening Postsecondary Educational Pathways for Black and Latinx Boys and Young Men

Personal Reflections, Professional Experiences, and Research-Based Insights

RODERICK L. CAREY

Achieving postsecondary educational goals can be daunting for racially and economically marginalized adolescents. Systemic and interpersonal barriers to educational, professional, and personal fulfillment meet them often along the PreK–12 pipeline. Few groups face these realities more than Black and Latinx boys and young men from low-income communities (Brooms, 2021; Carey, 2016; Clark et al., 2024; Harper & Newman, 2016; Huerta & Martinez, 2022; Knight-Manuel et al., 2019). Helping this unique group manifest bright futures demands educational stakeholders be attuned to the macro- and microlevel challenges they face. It also demands that interventions complement, and not discredit, the wealth of know-how and assets Black and Latinx family and community members use to forge youths' futures.

In this chapter, I reflect on my own educational journey to contextualize my mission to identify what matters for supporting Black and Latinx boys on their postsecondary future paths. Importantly, I describe my journey, as I experienced it as a child, teen, and young adult. Later, I deploy theories and more recent illuminations to unpack my journey and illustrate how my social class privilege afforded me college-going opportunities that were denied to others in my racial and gendered group. I then discuss how I contributed to widening students' postsecondary educational pathways during my tenure as a teacher and mentor to Black and Latinx students. Throughout this chapter, I share theoretical insights, research-based findings, and the voiced perspectives of Black and Latinx boys themselves. I do so while offering critical hindsight on my personal and professional journey, my students' journeys, and to shed light on interventions for widening postsecondary pathways for Black and Latinx boys and young men. This chapter concludes with critical reflection questions for youth workers and educational stakeholders.

Encountering College Early, Often, and Everywhere: A Personal Reflection

Throughout childhood, my mother ventured to US college campuses a few times a year to recruit Black and Latinx chemistry and chemical engineering majors for a major chemical corporation in Wilmington, Delaware. When she returned home, she often brought me college t-shirts, pennants, posters, and other swag (e.g., pens, folders, and spiral-bound notebooks, mostly). She gifted me these items because she knew how much I loved souvenirs. She also did so to spark my college-going aspirations.

Since I attended a Catholic school that required its students attend in uniforms, I wore the college t-shirts after school, to summer camp, and to extracurricular activities. I felt sophisticated completing class assignments with the pens and notebooks that read *Morgan State*, *Cornell*, *Carnegie Mellon*, and *North Carolina A & T*. I taped the college pennants and posters to the walls in my room alongside magazine cutouts of Black celebrities and historical icons. With each work trip, more and more college stuff would arrive. Cousins and aunts also mailed me flags and stickers of their alma mater; this was a whole family effort.

With reckless abandon, I taped and layered college materials till I fashioned a massive wall collage that featured the colors, logos, seals, and mascots of dozens of US colleges and universities. I positioned trophies and ribbons from swim team, Boy Scouts, and baseball on the shelves that flanked the college imagery. Except for a smattering of WWF posters of my favorite wrestlers, my room overflowed with testaments to childhood achievements. My shrine to little Black boy excellence signaled an expected future self, perhaps at one of the dozens of colleges or universities that were literally in front of me, on my wall, in my grasp.

While my father was the first in his family to attend and graduate from college, my mother (and her siblings), her mother (and her siblings), and her grandfather were all college graduates. Each college graduate passed down knowledge, resources, and wisdom to the next generation and to the next, which we used as "capital" for navigating the college process (Carey, 2016; Sewell, 2024; Yosso, 2005). I would go on to become a fourth-generation college graduate, so our home featured plenty of relatives' graduation photos taken on palatial campuses. Around were also other reminders of my family's college convictions. There was the college textbook on my parents' bookshelf—my dad's from the 1950s—wrapped in a Central State College (now named "Central State University") maroon and gold book cover. Blue and gold glassware that read "Fisk University"—my mom's alma mater—sat on the fireplace mantel adjacent to an ivory-colored stein from my aunt's doctoral institution: "Harvard." My dad attended UPenn for one of his two master's degrees. It wasn't uncommon to catch me flipping through his copy of the *Pennsylvania Gazette* and other alumni publications that arrived quarterly.

In addition, I encountered college-educated Black folks at Bethel AME Church in Wilmington, Delaware. They drove to choir rehearsal in cars with fraternity or sorority Greek letters etched into license plate holders. When our youth group took summer trips to waterparks, many adults had "Howard University" on their shirts or "Spelman College" on wide brim hats.

Black college students and recent grads worked at the Walnut Street YMCA after-school programs and camps I attended. This was the late 80s and early 90s. They dressed vibrantly, juxtaposing African heritage roots wear, designer-label hip-hop styles, and college paraphernalia in ways that validated the multifaceted contours of what it meant to be Black, young, educated, and cool. They taught us dances and showed us how to step like the Kappas at Delaware State College (now named "Delaware State University") and the AKAs at the University of Delaware.

Some of these youth workers attended a local community college. They arrived at the YMCA with giant textbooks, which they'd sometimes pull out to pore over alongside of us during quiet homework time. I was awestruck by college books. They were wider, thicker, and drabber than my colorful grade school textbooks. They featured unfamiliar titles—*Anatomy*, *Microeconomics*, *Political Science*—and were filled with long bodies of text on white pages interspersed with pictures and graphs. College books were daunting and intimidating; I was, and remain, a slow reader. Yet, seeing them engage with those texts—even just carry them around proudly—let me know I could and would do the same one day. These Black adult youth workers, with their books, styles, and presence, cultivated possibilities for us. They looked like us, spoke with our words, validated our present lives, role-modeled beautiful futures we were eager to attain, and in doing so, made college real, relevant, and present.

Years later, I was equipped when it came time to decide on a college. I was steeped in familial expectations and garnered "intergenerational capital transmission" (Sewell, 2024) from a variety of family members. My parents were HBCU graduates (for more on the importance of these institutions, see Britton et al., 2023; Commodore & Njoku, 2020; Johnson & McGowan, 2017; Mobley, 2017; Williams et al., 2019; Williams et al., 2022), and I had role models from the community and from my many after-school activities. I also attended an all-boys Catholic college-preparatory high school where nearly all of the graduates attended college or trade school. College matriculation was the norm at Salesianum School, which remains top-notch in academics, athletics, and the arts. Its near 100% college acceptance rate attracted families. Yet, it was widely assumed among community members that most of those boys—many the products of middle- and upper-middle-class white families—would have gone to college whether they attended Salesianum or not. Their families, like mine, would have made sure of it.

Possibilities and Pitfalls for College Pathway Making in the Nation's Capital

I grew up experiencing moments of anti-Black subjugation in predominantly white schools and organizations. The impacts of such racial isolation were buffered by "navigational capital"—the skills to maneuver places unintended for people of Color (Yosso, 2005)—that my family offered through their examples and messaging (see also Sewell, 2024). By the early 2000s, I was living and learning in the Boston area. Garnering inspiration from childhood experiences in school and youth programs, the field of education came into focus as my life's calling. I graduated with my bachelor's (Boston College) and master's degrees (Harvard Graduate

School of Education), both in education, having spent summers as a camp counselor at the same programs that I attended.

I taught high school English in predominantly Black and Latinx Washington, DC, public charter schools for four school years (2005–2009). As my 10th grade World Literature course students tackled *The Epic of Gilgamesh* and *Oedipus Rex*, they bore the weight of growing up amid anti-Black violence, experienced as economic subjugation and neighborhood strife. However, their communities were historically—and presently—beacons of cultural creativity and resilience. Along with the indelible impacts of Howard University and its alumni on Washington, DC, Black Washingtonians like Georgia Douglass Johnson, Alain Locke, Carter G. Woodson, Duke Ellington, and other radical Black creators cemented DC's place as a site for Black creative excellence and resistance movements.

DC's culture mesmerized me, and my students eagerly taught me all that made "Chocolate City" exceptional. They educated me about go-go, a unique form of funk music, which emerged out of the Black community and catapulted DC's culture and its sonic contributions to the forefront of popular music in the late 1970s. After I expressed my intrigue, students excitedly brought me the latest go-go CDs and showed me the accompanying dances. My students loved that I loved their music. This mutual admiration helped us forge deeper relationships.

Washington, DC, known for its museums and memorials, was also infamous for its drug economies and widespread economic stratification. The impacts from rampant incarcerations and street violence, which came about during the crack cocaine epidemic of the late 1980s, echoed for many years. My students had their potential dampened by the trauma and vulnerability they encountered growing up in historically looted communities, stripped of locally owned businesses, affordable housing, well-paying jobs, and safe and healthy recreation. They attended schools governed by neoliberal standardization measures that suffocated their learning at every turn. Their schools were situated in rapidly gentrifying Black neighborhoods and teemed with passionate, but novice teachers, like me.

These students sought out a college education or postsecondary training while surviving pervasive systemic injustices. Supporting my students' journey toward their unique future pathways brought to light so many of the privileges I was afforded growing up immersed in college-going messaging, imagery, and supports. Their college pathways were not laid out as smoothly as mine was. But, they had cadres of committed and resilient family members, feverishly devoted to their children's future well-being.

Collaborating with Washington, DC, Families for "Better" Black Futures

My students' parents, grandparents, extended relatives, and fictive kin poured all they had into their children. Their enthusiasm for their children's educational goals was evidenced at sporting events, family and teacher nights, and community gatherings we hosted. Family members toiled to ensure their children had a chance at finding their "better": a better education, a better job, a better shot at a better life. "Better" couched the dreams and ambitions of their children's unseen futures, which were often unattainable by older relatives due to structural constraints and limited opportunities.

From my vantage, "better" meant different things to different students. For some, it was about ownership. They wanted to own not only houses or cars but also barbershops, salons, restaurants, or other businesses. Some wanted college-based careers (e.g., accountant, physician, veterinarian) that were beyond the grasp of family members. They wanted careers they loved, not just ones that paid the bills. Many aspired to make their communities healthier and safer and knew a postsecondary education would provide the skills to do just that. Despite holding pride for their city, some desired to move away, or to just see more of the world. Many others couldn't conceptualize what they wanted to go toward. But they knew what they wanted to avoid. They didn't want to live paycheck to paycheck; they didn't want to end up a victim to the streets. In sum, "better" took on multiple forms, but it was rooted in satisfaction, financial stability, safety, and a type of life comfort that evaded many of their family members.

In addition to family members pushing youth toward their version of "better," they had an entire ecosystem of supports ranging from pastors and faith communities who ministered to them, neighborhood civic leaders who provided outreach, and athletic coaches who engaged their psychic and physical energy in positive ways (see Akiva & Robinson, 2022; Velez et al., 2024). They also had us: an ambitious, yet somewhat naïve, teaching force, determined to go to whatever lengths needed to make college going a reality for them.

Making College Real, Relevant, and Present for My Students

My teaching colleagues and I collaborated to implement a schoolwide "college-going culture." Schools with these cultures deploy intentional imagery, frequent messaging, and experiences (e.g., on-campus college visits, field trips) to spark and sustain students' postsecondary educational aspirations (Farmer-Hinton, 2011; Howard et al., 2016; Knight & Marciano, 2013; Knight-Manuel et al., 2019; McDonough, 1997). We decorated the hallways and classrooms with college pennants and posters and invited college representatives to speak with students. We exposed students to Black fraternity and sorority life and wore paraphernalia to inspire them. We taught them how to step like the Kappas and the Deltas. We ushered students onto college tours and mandated that they apply to at least three colleges. We, like other Washington, DC, charter schools, had a 100% college acceptance rate. Although some of the institutions had open enrollments and noncompetitive application policies (e.g., community colleges), this 100% rate was considered the "hallmark of a great school," one that we were fanatically—and admittedly, overzealously—ardent about upholding.

In addition to helping them solicit recommendation letters and maneuver online application portals, college counselors spent hours supporting students and families as they applied for financial aid and scholarships. Teachers provided graduating seniors other tangible supports. Each was "adopted" by in-school "parents"—generous teachers—who paid out of pocket for college-related supplies to ensure students had a good start.

Teachers filled a laundry hamper or a storage bin with supplies and dorm items; some purchased their "adopted senior" a coveted laptop. We presented these gifts along with recognitions and awards in a tear-filled ceremony attended by families. Teachers fostered deep, long-lasting relationships with students, and this adoption practice was logical given our school's close-knit community. I adopted two seniors—both quiet, often overlooked Black boys—myself. One was a boy I coached and admired for his gentle strength on and off the field. The other was from my World Literature class. He was the oldest of four boys, and I knew his mother would appreciate whatever supports I provided him.

I bought each a large plastic storage bin and spent well over $100 dollars of my novice teaching salary filling them with bedding, toiletries, and an additional $100 cash for books, travel, or other necessities. I took these bins to the auditorium and lined them up on stage with other senior gifts during our recognition night. We covered the front of the stage with desk supplies, colorful bedding sets, luggage, and white boards. Seniors lugged these bins out of the school building into cars, sometimes on the bus or subway, and rode back to their homes.

It was an impressive display of generosity and hope. It was a palpable investment in our adoptees' futures. Importantly, since we created a family with students, we shared responsibility for ensuring their smooth transition to college. We were not attempting to be "saviors" or replace their families, although, sometimes it felt like we thought we knew what was best for those who Lisa Delpit (2006) called "other people's children." However, while the tradition of adopting seniors was tinged with "saviorism," families respected the loving relationships we fostered with their children and seemed appreciative of the material help.

Home from College and Unlikely to Return

Despite the posters, pennants, and our supports, our graduates came home from college after a year, or even after a semester, never to return. I'd see 18- and 19-year-old former students at football games or walking the hallways to visit their teachers. It felt both good and painful to see them; these were our shining stars, our role models for students behind them, now returned home. They would narrate college challenges to drained and disappointed but empathetic teachers. Some failed courses and lost scholarships. Some felt overwhelmed and squeezed by new social demands. Some felt ostracized due to race and social class differences between themselves and their new peers (Williams & Martin, 2022). Others struggled to find their purpose and came home to regroup. However, on the whole, most returned home from college due to insurmountable economic stress, a reality many Black and Latinx collegians from low-income communities experience across the United States (see Brooms, 2021; Huerta & Martinez, 2022; Jack, 2019; Scott et al., 2021; Williams & Martin, 2022).

Despite our best efforts to get them to college and serve as "adoptive parents," students from systemically oppressed families, who struggled to meet their basic needs, experienced unbearable pressures to attend classes and scramble for book and dorm fees. One of my adopted seniors attended the University of Maryland Eastern Shore, an HBCU in a rural county and nearly two hours drive from the rented house he shared with his mother and three younger brothers. His family tried to make up the difference between his loan allotments and remaining balance. When the water was disconnected at his family's home, he reached his breaking point, deciding he could no longer stay away while his family struggled. He eventually completed one year of college, moved home to work, and never finished his degree program.

Why Did Black and Latinx Young Men of Color Leave College?

Accounts like these were common. Yet, economic challenges were not the only factors preventing Black and Latinx young men from college success. Some young men struggled with the newfound challenges and pressures posed by college life. A high school football star was forced to sit the bench in college. After quitting the team in protest, he lost the team comradery, adulation from peers and fans, and daily accountability from coaches that he needed to stay on the right path. His departure from the team put him on a downward social and academic spiral that spurred his decision to transfer to another college and ultimately drop out. Others ended up on academic probation after failing classes, eventually leading them to lose financial aid.

After departing college degree programs, some merely shifted their interests away from college-based careers to the military, policing, or firefighting. And some found their "better" through satisfying employment pathways beyond the realm of college and college-based careers in service industry professions. But the majority languished in low-pay employment after leaving college, which haunted me.

I first turned the inquiry to the colleges themselves. How did colleges and universities, which prioritize recruiting racially and ethnically diverse students, fail our graduates upon arrival? What were student affairs personnel doing to support their transitions and retain them once we—the educators, community stakeholders, and family members—got them there (see Cabrera et al., 2022; Harper & Newman, 2016; Jett, 2022)?

In addition to leaving me haunted by these questions, students' accounts inspired me to learn more about why *our* efforts missed the mark. What did *we* do wrong as teachers, coaches, and mentors? We were great at getting students accepted into college, which itself was no small feat. However, the boys especially rarely ascended very far through degree programs. And I wanted to know why. Did we place them into the wrong institutions? Did we not prepare them to interpret and negotiate the challenges and stressors of daily college life (see Taylor & Williams, 2022)? Did we not attune ourselves to students' goals and ambitions beyond just college (see Carey, 2022; 2024)? I left the classroom for a PhD program to answer these questions and help educators guide marginalized students toward actualizing their future goals.

The Postsecondary Future Selves of Black and Latinx Boys

After completing doctoral coursework and qualifying exams, I focused on learning about the ways educators prepare Black and Latinx boys and young men for life after high school. I spent the 2013–2014 school year conducting ethnographic dissertation research at Metropolitan Collegiate Public Charter School (a pseudonym), a mid-Atlantic urban US school that served nearly 1,000 students across three divisions: elementary, middle, and high school. My research site, which I also call Metro Collegiate or Metro, mirrored schools in which I taught. It served a majority Black and Latinx student population, and its educators directed tremendous efforts toward guiding students onto college pathways. One hundred percent of seniors gained college acceptance yearly, which was a key organizational goal and touchpoint for school marketers.

I focused closely on how a group of Black and Latinx adolescent boys in Metro's high school division conceptualized their future postsecondary prospects based on the influences of their college-going culture. Were elements of this college-going culture "working" to mold their unique aspirations? While my research was neither longitudinal nor predictive, I was curious about how present-day motivational forces shaped participants' mindsets and behaviors and put students on pathways toward optimal futures on their terms.

In formulating my study, I drew from psychological theory to develop "postsecondary future selves" (Carey, 2015; 2022; 2024). This concept references what students conceptualize as possible, likely, and expected for their life after high school graduation. College is but one domain—one milestone—of a broader postsecondary life trajectory that may be unseen or unimagined for youth from racially and economically marginalized communities (Carey, 2022). Although high schools like Metro Collegiate focused on college access, they did so using mass counseling approaches (see Gast, 2021) that overlooked nuanced factors driving students' future orientations. Instead of imprecise catch-all counseling, students need developmentally appropriate (see Savitz-Romer & Bouffard, 2012; Schneider & Stevenson, 1999) and culturally attuned (Knight-Manuel & Marciano, 2013; Welton & Martinez, 2014) supports to foster linkages between their college ambitions, career aims (see Lindstrom et al., 2022), and other future life goals.

As such, postsecondary future selves take up youths' futures given three domains: college (i.e., postsecondary education, be it through advanced vocational training or 2- or 4-year colleges or universities), career (i.e., occupation and employment trajectory), and condition (i.e., expected financial stability, relational and familial prospects, future living arrangements, happiness, and joy; Carey, 2015; 2022; 2024). Importantly, scholars more often take up the factors that compel Black and Latinx adolescents toward college and career aims (Brooms, 2022; Clark et al., 2024; Goings & Sewell, 2019; Hines et al., 2019; Hines et al., 2020; Howard et al., 2019; Kolluri, 2022; Warren, 2017). Yet, the condition domain (e.g., expected financial stability, relational and familial prospects, future living arrangements, happiness, and joy) remains less explored, especially when tied to Black and Latinx adolescent boys' college and career ambitions (i.e., If I go to college, what type of career and life condition do I expect?).

In developing their postsecondary future selves, youth require "future orientations" or thoughts, dreams, and expectations for possible events that influence, motivate, and guide their goal attainment (Nurmi, 1991). They also need a grounding in "possible selves," in that they think about their present potential and what they deem likely for their futures (Dunkel & Kerpelman, 2006; Gibbs Grey, 2022; Markus & Nurius, 1986; Oyserman, 2015). Possible selves reflect complementary variations of their self-concept: the *feared self, hoped for self*, and *expected self* (Markus & Nurius, 1986). Black and Latinx boys from low-income communities may be motivated toward or away from college, career, or certain life conditions owing to the feared self (e.g., I dread what will happen with my life if I miss out on college), the hoped for self (e.g., I wish to play professional basketball and earn a lucrative salary), or the expected self (e.g., I anticipate that attending college will help me attain my career and life goals).

The concept of *postsecondary future selves* was not only theorized from psychological constructs, it was inspired by my lived experiences and career as an educator in college-going schools. Due to extreme fortune, my community and family nurtured facets of my postsecondary future self into some semblance of alignment early in life. Yet, countless students that I worked with—even later in their high school years—faced challenges finding alignment between college ambitions, anticipated careers, and their expected life condition. In many ways, creating postsecondary future selves was an attempt at making sense of my educational, professional, and personal journey while also building the type of theoretical tool, or heuristic, that I needed to better meet the needs of my students in Washington, DC.

The Need to Broaden College-Going School Cultures: College, Career, and What Else?

Metropolitan Collegiate's college-going culture looked and felt like other schools engaging similar processes (e.g., college-going visuals, mandating college field trips; Farmer-Hinton, 2011; Gast, 2021; Noll, 2022). In many ways, Metro devised what Gibbs Grey (2022) called a "Community of Possibility," where educators fortified the possible selves of students so that they saw themselves as future college students. However, Metro's "college for all" messaging and mass counseling tactics were overzealous and incongruent with participants' ambitions at times, a result also seen in my own professional experiences as a teacher and in other studies (see Gast, 2021; Noll, 2022; Rodriguez, 2023).

Although some participants welcomed the college-going supports, others critiqued and even resisted them. An example from an interview I conducted with a 17-year-old, 11th grade Salvadoran boy, who chose the pseudonym Perdido, sheds light on such critiques. His chosen pseudonym—Spanish for lost, wandering, astray—reflected Perdido's challenges finding responsive academic and social supports, which fueled his uncertainty for life after high school. Perdido's appraisal shows both how educators' myopic college-going foci overlooked other elements of his postsecondary future self, and how resistant he was to falling in line with a vision for his life that misaligned with his ambitions.

> PERDIDO: I have an idea what a good life is for me. So I don't see college or anything like we're taught to believe as always being good, you know. I gotta figure out my good life, because it's my life, so I'll be happy.

> CAREY: Well, what are the things that you're taught to believe?

PERDIDO: All right, go to high school, then college. Get a college degree. Then get a job, then a good job and make money. Then make good money, you know, and then you'll have a good life. It's as simple as that. That's broken down to basics. And they want you to like follow that. When you go to [Metro], you're taught to follow this . . . And it's the college part that doesn't appeal to me, and I don't like feeling controlled.

Perdido considered going to college after working with his hands for a few years, but he was resistant to relenting to Metro's college-going pressures. He had other noncollege goals for his postsecondary future self that would lead to his version of a good life, goals that Metro neither cultivated nor supported.

Other participant accounts revealed how the school's myopic emphasis on college-going drowned them in the "what" and "how" of college (e.g., What is a college degree, and how do I get one?), giving little air to the "why" (e.g., Why should I spend my time, energy, and my family's money on a college degree as opposed to other, more immediate, goals?). Personally, the "why" was evident in ample familial examples. My parents, and many cousins, aunts, and uncles, had satisfying careers and life conditions (e.g., home ownership, time, and some money to travel) that I linked to their college degree attainment. My dad spent much of his career as a social worker, community activist, and local historian; my aunt and uncle were both K–12 educators. From them and others, I absorbed that going to college was not just about gaining a lucrative career. It was about studying something that interested you to live a satisfying life and give back to your communities. It was about merging your deepest passions with civic and professional possibilities.

Like my research, Arce and Carpenter's study in chapter 2 of this volume critiqued prescriptive and traditional college readiness programs that ignore noncognitive variables that shape students' ambitions and pathways. To replace traditional programs, which often focus on individual, achievement-focused endeavors, Arce and Carpenter advocate for a critically conscious college knowledge framework (C^3K) that helps students see how their lives are linked with broader social systems. C^3K also helps students see their college ambitions as tied to not just individual but communal uplift and offers perspectives on the "why" that sparks college-going processes for many students of Color.

In reflecting on my own professional journey, the "why" was rarely considered when I taught in schools like Metro. We made far too many assumptions: that college was always the best option for every kid, that students and their families believed this to be true and knew what they were putting their energy toward. Yet, such assumptions fueled imprecise interventions that focused lopsidedly on the "what" and "how."

In my research, considering the "why" of college-going would have compelled Metro to closely consider students' "career" and "condition" goals, which were often undiscussed and unexamined (see Carey, 2024). Considering the "why" would also demand a closer attention to students' versions of the "better" life they both envisioned and sought to actualize on their terms. Despite Metro's supports, participants often misunderstood the relationship between certain college majors and careers (Carey, 2022; 2024). They also had hazy ideas at best, and inarticulable visions at worst, for their future life conditions. Their lack of clarity could have been a result of growing up with few career role models and few examples of the adult lives they desired (e.g., visions for their homelife, romantic partnering, leisure, and joy).

But educators could have done more to support their imagining and helped students in building "aligned ambitions" (see Schneider & Stevenson, 1999), where college, career, and condition goals overlapped. By narrowing supports on college access, educators overlooked other elements of students' "postsecondary future selves," which may land students on pathways out of sync with their other goals, latent interests, and existing priorities.

The Importance of Family Influence on Black and Latinx Boys' Future Ambitions

Findings from my study also showed how important families are in motivating, inspiring, and supporting various domains of Black and Latinx boys' postsecondary future selves. Researchers studying the experiences of both Black (George Mwangi et al., 2017; George Mwangi et al., 2020; Hines et al., 2020; Holland, 2017; Johnson & McGowan, 2017; Rhoden, 2017) and Latinx (Ballysingh et al., 2021; Carrión & Torres, 2023; Conchas & Acevedo, 2020; Covarrubias, 2021; Patrón, 2020; Tichavakunda & Galan, 2023) students have pointed to the tangible (e.g., financial resources and information) and intangible (e.g., emotional and motivational supports) mechanisms families deploy to bolster their children's educational trajectories.

Despite limited "college knowledge" and financial resources, nuclear, extended, and fictive kin family members offered participants supports and wisdom in other ways through what I call "college-going familial capital." This form of capital, unlike that which is determined valuable solely by white middle and upper classes (Bourdieu & Passerson, 1977), draws upon cultural values from families and communities of Color. College-going familial capital accounts for "the rich knowledge, information, inspiration and resources students of Color gain from their families (nuclear, extended, and fictive kin) that serve as rationale, motivation, and support for securing postsecondary educational attainment" (Carey, 2016, p. 720).

To theorize college-going familial capital, I drew from the lived experiences of Latinx (i.e., Salvadoran) and Black (i.e., African American) boys (Carey, 2016). As such, it harnesses the knowledge and wisdom elicited from the Latinx norm of *familismo*, or the centrality of familial needs over individual desires (Marín & Marín, 1991; Smith-Morris et al., 2013). It also summons resources that youth garner from "fictive kin," or those unrelated by birth, marriage, or adoption, but who still count as family (George Mwangi, 2015). College-going familial capital also takes up asset-based theoretical approaches to communities of Color, including "funds of knowledge" (Moll et al., 1992; Rios-Aguilar & Kiyama, 2012) and community cultural wealth (Yosso, 2005).

Participants had grandparents and godparents (e.g., fictive kin) who graduated college and offered key forms of college-going familial capital. However, college-going familial capital was passed down not just from family who attended college. It also emerged from those unable to attend college or complete it. In many ways, these familial knowledge bases—these forms of college-going familial capital—went overlooked by educators at Metro Collegiate. Educators pushed Metro's students to use college as a mechanism for social mobility, to arise from the poverty and violence they experienced living in their neighborhoods, and use their educations to transcend their families and communities, not give back to them. Since students' mostly low-income families had less college experience, school stakeholders deemed them irrelevant for providing college-going supports. They were another barrier to overcome. However, family members, not just parents, of participants inspired their boys and bolstered their college aspirations. Samuel, a 17-year-old Black boy whose father was separated from his mother and estranged from his children, sustained college-going ambitions due to his uncle's inspiration. When I asked Samuel who motivated him to go to college, he noted the following:

My mom does it, but on a consistent basis, the person who has made me keep college in my head is my uncle, which is now my only male role model in my life. He has talked about [college], and he's praised me for doing good in school. When I'm doing good in school, he's the person that gives me rewards. He worries about us [Samuel, his twin brother, and older sister] just like his children. And when he knows that I'm doing good, he'll do things for me, like give me rewards and stuff.

Samuel's uncle cared deeply for the academic well-being and future trajectories of Samuel and his siblings. Yet, Samuel's uncle never attended college and knew little about the intricacies of financial aid and the application process (see Carey, 2022, for more insights on Samuel's uncle). He used what he had to motivate his nephews' and niece's educational ambitions. Findings like this show how participants' families, like those described in other studies of Black (Brooms, 2022; McArdle & Turner, 2021) and Latinx (see Garcia et al., 2020; Sáenz et al., 2018) youth, were not hindrances; they were key motivators. Educators could have leveraged untapped familial resources to implement more culturally attuned college-going support practices.

As I look back on my own teaching experiences in Washington, DC, I similarly recognize that as my colleagues and I attempted to normalize college going, we could have drawn upon the cultural know-how and other assets imbued in the Black and Latinx family and community members who surrounded our students (see Boettcher et al., 2022; Carey, 2016; George Mwangi et al., 2017; Knight-Manuel & Marciano, 2013; Sewell, 2024; Welton & Martinez, 2014). We worked closely with families; they sent their children to us intentionally to guide their children along college pathways. But we did not spend enough time working to fathom what college actually meant to families and their children. Young men, especially, were prone to falling off college pathways. We misunderstood racialized and gendered pressures shaping how young men conceptualized futures (e.g., protecting the family, academic and social barriers, conflicting priorities).

Anticipating and Maneuvering Barriers to College Access

As Black and Latinx boys and young men weigh the fiscal and social costs of college going, they do so against more immediate financial pressures and familial responsibilities (Carey, 2018; 2021). Those from low-income families may weigh longer-term college plans against more efficient mechanisms to financial and career stability. They may also matriculate at shorter-term vocational certificate programs or join the military (Carey, 2018; Martinez & Huerta, 2020; Noll, 2022).

Researchers have also shown that Black (Carey, 2019; Means et al., 2016; Reid & Moore, 2008) and Latinx (Acevedo-Gil, 2019; Carey, 2019) students constrain their ambitions due to feeling unprepared by their schools and marginalized in their communities. In a rural all-Black school, Castro (2021) documented how racism and systemic disinvestment undermined an intervention to reduce community college remediation rates. Castro's participants believed school failed to adequately prepare them for college. When a college intervention came along, students resisted it, because they believed it would fall short and merely set them up for more failure at the collegiate level.

Marciano's (2021) study of Black and Latinx high school students revealed that participants demonstrated a keen awareness of the college-readiness barriers they faced. Such inequities were acutely felt in the lack of access to high-level courses like pre-calculus, which led participants to feel both disadvantaged and unprepared for college. In Acevedo-Gil's (2019) study of low-income Latinx students, participants interpreted college-going prospects through the lens of *la facultad*, or the ability to anticipate institutional barriers. This "sixth sense" emerged at the nexus of school-based college messages including the low expectations of counselors and a keen awareness of their own interests. *La facultad* afforded students the ability to see beneath the surface of college (mis)information garnered from their underresourced school and anticipate obstacles. Findings like those in these studies show how and why Black and Latinx students approach college with trepidation, regardless of school supports.

The College-Going Dilemmas of Black and Latinx Boys

Like the studies reviewed in the prior section, participants in my study formulated self-appraisals about whether college was best for them by weighing and interpreting both pressures from school and family through the lens of their own perceived academic and social strengths. As a result of their evaluations, participants revealed "college-going dilemmas" that were initiated by internal and external factors (Carey, 2018; 2019). Internal dilemmas were rooted in familial factors like the fear of changing or being set apart from family members (Carey, 2018) and cognitive, academic, and personality-based attributes like doubting whether they were smart enough for the demands of college (Carey, 2019).

External dilemmas emerged from individuals, situations, or systems around them. These were tied mainly to perceived family responsibility. Participants worried about what would happen to certain family members if they left for college and questioned if assuming vast college student loan debt was best for their family's well-being (Carey, 2018; 2019). Returning to Perdido's experiences, we can see how internal and external dilemmas converged in shaping notions about whether college attendance was best for him and his family in the following: "I'm not prepared at all for college really. If I went to college, I'll be wasting my money and my parents' money too. That's another thing about college man, I gotta pay to get my education. . . . But I can't study. I can't stay focused enough to study. So till I figure out why I can't stay focused I can't really fix that staying focused problem." Internally, Perdido anticipated possibly lacking the focus to complete and succeed with his college coursework, which would lead to his failure. Simultaneously, external financial constraints induced him to avoid college to not place himself and his family in deeper economic stress.

These findings also show how Latinx participants drew on cultural values and "foregrounded family" (Carey, 2021) while making college-going-related decisions. When participants foregrounded their family, they endorsed *caballerismo*, or gendered cultural norms of heroic humility, family responsibility, and ethics passed down to them from their fathers (Arciniega et al., 2008). Whether or not the Salvadoran boys in my study pursued college or decided to forgo it, their family's well-being—and not their own individualist desires—was at the center.

In sum, Black and Latinx youth from low-income communities approach college with layers of not just hope but also trepidation informed by their perceived responsibility to family. If internal and external dilemmas are left unresolved, youth may be unprepared to manage their family's needs while grappling with the academic rigors and financial stress of college. Students may also formulate inaccurate or false college-related identities that could derail their college education and their young adult life trajectories as a result (see Duncheon & Relles, 2019).

Looking back, I entered college worried about making friends, being smart enough for college, and choosing the right major. Due to financial aid, scholarships, and most importantly, my parents' financial backing, I did not worry about paying tuition or dorm fees. My dilemmas—questioning my intelligence or ability to make friends—were assuredly racialized and gendered especially at an elite predominantly white institution like Boston College (BC). Countless times I was assumed to be a BC football player; such encounters fueled internal conflicts about my placement in such an environment, my identity, my reason for even being there. However, my dilemmas were not compounded by guilt for leaving home or uncertainty spurred by familial financial strain.

What PreK–12 Schools Can Do: A Conclusion

Writing from personal reflections, professional experiences, and research-based insights helped shed light on various factors that shape my under-standings of what matters for fostering Black and Latinx adolescent boys' futures. My reflections illuminated how my middle-class family, community members, and even after-school care youth workers normalized college going for me. Thanks to them, I encountered college early, often, and everywhere. Interestingly, my family did not rely on schools to teach me about college going or expose me to college-based careers. School actors simply mirrored back, reinforced, and complemented messages I garnered from college-educated family and mostly Black community members.

My tenure teaching in college preparatory public schools in Washing-ton, DC, awakened far broader understandings of the intricate processes that underscore what happens as Black and Brown adolescents venture onto postsecondary life paths. Made more apparent was the strength and resilience of Black and Latinx families from communities facing seem-ingly insurmountable economic stressors. Also evident was their devotion to supporting their children's college pathways in unique and culturally specific ways that defied forms of economic subjugation set up to keep them marginalized.

My research uncovers the need for educators to work strategically with students' families to ensure college-going supports draw upon their cultural assets and account for collective familial desires. Metro's impact—its college imagery and messaging—was overshadowed by the influence of family-based realities on participants' future mindsets. By not attending to what participants offered via college-going familial capital (Carey, 2016), and overlooking the socioaffective concerns spurred on by college-going internal and external dilemmas (Carey, 2018; 2019), Metro's college-going culture missed crucial opportunities to better align school practices with the interests and needs of their racially and ethnically diverse student population.

My practice and research experience also revealed the cost of myopically emphasizing college while overlooking the other life goals of Black and Latinx adolescents. When stakeholders do so, they miss opportunities to help youth clarify how their college ambitions align with and gain meaning in relationship to their career and life condition goals. Instead of mass counseling practices (see Gast, 2021), more wholistic and tailored approaches for guiding students to their own bright futures are needed. In this vein, college-going supports need also be developmentally attuned by considering the needs of adolescence, a time when youths' abstract thinking expands to account for not just college but other life goals (e.g., career and life condition) that inform and shape present-day dispositions (see Carey, 2022; Savitz-Romer & Bouffard, 2012).

Finally, families wanted their boys to find pride and fulfillment in their life, and they used messaging like "be somebody" or find "success" to spur on their ambitions (Carey, 2022). However, Metro could have done so much more to help the boys figure out who that "somebody" is or what "success" meant on their terms. A good starting place would have been helping students thread crucial linkages between college majors, career trajectories, and life conditions to complement familial messaging.

Critical Reflection

Widening postsecondary educational pathways for Black and Brown adolescents is contingent upon stakeholders understanding youths' lived realities, fostering their mindsets, and tailoring supports to the unique needs of youth and their families so they can find paths that align with their interests and unique potentials. It is also essential that educators and youth workers delve into their own lived experiences through personal reflection to unearth gaps in their understandings and build better relational bridges with youth. Thus, to better realize the future trajectories of Black and Latinx boys and young men, and determine ways to support them, take some time to reflect on your own path with the following:

1. As a child, what did you want to be when you grew up? How did this desire morph over the years, and why? Draw

or describe the images that come to mind when you reflect on the following: "I first became cognizant of college . . ." How was college going made "real, relevant, and present" for you when you were growing up? Who spurred these realities for you? Feelings often spur motivations. So, how do you remember feeling?

2. Do you feel like family, teachers, or community members pushed you toward "better"? If so, what did "better" mean for those who encouraged you? How did you know? What were some of the ways your family supported your educational pathway? What did this support feel like? And were you cognizant of these supports at the time?

3. How did the schools you attended support your college-going pathways? What were the most effective support mechanisms for you? Which were not helpful, and why?

4. The notion of *postsecondary future selves* takes up your college aims, career goals, and your expected life condition (see Carey, 2022; 2024). Why is it so difficult for youth to imagine themselves into their postsecondary future selves? What barriers keep youth from imagining bright futures on their own terms? What are some of the ways you were able to imagine yourself in your own postsecondary future self? What worked for you, and why? How do you define success? What or who influenced your definition?

References

Acevedo-Gil, N. (2019). College-going facultad: Latinx students anticipating postsecondary institutional obstacles. *Journal of Latinos and Education, 18*(2), 107–125. https://doi.org/10.1007/s11256-020-00585-9

Akiva, T., & Robinson, K. H. (Eds.). (2022). *It takes an ecosystem: Understanding the people, places, and possibilities of learning and development across settings.* IAP.

Arciniega, G. M., Anderson, T. C., Tovar-Blank, Z. G., & Tracey, T. J. (2008). Toward a fuller conception of Machismo: Development of a traditional Machismo and Caballerismo Scale. *Journal of Counseling Psychology, 55*(1), 19–33. https://doi.org/10.1037/0022-0167.55.1.19

Ballysingh, T. A., Rangel, V. S., Gonell, E. A., & Sáenz, V. B. (2021). Mechanisms of matriculation: School counseling resources and college going for

Latino men. *Professional School Counseling, 25*(1_part_4). https://doi.org/10.1177/2156759X211040033

Boettcher, M. L., Lange, A., Hanks, S., & Means, D. R. (2022). Rural Black and Latinx students: Engaging community cultural wealth in higher education. *Journal of Research in Rural Education, 38*(1), 1–15. https://doi.org/10.26209/jrre3801

Bourdieu, P., & Passeron, J. (1977). *Reproduction in education, society and culture.* Sage.

Britton, T. A., Rall, R. M., & Commodore, F. (2023). And still, I rise: A theory of institutional resilience at historically Black colleges and universities. *Journal of Negro Education, 92*(1), 77–93.

Brooms, D. R. (2021). *Stakes is high: Trials, lessons, and triumphs in young Black men's educational journeys.* State University of New York Press.

Brooms, D. R. (2022). "I didn't want to be a statistic": Black males, urban schooling, and educational urgency. *Race Ethnicity and Education, 25*(3), 351–369. https://doi.org/10.1080/13613324.2020.1803821

Cabrera, N. L., Karaman, A. K., Ballysingh, T. A., Oregon, Y. G., Gonell, E. A., Lopez, J. D., & Deil-Amen, R. (2022). Race without gender? Trends and limitations in the higher education scholarship regarding men of color. *Review of Educational Research, 92*(3), 331–369.https://doi.org/10.3102/00346543211054577

Carey, R. L. (2015). *"Making our lives": The contributions of urban high school cultures to the future selves of Black and Latino adolescent boys* [Doctoral dissertation, University of Maryland College Park]. https://doi.org/10.13016/M2005J

Carey, R. L. (2016). "Keep that in mind . . . You're gonna go to college": Family influence on the college going processes of Black and Latino high school boys. *Urban Review, 48*(5), 718–742. https://doi.org/10.1007/s11256-016-0375-8

Carey, R. L. (2018). "What am I gonna be losing?" School culture and the family-based college going dilemmas of Black and Latino adolescent boys. *Education and Urban Society, 50*(3), 246–273. https://doi.org/10.1177/0013124517713112

Carey, R. L. (2019). Am I smart enough? Will I make friends? And can I even afford it? Exploring the college going dilemmas of Black and Latino adolescent boys. *American Journal of Education, 125*(3), 381–415. https://doi.org/10.1086/702740

Carey, R. L. (2021). Foregrounding family: How Salvadoran American boys interpret and formulate college-going mindsets at the nexus of family, school, and the self. *Anthropology & Education Quarterly, 52*(3), 294–314. https://doi.org/10.1111/aeq.12372

Carey, R. L. (2022). "Whatever you become, just be proud of it": Uncovering the ways families influence Black and Latino adolescent boys' postsecondary future selves. *Journal of Adolescent Research, 37*(1), 59–97. https://doi.org/10.1177/07435584211018450

Carey, R. L. (2024). The postsecondary future selves of Black and Latinx boys: A case for cultivating more expansive supports in college-going schools. *American Educational Research Journal, 61*(2), 248–286. https://doi.org/10.3102/00028312231214477

Carrión, A. E., & Torres, M. (2023). Leaning on family: Examining college-going and help-seeking behaviors of Latino male high school students through dichos, consejos, and community cultural wealth. *International Journal of Educational Research, 122*, 102256. https://doi.org/10.1016/j.ijer.2023.102256

Castro, E. L. (2021). "They sellin' us a dream they not preparin' us for": College readiness, dysconscious racism, and policy failure in one rural Black high school. *Urban Review, 53*(4), 617–640. https://doi.org/10.1007/s11256-020-00585-9

Clark, J. S., Wint, K. M., & Brooms, D. R. (2024). Conceptualizing possibilities for Black boys through the educational continuum. *International Journal of Qualitative Studies in Education, 37*(6), 1720–1735.

Commodore, F., & Njoku, N. R. (2020). Outpacing expectations: Battling the misconceptions of regional public historically Black colleges and universities. *New Directions for Higher Education, 2020*(190), 99–117. https://doi.org/10.1002/he.20370

Conchas, G. Q., & Acevedo, N. (2020). *The Chicana/o/x dream: Hope, resistance, and educational success.* Harvard Education Press.

Covarrubias, R. (2021). What we bring with us: Investing in Latinx students means investing in families. *Policy Insights from the Behavioral and Brain Sciences, 8*(1), 3–10. https://doi.org/10.1177/2372732220983855

Delpit, L. (2006). *Other people's children: Cultural conflict in the classroom.* New Press.

Duncheon, J. C., & Relles, S. R. (2019). "A ditcher and a scholar": Figuring college-going identities in an urban magnet high school. *Teachers College Record, 121*(1), 1–36. https://doi.org/10.1177/016146811912100106

Dunkel, C., & Kerpelman, J. (2006). *Possible selves: Theory, research and applications.* Nova.

Farmer-Hinton, R. L. (2011). On being college prep: Examining the implementation of a "college for all" mission in an urban charter school. *Urban Review, 43*, 567–596. https://doi.org/10.1007/s11256-010-0168-4

Garcia, N. M., Irizarry, J. G., & Ruíz, Y. (2020). *Al esconder*, hide and seek: RicanStructing college choice for Puerto Rican students in urban schools. *Race Ethnicity and Education, 23*(1), 1–20. https://doi.org/10.1080/13613324.2019.1631779

Gast, M. J. (2021). "You're supposed to help me": The perils of mass counseling norms for working-class Black students. *Urban Education, 56*(9), 1429–1455. https://doi.org/10.1177/0042085916652178

George Mwangi, C. A. (2015). (Re)Examining the role of family and community in college access and choice: A metasynthesis. *Review of Higher Education, 39*(1), 123–151. https://doi.org/10.1353/rhe.2015.0046

George Mwangi, C. A., Daoud, N., English, S., & Griffin, K. A. (2017). "Me and my family": Ethnic differences and familial influences on academic motivations of Black collegians. *Journal of Negro Education, 86*(4), 479–493. http://doi.org/10.7709/jnegroeducation.86.4.0479

George Mwangi, C. A., Malcolm, M., & Thelamour, B. (2023). Our college degree: Familial engagement in the lives of diverse Black collegians. *Race Ethnicity and Education, 26*(7), 872–891. https://doi.org/10.1080/13613324.2020.1842347

Gibbs Grey, T. (2022). Reppin' and risin' above: Exploring communities of possibility that affirm the college-going aspirations of Black youth. *Urban Education, 57*(7), 1177–1206. https://doi.org/10.1177/0042085918804020

Goings, R. B., & Sewell, C. J. (2019). Outside connections matter: Reflections on the college choice process for gifted Black students from New York City. *High School Journal, 102*(3), 189–209. https://doi.org/10.1353/hsj.2019.0006

Harper, S. R., & Newman, C. B. (2016). Surprise, sensemaking, and success in the first college year: Black undergraduate men's academic adjustment experiences. *Teachers College Record, 118*(6), 1–30. https://doi.org/10.1177/016146811611800609

Hines, E. M., Cooper, J. N., & Corral, M. (2019). Overcoming the odds: First-generation Black and Latino male collegians' perspectives on pre-college barriers and facilitators. *Journal for Multicultural Education, 13*(1), 51–69. https://doi.org/10.1108/jme-11-2017-0064

Hines, E. M., Harris, P. C., Mayes, R. D., & Moore, J. L., III. (2020). I think of college as setting a good foundation for my future: Black males navigating the college decision making process. *Journal for Multicultural Education, 14*(2), 129–147. https://doi.org/10.1108/JME-09-2019-0064

Holland, N. E. (2017). Beyond conventional wisdom: Community cultural wealth and the college knowledge of African American youth in the United States. *Race Ethnicity and Education, 20*(6), 796–810. https://doi.org/10.1080/13613324.2016.1150823

Howard, T. C., Flennaugh, T., & Tunstall, J. (Eds.). (2016). *Expanding college access for urban youth: What schools and colleges can do.* Teachers College Press.

Howard, T. C., Woodward, B., Navarro, O., Huerta, A. H., Haro, B. N., & Watson, K. (2019). *Teachers College Record, 121*(5), 1–32. https://doi.org/10.1177/016146811912100504

Huerta, A. H., & Martinez, E., Jr. (2022). Strategies and support services for community college Latino/x men on academic probation. *Journal of Diversity in Higher Education, 15*(4), 406–411. https://doi.org/10.1037/dhe0000418

Jack, A. A. (2019). *The privileged poor: How elite colleges are failing disadvantaged students.* Harvard University Press.

Jett, C. C. (2022). *Black male success in higher education: How the mathematical brotherhood empowers a collegiate community to thrive.* Teachers College Press.

Johnson, J. M., & McGowan, B. L. (2017). Untold stories: The gendered experiences of high achieving African American male alumni of historically Black colleges and universities. *Journal of African American Males in Education, 8*(1), 23–44.

Knight, M. G., & Marciano, J. E. (2013). *College-ready: Preparing Black and Latina/o youth for higher education—A culturally relevant approach.* Teachers College Press.

Knight-Manuel, M. G., Marciano, J. E., Wilson, M., Jackson, I., Vernikoff, L., Zuckerman, K. G., & Watson, V. W. (2019). "It's all possible": Urban educators' perspectives on creating a culturally relevant, schoolwide, college-going culture for Black and Latino male students. *Urban Education, 54*(1), 35–64. https://doi.org/10.1177/0042085916651320

Kolluri, S. (2022). Men don't ask for directions: Gendered social capital and the path to college at an urban high school. *Education and Urban Society, 54*(4), 446–471. https://doi.org/10.1177/00131245221142563

Lindstrom, L., Lind, J., Beno, C., Gee, K. A., & Hirano, K. (2022). Career and college readiness for underserved youth: Educator and youth perspectives. *Youth & Society, 54*(2), 221–239. https://doi.org/10.1177/0044118X20977004

Marciano, J. E. (2021). "I think we're all teachers even though we're students": Examining youth perspectives of peer support for college readiness in an urban public high school. *Journal of Urban Learning, Teaching, and Research, 16*(1), 23–42.

Marín, G., & Marín, B. V. (1991). *Research with Hispanic populations.* Sage.

Markus, H., & Nurius, P. (1986). Possible selves. *American Psychologist, 41*(9), 954–969. https://doi.org/10.1037/0003-066X.41.9.954

Martinez, E., Jr., & Huerta, A. H. (2020). Deferred enrollment: Chicano/Latino males, social mobility and military enlistment. *Education and Urban Society, 52*(1), 117–142. https://doi.org/10.1177/0013124518785021

McArdle, E. E., & Turner, J. D. (2021). "I'm trying to beat a stereotype": Suburban African American male students' social supports and personal resources for success in AP English coursework. *Teachers College Record, 123*(4), 1–44. https://doi.org/10.1177/016146812112300403

McDonough, P. M. (1997). *Choosing colleges: How social class and schools structure opportunity.* State University of New York Press.

Means, D. R., Clayton, A. B., Conzelmann, J. G., Baynes, P., & Umbach, P. D. (2016). Bounded aspirations: Rural, African American high school students and college access. *Review of Higher Education, 39*(4), 543–569. https://doi.org/10.1353/rhe.2016.0035

Mobley, S. D., Jr. (2017). Seeking sanctuary: (Re)claiming the power of historically Black colleges and universities as places of Black refuge. *International*

Journal of Qualitative Studies in Education, 30(10), 1036–1041. https://doi.org/10.1080/09518398.2017.1312593

Moll, L. C., Amanti, C., Neff, D., & Gonzalez, N. (1992). Funds of knowledge for teaching: Using a qualitative approach to connect homes and classrooms. *Theory into Practice, 31*(2), 132–141. https://doi.org/10.1080/00405849209543534

Noll, L. A. (2022). Accountability and (in)congruence in a no-excuses school college-going culture. *American Educational Research Journal, 59*(1), 112–145. https://doi.org/10.3102/00028312211057303

Nurmi, J. E. (1991). How do adolescents see their future? A review of the development of future orientation and planning. *Developmental Review, 11*(1), 1–59. https://doi.org/10.1016/0273-2297(91)90002-6

Oyserman, D. (2015). *Pathways to success through identity-based motivation.* Oxford University Press.

Patrón, O. E. (2020). "The revolution begins at home": Exploring educational aspirations between Latino male collegians and their families through a reciprocity of relationships. *International Journal of Qualitative Studies in Education, 33*(4), 446–464. https://doi.org/10.1080/09518398.2019.1681545

Reid, M. J., & Moore, J. L., III. (2008). College readiness and academic preparation for postsecondary education: Oral histories of first-generation urban college students. *Urban Education, 43*(2), 240–261. https://doi.org/10.1177/0042085907312346

Rhoden, S. (2017). "Trust me, you are going to college": How trust influences academic achievement in Black males. *Journal of Negro Education, 86*(1), 52–64. https://doi.org/10.7709/jnegroeducation.86.1.0052

Rios-Aguilar, C., & Kiyama, J. M. (2012). Funds of knowledge: An approach to studying Latina(o) students' transition to college. *Journal of Latinos and Education, 11*(1), 2–16.

Rodriguez, G. (2023). Complicating college access: Understanding compliance and resistance for Latinx youth in suburbia. *Anthropology & Education Quarterly, 54*(4) 349–371. https://doi.org/10.1111/aeq.12461

Sáenz, V. B., García-Louis, C., Drake, A. P., & Guida, T. (2018). Leveraging their family capital: How Latino males successfully navigate the community college. *Community College Review, 46*(1), 40–61. https://doi.org/10.1177/0091552117743567

Savitz-Romer, M., & Bouffard, S. (2012). *Ready, willing, and able: A developmental approach to college access and success.* Harvard Education Press.

Schneider, B. L., & Stevenson, D. (1999). *The ambitious generation: America's teenagers, motivated but directionless.* Yale University Press.

Scott, S., Johnson, J. M., Hardaway, A., & Galloway, T. (2021). Investigating Ivy: Black undergraduate students at selective universities. *Journal of Postsecondary Student Success, 1*(2), 72–90. https://doi.org/10.33009/fsop_jpss128468

Sewell, C. J. P. (2024). Passing the torch: Intergenerational capital transmission and the Black legacy experience at a PWI. *Race Ethnicity and Education, 27*(4), 453–473. https://doi.org/10.1080/13613324.2023.2268002

Smith-Morris, C., Morales-Campos, D., Alvarez, E., A. C., & Turner, M. (2013). An anthropology of familismo: On narratives and description of Mexican/Immigrants. *Hispanic Journal of Behavioral Sciences, 35*(1), 35–60. https://doi.org/10.1177/0739986312459508

Taylor, L. D., & Williams, K. L. (2022). Critical sensemaking: A framework for interrogation, reflection, and coalition building toward more inclusive college environments. *Education Sciences, 12*(12), 877. https://doi.org/10.3390/educsci12120877

Tichavakunda, A., & Galan, C. (2023). The summer before college: A case study of first-generation, urban high school graduates. *Urban Education, 58*(8), 1–29. https://doi.org/10.1177/0042085920914362

Velez, G., Mancheno, V., & López, S. (2024). Mapping ecosystems: Building an understanding of an urban network of supports and resources for Black and Latino/a students. *Urban Education.* Advance online publication. https://doi.org/10.1177/00420859241244768

Warren, C. A. (2017). *Urban preparation: Young Black men moving from Chicago's South Side to success in higher education.* Harvard Education Press.

Welton, A. D., & Martinez, M. A. (2014). Coloring the college pathway: A more culturally responsive approach to college readiness and access for students of color in secondary schools. *Urban Review, 46*, 197–223. https://doi.org/10.1007/s11256-013-0252-7

Williams, B. M., & Martin, G. (2022). Exploring the rhetoric of social class among first-generation, low-income college students in US higher education. *Higher Education Research & Development, 41*(6), 2094–2107. https://doi.org/10.1080/07294360.2021.1967885

Williams, K. L., Burt, B. A., Clay, K. L., & Bridges, B. K. (2019). Stories untold: Counter-narratives to anti-Blackness and deficit-oriented discourse concerning HBCUs. *American Educational Research Journal, 56*(2), 556–599. https://doi.org/10.3102/0002831218802776

Williams, K. L., Mobley, S. D., Jr., Campbell, E., & Jowers, R. (2022). Meeting at the margins: Culturally affirming practices at HBCUs for underserved populations. *Higher Education, 84*(5), 1067–1087. https://doi.org/10.1007/s10734-022-00816-w

Yosso, T. J. (2005). Whose culture has capital? A critical race theory discussion of community cultural wealth. *Race Ethnicity and Education, 8*(1), 69–91. https://doi.org/10.1080/1361332052000341006

Chapter 7

Breaking the Chains of Intergenerational Poverty and Becoming a First-Generation Warrior

Anastasia (Stasia) Morton

I grew up in a family that valued education, with loved ones, allies, and community members often telling me I had potential. Like most teens in my situation, I did not see this comment as encouragement. Instead, I gave my mother hell and was highly reluctant to listen to the lessons she and others attempted to teach me.

I once believed I would not live past 18, so I never prepared for adulthood. Transitioning to adulthood revealed narrow and restricted paths to success. In this experience, I learned the harsh reality of discrimination and poverty. The cycle of generational poverty and society's low expectations trapped me in a box like a prisoner locked behind bars.

Audre Lorde's work empowered me with the language to articulate my experiences, bridging the connection to my struggles and the skin and class I was born into. Both of her works, *The Collected Poems* (2000) and "The Transformation of Silence into Language and Action" (1984), exemplify her urging the reader to use their strength to serve their vision and purpose, making fear less critical and empowering them. This sentiment resonates with my ongoing struggle to balance fear and belief in my ability to succeed in college. In my community, college degrees were few and far between. Those of us who dodged the school-to-prison pipeline vowed to secure a job or join the military as the safe bet for a future. My under-funded school left me unprepared for an "alternative" academic future, yet I dared to use my strength to serve a different vision for my life. Similarly, in chapter 6, Roderick Carey shares his experience teaching high school students of Color in Washington, DC. He discusses how, despite facing systemic injustices and challenges in accessing college pathways, students still sought college education or postsecondary training. Carey praises the committed and resilient family members who support students' pathways to a "better" life and future well-being.

My life experiences, including my culture, language, and consumed media, differed significantly from the resources and environment I encountered while learning and studying among third- and fourth-generation white college graduates on campus. This stark contrast made it challenging to adapt and find my place. As a first-generation and low-income new adult and woman of Color, I came from generations of hard-working people with excellent work ethic, resilience, and perseverance. Ironically, having this high work ethic made it extremely difficult for me to find my voice (Perdomo, 2012) and not rub people the wrong way. Regardless of intentionality, interrupting stereotypes in real time can trigger the insecurities of white supremacy. Shattering the glass ceiling can make others feel uncomfortable and inferior, as John Bracey (2014) described in *How Racism Harms White Americans*. This is why we must teach first-generation learners of Color about the toxic power dynamics they must deal with in academic, personal, and professional war zones, where fighting is passive but aggressive warfare. Perdomo (2012) describes the delicate balance between the raw tongue, instructional voice, and symbolic voice while effectively conveying one's narrative of race, class, and gender in their life. Whereas some students have cultural/societal boundaries imposed on them to contain and/or control their verbal expressions, others were encouraged to express their full voice in their creativity. My experience of transitioning from nontraditional to traditional thought and practice left me feeling like I was at war with myself, who I was, who I wanted to be, and what it would cost me personally to become them. Finding my instrumental voice helped me express my range of intellect, leadership, and critical thinking skills and openly share my perspectives. By skillfully blending raw tongue and instructional voices, I have developed a symbolic voice that embodies my self-identity, self-awareness, and appreciation of my multiple identities. This chapter is written for the following generation of First-Generation Warriors.

Breaking the Chains of Intergenerational Poverty

The humanity of Ubuntu (Metz, 2007) "I Am Because You Are" has left footprints in my soul. It provided the realization that I stand on the shoulders of those who pushed me to take advantage of opportunities they were denied. In the same way that Christine Sleeter (2013) acknowledged inheriting footholds and cushions, I want to thank all the people who paved the path for me to be where I am today. Valuing my future and seeing where my potential could lead me was like a shovel leaving a trail for the next person to follow. People like me bring their own cultural wealth (Yosso, 2005), like the linguistic capital of speaking multiple languages, the navigational experience of figuring out the college application process independently, and aspirational capital because they are intentional about setting and reaching their goals. My learning journey has been an experience in survival, requiring intense resilience to navigate cultural, institutional, and experiential challenges. This survival tool is an ode to all the coffins that laid the foundation for me to be here. Because of the mentors and educators I have had in my life both inside and outside academia, I took a leap of faith in applying as a nontraditional student to a community college. Real soldiers do real things on the road to power, respect, and financial security. This is a shoutout to the teachers found on the streets but not welcomed in the classroom. This includes my two grandmothers, both of whom I identify closely with. Before I knew what an educator was, my grandmother formed the mold, making it my default. It was ingrained in me—in my muscles, in my memories. Not a day goes by when their work does not influence my educational practices. These two women are a massive part of why I can think differently and successfully navigate professional spaces. I have tried to carry their influence forward to generations after me.

My Grandmothers' Generational Link to the Chain

Each of my grandmothers had a significant influence on me. Doris "NaNa" Moore was a self-proclaimed hustla. With only elementary school education, graduating high school or even envisioning college was not an option. As a mother, her goal was for each generation after her to be better than the one before them. She championed a financial literacy mindset and always preached that you should turn a talent into an income. And she led by example by sewing and selling stockings. She taught me how to cook so that I could always feed my family and fall back on it as a means of income if need be. She was a young mother who raised her children by herself while holding down two jobs, maintaining several side hustles, and throwing regular rent parties that welcomed the whole community.

NaNa always took care of her family and the house. She taught me how to think about money and manage a household, how to be a community organizer, and how to be a mentor as the oldest cousin and granddaughter—all transferable skills. Today, her lessons show up in my work as an event planner, educator, dialogue facilitator, and role model. I am a person who can take care of the house and think about all the intricate details necessary to start and complete a task. I can keep an audience engaged, be an excellent host, organize a group gathering, and use an endless number of other practical and soft skills.

Loretta "Grandma" Morton got kicked out of high school two weeks before graduation when they found out she was pregnant. Graduating high school and attending college was not an option. Since 1970 she has been widowed twice. She taught her children to strive for excellence. Her motto of reliance was, "I can complain, but I won't." In 1980, she moved back to Virginia and began a day care center from her home. Over 50 children entered her doors and were surrounded by love, education, and happiness. Grandma had a gentle but firm way of making you listen and follow directions. She made you think you had choices and options (although in the end, you did what she said). She got you to agree without feeling like you gave up everything in the process.

Every summer, she, my cousins, and I taught kids the ABCs, numbers 1–10, and all toddlers left fully potty trained. She had a very efficient system with a designated time for everything from nap time to mealtime to potty time. Everything was organized and done uniformly.

My grandmother taught me time management, productivity, organization, planning, and execution. She helped sharpen my executive functioning skills. Looking back now, I see how: Knowing that the babies would have to go down for a nap at a particular time meant that all of the blankets had to be laid down before that time. Ten to fifteen minutes before eating, the table must be set. The bathrooms had to be ready for use before everyone woke up from their nap. All of these things were done consistently. So, from a young age, it was ingrained in me to think five steps ahead. I learned to execute plans thoroughly and effectively from an early age. As a result, I developed skills that I still use today. I utilize these skills in various areas, including classroom management, curriculum development, participant-centered engagement, and professional development training for educators and administrators.

MY PARENTS' GENERATIONAL LINK TO THE CHAIN

I was born in Queens, but Brooklyn raised me. My cycle of socialization (Harro, 2000) included the gender and racial biases, assumptions, and unquestioned stereotypes of the 1980–1990 crack era (Hartman & Golub, 1999). Sculpted with the clay of an economic status defined by Reaganomics (Morgan, 2008), I was molded by the streets. I consider myself both lucky and unlucky to have been born into an underprivileged reality. Lucky because my journey started among the richly diverse people and varied cultures of almost every borough of New York City. Unlucky because the love and support I received were encased within systemic oppression and a personally traumatic existence.

I was introduced to the world by predetermined discrimination, racism, colorism, and generational poverty. Shackled by chains of generational poverty like an umbilical cord attached to a newborn baby, I made my entrance into the world. My grandmothers valued education so everyone under their roof valued education as well. Being reduced to a statistic was unacceptable regardless of external circumstances. Both my parents graduated from high school with the intention of going to college. However, they could not make it happen, not due to incompetence or lack of effort, but because of the impact of the times and a shift in priorities. After high school, motherhood took priority for my mother and drug dependency took priority for my dad.

I learned transformative lessons from others that helped me avoid pitfalls and generational curses. I am grateful for those who have shared their struggles with me, allowing me to learn from their mistakes. In the 1990s, I began the next chapter in my life by leaving my comfort zone in Cambria Heights. I immersed myself in the street culture of Coney Island houses in Brooklyn, New York. My challenges included avoiding teen pregnancy, drug addiction, and the school-to-prison pipeline. Despite the daily minefield of obstacles, I remained motivated and focused on academic success. My parents, who did not finish college, transferred their dreams of a better future to their children.

MY GENERATIONAL LINK IN THE CHAIN

Nin (n.d.) once said, "It was life that beat her, but it was culture and society that paralyzed her." Since my early days, it has been abundantly clear that society holds little to no regard for Black girls' tears, sorrow, pain, and well-being. Therefore, I knew I alone would have to safeguard my mental, spiritual, physical, and financial health. My beliefs, morals, and values were shaped by misunderstanding, insecurity, and others' perception of me as an "angry Black girl." Like a scarlet letter on my person, eventually, I was branded as a defiant, disrespectful, and disobedient "young lady." It was a struggle to stay positive and when I looked in the mirror, all I saw was what author Donald Goines (1972) describes as a "Black girl lost." As a woman of Color, I have learned to anticipate and overcome the challenges of pursuing the American Dream. Imprisoned by stereotypes, I witnessed and experienced the consequences of biases and perpetual disadvantage. Not daring to even dream of greatness or any semblance of it, I graduated from high school as the result of a relentless struggle. When I think back to my high school experience and who was supposed to help me access college, two things immediately come to mind. First is the one and only time I met my guidance counselor. I believed her job was to push me to be the best version of myself. But that day she advised me that although I had an excellent score on my SAT, I should not bother considering college. When she saw where I came from and decided how my story would end, she had already determined my life trajectory. I'll never forget the feeling I left the room with. Second, a hero named Miss Oliver desperately pointed out that I was wasting my potential by not maximizing my opportunities, gifts, and talents. She took me on a college tour to get a glimpse of what my future could be like. All available if I just took advantage of the untapped resources, skills, and drive inside me.

Having worked hard to finish high school and now with the responsibilities of motherhood, at the age of 22, I could not imagine anything different. This new territory was unfamiliar, and I felt unprepared. As someone who usually transcends the limits of their comfort zone, I moved from survival mode to thriving mode despite extreme fear. I could not see myself starting college, let alone finishing it.

Breaking the Chain

Behind the person you see today stands my son Brendon Jerome Stephen, the driving force behind my growth and development. Motherhood is a double-faced coin—on one side, it demands selflessness and sacrifice to secure a brighter future for your offspring; on the other side, it necessitates a steadfast commitment to considering the long-term consequences of your choices on your child's well-being and success. It takes great courage and strength to flip between both sides of this coin, but it is essential for shaping our children's future. My son's birth inspired me to consider the legacy I wanted to leave behind. This realization intrinsically motivated and empowered me to break free from the chains of poverty and plan my path toward my purpose with strategic intentionality. My college success journey is rooted in my family's foundation.

Their deep appreciation for Black excellence and history helped me recognize my cultural traditions of resilience, grit, self-efficacy, curiosity, self-control, zest, and social intelligence, as described by Paul Tough in his book *How Children Succeed* (2012). I am eternally grateful to my loved ones for laying the groundwork that would equip me with the tools I needed to excel in the future. It was their unwavering support and guidance that taught me the importance of a strong work ethic and propelled me toward success. As I entered college, I naïvely believed it was the ultimate challenge. However, I soon realized that it was merely a boot camp for the true battlefield—the professional realm. Thanks to the foundation laid by my loved ones, I am trained to face this next chapter with confidence and determination. My journey toward academic excellence and financial uplift through college access began when I started community college in New York. While at La Guardia Community College, I was accepted into the Accelerated Study in Associates Program (ASAP) and guided by Dr. Pisco. She changed my life with a coffee bean. In a classroom exercise, she distributed coffee beans and asked us to share our thoughts. I shared that I saw the blood, sweat, and tears of the people who harvested and transported the coffee to my table. Her response to my comment was the most profound affirmation I had ever received. This unexpected positive feedback shocked me. In that moment, Dr. Pisco demonstrated the transformative power of nonoppressive, joyful, and liberating education. This experience ignited a passion for education I had never felt before. It also erased the trauma I endured in the educational system. Her gift of critical thinking and problem-solving changed my perspective and since then I have thirsted for education. Being on the dean's list for the first time propelled me into the Phi Theta Kappa Honor Society.

Mentors like Ingrid DeLeon challenged me to dream big and stood by me when I adamantly resisted, out of fear, applying for the Kaplan Leadership Scholarship. Becoming a Kaplan Scholar, I learned from Dr. Nancy Sanchez, Jennifer Benn, and my fellow cohort members the transformative power of altering one's way of thinking, propelling one from poverty to unimaginable success.

As a proud community college graduate, I took a leap of faith, uprooting my life and my son from New York City. I trusted Dr. Yedalis Ruíz Santana's guidance, especially when she served as my Mount Holyoke College tour guide. Her invaluable insights helped me transition from feeling like an outsider to envisioning myself as a Mount Holyoke College graduate. Encouraged by the wisdom and advice of those who walked the path before me, I transferred to Mount Holyoke College as a Frances Perkins Scholar. There, I diligently worked to complete my bachelor's degree in psychology and educational studies. My accomplishments would not be possible without the unwavering support of the team "No Sleep." My mentors and my community's supportive system have been invaluable to me.

Stasia's Journey to the Table

In the play *Man and Superman*, George Bernard Shaw (1856–1950) is widely quoted for saying, "If youth is wasted on the young, then wisdom is wasted on the old." Starting college after many gap years, I did not really comprehend the impact of my voice, choices, and opportunities. Students of Color like me face barriers in gaining college admission, staying in college, and graduating with a degree. Because we are working, trying to maintain a household, juggling a career, and still striving to maintain a GPA that will get us admitted into college, dropping out seems like the easier solution compared to continuing to get up and grind it out. The thought of graduating with a degree feels so far off. You have to persevere through many tears and sleepless nights, enduring moments of feeling like a disappointment, to eventually walk across the stage, shake someone's hand, and receive your degree. This is what I mean when I say this statement. However, these struggles are not just about upward social mobility; they are about the freedom to choose our paths, explore our interests, enter positions of power, and feel a sense of belonging at the table. If I could speak to a past version of myself about college access, and preparing mentally for the academic nuances along the journey, what I would share is: When in Rome, do as the Romans do. With the added caveat: "First you have to dream of a 'want' to go and get admission to Rome," and, "Yes, beloved, one day you will want to leave Rome to go to Jamaica and/or Brooklyn" —Saint Ambrose (n.d.) and Stasia.

The traditional "do as the Romans do" is invoked to connect to the gifts of flexibility and adaptability to change. As in the pandemic, transitioning from in-person to virtual to hybrid, you must learn to survive outside your comfort zone and thrive in your panic zone. As a single mother in my late 20s to early 30s on a scholarship, juggling multiple identities and economic realities, I truly struggled to maximize every moment. I will clarify my thought process on college access within this framework.

But First You Have to Dream of a "Want" to Go and Get Admission to Rome

Having to navigate through the admission process and trying to obtain acceptance into various colleges is like dreaming that you might "want" to get to Rome.

In This Framework, "Do as the Romans Do"

Speak to the Romans once you're in Rome. Do as they do so you can adjust and blossom while living there. This is similar to the shift in paradigms, learning habits, attitudes, and strategies that need to be applied while in college until the day you walk across the stage to claim your degree.

At Some Point You Will Want to Leave Rome to Go to Jamaica and/or Brooklyn

This is the mindset of leaving college and transitioning to being professionally employed. Here you will be walking into the warfare of trying to successfully sustain upward mobility, maintaining a sense of respect, feeling valued, heard, and welcomed. As well as having your opinions and thoughts comprehended and executed professionally. The messages, strategies, and vignettes shared in this section are things I wish I knew before I started my journey to use college as a vehicle to access generational wealth with my associate degree in liberal arts from LaGuardia Community College and a bachelor's degree in psychology and educational studies from Mount Holyoke College.

I fought through numerous obstacles, including impostor syndrome, which nearly forced me to abandon my dreams. Financial insecurity almost pushed me to drop out because of fear of losing my safety net of stability I had known all my life. Food insecurity almost convinced me to give up my ambitions, as affording food and college was a daily challenge. The following tools equipped me with the power to say "f(orget) this, two tears in a bucket," push through to graduation, and walk across that stage to where my degree was waiting for me. This success elevated me to the status of a "First-Generation Warriorhood." I was ready to transition into professional warfare where the assignment was to sustain gainful employment and financial security. I wanted to make space for the next group of First-Generation Warriors to follow and use the power of my voice and position for good. I represent for all the graves and those souls who did not get the chance to escape the prison pipeline, make it out of the hood, or make it past 18. I urge you to do the same and apply these helpful hints to this metaphorical battlefield. Applying these ideas to present and future circumstances is essential to paving a trail for the next generation to navigate through "Rome."

First-Generation Warriors

Asking yourself what defines a First-Generation Warrior may naturally lead to exploring the characteristics and experiences that set these individuals apart from their peers. Like any advertisement for an elite squad, the First-Generation Warrior cohort consists of members with unique characteristics and commonalities. These characteristics will help the squad succeed in the face of various obstacles and challenges. On paper, First-Generation Warriors are a combination of anyone who easily understands the universal experience of:

- Surviving intergenerational poverty

- Experiencing the legacy of incarceration, selling drugs, and/ or minimum wage jobs

- Growing from generations of unfilled dreams

- Seeing friends die or go to jail

- Not expecting to live past 18 years old

- Fighting others' perception of ability based on skin color and socioeconomic status

- Making the most of underfunded and underresourced schools

- A lack of preparation for postsecondary academic excellence

- Not planning or knowing how to plan for financial stability

- First in the family to stay in school and graduate from college

- Living with survivor's guilt because you made it out . . . alive

- Carry triumph and fear that your past will overshadow the future you are building

If these "qualities" mirror your experience, you too might be a First-Generation Warrior.

Below the surface, First-Generation Warriors refer to people without a caregiver who can understand the jargon of the common application process during high school senior year. First-Generation Warriors describe a person who has gone through the college application process alone. First-Generation Warriors indicate a person who fully understands the struggle of explaining to their parents why a W-2 income tax document is imperative for filling out the FAFSA by the deadline. First-Generation Warriors are individuals who can comprehend the constant second-guessing of the choice of future financial stability over earning a living in the present. First-Generation Warriors need someone to lead them through the process of applying for desperately needed scholarships and loans. First-Generation Warriors:

- Have the capacity and tenacity to overcome obstacles and challenges

- Strategically envision a better future

- Refuse to let current reality distract from the goal of graduating from college

- Achieve desired outcomes while learning from the experience

As a First-Generation Warrior, I understand how it feels to envision a future that feels nowhere near your current line of sight. If any of these things mirror your experience, you may be a candidate to become a First-Generation Warrior. Being first-generation and not having the tools to navigate collegiate and professional spaces while struggling with impostor syndrome is a constant internal battle. Having earned every opportunity I was afforded, I understand the realities of nepotism, entitlement, and privilege. These realities exist especially in predominantly white college and career environments. Breaking the chains of intergenerational poverty requires removing locks shaped by low income and socioeconomic status.

Finding My Voice

Having a family with a history of college graduates offers invaluable rewards for a college student. Discussing ways to navigate the admissions process, classrooms, dining halls, and campus life is a standard topic during family conversations. Strategies for coping with pressures and rigor are shared, which helps build a foundation and capacity for academic merit. Empathizing with the stress of studying for midterms and finals can be what a newly minted adult needs to stay in college. Financial preparation is also discussed, including planning for tuition and housing costs and saving for future expenses like meal plans to prevent food anxiety. These resources eliminate financial insecurity, allowing the next generation to focus solely on education, social networking, and financial upliftment.

To quote legendary hip hop artist Christopher Wallace (1997) (the Notorious B.I.G.), "I've been in this game for years . . . so I wrote me a manual." With the right tools and navigational skills, anyone can succeed and transform survival skills into cultural capital. Later in this chapter, I share tools I used to escape poverty and excel inside and outside the college classroom. These tools provide specific ways to become solution-oriented while still being authentic. I hope this serves as a navigational guide, similar to Victor Hugo Green's (1936) *The Negro Motorist Green-Book*, shedding light on ways to prepare first-generation warriors to sit at the table with second- and third-generation nepotists assertively.

The PWIT College Access Toolkit: A Practical Toolkit for PWIT and PWITFC

The information in the remainder of this chapter is targeted at individuals who have faced financial challenges and have not had access to resources.

It offers practical ways to help first-generation students of Color get into college and break the chains of poverty. Everyone absorbing these gems of advice traveled individually to this section. Whether you found the work by chance or not. Welcome! Honor the journey and take the tools with you to the next step. The text speaks directly to first-generation students of Color who are looking for ways to:

- Relinquish the weight of stereotypes of academic under-achievement

- Evade teen pregnancy stigmas and the school-to-prison pipeline

- Break the locks on the chains holding them captive to poverty

Each tool I share comes from a different obstacle I have faced. These experiences include college access, career exploration, and establishing themselves in life. These lessons taught me to stay professional and employable. At points in this section, I will call attention to Potential Warriors in Training (PWIT) and explicitly suggest methods of application. I will also sometimes refer to loved ones, mentors, educators, community members, support networks, allies, and fans of First-Generation Warriors as the Potential Warriors in Training Fan Club (PWITFC) members.

Hey PWITFCs, here is a way to move from theory to practice: motivational interviewing broadens scholars' perspectives by considering different paradigms and viewpoints. This strategy allows them to come up with their own answers. Furthermore, scholars execute their tasks freely and with intrinsic motivation, which is a bonus.

After reading the subsequent tools, I want you to be able to apply these strategies when facing your own obstacles. I want you to explore where you can shine and bring your talents and skills. Discover what you want and why. This section uses storytelling to raise awareness and share lessons and tips. I hope you enjoy reading it!

All the PWITs in the building: High school classrooms may often be filled with students who share similar backgrounds. College campuses are diverse, with people from various backgrounds, socioeconomic classes, ethnicities, and races, which can help individuals become less judgmental. Comprehending this information provides you with self-efficacy skills and flexibility in navigating educational minefields.

The following tools can provide First-Generation Warriors like me—and Second-Generation Warriors[1] like my son—with the opportunity for long-term employment and more financial stability. The framework is inspired by our story, and the categories will give you a chance to level up and build capacity. The anecdotes and subtext will be the lens through which we view the college access process as defined by me.

- Level 1—GETTING IN: "But first you have to dream of a 'want' to go and get admission to Rome" (table 7.1)

- Level 2—GETTING THROUGH: "Do as the Romans do" (table 7.2)

- Level 3—GETTING OUT: "At some point, you will want to leave Rome to go to Jamaica and/or Brooklyn" (table 7.3)

Table 7.1. Level 1: Getting in(to college). Also known as "But first you have to dream of a 'want' to go to Rome."

On the Surface: Desiring More	In his 2011 work, Maymind referenced Shinran, the founder of Japanese True Pure Land Buddhism (Jōdo Shinshū). Shinran believed in the Buddhist theory that the root of all suffering is "desire," also known as tanhā. This desire comes in different forms, one of which is described as the Three Poisons. Desiring more in life led me to question everything and gain more control over my destiny, but that process was filled with hardships and pitfalls along the way. Access to higher education is a multilayered process and varies for everyone. I started my journey at a community college as a first-generation student, who then transferred and graduated from a 4-year institution. My journey getting into college, being in college, and graduating from college as a nontraditional student was very different than what my son is experiencing now. As I recently sent him off to school, I thought about him as a loved one, a fan, and my support system through my school days, and I realized he is now a Second-Generation Warrior, the child of someone who desired more.

On the Surface: College Admission Process	College admission involves a slew of tedious tasks. These tasks include but are not limited to maintaining a certain grade point average, getting recommendation letters, completing applications, writing personal statements, as well as filling out the Federal Application for Financial Student Aid (FAFSA)—each with its own deadline. Regardless of feeling unprepared, dream big and step outside your comfort zone to envision your future as a college graduate.
	CommonApp.org allows you to apply to multiple colleges at once, but ensure your desired college is included as some require separate applications.
	Personal Statement: 650-word essay about you and your personal, academic, and professional development.
	Maintaining a certain GPA: 3.0 to be safe
	Completing the FAFSA: https://studentaid.gov/h/apply-for-aid/fafsa
	Recommendation letters: Letters from teachers, mentors, and guidance counselors highlighting your strengths and versatility
Below the Surface: What Is Your Brand?	Identifying your brand and/or rebranding yourself after high school maximizes your college experience. This involves strategic planning and determining how to achieve and reach your goals. "I want to be known for . . . (fill the blank)." "I want to graduate with a high school diploma, transfer to a community college, and graduate in two years."
	To the PWIT: Be committed. Make sure that when you are in class, you are known for asking questions that deepen your thinking. Sit in the front of the classroom. Strategically look for moments to get to where you want to be. This process starts with interviewing yourself:
	• What were you known for in high school?
	• While you are on campus, what are you known for?
	• What do you want to be known for?*
	• Who will enter the classroom or office today?
	*For example, I want to be known for heading up the debate team or leading the majorettes. Or, I want to be known for graduating with a master's degree.

continued on next page

Table 7.1. Continued.

Below the Surface: Setting Up a Foundation for Future Success	When I started college, my main goal was to set an example for my son to follow. I aimed to give him the chance to succeed in any path he chooses. I found inspiration in Strode's quote, "Do not go where the path may lead, go instead where there is no path and leave a trail," which is a central theme in her poem "Wind-Wafted Wild Flower," emphasizing individuality and nonconformity (Strode, 1903, p. 489).
	I want to talk directly to PWITFCs, who have strategically set up a way for your loved ones to financially take on college responsibility but do not possess the skills to help them navigate the admission process. Your love, support, and compassion will motivate them to remain focused at this stage of life. Empower PWITs to maximize their potential and succeed as young adults by providing them with the necessary tools and resources. Help them maximize opportunities. Although I know they might not do what you want, still give 200%.
	To the PWIT, this advice is meant to walk hand in hand with you as you explore the benefits of a college degree from different vantage points and paradigms.
Below the Surface: Old School vs. New School	Traditional education frameworks emphasize core skills during students' formative years. However, the foundation and examples set by one's family are equally critical to shaping one's outlook and approach to the world. These combined influences provide invaluable lessons that can enhance the college experience. Using these tools to create your own path and blend your old and updated identities is essential. Discover where your strengths lie and how to leverage your unique talents and skills within your college community. Remember that your old and transformed selves can coexist during this journey. Strive to find a balance between your past and present selves. Both shape who you are and where you're headed.
	PWIT, listen up . . . This skill will help you strengthen your self-image, resist emotional irregularity, achieve long- and short-term goals, and collaborate professionally in an authentic way.

Below the Surface: Fort Knox	As a first-generation student, it is easy to underestimate the value of your experiences and ideas. However, it is imperative to recognize that you have unique gifts worth protecting. Your insights and perspectives are valuable and could be just what someone else needs to hear. Guard your brilliance like gold at Fort Knox. Be aware of those who may use your ideas to advance their own agenda. Your trash could be someone else's treasure. Protect yourself from creative and intellectual property theft, safeguard your ideas, and always give yourself credit for your accomplishments and cultural capital. Never underestimate your impact and contribution to society. You are more than enough, and your brilliance deserves to be recognized and celebrated.

Source: Created by the author.

Table 7.2. Level 2: Getting through (college). Otherwise known as "Do as the Romans do."

On the Surface: Belonging	First-generation students of Color face stereotypes and impostor syndrome on campus, in the classroom, dorms, and dining halls. People assume you don't belong in the space—that you're here because of your skin color and economic background. First-generation students of Color carry a different burden with the skin they are in and take obstacles personally. The presence of stereotypes leads them to wonder if they belong.

To the PWIT in the building: The most professional advice I can give you is do not believe the hype. You deserve to be there just as much as anyone. This is why you need to make your voice count. Create a network and refine what you want to be known for. Figure out your brand and what it stands for. |

continued on next page

Table 7.2. Continued.

| On the Surface: Interview Mode | According to Law 19 from *The 48 Laws of Power*: "There are many different kinds of people in the world, and you can never assume that everyone will react to your strategies in the same way. Deceive or outmaneuver some people and they will spend the rest of their lives seeking revenge. They are wolves in lambs' clothing. Never offend or deceive the wrong person" (Greene, 1998, p. 138). Awareness of potential consequences and mindfulness of others is crucial to avoiding burned bridges. Treat every encounter as a job interview, reflecting your personal brand through your words and actions, whether in the classroom, workforce, or community. Millennials and Gen Z would probably compare this phenomenon to "shares" or "likes." Remember that you are constantly judged, so speaking and acting in a way that guarantees a positive reference is essential. I considered every encounter an interview and a chance to work with someone in the future. However, it's also a chance for them to work with me in the future. With this mindset, I always stay on point and put my best self forward.

Attention PWITFC: Mastering "interview mode" is an effective tool for helping First-Generation Warriors become successful adults. |
|---|---|
| On the Surface: Maximize Every Opportunity | Throughout years of working with high school students, I've observed that many scholars do not comprehend the monetary value of knowledge until senior year when they must consider how much a semester of tuition costs. They metaphorically rip up money for years because they undervalue education. As a scholarship recipient, I felt a duty to seize every opportunity my free education provided. Learning to level up in class prepared me to be courageous and speak for those without a seat at the table. Someone invested in my future and the future generations to follow. So, I used my voice to advocate for the voiceless and break unproductive habits.

PWIT: Don't play around with your time; you won't be in "Rome" forever. Make sure you are attending talks, getting tutoring, and regularly visiting the writing center and teacher office hours. |
| Below the Surface: Zero to Hundreds Fast | Unfortunately, having the highest grades or the most impressive work ethic does not always get you to the finish line. Society judges based on visible traits, such as race, gender presentation, hair texture, sexuality, and fashion sense. This leads to assumptions about expectations and limitations. More often, it is about who you know. Making a positive impression can mean a |

Below the Surface: Zero to Hundreds Fast (cont.)	positive recommendation letter for your common app, grad school application, and/or job. This tool will help you navigate personal and professional group dynamics regardless of your visible or invisible fears. When applied correctly, this tool will raise your self-esteem, build confidence, and improve your participation in and understanding of group dynamics. You pay tuition for networking opportunities. Networking is about coming to college knowing 0 and leaving knowing at least 100 future business contacts.
	PWIT should pay special attention to this next point: Networking is vital. College campuses are electric communities where everyone is there to "take care of business." Students are driven to succeed by parental pressure, personal ambition, or other motivators. Dorm life provides opportunities to network and form connections that may lead to future collaborations. Joining organizations and fraternities/sororities can be seen as informal job interviews. Building relationships and finding mentors are key to success. Maintaining positive relationships and leaving a trail for others to follow are essential.
Below the Surface: Graduation Is the Goal	Power moves toward success and requires strategic planning and foresight, combined with a growth mindset. Stereotype threat can affect academic, personal, and professional success. Claude Steele (2010) explains how stereotype threat can impact your self-esteem, sense of purpose, and outlook on your future. These strategies enrich the toolbox I know First-Generation Warriors are assembling. They are situational, and their relevance should be considered depending on their circumstances. "Focus on the Goal and Learn from the Journey." College education costs more than just dollars and cents; there is more personal cost than just tuition. Higher education costs emotional, mental, and spiritual currency. The institution often views high-achieving, assertive, and goal-oriented college students of Color as too aggressive, challengers of academic tradition, defiant, and unappreciative of the opportunity they've been given.
	PWIT soon realize that access has given them a false sense of belonging and a false belief in the American Dream. When in Rome, do the bid. Don't let a bid ruin you. A negative self-image can infect your task execution, skew your vision, interrupt your brilliance, and inhibit your ability to shine as brightly as you can, which can manifest as impostor syndrome. Ensure you feel confident when looking in the mirror. Your thoughts are your capital and they shape your choices.

Source: Created by the author.

Table 7.3. Level 3: Getting Out. "At some point, you will want to leave Rome to go to Jamaica and/or Brooklyn."

| On the Surface: Professional Warfare | First-generation students often do not have the privilege of effortlessly providing and securing financial and career opportunities for their relatives, friends, and/or partners, as this is commonly a benefit of those who have access to channels of nepotism. White supremacy populates the professional realm with employees who can boast about having their uncle, brother, cousin, godfather, wife, or husband help them get closer to achieving their goals. First-generation legacy includes power, influence, and connection. Nepotism (Hildreth et al., 2016) pipelines into a long line of legacy from which first- and second-generation families do not benefit. Nepotism stands on the shoulders of the powerless. Where there is nepotism, there will always be a need for affirmative action. This is because some people are born with the privilege of walking around the world "willfully ignorant and uninterrupted." If you were born into a specific class, are of a certain race, and are of a particular gender, you are allowed to be innocent past adolescence, sometimes even until adulthood. As a woman of Color, my innocence was stolen at a young age, leaving me without that opportunity to exist in the world uninterrupted. That said, it was a total cultural shock entering college as a mother and veteran in the work field to find that white supremacy shielded "others" from facing the same harsh realities and limitations of the world.

Preparing first-generation students to thrive in professional settings is warfare. It is necessary to enrich the growth mindset of second-, third-, and fourth-generation poverty to sit at a table with second-, third-, and fourth-generation wealth and have their voices heard without feeling like what Parkman (2016) describes as the "impostor phenomenon." Applying these tools can bridge the gap between theory and practice. This will enable one to thrive in professional environments rife with nepotism and white supremacy, especially after finishing college. |
| On the Surface: Leave a Trail | *The Souls of Black Folk* by W. E. B. Du Bois (1903) warns of double consciousness. When first-generation high school graduates, college graduates, and professionals dare to dream beyond their stagnating stereotypes, they face the challenges of juggling multiple identities and realities. The poem "We Wear the Mask" by Paul Dunbar (1913) explains the internal war we face when reflecting on who we were, who we wanted to be, and what it would cost |

On the Surface: Leave a Trail *(cont.)*	personally, as we pursue the "American Nightmare." Because many first-generation people do not have somebody gifting them wealth, you need to create your own generational wealth. Achieving financial freedom involves maintaining gainful employment and financial stability.
Below the Surface: Snakes in the Grass	Listen up First-Generation Warriors, this is the direction I want to lead you in: Protect your ideas. They are your intellectual property and can open doors of opportunity. Be mindful of who you're dealing with in personal and professional settings. The concept of first-generation warfare involves protecting your growing knowledge base, including recognizing and overcoming feelings that lead to undervaluing our own ideas and cultural capital. Protecting your ideas from those who may benefit from your generosity is crucial, especially for co-workers or colleagues you cannot trust. In the same way, snakes wait for an opportunity to strike—they lie in wait to strike. Territorial king cobras, solitary anacondas, and stealthy rattlesnakes must not be confused for a gentle bunny. Recognizing different personality types is crucial to survival. We can avoid unnecessary pain and conflict by accepting others for who they are and making informed choices based on their behavior. When I refer to 'snakes in the grass,' I want to emphasize that people's behavior patterns tend to be consistent over time. The saying, "You were who you were yesterday, and you will probably be that way tomorrow," highlights the importance of recognizing someone's character and treating them accordingly. Similarly, "They have been that way their whole life" reinforces the value of knowing who you are dealing with, not who you desire to deal with. Consider, the cautionary tale of the Scorpion and the Frog (Aesop, 1981). As the story unfolds, a scorpion asks a frog for a ride across a river, promising not to harm the frog. The frog agrees, but the scorpion stings the frog midway, dooming them both. The scorpion says, "It's in my nature," when asked why it betrayed its promise. The fable teaches us that some people cannot resist hurting others. It also sheds light on the personal interactions surrounding the "snakes in the grass" metaphor (Silverman & Kanarek, 2013) and warns us that we may be taken advantage of if we don't realize our value and worth. As a First-Generation Warrior, your ideas are your currency. First-generation warfare helps us protect our knowledge base and cultural capital. If you misjudge the situation, use emotional intelligence to regroup, reconsider, and rethink how you are handling the behavior.

Source: Created by the author.

Closing Remarks

My learning journey has required intense resilience to navigate cultural, institutional, and experiential challenges. My journey through college was inspired by my brother Jerille's message about having the drive and keeping a sense of agency alive when it comes to attaining my life goals. I hope some readers will see themselves in this story and feel inspired to finish high school, pursue higher education, and achieve a fulfilling career.

Dr. Ron Ferguson (The Gazette, 2020), director of the Harvard Achievement Gap Initiative, describes a highly successful person as having a combination of smarts, purpose, and a sense of agency—that feeling of being able to control one's own actions and their impact on the world around them. My name is Anastasia Danelle Morton, a powerful name gifted to me by my mother. She named me after the Russian princess, thinking of her legacy. Anastasia can be translated to mean "the bird, the phoenix," representing a fire of hope that never dies because it will always rise again from the ashes. As I pursue success, I lead by example, using the tools I've learned to achieve my family's mission of generational progress.

Critical Reflection

1. What are your reactions to the First-Generation Warrior concept? What resonates or is dissimilar to your understanding of first-generation students based on your own personal experiences, professional experiences, existing research, and so forth?

2. What stage of the journey (desiring "Rome," in "Rome," or leaving "Rome") are you at in your life, whether college related or otherwise? What tools are you using and/or might you apply from this chapter on your journey?

Note

1. Second-Generation Warriors come from families who have broken the chains of generational poverty, attained financial stability, and have had parents pave the way for them to pursue higher education. Their parents may feel a responsibility

to and are successful at equipping their children with the skills and tools they need to flourish independently. However, despite great achievements, their children will undoubtedly encounter obstacles as they strive for independence and establish their unique identities. Parents can support their Second-Generation Warriors by encouraging them to discover their own path forward. As they step out of the shadows and seek to prove themselves, networking is a skill and a strategy that can offer opportunities to connect with like-minded people, particularly in light of society's assumptions and judgments based on race and family background.

References

Aesop. (1981). *Aesop's fables* (1st ed.). Illustrated by Heidi Holder. Viking Press.

Ambrose of Milan. (n.d.). When in Rome. In William W. Goodwin (Ed.), *The proverbia sententiaeque latinitatis medii aevi* (vol. 1, pp. 45). Harvard University Press.

Bracey, J. (2014). How racism harms white Americans. In M. K. Asante Jr. & E. N. Ntiri (Eds.), *The African American experience: Psychoanalytic perspectives* (pp. 123–134). Routledge.

Dunbar, P. (1913). We wear the mask. In *Lyrics of lowly life* (Lit2Go Edition). Retrieved January 23, 2023, from https://etc.usf.edu/lit2go/187/lyrics-of-lowly-life/3819/we-wear-the-mask/

The Gazette. (2020, October 26). *Iowa ideas 2020: Dr. Ronald F. Ferguson discusses the achievement gap in education* [Video]. YouTube. https://www.youtube.com/watch?v=vdkVL2lwogg

Goines, D. (1972). *Black girl lost*. Holloway House.

Green, V., & Co. (1936). *The Negro motorist green-book*. (1936). [Periodical] Retrieved from the Library of Congress: https://www.loc.gov/item/2016298176/

Greene, R. (1998). *The 48 laws of power*. Penguin Books.

Harro, B. (2000). The cycle of socialization. In M. Adams, W. J. Blumenfeld, R. Castañeda, H. W. Hackman, M. L. Peters, & X. Zúñiga (Eds.), *Readings in diversity and social justice* (pp. 15–21). Routledge.

Hartman, D. M., & Golub, A. (1999). The social construction of the crack epidemic in the print media. *Journal of Psychoactive Drugs, 31*(4), 423–433. https://doi.org/10.1080/02791072.1999.10471772

Hildreth, J. A. D., Gino, F., & Bazerman, M. (2016). Blind loyalty? When group loyalty makes us see evil or engage in it. *Organizational Behavior and Human Decision Processes, 132*, 16–36. https://doi.org/10.1016/j.obhdp.2015.10.001

Lorde, A. (2000). *The collected poems of Audre Lorde*. W. W. Norton.

Lorde, A. (1984). *Sister outsider: Essays and speeches*. Crossing Press.

Metz, T., 2007. Ubuntu as a moral theory: Reply to four critics. *South African Journal of Philosophy, 26*(4), 369–387. https://doi.org/10.4314/sajpem.v26i4.31495

Morgan, I. (2008). Reaganomics and its legacy. In C. Hudson & G. Davies (Eds.), *Ronald Reagan and the 1980s* (pp. 145–162). Studies of the Americas. Palgrave Macmillan. https://doi.org/10.1057/9780230616196_7

Nin, A. (n.d.). "It was life that beat her, but it was culture and society that paralyzed her."

Parkman, A. (2016). The impostor phenomenon in higher education: Incidence and impact. *Journal of Higher Education Theory and Practice, 16*(1), 51–60. https://doi.org/10.33423/jhetp.v16i1.401

Perdomo, S. A. (2012). *Unpacking voice and silence: A phenomenological study of Black women and Latinas in the college classroom* [Doctoral dissertation, University of Massachusetts Amherst]. Open Access Dissertations. https://doi.org/10.7275/3291766

Shinran (1173–1263). (1984). *Tannisho: A Shin Buddhist classic.* Buddhist Study Center Press.

Silverman, K., & Kanarek, J. (2013) The scorpion and the frog: A false narrative of human nature. In *The Intellectual Standard, 2*(1), 6–9. https://digitalcommons.iwu.edu/tis/vol2/iss1/2

Sleeter, C. (2013). Inheriting footholds and cushions: Family legacies and institutional racism. *Counterpoints, 449,* 11–26. https://doi.org/10.2307/42982062

Steele, C. M. (2010). *Whistling Vivaldi: How stereotypes affect us and what we can do.* W. W. Norton.

Strode, M. (1903). Wind-wafted wild flowers. *The Open Court, 1903*(8), 489.

Tough, P. (2012). *How children succeed: Grit, curiosity, and the hidden power of character.* Houghton Mifflin Harcourt.

Wallace, C. (1997). Ten crack commandments [Song]. On *Life After Death.* Bad Boy Records.

Yosso, T. J. (2005). Whose culture has capital? A critical race theory discussion of community cultural wealth. *Race Ethnicity and Education, 8*(1), 69–91. https://doi.org/10.1080/1361332052000341006

Chapter 8

"By Us, for Us"

A Student Bridges Approach to Access and Retention
among Historically Underrepresented Populations

OLGA M. CORREA AND KELSEY RUIZ

*A note to our readers: The following chapter is not a complete depiction of
our voice or scholarly work alone.*

*Our chapter is for those who have experienced silence, exclusion, or
misrepresentation while pursuing postsecondary education. Our chapter is
dedicated to women of Color who faced systemic barriers to access and
navigate college, and to our community.*

This was created by us, for us.

Trends of access, retention, and success within public higher education are
severely impacted by persistent systemic disparities and inequitable K–12
policies and practices. Organizational leaders across varying sectors in the
United States have created precollege programs that offer supplemental
support to students of Color, low-income students, and first-generation
students, who often face the brunt of these realities and have thus been
historically underrepresented[1] in enrollment at colleges and universities
(Gandara, 2002; Welton & Martinez, 2014). Contributions from federal-
and state-granted programs, local community organizations, and postsecondary institutions provide underrepresented students with knowledge

and materials that are missing or insufficient in the K–12 trajectory to navigate the college application process and understand the differences between secondary and postsecondary education (Carpenter, 2019; Means et al., 2019; Perna, 2002; Welton & Martinez, 2014). Students are exposed to academic and career pathways, improving academic preparation, and financial aid resources to alleviate cost barriers. While this work is vital to improving upward mobility, the prevalent narrative in educational research tends to offer deficit-based portrayals of students of Color, low-income students, and first-generation students as vulnerable and at-risk because of limited social, educational, and cultural capital (Garcia & Guerra, 2004; Valenzuela, 1999; Villalpando & Solórzano, 2005). These are skewed perceptions and incomplete pictures that do not account for the systems of inequity sown into the fabric of our nation, actively working to exclude students from educational opportunities.

This chapter will introduce Student Bridges,[2] a student-led university agency created *by* students of Color, *for* students of Color, at a predominately white institution (PWI) in western Massachusetts. Inspired by firsthand experiences, Student Bridges staff and general members build a sense of comradery because of the hardships they face in preparation for the college application process and after gaining access to higher education spaces. Through a *critical* community engagement model, undergraduate students commit to identifying the sociohistorical factors that influence students' pathways and barriers to quality education, elevating asset-based approaches, and advocating for equitable policies and practices. Often, traditional community engagement models reinforce unequal power dynamics and provide temporary solutions to oppressive conditions (Candelario, 2018; Mitchell, 2008; Wade, 2001). Student Bridges' *critical* model allows for a communal classroom space, where students' cultures and upbringings are at the center, to enhance the likelihood of collective effort in creating and sustaining a learning community (hooks, 1994). Coupling students' analytical skills, academic disciplinary strengths, youth development skills, and their understanding of societal problems leads to implementing real solutions with and within the communities they are entering as members of the SB staff or students in a community engagement course.

Told from the perspective of Student Bridges staff, past and present, the narratives collected for this chapter will provide a nuanced view often undervalued or absent from educational discourse surrounding access to quality education. While we are honoring the work that SB has led since its founding in 2006, it is important to note that the authors are speaking from their perspectives as members of the agency during the 2019–2022 academic years. The authors emphasize the placement of the agency within the larger university structure and illustrate how agency administrators and student staff managed the unforeseen challenges of a pandemic and shift to remote learning. SB's goal is to acknowledge the complexities of navigating institutions of higher education as members of historically underrepresented communities, transform practice and policy, and contribute to the emerging body of literature related to college access and critical community engagement.

Creating a *Bridge* to College Access

The founding of the Student Bridges Agency transpired as a response to the worsening racial climate present at the University of Massachusetts (UMass) Amherst in the late 20th century. The Mill House Incident of 1970, the racial riot after Game 7 of the 1986 World Series, and the racially motivated attack on a resident assistant in 1992 sparked social unrest among the campuses' students of Color (Depalma, 1992; McGrath, 2020; World Series, 1986). While UMass Amherst was founded as a land-grant university with a mission to "provide teaching, research and public service to benefit people in Massachusetts, the nation, and the world," these events were a stark reminder of higher education's legacy of racial discrimination and disregard for inclusion and belonging for students of Color, first-generation college students, and low-income students (UMass Amherst, 2018, p. 1). Further, in 1996, university administrators decided to deemphasize race in the undergraduate admissions process, leading to a decline in first-year student enrollment rates among Black/African American, Latinx, Asian/Pacific Islander, and Native American students in the years that followed. This administrative decision consequently added to existing obstacles for students to earn admissions to any higher education institution. Students understood how systemic and institutional barriers limit access to tangible resources, such as higher-level courses in K–12, college-preparatory curriculum, and school counselor information that leads to eventual college enrollment (Welton & Martinez, 2014). Thus, a network of UMass students conducted interviews with students, faculty, and staff across campus to develop a plan for a student-to-student outreach program to provide direct resources and expand pathways to higher education for local communities. In particular, because university administrators were not putting much effort into addressing the inequities that were impacting communities of Color in the local communities of Holyoke and Springfield, UMass students were intentional about making their needs more visible. SB works collaboratively with local schools in Holyoke and Springfield because of the large population of students of Color, first-generation-to-college students, low-income students, and English-language learners attending (MDESE, 2022). The college-student-to-high-school-student approach created "bridges between UMass students and working-class communities" to develop and maintain mutually beneficial relationships (Student Bridges Agency, 2021). The Student Government Association (SGA) approved the proposal and provided $100,000 in funding for the Student Bridges Pilot Program.

UMass students established reciprocal relationships with local communities and engaged in policy evaluations and advocacy to effect long-term, systematic enhancement of outreach efforts for underrepresented students. After a successful pilot program, the SGA granted independent agency status to Student Bridges in September of 2006. At UMass, agencies are defined as permanent, co-curricular organizations, operating under the guidance and supervision of a full-time staff member or graduate student assistant, which provides services to UMass Amherst students, including but not limited to advocacy, activities, or media (UMass Amherst, 2020). As such, the agency became eligible to request annual funding from the Student Activities Trust Fund to cover staff payroll, campus and community event expenses, course material, and transportation to/from community partner sites. The founding mission of Student Bridges holds true today: "to increase college access and success for underrepresented students by building partnerships with local schools and community organizations, offering college awareness preparation and success activities, and advocating for enhanced institutional and public policies and practices" (Student Bridges Agency, 2021). Currently, the agency sits within the Advocacy, Inclusion, and Support Programs cluster of the Division of Student Affairs and Campus Life. SB's office is located in the Student Union Building and is known as a space where students can be in community with peers, engage in meaningful conversations about issues pertaining to educational equity and social justice, and learn about resources on campus. In an interview for the agency's web series video, an SB staff member reflected on the "overall vibe" of the office: "The SUB [Student Union Building] is always packed, so coming in here it's really nice to know there's always space for you. And then getting to interact with your friends or meet new people with similar stories to mine. I live all the way in [residence hall] so I don't see certain people often, but I get to see them here."

Within and beyond the walls of its office, SB's existence as a student-led agency stands as an impactful part of students of Color, first-generation, and low-income students' experience at a PWI where they are underrepresented among the undergraduate student population.

Learning with/within Communities

Providing opportunities to develop greater pedagogic, leadership, and critical thinking skills in an empowering environment is a complex goal. To attain this goal and further enhance learning opportunities with/within communities, SB began to offer multiple service-learning courses to engage undergraduate and graduate students as tutor mentors both in the classroom and within the community. Mitchell et al. (2012) define service-learning as a "pedagogical strategy that employs community service and reflection on service to support students in meeting academic learning goals and developing greater community and social responsibility" (p. 612). This approach is known to increase engagement, influence attitudes toward community service and social justice, help cultivate professional skills, and impact students' understanding of the structural causes of social problems (Becker & Paul, 2015). At UMass Amherst, the office of Civic Engagement and Service Learning (CESL) oversees the university's formal service-learning curriculum, offering individual credit-bearing courses and a certificate of completion. Of these courses, there are four courses taught by SB staff: Learning through Community Engagement, Advanced Community Service Learning, Peer Mentorship for College Success, and a Critical Reflection Seminar. To foster a classroom community where students are able to interrogate sources of power as they relate to educational equity and access, SB staff shifted to a critical communication engagement model utilizing asset-based approaches and critical frameworks.

FROM SERVICE-LEARNING TO *CRITICAL* COMMUNITY ENGAGEMENT

Wade (2001) and Mitchell (2008) describe how the outcomes-based goals of traditional service-learning can reinforce unequal power dynamics and provide temporary solutions that do not address oppressive conditions. This inspired SB staff to develop a *critical* community engagement model to bridge academic theory and pedagogical practice through critical reflection and asset-based approaches that counter dominant deficit-based perspectives of students of Color, low-income students, and first-generation students. Critical reflection is a "meaning-making process" that helps us articulate questions, confront bias, examine causality, contrast theory with practice, and identify systemic issues—all of which helps foster critical evaluation and knowledge transfer (Ash & Clayton, 2009, p. 42; Knight et al., 2004). Students in the class reflect individually for journal assignments and with each other during class discussions. Critical dialogue is beneficial for educators who want to approach their classes in a way that unveils oppression and allows students to humanize one another and challenge the prevailing ideology. This component of the curriculum was developed by director and faculty advisor Dr. Yedalis Ruíz Santana to create collaborations between the SB undergraduates, higher education administration graduate students, and Holyoke/Springfield high school students around college access.

Approaching community engagement with an asset-based approach is essential as it pertains to the college-going process. Scholars have spoken out against previous research blaming the families of students of Color for their child(ren) not being academically or socially prepared, not taking the application process seriously, and not encouraging child(ren) to pursue education away from home (Liou & Rojas, 2020; Villalpando & Solórzano, 2005). These examples of deficit thinking do not account for how systems of oppression exclude parents/guardians from gaining the social capital to properly support their students' academic pathways. Therefore, counternarratives, culturally relevant pedagogy, and asset-based approaches aid in discrediting these negative portrayals (Harper, 2010; Ladson-Billings,1995; Yosso, 2005; Welton & Martinez, 2014). A former undergraduate program coordinator emphasized, "The counter stories that are promoted and nurtured by spaces such as Student Bridges are personally important to me because of the harsh realities I was exposed to growing up as a Black man in Boston." Being part of a staff that validated his racial identity and working in an environment that fostered community was essential to feeling a sense of belonging at a PWI.

SB staff provide students the necessary tools and resources to supplement the knowledge that students and families carry as they navigate the college-going process and eventually earn their degree. Additionally, service-learning discourse is often tainted by a pedagogy of whiteness,[3] "strategies of instruction that consciously or unconsciously reinforce norms and privileges developed by, and for the benefit of, white people in the United States" (Mitchell et al., 2012, p. 613). The work of students of Color is often overshadowed or trivialized by service completed by white faculty and students. SB's model decentralizes whiteness and emphasizes a collaborative approach to college access by following hooks's (1994) ideology of a communal classroom to develop trust for long-term, authentic, and sustainable efforts with local schools and community organizations. A former undergraduate staff shared, "Community engagement led by people of Color is a more genuine experience that allows for better outcomes since people have similar backgrounds and can relate to the issues brought forth. It is difficult for white faculty and students to overcome this due to the fact that experiences differ tremendously, which takes away from the purpose of the community engagement." Their sentiments echo the ways in which Student Bridges staff and students are leading community engagement work because it is personal to them, and they understand how essential it is to lay pathways of success for future generations.

Figure 8.1. SB Access and Success model. *Source*: Created by the authors.

Figure 8.1 reflects the authors' visual interpretation of the SB Access and Success model: a collaborative structure, preparatory mentoring, access and retention programming, and policy advocacy. The following sections will detail how these pedagogical practices and guiding principles all function within asset-based approaches and critical community engagement to promote access and success among historically underrepresented students.

COLLABORATIVE STRUCTURE

SB staff are predominantly students of Color, low-income students, and first-generation students, and therefore are proximate to the pressing concerns of college access, retention, and success. The staff is composed of undergraduate and graduate students representing a range of academic disciplines and professional staff. While everyone holds their own position and responsibilities, the agency's organizational model functions in a way that promotes collaboration over hierarchy to move the mission forward. There are 14 undergraduate coordinators who focus on specific areas of programming, community partnerships, student recruitment, and campus and community outreach. The agency also includes one full-time director/faculty advisor who oversees the logistical and administrative aspects of the agency, and one graduate program coordinator that supports agency programming, advising, and course curriculum development. The director/faculty advisor and graduate program coordinator collaborate to identify campus and community-based resources for professional training and development to ensure the SB student staff are exposed to and have access to opportunities to improve upward mobility beyond their time with the agency. These efforts are aligned with a commitment to educational equity and social justice and can help to eliminate employment disparities in the community by ensuring student staff have resources, tools, and training to be competitive in the job market.

SB's organizational logistics are intentional to further student-led access because staff are trained to utilize a critical lens to identify and challenge educational inequities and humanize the college-going experience for themselves, their undergraduate peers, and high school students. SB students acknowledge the historical context necessary to challenge dominant narratives and ideas about marginalized communities, decentering the white perspective, and reshaping how members of the communities talk about themselves to highlight the strengths they carry with them to/through college and beyond. Given the legacy of white supremacy and anti-Blackness across higher education, staff constantly assert the role of the agency to challenge any threats that would limit campus and community outreach to support students. A 2018 SB applicant shared, "College accessibility is an issue that is important to me. I identify strongly with how SB connects underrepresented students with resources, especially for high school students who do not have access to things students in wealthy suburbs have"; this student observed the care put forward by Student Bridges during events and community engagement sessions with high school students. Additionally, undergraduate SB staff facilitate the hiring process for undergraduate, graduate, and professional staff positions. This framework emphasizes a student-centered approach to dismiss power relations that may stifle student voices and lived experience in traditional hiring practices.

PREPARATORY MENTORING

SB's critical community engagement model offers different levels of college-preparatory mentoring between undergraduate, graduate, and high school students who are underrepresented in higher education. By building trusting and sustainable social networks, students are more likely to fulfill their academic and career goals because encouragement promotes higher aspirations and retention (Scisney-Matlock & Matlock, 2001). Tierney and Garcia (2014) expand upon the importance of social support services, including mentoring programs, because they provide personalized attention and serve as a safe space where students can connect with and learn from peers who share common backgrounds and experiences about how to navigate the institution and college life. UMass students who participate in the Learning through Community Engagement (SRVCLRNG 293) and Advanced Community Service Learning (SRVCLRNG 393) courses spend each semester building rapport with each other through check-in questions, discussion of writing prompts, adding music to a class playlist, and sharing general updates about their day. These pedagogical practices are central to SB's mission because students become critical of the status quo and ultimately challenge unjust structures and oppressive institutional operations (Marullo, 1999; Mitchell, 2008; Reed-Bouley et al., 2015). The number of topics that support our examination of how historical and social structures create systems of inequality for historically underrepresented students are daunting. Through readings about diversity and social justice (Adams & Bell, 2016), abolitionist teaching (Love, 2019), and the Latinization of

US schools (Irizarry, 2011), students and the teaching team engage in critical dialogue about how oppressive systems were designed and continue to transpire over the years via policies and practices that perpetuate educational inequality. Establishing a foundational sense of community thus supports our ongoing efforts. Additionally, the classroom structure is nonhierarchical; the director/faculty advisor and the undergraduate and graduate students teach and learn from each other, critically engage and reflect on issues of college access and success, while simultaneously reflecting on and assessing personal privileges and accepting a continuing responsibility for professional and personal development.

SB's pedagogical practices are mirrored during after-school programming with middle and high school students made possible by long-standing relationships with school administrators, school counselors, teachers, and community organizations. The after-school program with a local high school was an intentional initiative developed by Dr. Chrystal George Mwangi and Dr. Yedalis Ruíz Santana via the College Access Program (UCAP). As discussed by Arce and Carpenter in chapter 2 in this volume, UCAP was implemented in a unique way to lead to approaches that were intentional in acknowledging and resisting the ways in which structural inequities influence educational pathways for Students of Color. SB's efforts formed a sort of continuum of mentorship as high school students participating in UCAP engage with undergraduate and graduate students from UMass through culturally relevant college-readiness programming and conversations surrounding academic and career goals. SB staff plan lessons and activities collectively to demystify the college application process and college life via activities about decision-making factors when applying to various institutions, preparing to talk to parents/guardians about the location of certain schools, and about the overwhelming discussion of associated costs to earn a degree. These conversations look different for students of Color, low-income students, and first-generation students because of cultural upbringings. Instead of being looked down on, asset-based approaches such as Yosso's (2005) community cultural wealth (see chapter 1 in this volume for a description) guide SB staff in highlighting the strengths students bring and how to elevate them when talking to family members to be better prepared for the college process. During one discussion about the "superpowers" students of Color each carry, one high school student was shocked to think that being bilingual was an asset because "our teachers usually tell us not to speak Spanish or they look at us funny." We were able to alter the way the student thought about their culture by highlighting how adding the ability to speak, write, and read in a second language onto their college applications can make them stand out as an applicant.

Preparatory mentorship promotes access, retention, and success because many of the students who participate with our program identify as students of Color, low-income students, and will be the first in their families to pursue a college degree. Many of the schools SB works with are also underfunded, influencing the available resources and overall educational opportunities available to students. Students who participate in the after-school program gain secondhand knowledge of college life and enhance skills to reach their own academic and career goals (McCombs et al., 2017). While college preparation is often placed in the hands of school counselors, underfunded schools struggle with financial barriers and high turnover, limiting the number of counselors available to mentor students regarding college and there is not enough time to provide extensive support to each student and their families (Avery et al., 2014; Huang et al., 2008). SB's connection to students, and ability to meet students where they are, becomes vital to their development and to forming meaningful connections they would otherwise not be exposed to while figuring out their plans for life after school. Moreover, an undergraduate student stressed the significance of mentorship for students of Color in particular: "I believe that a mentor or role model that resembles an individual's identities, struggles, and cultures can alter and improve the internalized thinking of the self and future possibilities." This level of social support becomes a contributing factor in a student's decision to attend college because the relationships are formed without power dynamics and students find commonality with Student Bridges staff and students.

Access and Retention Programming

Student Bridges staff plan and implement comprehensive initiatives and programming for the campus community to promote access and retention via critical dialogue among students, administrators, and faculty. Many predominantly white institutions (PWIs) encounter issues in retaining and graduating students of Color, emphasizing the need for events that are inclusive and shine a light on diverse cultures and upbringings (McClain & Perry, 2017). SB's events are aligned with asset-based approaches as we center the experiences of students of Color, low-income students, and first-generation students, all while leading engaging and inclusive programs.

These opportunities promote retention among UMass students because they feel inspired to be in community with students like themselves, while also giving back to local communities to provide the type of preparatory support they did not have themselves. A former retention mentorship coordinator on the staff shared:

> I transferred here [UMass Amherst] because I wasn't really connected to my last institution. And to be honest, things weren't going so great here either but my friend told me about the [Club and Agency Fair] and I walked up to the Student Bridges table to learn more. I had volunteered at the Boys and Girls Club before so I thought I'd have some experience working with younger students and I ended up applying for the position I have now. So now I'm co-teaching a class about mentorship and campus resources which is teaching me a lot and helping me help other students who may be lost like I was when I first transferred. (Personal Communication, 2021)

Their sentiments are an example of how many students become involved with SB after participating in a campus event or taking one of the community engagement courses. Events are facilitated by the Community Outreach and College Awareness (COCA) coordinator, an area focused on programs that provide local schools and community-based organizations college awareness and preparation workshops as well as unique tours of the UMass campus. A variety of campus events are organized, including a career-readiness series, an SB alumni panel, a culturally responsive movie night, and an I'm So College! community outreach event. The community engagement Peer Mentorship for College Success course influences retention as undergraduate students are paired and tasked with holding each other accountable toward academic and social goals throughout the semester. One undergraduate student in the course reflected about their own experience with access to educational opportunities writing:

> As a young Black college student, there are not a lot of resources you can turn to unless you do the research which can be a lot with having to do homework or deal with family business, so it's easy to just give up. This class is teaching me how to be more prepared and how to prepare future students like me to know where to go and how to get there because college is a whole new world from high school especially for students like us.

Their thoughts echo SB's mission to encourage students to engage in problem-solving techniques and resource acquisition to seek the tools to succeed. The university offers many resources across campus, but it can often feel overwhelming for students who are the first in their family to attend college to seek out help. Ladson-Billings (1995) and Paris and Alim (2017) also contend that these efforts can maximize students' potential by coupling material resources with culturally relevant and sustaining approaches that incorporate the existing cultural capital of students of Color. The SB staff works together to ensure that their line of events, programming, and overall community engagement sufficiently reflect students' identities.

POLICY ADVOCACY

Student Bridges collaborates with campus stakeholders and registered student organizations (RSOs) to learn how to advocate for policies and practices that support college access and success for students of Color through workshops and special programs. In turn, these efforts inform institutional policies and practices that may impact demographic shifts related to enrollment, retention, and success. These efforts include supporting students who have issues with affordability, academic preparation, social capital, parental support, transportation, child care, and learning accommodations. SB staff develop programming and social media content that advocates for policies and practices to improve existing campus resources. Advocating for policies related to access and equity in higher education benefits people of all backgrounds, especially underrepresented communities and those silenced or threatened by an increasingly divisive geopolitical climate (Student Bridges Agency, 2021). Collaborating with other advocacy bodies and coalitions, including the Student Government Association and the Center for Educational Policy and Administration is central to SB's mission. The Policy Advocacy Coordinator attends their general body meetings to stay up to date with local and state-level policy and upcoming campus and community campaigns. Relaying these updates to the SB staff and general SB community encourages students of Color to make their voices heard in agreement or against policies that influence their experience as students.

SB aims to expand its policy and advocacy beyond students on campus to include local communities. In December 2019, SB staff learned about a local high school's proposed new policy requiring school administrators to conduct regular searches of students' belongings. An increase in surveillance measures paradoxically fosters hostile environments that may lead to more disorder, dysfunction, and may contribute to the school-to-prison pipeline (Nance, 2017). Since this local high school served predominately underrepresented students, SB staff were prompted to attend an open forum to support the high school students due to the inherent bias of such policies. For high school students to see SB undergraduate and graduate staff in attendance was a meaningful reminder of the commitment to community.

Crisis and Unprecedented Challenges

Coming together to address the impact of the COVID-19 pandemic is a prime illustration of SB's commitment to campus and community engagement. SB staff members were individually affected by the shift to remote learning, sudden moves off campus, and health emergencies with family members. Nonetheless, the agency continued to offer programming through virtual platforms and work alongside local communities, all while addressing heightened educational disparities and financial constraints. Years of developing intentional relationships allowed SB to gain extensive understanding about the cultural context of local communities. These relationships, as well as the presence of staff members who were close to the communities that were impacted, aided in the transition to remote learning. SB was able to meet the needs of the community and provide spaces of support because staff were closely linked to the needs of the communities.

MARCH 2020

The world shifted significantly with the abrupt transition to remote living and learning due to the COVID-19 pandemic. Burch and Jacobs (2021) described how the onset of the pandemic raised Americans' levels of anxiety because of a variety of health inequalities, rising financial worries, disruptions in education, and ongoing police brutality. However, before the pandemic, communities of Color were already facing these difficulties at disproportionate rates. Notably, George Floyd's death at the hands of prejudiced law enforcement marked the beginning of what many white Americans recognize as a public health issue: institutional racism (Roberts,

2021). Student Bridges remained committed to holding space; in a social media message, staff reminded students that SB is a home for support in navigating the emotionally taxing events that stem from systemic issues.

The likelihood of residing in densely populated areas around the country that were affected by COVID-19 was considerably increased among Black/African American and Latinx communities (Ramprasad et al., 2022). Moreover, Smith and Reeves (2020) found that Black, Hispanic, and Asian students were more likely than white students to live in a remote-only school district. Remote instruction made learning more difficult for students of Color, considering limited access to a personal computer or reliable wi-fi in their homes (Hickman, 2021). As the pandemic progressed, the challenges involved with participating in remote learning platforms contributed to students' inability to apply to college. The National Student Clearinghouse indicated that in spring 2021 the number of students applying for undergraduate admission dropped to 4.9% (Camera, 2021). However, for students of Color and low-income students, the likelihood of applying to college decreased more significantly (Camera, 2021). The pandemic demonstrates how educational paths for communities of Color were even more adversely affected, necessitating the development of new outreach strategies and engagement initiatives to meet students where they were. Due to the heightened racial and educational disparities, Student Bridges' priority was to ensure that staff could continue facilitating community partnerships and engagement, without it being an added burden to our UMass and local high school students. The staff focused on advocating for continued staff employment and creating an interactive curriculum for our virtual learning space.

ADVOCATING FOR STUDENT EMPLOYMENT

The onset of the pandemic also forced an economic shutdown, leading to students being displaced from their campus housing and forcing UMass administrators to reassess funding availability due to the expected decreases in student enrollment. All SGA-funded organizations were asked to assess their budgets and provide rationale for continuing to use their payroll funds for the remainder of the semester, a practice that continued into the 2020–2021 academic year. In a detailed email, the SGA secretary of finance asked agency directors to include:

- The names of employees on agency payroll who are able to continue to do work relevant to the mission and goals of the agency remotely;

- Responsibilities & Hourly allocations;

- A list of students who have chosen not to work. (Email Communication, March 2020)

The assumption was that only essential staff who had work to do in-person should stay employed. The director and faculty advisor at the time led the development of an innovative plan to continue meeting the needs of campus and local high school students through a virtual platform. The staff successfully secured SB's Student Affairs Trust Fund (SATF) balance to continue paying undergraduate staff for remote community engagement, office hours, lunch discussions on social media platforms, and overall virtual support to connect students with campus resources. SB mobilized efforts to ensure UMass students who needed to stay on campus from March 2020 through May 2020 were granted access to residence halls, connected with the Dean of Students Office and Student Legal Services for rent assistance, and most of all, continued to provide high school students a stable after-school program despite the surrounding uncertainty.

VIRTUAL COMMUNITY ENGAGEMENT

During a time of community social isolation and grief, agency staff successfully continued programming, coursework, and community engagement initiatives through a virtual platform to hold space for students and ensure a sense of community throughout the difficult circumstances. Shifting the community engagement component to a remote platform was essential because many after-school programs were forced to shut down due to safety protocols and overall uncertainty on the status of COVID-19. Despite SB's efforts, the remote world was overwhelming for many students, considering the virtual classroom was the first time students had their classmates and teachers *inside* of their homes. High school students entered SB's virtual after-school program after a day of remote learning where teachers expected high levels of engagement, forced students to have their cameras on or risk losing participation credit, and discouraged background interruptions. A myriad of op-ed authors uncovered that as Black students shifted from the classroom to online learning, harsher disciplinary measures that had been carried out against them at school followed them home (Cohen, 2020; Collins, 2021).

Unsurprisingly, students joined our sessions hesitantly because of limited privacy; their siblings were playing or doing homework in the same room or parents/guardians were working from home in the background. As one 11th grade student noted, "My teacher got upset with me because my mother was cleaning in the background, which she said was distracting to other students." She explained that even after staying on Zoom the remainder of the class time, she did not receive credit for the day. Students' narratives about their negative experiences further influenced our approach to virtual learning. In our SB courses and after-school program, we expressed to our high school students that they were not required to turn on their cameras, but of course encouraged them to have them on if they felt comfortable. At first many students had their cameras turned off, and after developing trust with our SB staff and undergraduate students, the students gradually put their cameras on to participate. Because the homes and lives of their peers and educators were similar to their own, students discovered that they felt safe in our SB courses and, in many cases, found community.

As access barriers to higher education grew, Student Bridges assisted students navigating college applications and exploring college options. For many students, it was difficult to see themselves going to college because there was a lack of educational, emotional, and financial support provided to them during COVID-19. The SB staff and the UMass undergraduate and graduate students who were enrolled in the service-learning courses also received the same amount of support from SB, as it was a challenging transition for them to apply to graduate school or full-time employment during a time of uncertainty. SB's response to the COVID-19 outbreak heightened the agency's commitment to the community.

Student Bridges was able to manage outreach efforts and stay engaged while those from advantaged backgrounds had the resources to tackle problems that affected college access in this pandemic context. Connecting students and families to resources during COVID-19 was a new experience for everyone, yet Student Bridges staff stayed true to the principles of mentorship, community outreach, advocacy, and retention through all initiatives. Students at UMass Amherst and in local high schools remained aware of our mission and developed a sense of commitment to making a difference through their involvement. Despite in-person interaction improving with the COVID-19 pandemic over time, the agency continued to offer both in-person and virtual modalities because SB staff noticed that providing students with virtual platforms for college preparation expands access to information and college preparation. Our experiences during the onset of COVID-19 are an illustration of the several occasions we brainstormed, utilizing the potential and possibilities of each difficulty our students and the agency met to ensure we expanded access to higher education.

Closing Thoughts

Telling the story of the Student Bridges Agency, from its founding to the present day, is the first step in sharing an approach to college access facilitated *by* students of Color *for* students of Color. Education scholar Ladson-Billings (1998) reminds us that, "historically, storytelling has been a kind of medicine to heal the wounds of pain caused by racial oppression" (p. 14). Sharing the story of Student Bridges is vital in the fight for educational equity because we are showing the world, *starting with our readers*, that though it is challenging to go against the systemic racism permeating higher education, there are spaces where students with marginalized identities are coming together for comfort and support and to address these policies and practices collectively (Agyei, 2020). Approaching our work critically comes with providing our students with the context on how to push back from dominant narratives and ideas on the communities we are a part of, decentering the narrative from the white perspective and instead shaping the ways in which we speak about ourselves and community to be held in an asset-based lens.

Major disruptions have shaken communities in the past, at times disproportionately impacting populations with limited access to resources. Educators and college access practitioners can learn from Student Bridges' response to the COVID-19 pandemic and how it reflects a larger life cycle. Even though remote college access was not the sole plan for SB prior to the COVID-19 pandemic, staff took advantage of the opportunity to connect and expand college resources for students because we saw how providing students with options to be a part of SB virtually and in-person was successful. The pandemic has taught SB staff to be innovative to meet the needs of students while upholding the SB model of having students *come as they are*. SB encourages students to come as they are, to enter the space authentically and to take up space and share their narratives without being pressured to participate in dialogue, particularly if they are not in the right emotional or mental state to do so. Whether a student is having a good or terrible day, SB accepts everyone who enters in any capacity or circumstances.

In many ways, due to systemic racism, our students and staff have been doing the work to dismantle a system that was not designed for communities of Color. A significant portion of the problem at hand stems from the fact that many of us, including the authors of this chapter, struggled in college to earn a college degree, not because we lacked intelligence but because we entered into an elitist space that was intended for a different group of people. However, after making it into higher education, we have dedicated ourselves to ensure that, ideally, the following generations struggle *a little less*. "A difficult concept to consider . . . is the acceptance of struggle," shared one of our undergraduate students in a final paper reflection. He continued, "It is pretty obvious how deeply ingrained racism and discrimination are in our society. Our country was literally built on it. So, the work to dismantle and reconfigure our country would require a great deal of time and struggle to rework everything that has made it what it is." At Student Bridges, we push back and resist existing systems of oppression to be a figure of representation and mentor for students who, like ourselves, did not have anyone to show them the way to access and navigate higher education. This chapter calls on educators and practitioners to think critically about why they engage in college access work with communities of Color and to ensure that their model of programming and curriculum centers students of Color as experts of their own lived realities.

Critical Reflection

1. How would a student-led agency that is dedicated to increasing college access, retention, and success function on your campus? What is beneficial from student/community-led and informed practices?

2. What makes critical community engagement different from traditional service-learning models? How would a critical approach promote college access, retention, and success among historically underrepresented students in your setting?

3. How can educators in your setting elevate students' race, ethnicity, and/or socioeconomic status as an asset throughout the college application process? How can these lessons play out in the students' educational trajectory (retention and success)?

4. What are your intentions for facilitating critical community engagement alongside youth/communities of Color at your institution and with/within local communities?

Notes

1. The authors utilize the term *historically underrepresented students* in alignment with the Student Bridges' goal of using the term to account for the intersectional experiences of students who have been impacted by disparities and other barriers that impeded their access to resources, quality education, and thus access to higher education. Students who have been historically underrepresented in higher education are often students of Color, low-income students, LGBTQIA students, and Dreamers/DACA students. The authors will use *students of Color* when appropriate and *historically underrepresented* to emphasize how systemic barriers limit postsecondary enrollment of the student populations described in this chapter.

2. Throughout the chapter, the authors refer to Student Bridges, as such, as "SB" or "the agency."

3. Whiteness is a racial discourse, whereas the category *white people* represents a socially constructed identity, usually based on skin color. Whiteness is not a culture but a social concept (Leonardo, 2009, pp. 169–170).

References

Adams, M., & Bell, L. A. (Eds.) (2016). *Teaching for diversity and social justice: A sourcebook* (3rd ed.). Routledge.

Agyei, A. (2020). A dollar and a dream: Creating culturally responsive structures of support for Black students [Unpublished master's thesis, University of Massachusetts Amherst].

Ash, S. L., & Clayton, P. H. (2009). Generating, deepening, and documenting learning: The power of critical reflection in applied learning. *Journal of Applied Learning in Higher Education, 1,* 25–48. https://scholarworks. iupui.edu/bitstream/handle/1805/4579/ash-2009-generating.pdf?sequence= 1&isAllowed=y

Avery, C., Howell, J. S., & Page, L. (2014). *A review of the role of college counseling, coaching, and mentoring on students' postsecondary outcomes: Research brief.* College Board. https://eric.ed.gov/?id=ED556468

Becker, S., & Paul, C. (2015). "It didn't seem like race mattered": Exploring the implications of service-learning pedagogy for reproducing or challenging color-blind racism. *Teaching Sociology, 43*(3), 184–200. https://doi.org/10.1177/0092055X15587987

Burch, A. E., & Jacobs, M. (2021). COVID-19, police violence, and educational disruption: The differential experience of anxiety for racial and ethnic households. *Journal of Racial and Ethnic Health Disparities, 9*(6), 2533–2550. https://doi.org/10.1007/s40615-021-01188-0

Camera, L. (2021, July 19). *Financial aid applications drop among 2021 high school graduates.* Retrieved May 19, 2022, from: https://www.usnews.com/news/education-news/articles/2021-07-19/financial-aid-applications-drop-among-2021-high-school-graduates

Candelario, G. E. B. (2018). Saber es poder: Teaching and learning about social inequality in a New England Latin@ community. In M. Castañeda & J. Krupczynski (Eds.), *Civic engagement in diverse Latinx communities: Learning from social justice partnerships in action* (pp. 179–200). Peter Lang.

Carpenter, A. J. (2019). *Bridging the gap: Cultural wealth and college transitions for Upward Bound students.* [Doctoral dissertation, University of Massachusetts Amherst]. https://doi.org/10.7275/rmpz-ra19

Cohen, J. S. (July, 2020). *A teenager didn't do her online schoolwork. So a judge sent her to juvenile detention.* ProPublica. https://www.propublica.org/article/a-teenager-didnt-do-her-online-schoolwork-so-a-judge-sent-her-to-juvenile-detention

Collins, C. (2021). *It was all about control.* Learning for Justice. https://www.learningforjustice.org/magazine/spring-2021/it-was-always-about-control

Depalma, A. (1992, October 18). Massachusetts campus is torn by racial strife. *New York Times.* Retrieved from: https://www.nytimes.com/1992/10/18/us/massachusetts-campus-is-torn-by-racial-strife.html

Gandara, P. (2002). Meeting common goals: Linking K–12 and college interventions. In W. G. Tierney & L. S. Hagedorn (Eds.), *Increasing access to college: Extending possibilities for all students.* State University of New York Press.

Garcia, S. B., & Guerra, P. L. (2004). Deconstructing deficit thinking: Working with educators to create more equitable learning environments. *Education and Urban Society, 36*(2), 150–168. https://doi.org/10.1177/0013124503261322

Harper, S. R. (2010). An anti-deficit achievement framework for research on students of color in STEM. *New Directions for Institutional Research, 148,* 63–74. https://doi.org/10.1002/ir.362

Hickman, L. (2021, July 14). *Opinion: Why Black families have found some benefits in distance learning.* The Hechinger Report. Retrieved May 19, 2022, from: https://hechingerreport.org/opinion-why-black-families-have-found-some-benefits-in-distance-learning/

hooks, b. (1994). *Teaching to transgress education as the practice of freedom.* Routledge.

Huang, D., Leon, S., La Torre, D., & Mostafavi, S. (2008). *Examining the relationship between LA's BEST program attendance and academic achievement of LA's BEST students.* (CRESST Report No. 749). National Center for Research on Evaluation, Standards, and Student Testing.

Irizarry, J.G. (2011). *The Latinization of U.S. schools: Successful teaching and learning in shifting cultural contexts.* Paradigm.

Knight, M. G., Norton, N. E., Bentley, C. C., & Dixon, I. R. (2004). The power of Black and Latina/o counterstories: Urban families and college-going processes. *Anthropology & Education Quarterly, 35*(1), 99–120. https://doi.org/10.1525/aeq.2004.35.1.99

Ladson-Billings, G. (1995). Toward a theory of culturally relevant pedagogy. *American Educational Research Journal, 32*(3), 465–491. https://doi.org/10.3102/00028312032003465

Ladson-Billings, G. (1998). Just what is critical race theory and what's it doing in a nice field like education? *International Journal of Qualitative Studies in Education, 11*(1), 7–24. https://doi.org/10.1080/095183998236863

Leonardo, Z. (2009). *Race, whiteness, and education.* Routledge.

Liou, D. D., & Rojas, L. (2020). The significance of the racial contract in teachers' college expectancies for students of Color. *Race Ethnicity and Education, 23*(5), 712–731. https://doi.org/10.1080/13613324.2018.1511529

Love, B. (2019) *We want to do more than survive: Abolitionist teaching and the pursuit of educational freedom.* Beacon Press.

Marullo, S. (1999). Sociology's essential role: Promoting critical analysis in service-learning. In J. Ostrow, G. Hesser, & S. Enos (Eds.), *Cultivating the sociological imagination concepts and models for service-learning in sociology.* American Association of Higher Education.

Massachusetts Department of Elementary and Secondary Education. (2022). School and district profiles. https://profiles.doe.mass.edu/general/general.aspx?orgtypecode=6&orgcode=02810510

McClain, K. S., & Perry, A. (2017). Where did they go: Retention rates for students of Color at predominantly white institutions. *College Student Affairs Leadership, 4*(1), article 3.

McCombs, J. S, Whitaker, A. A, & Yoo, P. Y. (2017). *The value of out-of-school time programs.* RAND Corporation. https://doi.org/10.7249/PE267

McGrath, C. (2020, February 7). The new Africa house: Yesterday, today and tomorrow. *Massachusetts Daily Collegian.* https://dailycollegian.com/2021/02/the-new-africa-house-yesterday-today-and-tomorrow/

Means, D. R., Hudson, T. D., & Tish, E. (2019). A snapshot of college access and inequity: Using photography to illuminate the pathways to higher education for underserved youth. *High School Journal, 102*(2), 139–158. doi:10.1353/hsj.2019.0003.

Mitchell, T. D. (2008). Traditional vs. critical service-learning: Engaging the literature to differentiate two models. *Michigan Journal of Community Service Learning, 14*(2), 50–65.

Mitchell, T. D., Donahue, D. M., & Young-Law, C. (2012). Service learning as a pedagogy of whiteness. *Equity & Excellence in Education, 45*(4), 612–629. https://doi.org/10.1080/10665684.2012.715534

Nance, J. (2017). Student surveillance, racial inequalities, and implicit racial bias. *Emory Law Journal, 66,* 765–837. https://scholarship.law.ufl.edu/cgi/viewcontent.cgi?article=1793&context=facultypub

Paris, D., & Alim, H. S. (2017). *Culturally sustaining pedagogies: Teaching and learning for justice in a changing world.* Teachers College Press.

Perna, L. W. (2002). Pre-college outreach programs: Characteristics of programs serving historically underrepresented groups of students. *Journal of College Student Development, 43*(1), 64–83.

Ramprasad, A., Qureshi, F., Lee, B. R., & Jones, B. L. (2022). The relationship between structural racism and COVID-19 related health disparities across 10 metropolitan cities in the United States. *Journal of the National Medical Association, 114*(3), 265–273. https://doi.org/10.1016/j.jnma.2022.01.008

Reed-Bouley, J., & Kyle, E. (2015). Challenging racism and white privilege in undergraduate theology contexts: Teaching and learning strategies for maximizing the promise of community service-learning. *Teaching Theology & Religion, 18*(1), 20–36. https://doi.org/10.1111/teth.12260

Roberts, J. (2021, June 9). *Pandemics and protests: America has experienced racism like this before.* Brookings. https://www.brookings.edu/blog/how-we-rise/2021/06/09/pandemics-and-protests-america-has-experienced-racism-like-this-before/

Tierney, W. G., & Garcia, L. D. (2014, October). *Getting in: Increasing access to college via mentoring. Findings from 10 years of a high school mentoring program.* Pullias Center for Higher Education, University of Southern California. https://files.eric.ed.gov/fulltext/ED559562.pdf

Scisney-Matlock, M., & Matlock, J. (2001). Promoting understanding of diversity through mentoring undergraduate students. *New Directions for Teaching and Learning, 2001*(85), 75–84. https://doi.org/10.1002/tl.8

Smith, E., & Reeves, R. V. (2020, September 23). *Students of color most likely to be learning online: Districts must work even harder on race equity.* Brookings. Retrieved May 18, 2022, from: https://www.brookings.edu/blog/how-we-rise/2020/09/23/students-of-color-most-likely-to-be-learning-online-districts-must-work-even-harder-on-race-equity/

Student Bridges Agency. (2021). *Student bridges access & success.* https://student-bridgesagency.org/

University of Massachusetts Amherst. (2018). *NEASC accreditation self-study. Standard one: Mission and purpose.* Retrieved from: https://www.umass.edu/archive-planning/sites/default/files/Standard-1-Mission-and-Purposes.pdf

University of Massachusetts Amherst. (2020, December 19). *Agencies.* Retrieved May 26, 2022, from: https://www.umass.edu/sga/agencies/

Valenzuela, A. (1999). *Subtractive schooling: Issues of caring in education of US-Mexican youth.* SUNY Press.

Villalpando, O., & Solórzano, D. G. (2005). The role of culture in college preparation programs: A review of the research literature. In W. G. Tierney, Z. B. Corwin, & J. E. Colyar (Eds.), *Preparing for college: Nine elements of effective outreach* (pp. 13–28). State University of New York Press.

Wade, R. (2001). *And justice for all: Community service-learning for social justice* (Issue Paper for Service-Learning and Community Service). Education Commission of the States.

Welton, A. D., & Martinez, M. A. (2014). Coloring the college pathway: A more culturally responsive approach to college readiness and access for students of color in secondary schools. *Urban Review, 46,* 197–223. https://doi.org/10.1007/s11256-013-0252-7

World Series touches off racial clashes. (1986, February). *Harvard Crimson.* Retrieved from: https://www.thecrimson.com/article/1986/11/15/world-series-touches-off-racial-clashes/

Yosso, T. J. (2005). Whose culture has capital? A critical race theory discussion of community cultural wealth. *Race Ethnicity and Education, 8*(1), 69–91. https://doi.org/10.1080/1361332052000341006

Part III

Culture- and Family-Oriented Framings

"I Am from My Community"

BY A COLLECTIVE OF COLLEGE ASPIRANTS[1]

I am from loud talking and galaxy phones.
I am from apartment buildings and loud horns.
I am from hearing my mom hitting the pot with the spoon
    when cooking rice,
I am from always having dinner on holidays.

I am from "be careful who you be with . . ."
and the first time I started dribbling a basketball

I am from thanksgiving and cooking, from Carlos, Jessica,
    Maria, Jacob, and Taneka.
I am from "I love you's" and music playing.

I am from "go to college and make us proud because we
    couldn't do it."

I am from Puerto Rico, Jamaica, New York, Holyoke and Santo
    Domingo.
I am from my grandmom always caring for me.

I am from loud television and cellphones.

I am from "que Dios te bendiga,"
and "you have to work for what you want and need."

I am from the buildings, the free but controlled. I am from
    the concrete.
From smiles on the beaches and playing in the park.

I am from the cold where my people survive day by day.
I am from the talented and the brave and "love more than you
    hate, give more than you take."

I am from this Black and Brown community, and I will fight
    to make it better for everyone!

Note

1. A collective of excerpts from individual poems written by high school students of Color that the co-editors worked with weaved together as a reflection of their shared learning community, family practices, and cultures. The poems were inspired by the "I am from" poem by George Ella *Lyon*.

Chapter 9

College Choice as *Conocimiento*

Disentangling the Reflective and Cyclical Postsecondary Pathways of Latina/o/x Students

NANCY ACEVEDO

In this chapter, I intertwine my *testimonio* about my college-going experiences as they intertwine with my development of the college-*conocimiento* framework (Acevedo-Gil, 2017). A *testimonio* methodology serves to document the experiences of oppressed groups and challenge injustices (Booker, 2002). Cruz (2006) explains that "what testimonio does best is to connect with a reader or an audience, positioning a reader or an audience for self-reflection" (p. 31). While Cruz (2006) notes the need for the audience to connect with the *testimonio* on some level, it does not always occur, and she notes that "rejection of this positioning might come from a reader's or an audience's inability to feel solidarity with the subject" (p. 31). I begin with my *testimonio* as an undergraduate student, before I could have imagined pursuing a PhD and developing a conceptual framework. I then continue the chapter by providing a broader understanding of Latina/o/x college choice literature. I continue by summarizing the college-*conocimiento* framework that resulted from my dissertation research and integrating my college choice *testimonio* throughout the seven stages. I then summarize literature that has been guided by the college-*conocimiento* framework and conclude with questions for readers to reflect on when thinking about college access for communities of Color.

Fostering College Choices as a
First-Generation Chicana Student

In my undergraduate years, I would take both education and Chicano studies courses where the emphasis was on the importance of first-generation students having access to "cultural capital" and information to improve college-going rates for Latina/o/x students. Therefore, when I became a TRIO college advisor for an underresourced high school in East Oakland, I ensured that all students enrolled in the program had access not only to information but also to individualized college advising and guidance with the college application process. I was motivated because I knew I had the best intentions for students and would advocate for them with teachers and college admission officers. I felt empowered as I sat in my cubicle and carried around my copy of Gloria Anzaldúa's (1989) Borderlands to read for class as I waited for students to show up for our individual meetings. By the end of the year, I was certain that I had addressed the "information gap" discussed in my courses because so many of the students had accepted admission offers from four-year colleges.

However, when it was time for me to follow-up and lookup the Student Clearinghouse enrollment data for each participant, I was surprised to see that students who were admitted to 4-year colleges were either enrolled in community college or not at all. When I shared my disbelief with my supervisor, she shared, "That happens every year." I could not understand what had occurred but I spent my years as a master's student attempting to learn more about the issue through qualitative data. When applying for PhD programs, I met with Dr. Danny Solórzano[1] and shared my master's thesis topic with him—Latina/o/x students earning admission to 4-year colleges but not enrolling. He was surprised and impressed that I had selected such an innovative topic. Shortly after that summer, I learned about the emerging concept of "summer melt" (Arnold et al., 2009) and was in disbelief that my master's thesis was so timely.

As impressive as my research topic was to Dr. Solórzano, it was never approved by Graduate Studies at San Jose State University. I was told there were grammatical and syntax mistakes, such as split infinitives. I was asked to hire a professional editor to address the concerns. *Given my low-income background and first-generation college student status, I had no idea where to begin with that process. I did not understand how I was supposed to afford an editor and ask that they fix my mistakes in only a couple of weeks. Thankfully, I had taken an additional course, just for fun, which meant that I could still graduate with the master's degree in time to begin my PhD coursework.*

During my first quarter at UCLA, I made sure to visit the graduate student writing center almost weekly to understand what I was doing wrong in my writing. I learned about split infinitives. I wondered why no one had ever explained to me my writing shortfalls? Thankfully, on day 1 of her class, Dr. Pat McDonough taught the need to establish arguments with evidence and warrant. Then, in his writing course, Dr. Mike Rose continued to develop my experience as a writer; I learned that I had to slow down and edit my work, I had to explain to the reader the connections that, to me, seemed like common sense and self-explanatory. These moments along my journey as a first-generation Chicana student from a low-income background contributed to my abilities to not only conduct research but also to analyze and write the findings, which resulted in my developing the college-conocimiento framework (Acevedo-Gil, 2017) from my dissertation.

Latina/o/x College Access and College Choice

With over 62 million individuals, Latina/o/x are the largest nonwhite ethnic/racial group in the United States and represent 19% of the US population (US Census, 2023). Moreover, Latina/o/x students represent one in four elementary school students nationwide (Fabina et al., 2023). Despite experiencing inequitable access to educational resources, Latina/o/x students maintain college aspirations (Conchas & Acevedo, 2020).

The general narrative in the field of education is that Latina/o/x are more likely to choose community colleges after high school (Nora et al., 2018). However, state context matters (Zerquera et al., 2018) and the college choice process for Latina/o/x students is complex (Hurtado & Carter, 1997; Nuñez, 2009; Rios-Aguilar & Kiyama, 2012). More research is needed to clarify the college choice process. Traditional college choice frameworks do not include the Latina/o/x student experience, may not align with community college choice (Hurtado & Carter, 1997; Nuñez, 2009), do not consider social contexts (Rios-Aguilar & Kiyama, 2012), and do not account for interruptions after college enrollment (Cox, 2016).

Developing and Publishing College-*Conocimiento*

I continued my examination of the college choice process for Latina/o/x students throughout my years as a doctoral student and in my dissertation research. As an undergraduate student, I majored in Chicano studies and my master's degree was in Mexican American studies. Thus, I could not understand why, in the higher education courses, we would discuss the experiences of Latina/o/x students but never include any theoretical understandings from the field that connected with the ethnic/ racial identity development of students. I also did not realize I could ask such questions, but I had a feeling there should be a connection. In my personal life, I would reread texts foundational to Chicano studies. For instance, when I accompanied my sister to access information from a community college counselor during her enrollment process, I recall reading Borderlands *(Anzaldúa, 2002). I underlined key concepts of* nepantla *(a liminal state) and* atravesado *(transgressor) because there seemed to be a connection to the college-choice process that I was witnessing, but could not fully define.*

It was difficult to process the connections between traditional college choice theories with Chicano studies theories, particularly because I was grappling with collecting follow-up dissertation data and analyzing collected data, while applying to faculty positions and mothering Diana Isabella, my 9-month-old daughter. It was not until I sat in the hotel room at the Association for the Studies of Higher Education (ASHE) conference that I immersed myself in rereading Anzaldúan concepts, in preparation for applying for an ethnic studies faculty position. Within a few hours, I could see the connection between the experiences of the 47 Latina/o/x students whom I had interviewed and Anzaldúa's (2002) theory of conocimiento. *The next morning, I sat waiting for my breakfast meeting with Danny to discuss my dissertation progress and I wrote down on a napkin the seven spaces of college choice, in alignment with the theory of* conocimiento. *His reaction was surprising and validating because he was impressed by what I shared.*

    *After defending and filing the dissertation, I attempted to publish the college-*conocimiento *framework as an empirical study in top-tier higher education journals. However, I would revise and resubmit only to get rejected. Finally, I hired Dr. Aurora Chang as an editor to understand what I was doing "wrong" in the revision process. She explained that bridging two areas required that I first present a conceptual framework, separate from the empirical data. I could not understand why a conceptual framework would be more "valuable" than one based on empirical data. Dr. Chang clarified that the framework itself was a lot of new information to process because it included a field of study that was outside of higher education and the reader could not consume both the theoretical implications and the empirical findings. I made the required changes and, a few months later, college-*conocimiento *was accepted for publication. In the following section, I summarize the framework and interweave my personal experiences with college choice.*

College-*Conocimiento*

Given the call by Cox (2016) to examine college choice through a non-linear model, college-*conocimiento* (Acevedo-Gil, 2017) represents an interdisciplinary college choice framework tailored to the experiences of Latina/o/x students.[2] Informed by the college choice model (Perna, 2006) and *conocimiento* (Anzaldúa, 2002), college-*conocimiento* (see figure 9.1) entails seven cyclical and overlapping stages to examine Latina/o/x college choices (Acevedo-Gil, 2017). The seven spaces account for racialized access to college information (Deil-Amen & Turley, 2007; Palardy, 2014; Rendón et al., 2014).

In high school, I was an "ideal" college-going student; academically, I was ranked among the top 12 graduating students, served as a leader for various student clubs, volunteered with underserved elementary school students, and I was a Chicana from a

Figure 9.1. College-*conocimiento* framework. *Source*: N. Acevedo-Gil (2017), College-*conocimiento*: Toward an interdisciplinary college choice framework for Latinx students, *Race Ethnicity and Education, 20*(6), 829–850, https://doi.org/10. 1080/13613324.2017.1343294 /Taylor & Francis Ltd., http://www.tandfonline.com. Used with permission.

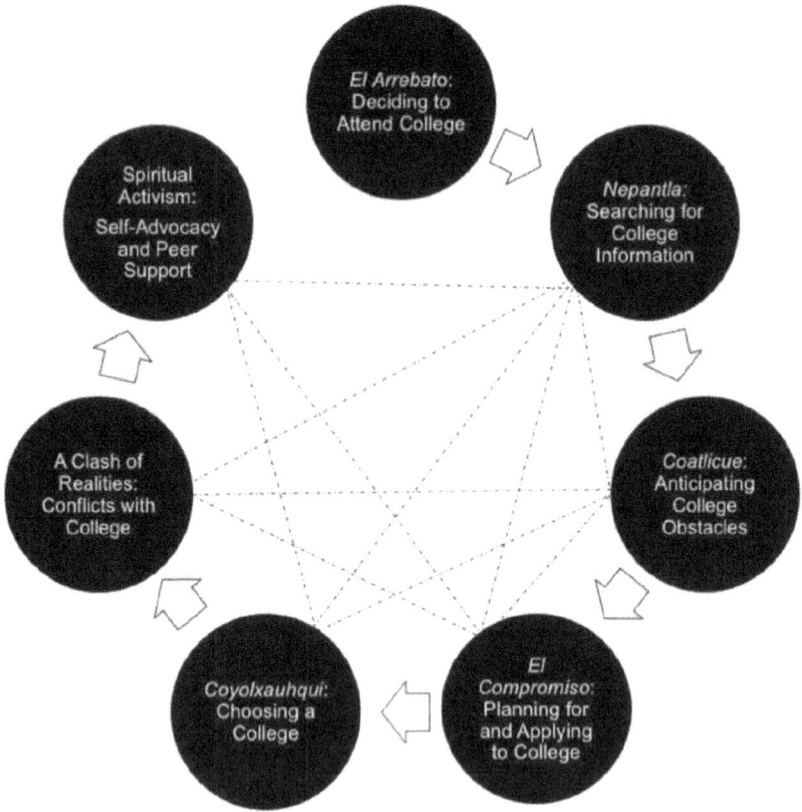

low-income household, whose Mexican immigrant parents did not graduate high school and worked in the agricultural fields. Up until senior year, I had followed the three-phase college choice model: by middle school, I knew I would attend a 4-year college because I had to earn a college degree so that I could secure a career. I assume the school counselor enrolled me in the UC Davis Early Academic Outreach Program, an outreach program funded by the UC system. Thus, I made sure to enroll in the

TRIO program when Rafael Rivera walked into my ninth-grade
English classroom recruiting students; I knew I needed help with
navigating the college admission process.

As stated in college-*conocimiento* (Acevedo-Gil, 2017), the process is
nonlinear and my experience exemplifies that I had not experienced the
first stage before entering the information phase. Instead, I was following a pathway because I had to attend college to secure a better future.
However, in the first stage on the pathway to *conocimiento*, **El Arrebato:
Deciding to Attend College**, a figurative earthquake dislocates an individual's reality, forcing her to alter her self-description and her position
within the world. This space serves as a moment for students to establish
college aspirations to pursue a college degree, even if it was not in their
plans prior to the eye-opening experience. This first stage also awakens
la facultad, the ability to see deeper than the surface of situations, which
represents a sixth sense of awareness (Anzaldúa, 2002). The sixth sense
of awareness supports students as they process information during the
second stage of the college-*conocimiento* framework: **Nepantla: Searching
for College Information**. This space is informed by Perna's (2006) college
choice model and acknowledges that information accessible to students
varies by student and the resources available in a school (Palardy, 2014).
If educators do not provide students with contextualized and comprehensive information, represents a lack of opportunity along the pathway to
college access. Therefore, the *Nepantla*: Searching for College Information
stage entails a student consuming college information after she chooses
to pursue a college pathway. In this stage, she searches for information
to pursue college and is open to learning about possible postsecondary
pathways. However, given the school and local higher education contexts
(Perna, 2006), the student can either gain an in-depth understanding of
all postsecondary options or receive limited information.

During ninth and 10th grade, I looked forward to Tuesdays when
I would get called out from class to attend college information
workshops led by Rafael. Around 11th grade, I had access to
college fieldtrips and was receiving information to distinguish
between the different college systems. We visited UC Davis and I
was bored; the campus felt too spread out. We visited UC Berkeley
and I loved it; it was gloomy, cold, and lively as students shared
flyers all along Sproul Plaza. Rafael made sure we knew about

the SAT requirements and had workshops where we would sign up for the exams. One of my best friends first told me about University of the Pacific (UOP)—she was not part of a college outreach program, so even though her GPA was higher than mine, she was ineligible to apply for the UC system because she did not know she had to take the SAT II. We had our plan; we would be roommates and have a smooth transition to college.

I was fortunate to have access to institutional agents who provided me with college information starting in middle school. In alignment with the college-*conocimiento* information stage, relatives, peers, and institutional agents tend to serve as primary sources of information for first-generation Latina/o/x students (Acevedo-Gil, 2017). When parents do not have a college degree, Latina/o/x high school students often turn to siblings, extended family members (Carolan-Silva & Reyes, 2013; Pérez & McDonough, 2008), and peers (Nuñez et al., 2008) for guidance. If a Latina/o/x student lacks other sources of information, peers can have a larger influence during the college information process (Nuñez et al., 2007), and having friends who plan to attend college influences the likelihood of choosing to attend a selective 4-year college (Arbona & Nora, 2007).

Nevertheless, future first-generation students often resort to institutional agents for college guidance (McClafferty Jarsky et al., 2009). The search for college information occurs within a K–12 context where both teachers (McCall et al., 2015) and counselors (Martinez, 2003; McDonough & Calderone, 2006; Vela-Gude et al., 2009) often do not view Latina/o/x students as college bound. Teachers tend to highlight behavior limitations of Latina/o/x students, instead of supporting a college pathway (McCall et al., 2015). Given the understaffing in Latino majority schools, counselors maintain high caseloads and Latina/o/x students are not likely to receive college information until 12th grade (Liou et al., 2009). When finally offering information, counselors will base the *type* of college information on a student's academic program (Liou et al., 2009).

Within a college-*conocimiento* framework, higher education contexts (Perna, 2006) influence the search for college information. High school leaders allow for-profit college outreach counselors to provide information and engage in fraudulent recruiting practices by misleading and misinforming low-income Latina/o/x students (Bailey et al., 2001; Oseguera & Malagon, 2011). Outreach counselors from community colleges can provide information to narrow students' choices to vocational pathways, despite student aspirations to earn a bachelor's degree (Acevedo, 2021). Nevertheless, college outreach program counselors guide a small portion of Latina/o/x students (Swail & Perna, 2002), which increases access to information (Pérez et al., 2015).

> *After reading that UOP brochure, I was certain that this private college would be the best decision for me. The UOP pamphlet stated they had a 14 student to one faculty ratio. I attributed that number to the level of support I would receive and believed that could be the only way I would succeed in college. I anticipated that my first-generation status and having English as my second language would loom over me in college. After admission, my friend's grandmother took us to visit UOP, but I did not feel right. I could not explain it at the time because the campus was beautiful and pristine; but it felt silent. It felt too quiet and all I could picture were the few thin white young women who were students. UOP did not feel like a place I wanted to be, but for some reason, my friend, also a young white woman, loved it. Even with the uncertainty, I was certain that UOP would be the correct choice because of the level of support promised by the brochure.*

While not everyone experiences the third stage of college-*conocimiento*, I did—as evidenced in my questioning the pathway that I had planned out so carefully. The third stage is **Coatlicue: Anticipating College Obstacles**. The college-*conocimiento* framework notes that, in the third stage, the student reflects on the college information received and questions whether she will be admitted to college, belong in college, and succeed in college. The *Coatlicue*: Anticipating College Obstacles stage explains that while Latina/o/x students consider academic and financial concerns, other intersectional experiences can inform the anticipation of potential obstacles (Acevedo-Gil, 2017). In particular, the *Coatlicue*: Anticipating College Obstacles stage centralizes the link between low academic expectations from counselors and reduced educational outcomes for Latina/o/x students (Conchas & Acevedo, 2020). Because high school counselors often have low expectations, underestimate students' academic potential, and attempt to limit the educational aspirations of Latina/o/x students (Martinez, 2003; McCall et al., 2015; Parker & Ray, 2017; Vela-Gude et al., 2009), it is plausible that Latina/o/x students reflect on the guidance received during the second stage and internalize academic self-doubt.

Furthermore, the majority of Latina/o/x college students come from low-income families (Postsecondary National Policy Institute, 2022) and college-*conocimiento* explains that Latina/o/x students reflect on information about college costs and financial aid to anticipate (in)abilities to afford college (Acevedo-Gil, 2019). While students may overestimate the costs of college, counselors can decrease the misinformation by providing accurate information, but the dismal number of counselors restricts the financial information that Latina/o/x students receive (González et al., 2003; McCall et al., 2015; McDonough & Calderone, 2006; Parker & Ray, 2017).

Through the two stages, a college-*conocimiento* framework posits an interconnectedness between a Latina/o/x student receiving information and assessing the information received based on her intersectional identities. Intersectionality (Crenshaw, 1989) is conceptualized as individual personal and social identities intersecting with power and privilege (Hurtado & Sinha, 2008). Because institutional systems receive individuals based on their social identity groups (e.g., race, gender, class, sexuality, and ability), these identities intersect and individuals experience contexts of power differently (Hurtado & Sinha, 2008). Intersectionality accounts for the interlocking oppressions experienced within connecting systems of oppression (Collins, 2000).

With college-*conocimiento* (Acevedo-Gil, 2019), I find that marginalized intersectional identities allowed Latina/o/x students to tap into *la facultad* (Anzaldúa, 2002). *La facultad* is accessible to individuals on the margins and represents a "sixth sense," the ability to view beneath the surface. Anzaldúa (2002) explains, "The urgency to know what you're experiencing awakens la facultad, the ability to shift attention and see through the surface of things and situations" (p. 547). Students may use *la facultad* to foresee likely college obstacles (Acevedo-Gil, 2017; 2019). As such, Latina/o/x students assess the information while reflecting on their individual identities (Acevedo-Gil, 2019). Such reflection informs the anticipation of postsecondary institutional obstacles, which students experience in college. I developed the concept of college-going *facultad*, defined as the ability to see beneath the surface of college information and anticipate college obstacles (Acevedo-Gil, 2019). *La facultad* in my college choice process was evidenced by knowing that I would not feel like I "belonged" in UOP along with knowing that I would need academic support.

By senior year, I had applied to eight public 4-year colleges, in addition to UOP. Rafael helped me choose what 4-year colleges to apply for and made me select between Los Angeles and Berkeley because I had four UC fee waivers. Looking back now, I realize that he was ensuring I selected at least one of the highly competitive UC campuses. After secondary review of my application, which included my math teacher, Mr. Duke, writing a letter of recommendation and my answering more questions about my educational experiences, I was admitted to UC Berkeley on the condition that I earned grades of B or better in every class. Nevertheless, I was prepared to ignore the feeling of discomfort I had felt on that campus and had set my mind to enroll in UOP for two key reasons: the student-to-faculty ratio and my best friend would be my roommate.

Again, in combination with my feeling uncomfortable on the UOP campus and my admission to UC Berkeley, I experienced the fourth stage of college-*conocimiento*. Within the college-*conocimiento* framework, in the fourth stage, **El *Compromiso* (The Compromise): Planning and Applying to College**, the student assesses previous and anticipated obstacles in the college choice pathway to determine the most appropriate college pathway. In this space, the student reflects on her experiences with college information and anticipated obstacles (Acevedo-Gil, 2019). In this reflection, she is motivated by counselors, family, peers, and community members to continue on her (altered) college pathway (McCall et al., 2015; Rendon et al., 2014). For instance, when Latina/o/x students faced obstacles while applying for college, they continue on their quest because they believed their pursuit of college would entail a higher purpose—to serve as an example for future Latina/o/x college students in their families and communities (Rendon et al., 2014). Thus, after reflecting on her need to continue, she establishes a postsecondary educational pathway.

Admission offers from all CSU and UC campuses were not important to me because I had made my decision that I would attend UOP. However, my cousin who had graduated from Humboldt State University and who was like an older sister to me called me the Sunday before the Student Intent to Register was due. She spent what felt like an hour lecturing me about why I had to accept admission to UC Berkeley. Finally, she said, "Try it for a year. If you do not like it, you can go anywhere else." With that piece of information, she convinced me. Had she not explained that I could make another choice if I was not happy, I would have chosen UOP.

When I went back to school, I met with my TRIO counselor and informed him that I had accepted admission to UC Berkeley. Although he had required that I use my fourth fee waiver to apply for admission at either UC Los Angeles or UC Berkeley, he had not followed up to guide my choice process—I imagine because the aim for college advisors is to get students admitted to college, not enrolled. At that point, I also asked him what would happen if I did not meet the conditional acceptance requirements that UC Berkeley had put in place when they sent the admission letter. He told me that if I did not meet the conditions, I would have to enroll in community college. I did not tell him that I was earning a C in physics because I chose not to turn in homework. Instead, I just acknowledged his statement then listened to what felt like a random lecture about Latina students being intelligent but ending up with men who are not good for them. When I had to ask my counselor for transcripts, she was surprised that I had applied to colleges because she was not involved with that process. She congratulated me and lectured me about never stopping my education to pay for a man's education because that is what happened to her. Now reflecting on these key college choice moments, it is interesting to see how gendered expectations were intertwined with the college guidance I was receiving from institutional agents.

The college-*conocimiento* pathway includes ***Coyolxauhqui*: Choosing a College**, which entails establishing a potential college student identity after receiving admission notices, redefining college realities, and choosing a postsecondary institution. In this space, the student also returns to the second stage of *nepantla* and sorts through various college information sources, including admission and financial aid offers, to choose an institution that aligns with her reality: a 4-year college, a community college, a for-profit vocational college, the military, or postponing college.

*In the summer, a friend from high school called me to explain she
was writing a letter to UC Berkeley admissions because she had
failed a course. That information made me call the admissions
office to inquire "hypothetically" about what would happen if I
did not meet the B grade conditions of admission. I was told to
send in a letter explaining why I had not met the conditions.
Because I could not think of an explanation to why I chose not
to do my homework for physics, which led to having below a B
in the course, I chose to ignore everything and hoped for the best.*

*That summer, I asked my parents to drive me to UC
Berkeley so that I could meet with a counselor to understand
what courses I would need to enroll in in the fall term. With
his paper map, my dad managed to get us to the campus, but
we got lost on campus. Finally, when I found the building and
walked into the counseling office, the white man seemed confused
as to why I was there; he was nothing like Rafael and offered no
guidance. Instead, he handed me a list of courses that fulfilled
the general education requirements (which I used all five years as
an undergrad student). It took us longer to find the appropriate
building than to meet with the counselor.*

*When the day to move into the dorms arrived, I was
bracing myself for being told that I would not be admitted
because I did not meet the conditional requirements. Thankfully,
everything went as smoothly as possible for a first-generation
college student who did not know there would be a difference
in twin-sized mattresses and whose fitted sheet was too short.
My roommate was an acquaintance from high school because
we chose to room together. We were not close friends but it was
comforting to have another first-generation student in that room.*

My experience with the sixth stage of college-*conocimiento* included questioning whether I would even be allowed into the campus and questioning
whether I belonged on that campus because it was challenging to navigate
as a first-generation college student. However, there was a sense of comfort
in knowing that I at least would have someone to help me transition to
the college. In the sixth space of college-*conocimiento*, **A Clash of Realities: Entering and Conflicting with College**, the student tests her college
choice and identity. This stage does not necessarily occur once the student

is accepted to college. This space can occur in various instances, such as when a student chooses a college major to pursue and tells an educator, when the student accepts admission to a college and shares the news with the counselor, or upon entering the college and meeting her professors. After choosing a college major and embracing an identity as a college student, her interactions with others and the institution can entail various conflicts. These interactions can influence the decision to continue on the pathway or choose a different college, which challenges the traditional three-stage college choice model (Hossler & Gallagher, 1987).

This space aligns with the previous framing of college choice as an ongoing process for Latina/o/x students that continues upon experiencing postsecondary interruptions (Acevedo, 2019; Bergerson 2009; Cox 2016). For instance, research highlights that despite accepting college admission, students experience "summer melt" (Arnold et al., 2009, p. 23) if they change their minds over the summer and decide not to enroll in the college. While a dearth in the Latina/o/x summer melt literature exists, Latina/o/x students "waver" throughout the summer (Arnold et al., 2009, 11), particularly with the COVID-19 pandemic effects (Resendez, 2022). The limited findings resonate with the notion of a nonlinear college choice process for Latina/o/x students, particularly those who experience summer melt. A second instance of a nonsequential college choice process occurs when the student encounters academic, financial, and social conflicts (Acevedo, 2019). Such conflicts, what Rendón and colleagues call "*choque/cultural collision(s)*' (2014, p. 5), are experienced by Latina/o/x students within college campuses.

> *My first semester, I was fortunate to be in a dorm hallway with majority first-generation students and majority students of Color, many who were Latina/o/x. It felt like a comfortable, welcoming space—the opposite of UOP. They proved to be an essential resource my first semester when the Introduction to Psychology class was canceled and I needed another class urgently to meet financial aid requirements. I was able to share freely with my hallway neighbors, and Chris mentioned that his 8:00 a.m. Chicano Spanish course was accepting more students. It was in this hallway that we would share resources, study together while doing laundry, celebrate each other's birthdays—we developed a community. I still cannot explain how so many students of Color were in one hallway when it was not a themed dorm, but they were instrumental in my retention during the first year.*

I joined the course and Josefina Parra was such a kind and caring professor who taught us so much more than written Spanish. She shared with us her educational journey and created a welcoming space, which was instrumental because even after missing class for a couple of weeks, she welcomed me and allowed me to make up the work I had missed. That was my introduction to Chicano studies, and it influenced my decision to enroll in all Chicano studies courses that fulfilled major or general education requirements. They were my "fun" classes that I looked forward to attending. It was also in these courses that I learned about the PhD pathway and finally understood the definition of research.

I was fortunate to have a community of peers supporting me as I developed into the seventh space of college-*conocimiento*. Without their own activation of supporting peers, I would not have had access to the guidance and information that I needed to successfully remain enrolled at the university. Instead, we had access to one another as a retention system. Within the seventh space of college-*conocimiento*, **Spiritual Activism: Self-Advocacy and Peer Support**, the internal transformation that occurs entails the student feeling like she belongs in college and engaging in self-advocacy, while the external transformation includes her supporting peers and other students. I frame the internal change of self-advocating on a continuum that ranges from the student bridging college aspirations with expectations while simultaneously seeking and offering resources. The student who reaches the space of spiritual activism engages in an internal transformation by realizing that obstacles will continue to arise and she can access resources to navigate the obstacles. However, the student does not have to complete the college-*conocimiento* pathway before she enacts her spiritual activism; instead, she can be in the seventh space at different points along her pathway as indicated by self-advocating and help-seeking behaviors. Educators can support low-income first-generation Latina/o/x students to navigate college choice by focusing on access to resources and self-advocacy (Espinoza, 2011).

Spiritual activism also includes outward actions, defined within college-*conocimiento* as supporting other students. External actions can include sharing information with her peers or fostering mutually supportive networks, fueled by the sense of responsibility to her family and community (Rendón et al., 2014). Thus, when choosing a college, peers greatly influence Latina/o/x students, especially when they lack access to college guidance from institutional agents (Nuñez et al., 2008; Sánchez-Connally, 2020). In essence, the push for social justice that Anzaldúa (2002) highlights can include Latina/o/x students supporting each other along the college choice pathway.

Discussion

In reflecting on the process of attempting to publish college-*conocimiento*, I found it most ironic when Drs. Nichole Garcia and Rebeca Mireles-Rios reached out to me and shared that during the peer review process, they were asked by the *American Educational Research Journal* to include my framework. That framework went from being rejected by the *Journal of Higher Education* to being acknowledged as key by a top education journal. I wonder what would have happened if I did not receive the advice from Dr. Cheryl Matias to hire an editor; she reframed my understanding of editors being only there to fix grammar and syntax problems and explained that many professors hire editors throughout the publication process. It was Dr. Chang who then explained the framework with empirical data would be "too much" for higher education scholars to process because I was bridging two different fields of study.

That first-generation-student identity lingers because I still find it a little surreal to see emerging and established scholars build on my framework that was rejected multiple times for publication. Although I developed college-*conocimiento* with first-generation low-income Latina/o/x students in mind, Garcia and Mireles-Rios (2020) engaged in *platicas* with their Chicano dads, informed by college-*conocimiento*. Using the framework contributed to their findings that "unearth intersubjective cultural knowledge and intergenerational strategies taught within the household, where gendered and raced differences emerge between college-educated Chicano fathers and their daughters" (p. 2082). Garcia and Mireles-Rios (2020) highlight that the framework can also apply to college-educated Latina/o/x students, not just first-generation students. Their study also emphasizes that more research is needed to examine the experiences of Latina/o/x students whose parents have graduated from college, particularly the role of fathers in the college choice process.

Puente (2022) used college-*conocimiento* when applying a critical race spatial analysis of the access to college-going opportunities for Latina/o/x students in rural agricultural areas of California. She found a reduced access to college information and guidance from teachers and counselors due to their inability to connect with students. The pandemic further constrained access to college guidance opportunities, which influenced Latina/o/x students to choose a community college over a 4-year college. In alignment with college-*conocimiento*, Puente (2022) was able to identify the decision as a strategic decision that aligned with their context and reality at the moment.

Finally, when applying college-*conocimiento*, Farrow and Coaxum (2021) highlighted the importance of recognizing religious identity as part of the intersectional identities that influence the college choice process for Latina/o/x students. By accounting for student identities Farrow and Coaxum (2021) found that Latina/o/x students chose college after considering how their spiritual needs would be met at the campus and made decisions with the intention that their religious communities would also benefit from their earning a college degree.

Conclusion

In considering both my personal journey and scholarly contributions, I am grateful for the continual access I have had to various levels of information, guidance, and support; I acknowledge the privileges I had in accessing those resources partly due to my white-passing skin tone and being viewed by the majority of my teachers as a "good" quiet girl that they could help. With that support, I was able to enter a postsecondary system and tap into my lens developed from my identities to interpret readings, social contexts, and empirical data and eventually develop a college-*conocimiento* framework. As an undergraduate, I aimed to pursue a pathway into academia with the intention to improve educational systems for low-income students of Color. Since then, I have adopted a racial realism lens. Bell (1992) noted that "even those herculean efforts we hail as successful will produce no more than temporary 'peaks of progress,' short-lived victories that slide into irrelevance as racial patterns adapt in ways that maintain white dominance" (pp. 373–374). I have also benefited from Stovall's definition of social justice. He delimits social justice to an "interruption to the status quo of substandard education for low-income/working-class Black and Latina/o students" (Stovall, 2016, p. 14). Thus, when engaging in any research, I am now more comfortable allowing myself to do the work as I see fit and to the best of my abilities with the intention of contributing toward "short-lived victories." While the journey of pursuing equity and access for all students does not stop with developing a framework, such perspectives allow me to understand that the long-term goal of social justice in education includes doing the work while we integrate our well-being and celebrate moments of joy.

Critical Reflection

I invite readers to reflect on the process and resources that they have had access to as they cross various boundaries when engaging in college-going practices and research.

1. If a theory is a lens with which we view the world, as Dr. Danny Solórzano explains in his presentations, then what lenses are we using to view college-going practices and research?

2. How can we navigate college-going spaces in a way that builds on the knowledge, experiences, and assets of students of Color?

3. How do we learn from other individuals in the field so that we can continue serving students to the best of our abilities?

4. How do we engage in this work in a way that interrupts the racist and sexist foundations of higher education institutions?

Notes

1. For more information, see Solórzano (2023).
2. This section is primarily informed by Acevedo-Gil (2017, 2019).

References

Acevedo-Gil, N. (2017). College-*conocimiento*: Toward an interdisciplinary college choice framework for Latinx students. *Race Ethnicity and Education, 20*(6), 829–850. https://doi.org/10.1080/13613324.2017.1343294

Acevedo-Gil, N. (2019). College-going *facultad*: Latinx students anticipating post-secondary institutional obstacles. *Journal of Latinos and Education, 18*(2), 107–125. https://doi.org/10.1080/15348431.2017.1371019

Anzaldúa, G. (1987). *Borderlands/la frontera*. Aunt Lute Press.

Anzaldúa, G. (2002). Now let us shift: Conocimiento . . . the path of inner work, public acts. In G. Anzaldúa & A. Keating (Eds.), *This bridge we call home: Radical visions for transformation* (pp. 540–578). Routledge.

Arbona, C., & Nora, A. (2007). The influence of academic and environmental factors on Hispanic college degree attainment. *Review of Higher Education, 30*(3), 247–269. https://doi.org/10.1353/rhe.2007.0001

Arnold, K., Fleming, S., DeAnda, M., Castleman, B., & Wartman, K. L. (2009). The summer flood: The invisible gap among low-income students. *Thought & Action, 25*, 23–34.

Bailey, T., Badway, N., & Gumport, P. J. (2001). *For-profit higher education and community colleges*. Retrieved from: https://files.eric.ed.gov/fulltext/ED463824.pdf

Bell, D. (1992). Racial realism. *Connecticut Law Review, 24*(2), 363–379.

Bergerson, A. A. (2009). College choice and access to college: Moving policy, research, and practice to the 21st century. *ASHE Higher Education Report, 35*(4), 1–141.

Booker, M. (2002). Stories of violence: Use of testimony in a support group for Latin American battered women. In L. H. Collins, M. R. Dunlap, & J. C. Chrisler (Eds.), *Charting a new course for feminist psychology* (pp. 307–320). Greenwood.

Carolan-Silva, A., & Reyes, J. R. (2013). Navigating the path to college: Latino students' social networks and access to college. *Educational Studies, 49*(4), 334–359.

Collins, P. H. (2000). Gender, Black feminism, and Black political economy. *Annals of the American Academy of Political and Social Science, 568*(1), 41–53. https://doi.org/10.1177/000271620056800105

Conchas, G. Q., & Acevedo, N. (2020). *The Chicana/o/x dream: Hope, resistance, and educational success*. Harvard Education Press.

Cox, R. D. (2016). Complicating conditions: Obstacles and interruptions to low-income students' college "choices." *Journal of Higher Education, 87*(1), 1–26. https://doi.org/10.1080/00221546.2016.11777392

Crenshaw, K. (1989). Demarginalizing the intersection of race and sex: A Black feminist critique of antidiscrimination doctrine, feminist theory, and anti-racist politics. *University of Chicago Legal Forum, 1989*(1), 139–167.

Cruz, C. (2006). *Testimonial narratives of queer street youth: Toward an epistemology of a Brown body* [Doctoral dissertation, University of California, Los Angeles 2006]. *Dissertation Abstracts International, 68*(2).

Deil-Amen, R., & Turley, R. L. (2007). A review of the transition to college literature in sociology. *Teachers College Record, 109*(10), 2324–2366. https://doi.org/10.1177/016146810710901001

Espinoza, R. (2011). *Pivotal moments: How educators can put all students on the path to college*. Harvard Education Press.

Fabina, J., Hernandez, E. L., & McElrath, K. (2023). *School enrollment in the United States: 2021*. US Census. https://www.census.gov/content/dam/Census/library/publications/2023/acs/acs-55.pdf

Farrow, M. J., & Coaxum, J., III. (2023). Breaking with an anticollege tradition: Latinx Pentecostal students and college choice. *Journal of Diversity in Higher Education, 16*(3), 356–368. https://doi.org/10.1037/dhe0000342

Garcia, N. M., & Mireles-Rios, R. (2020). "You were going to go to college": The role of Chicano fathers' involvement in Chicana daughters' college choice. *American Educational Research Journal, 57*(5), 2059–2088. https://doi.org/10.3102/0002831219892004

González, K. P., Stone, C., & Jovel, J. (2003). Examining the role of social capital in access to college for Latinas: Toward a college opportunity framework. *Journal of Hispanics in Higher Education, 2*(2), 146–171. https://doi.org/10.1177/1538192702250620

Hossler, D., & Gallagher, K. S. (1987). Studying student college choice: A three-phase model and the implications for policymakers. *College and University 2*, 207–221.

Hurtado, A., & Sinha, M. (2008). More than men: Latino feminist masculinities and intersectionality. *Sex roles, 59*(5), 337–349. https://doi.org/10.1007/s11199-008-9405-7

Hurtado, S., & Carter, D. F. (1997). Effects of college transition and perceptions of the campus racial climate on Latino college students' sense of belonging. *Sociology of education, 70*(4), 324–345. https://doi.org/10.2307/2673270

Liou, D. D., Antrop-González, R., & Cooper, R. (2009). Unveiling the promise of community cultural wealth to sustaining Latina/o students' college-going information networks. *Educational Studies, 45*(6), 534–555. https://doi.org/10.1080/00131940903311347

Martinez, M. D. (2003). Missing in action: Reconstructing hope and possibility among Latino students placed at risk. *Journal of Latinos and Education, 2*(1), 13–21. https://doi.org/10.1207/S1532771XJLE0201_3

McCall, J., Zarate, M. E., & Perez, W. Y. (2015). Sixth-grade teachers' perceptions of the college-bound student. In P. A. Pérez & M. Ceja (Eds.), *Higher education access and choice for Latino students* (pp. 11–25). Routledge.

McClafferty Jarsky, K., McDonough, P. M., & Núñez, A. M. (2009). Establishing a college culture in secondary schools through P-20 collaboration: A case study. *Journal of Hispanic Higher Education, 8*(4), 357–373. https://doi.org/10.1177/1538192709347846

McDonough, P. M., & Calderone, S. (2006). The meaning of money: Perceptual differences between college counselors and low-income families about college costs and financial aid. *American Behavioral Scientist, 49*(12), 1703–1718. https://doi.org/10.1177/0002764206289140

Nora, A., Carales, V. D., & Bledsoe, R. K. (2018). Hispanic community college students: A profile of theory and research. In J. S. Levin & S. T. Kater (Eds.), *Understanding community college* (2nd Ed., pp. 65–87). Routledge.

Nuñez, A. M. (2009). Latino students' transitions to college: A social and intercultural capital perspective. *Harvard Educational Review, 79*(1), 22–48. https://doi.org/10.17763/haer.79.1.wh7164658k33w477

Núñez, A. M., McDonough, P., Ceja, M., & Solórzano, D. (2008). Diversity within: Latino college choice and ethnic comparisons. In C. Gallagher (Ed.), *Racism in post-race America: New theories, new directions* (pp. 267–284). Social Forces Publishing.

Oseguera, L., & Malagon, M. C. (2011). For-profit colleges and universities and the Latina/o students who enroll in them. *Journal of Hispanic Higher Education, 10*(1), 66–91. https://doi.org/10.1177/1538192710392040

Palardy, G. J. (2014). High school socioeconomic composition and college choice: Multilevel mediation via organizational habitus, school practices, peer and staff attitudes. *School Effectiveness and School Improvement, 26*(3), 329–353. https://doi.org/10.1080/09243453.2014.965182

Parker, M. M., & Ray, D. C. (2017). School counseling needs of Latino students. *Journal of School Counseling, 15*(16), n16.

Pérez, P. A., & McDonough, P. M. (2008). Understanding Latina and Latino college choice: A social capital and chain migration analysis. *Journal of Hispanic Higher Education, 7*(3), 249–265. https://doi.org/10.1177/1538192708317620

Pérez, P. A., Rodriguez, J. L., & Guadarrama, J. (2015). Rising voices: College opportunity and choice among Latina/o undocumented students. In P. Perez & M. Ceja (Eds.), *Higher Education Access and Choice for Latino Students* (pp. 96–105). Routledge.

Perna, L. W. (2006). Studying college access and choice: A proposed conceptual model. In J. C. Smart (Eds.), *Higher education: Handbook of theory and research* (pp. 99–157). Springer.

Postsecondary National Policy Institute. (2022). *Factsheet, 2022.* Postsecondary National Policy Institute. https://pnpi.org/wp-content/uploads/2022/09/LatinoStudentsFactSheet_ September_2022.pdf

Puente, M. (2022). A critical race spatial analysis of rural Latinx students' college (in)opportunities and conscious choices during the COVID-19 pandemic. *Journal of Latinos and Education, 21*(3), 304–318. https://doi.org/10.1080/15348431.2022.2051040

Rendón, L. I., Nora, A., & Kanagala, V. (2014). *Ventajas/assets y conocimientos/knowledge: Leveraging Latin@ strengths to foster student success.* Center for Research and Policy in Education, University of Texas at San Antonio.

Resendez, J. (2022). *Latinx pandemic melt: A phenomenological study of summer melt during the COVID-19 pandemic.* (Publication No. 29061493) [Doctoral dissertation, University of California, San Diego]. Proquest.

Rios-Aguilar, C., & Kiyama, J. M. (2012). Funds of knowledge: An approach to studying Latina(o) students' transition to college. *Journal of Latinos and Education, 11*(1), 2–16. https://doi.org/10.1080/15348431.2012.631430

Sánchez-Connally, P. (2020). "Proving people wrong": The role of peers and resistance in shaping Latinx students' educational aspirations. *Journal of Education & Social Policy, 7*(1), 23–29.

Solórzano, D. G. (2023). My journey to this place called the RAC: Reflections on a movement in critical race thought and critical race hope in higher education. *International Journal of Qualitative Studies in Education, 36*(1), 87–98. https://doi.org/10.1080/09518398.2022.2042613

Stovall, D. O. (2016). *Born out of struggle: Critical race theory, school creation, and the politics of interruption.* State University of New York Press.

Swail, W. S., & Perna, L. W. (2002). Pre-college outreach programs: A national perspective. In W. G. Tierney & L. S. Hagedorn (Eds.), *Increasing access to college: Extending possibilities for all students* (pp. 15–34.) State University of New York Press.

US Census Bureau. (2023). *Quick facts.* Retrieved from: https://www.census.gov/quickfacts/fact/table/US/RHI725221

Vela Gude, T., Cavazos Jr., J., Johnson, M. B., Cheryl, F., Cavazos, A. G., Leslie, C., & Iliana, R. (2009). "My counselors were never there": Perceptions from Latino college students. *Professional School Counseling, 12*(4), 272–279. https://doi.org/10.1177/2156759X09012004

Zerquera, D. D., Acevedo-Gil, N., Flores, E., & Marantal, P. (2018). Repositioning trends of Latina/o/x student enrollments in community colleges. *Association of Mexican American Educators Journal, 12*(1), 86–106. https://doi.org/10.24974/amae.12.1.379

Chapter 10

Family Building

College Choice Process for Native American Students

Eliza Yellow Bird, Amanda R. Tachine,
and Nolan L. Cabrera

Eliza's Story

I grew up hearing my grandpa tell my siblings and me to get our education, that "education is the one thing they can't take from us." From a young age I knew that college was a part of my path; even with this knowledge it wasn't until late in my high school career that I started to think about my next steps. I went to my guidance counselor to figure out how to apply for college. She laughed off my future college plans and suggested I see if I could make it at the local community college first, instilling the idea in me that I was not college-ready. Even though I was at the top of my class, the tribal school I attended did not have a college-going culture and was not preparing us for those next steps with advanced classes or curriculum. My family was the support system that helped me with the application process; even though my parents had nontraditional paths into college, they were just as determined as I was. We put our heads together to find the best fit, somewhere with a strong Native community and support system. Sadly, my story is not unique, I've heard countless experiences of Native students reaching out to their guidance counselors and leaving feeling hopeless. It is why it is so important to fully understand

241

what the college choice process is for Native students and the role family plays within that decision, since I am only here today because of my family and their support.

Amanda's Story

As a Diné, I attended a reservation rural high school on the Navajo Nation. I loved my community and the education I received there, but it pains me to admit that I did not have a lot of knowledge about the college choice process. Although I was an academically strong student, I had a limited chance to learn about academic programs or scholarship opportunities since colleges rarely visited our school to recruit. I also recall talking with my guidance counselor only a few times about college. Nonetheless, I applied to three colleges (very late in the Spring semester) while I was a senior. I lived in a single-parent household with limited financial resources. Two institutions offered me some scholarship support (<$1,500/year), but the one college that did not offer me funding was the college that I decided to attend. I chose to attend Northern Arizona University because it was a 2-hour drive from my home community. I wanted to be close to home, to be able to visit my grandma, and feel the security of my home community while at college. Family and home were incredible drivers for me. Institutions of higher education must consider the powerful influences that home and family have on Native college students. This research explores this phenomenon in more depth.

Nolan's Story

When I was 12 years old, my father was at a conference in the Bay Area, and we visited Stanford University. I had an intuitive feeling that I would go to Stanford as an undergraduate even though I am not an intuitive person. Five years later, I applied to one school, Stanford, and was accepted early admission. How did that happen? I could take the Horatio Alger approach—I had perfect grades, high SATs, was a three-sport varsity letterman, student body president . . . blah, blah, blah. I knew plenty of people like that who applied and were rejected from Stanford. I could take the structural approach where my family, in particular my father, knew the dominant codes of society, providing me access to the necessary social and cultural capital to access elite education when most Brown boys were denied. I could take a magical realism approach where this was destined by powers beyond my control. I could take a lottery approach and say that among the qualified people who applied to Stanford, my admission was due to sheer luck. The truth is that I do not understand how my college choice process turned out the way that it did—in fact, to even call it a "choice" is probably a misnomer since the acceptance rate was 10.9% when I applied. I know that is more confusing than illuminating, but maybe that is the point.

⌒⌒

As the authors' stories highlight, the college choice process is complex and can be a challenge to navigate. College choice models describe the process as a series of prescribed steps to consider, but that misses some of the nuances that real life presents. This study will explore what college choice looks like for Indigenous students and their families, sharing a distinct lens to consider moving forward in academia.

Native[1] peoples are faced with a paradox. Pursuing higher education helps support Native Nation Building and tribal sovereignty (Brayboy et al., 2012), yet the pathway to the goal is frequently through settler, colonialist institutions (Tachine, 2022; Yellow Bird, 2020). There is currently little known about the unique experiences of Native students as they embark on their college choice processes; this study hopes to bring more insight into what this process entails for Indigenous students. In doing so, we heed the wisdom of Dr. Michelle Espino,[2] who reviewed an earlier draft of this chapter and offered the following important critique: Given how limited college choice is by issues of white supremacy and capitalist exploitation, can we reasonably call this process a "choice"? We do not pretend to have an answer to this question, but we do proceed acknowledging that there are *systemic monsters*[3] (Tachine, 2022) that Native students battle to pursue higher education that restrict college access and limit choice (Waterman et al., 2018). Iloh (2018) asserts that the concept of *choice* is too limited and problematic to account for the 21st-century context. Despite the problematic nature of the term *college choice*, we still seek to empirically explore and theorize what college choice looks like for Native students in their journeys to pursue higher education. We see this as a critical line of inquiry given the ongoing decreasing enrollment trends for Native students.

In 1980, the enrollment of Native students in degree-granting institutions was 83,900 and by 2009, 205,900 students were enrolled in degree-granting 4-year institutions (Nelson et al., 2021). However, there has been an alarming decline in Native student enrollments: in 2021 the enrollment numbers decreased to 121,100 (National Center for Education Statistics, 2022). This could be due to multiple factors, one of which being the way the federal government and institutions track students, not counting multiracial Indigenous students under the Native student metrics (Ford et al., 2021). For a community that is vastly diverse, this diminishes the accurate representation of Native students. While this is only one attribute and explanation for the decline, the decreased numbers in college enrollment highlights the imperative to better understand the influences and experiences of Indigenous students and their college choice process.

Connected to this enrollment disparity is that, too often, research provides no more than a footnote or asterisk about Native American students, indicating that the numbers are so small that they cannot be studied (Brayboy et al., 2012; Shotton et al., 2013). As a result, professionals in higher education seeking to increase the access and success of Native American students are offered little or no specific guidance about how to better outreach and serve Native students (Jackson et al., 2003; Waterman et al., 2018). Thus, it is not surprising that examinations of the college choice process for Native students are overlooked.

The purpose of this chapter is to move "beyond the asterisk" (Shotton et al., 2013) by generating data about the college choice process for Native American students at the University of Arizona (UA), exploring factors influencing Native American students' college choice. Ultimately, this study asked, What do current conceptions of college choice mean for Native American students?

Relevant Literature and Theoretical Framework

To contextualize this research, we begin by describing Native Nation Building (Brayboy et al., 2012) and a Native American Student College Choice model (Peters, 2018) as conceptual frameworks guiding this study, while deconstructing how early models do not consider Indigenous student experiences and frequently reinforce whiteness.

NATIVE NATION BUILDING: CENTERING INDIGENEITY

Native Nation Building is based on the premise that educational success within Native communities is vital to forming Native nations (Brayboy et al., 2012). Native Nation Building has been shaped by historical experiences that described the federal government's intent to fix the "Native problem" (Grinde, 2004). Formal education was introduced as a perceived ideal mechanism for the Native to "kill the Indian in him, and save the man" (Adams, 1995, p. 52). Young Native children were mandated to attend boarding schools where they were restricted from practicing their ways of life (Adams, 1995; Lomawaima, 1995) in order to assimilate into western culture. Today, many Native college students may have a family member (grandparent, uncle, aunt, even parent) who attended a boarding school; the stories of those experiences are "a legacy from which our students experience education" (Shotton et al., 2013, p. 12).

Despite the appalling origin of formal education mandated by the federal government, Native nations have remained grounded in their Indigenous ways of knowing and persevered through colonial irreverence, building stronger nations today (Brayboy et al., 2012; Tachine, 2022). Brayboy et al. (2012) in their monograph, *Postsecondary Education for American Indian and Alaska Natives: Higher Education for Nation Building and Self-Determination*, emphasized that educational success within Native communities is vital to forming stronger Native nations to be politically and economically autonomous nations. Tribal leaders acknowledged that education is key—as a leader stated, "It is very important that we hold education important to our children, to our tribal membership . . . we are not only expressing what we want for our education, for our children, but for the future—a better education" (US Department of Education, 2010, p. 1). With tribal leaders encouraging the youth to pursue higher education, it is even more imperative to better understand the complexities that entail the college choice process for Native students and their families.

NATIVE AMERICAN STUDENT COLLEGE CHOICE MODEL

While there are multiple college choice models, there currently is only one model (Peters, 2018) that specifically explores the Native American college choice process. Peters interviewed seven Native American students (six undergraduate and one graduate student) from 4-year institutions across North Carolina. From these interviews he developed a Native American

246 | Eliza Yellow Bird, Amanda R. Tachine, and Nolan L. Cabrera

Student College Choice model comprising four quadrants (1) family, (2) Native identity and community, (3) external factors, and (4) growth and opportunities. The first quadrant specified that family was integral for all major decisions throughout the college choice process. The second quadrant of the model, Native identity and community, was a significant part because students would select schools where they felt they could connect with community, feel a sense of "home" on campus, and that provided opportunities for them to continue to learn and develop their cultural practices. The third quadrant was external factors, which were a multitude of additional aspects that influenced their college choice process. Some examples of these factors were if the students were first-generation college students, if they were athletes, if they had visited the college, and so on. These factors contributed to the students' and families' process of deciding which school would be the best fit. The last quadrant was growth and opportunities. This area highlighted the students' motivation to attend college and how they saw college overall as an opportunity to grow and better themselves, their families, and communities. This fourth quadrant parallels Native Nation Building as many of the students saw education as a way to return to their community later to support their people. While there are other studies that have mentioned Native students' college choice process (e.g., Dillman, 2002; Fann, 2005; Nelson, 2015; Starks, 2010), Peters' model is the first to offer a conceptual framework that addresses Native students' college choice process and takes into account family, community, Indigenous identity, and additional factors that influence their college choice process.

For racial/ethnic groups, studies show that family and peer influence, access to resources, and proximity to home are all important factors in the college choice process of students of Color (George Mwangi, 2015; Hurtado et al., 1997; Pérez & McDonough, 2008; St. John et al., 2005). Although these studies offer further insight into the college choice process of students of Color, Native American students continue to be left out of the conversation (Hurtado et al., 1997; Perna, 2000). Additionally, for Native students specifically, these models do not adequately grasp the communal decision-making process as connected to their Indigenous identity that many Native students experience when considering college (Tachine, 2022).

Based on the frameworks of Native Nation Building and the Native Student College Choice model, there are key components missing from white-centered models including the collective, extended family-based dimension of college choice. These college choice models tend to be individualistic in their orientations. The foundation of these models normalizes a "cost-benefit" analysis, privileging individual gain as core factors in decision-making processes (e.g., Hossler & Gallagher, 1987; Perna, 2006). The whiteness embedded in this work is evident in the following juxtaposition. The classic Cartesian principle is "I think, therefore I am." Whereas, from an Indigenous paradigm, Yazzie Burkhart (2004) reframed that principle: "We are, therefore I am," emphasizing the orientation of interdependence in decision-making processes. The influence of the Cartesian principle on foundational higher education scholarship inadvertently reinforces whiteness through individualistic as opposed to collectivist paradigms (Cabrera, 2019). It does not mean that this work was irrelevant or fatally flawed. Rather, it was created without Indigenous students at the center of it. Peters (2018) centered his model on Native students' experiences and found that Indigenous identity and giving back to tribal communities were core components of their college choice process, both of which are missing from predominantly white college choice models. To address the scholarly limitations, we employ Indigenous theoretical frameworks from the Native American Student College Choice model (Peters, 2018) and Native Nation Building (Brayboy, 2012) to examine what Native students identified as being important in their college choice process as well as the purpose or motivation for their pursuits to attend college.

Methodology

This study utilized a sequential, explanatory mixed methods design where the quantitative component is completed first, and the qualitative follows as a form of critical elaboration (Plano Clark & Creswell, 2010). The qualitative component included a series of sharing circles (Tachine et al., 2016) with Native college students, and the quantitative component included a university survey for first-time, full-time freshmen. This created some interesting paradigmatic issues as the postpositivist method employed in the quantitative analysis (t-tests with Bonferroni corrections) demonstrated some important differences between Native and white students in terms of their college choice process. Yet, conforming to the survey constructs was a challenge as it was rooted in white college choice frameworks, which limited the depth of that initial analysis. Thus, the sharing circles methodology was not simply an extension of the quantitative analysis, but it offered robust insights that critically interrogated the quantitative approach and its embedded assumptions.

Data

Data for this project derived from two sources. The first data set is a universitywide survey offered to all first-time, full-time freshmen that focuses on a broad set of constructs, which included, but was not limited to, the college choice process and college goals/aspirations.

To yield greater numbers of student survey responses, partnering with the Native American Student Affairs (NASA) center and other Native American organizations was a tremendously valuable strategy. When sharing the research initiative many students appreciated the opportunity to contribute to a study that was going to provide avenues for making future Native American students' experiences at the UA more beneficial. That is, many participated because of the possibility of improving supports and opportunities for future Native students, which already highlights their interconnected worldview. This stands in stark contrast to their white peers who frequently need financial incentives to participate in surveys (Sax et al., 2003). Moreover, the UA Office of Student Affairs was making a move toward "data-driven decision-making." This meant students are inundated with requests for survey participation constantly, and low-income, first-generation students, and students of Color have the lowest response rates (Sax et al., 2003). Therefore, we had to be creative regarding our outreach strategies for participation. In terms of survey participation, there was a major push during NASA events so that Native students could be more than simply an asterisk (Shotton et al., 2013) within UA institutional analyses.

All first-time, full-time students attending the UA were invited to participate and the final sample yielded n = 5,176 students completing the survey representing 58% of the entering class and 124 Native American students representing 86% of the entering Native population. This high response rate was largely due to intentional outreach from NASA and other Indigenous organizations on campus. Due to the breadth of the survey, there was a great deal of missing data and sample size varied among the constructs. Regardless, the data allowed us to analyze trends and to find differences in the college choice process among Native American and white students, thereby leading into the qualitative analysis.

An important aspect of the qualitative component is the integrative perspective of Native students, which is a point of view profoundly grounded in interdependence (Fryberg & Markus, 2007). Thus, the format of the interviews was based on a conversational "sharing circle," focused on the sharing of different perspectives (Kovach, 2009; Tachine et al., 2016). The development of a sharing circle interview protocol was informed by scholarly literature and experiential practice as several of the research team members are enrolled tribal members and have worked closely with Native American college students. Utilizing tribal protocols, the second data set included conducting seven sharing circles with a total of 23 Native American undergraduate students who attended the UA. Students were recruited through their participation in NASA and may have influenced the unintended outcome of sampling a large portion of students who grew up on tribal reservations (n = 10, 43.4%). All names were replaced with pseudonyms. Students were traditional college age (18–24 years of age) and included 14 women and nine men as participants. Students represented diverse tribal affiliations, including Hopi, Navajo, and Pascua Yaqui.

Throughout the development of this research, we made considerable efforts to collaborate with local tribes to ensure that we were being culturally appropriate and creating spaces where tribal input was incorporated. We did this by having conversations with tribal education directors from the Hopi, Pascua Yaqui, Navajo Nation, and Tohono O'odham Nation. In this discussion, we asked whether the research we were interested in pursuing was valuable for them and their tribal members and also asked if they had any research concerns or needs that we could assist with. This collaboration and rapport building is important due to the history of misusing or abusing data collected (Walter et al., 2020). It was important to follow and respect tribal protocol regarding what IRB processes the tribal nations had in place for collecting the stories of tribal members. This study created the opportunity for greater reciprocity with these nations, which was important as "giving back" is a core value for many Indigenous peoples (Grande, 2004; Lopez, 2018; Lopez & Tachine, 2021; Reyes, 2016; Smith, 1999).

Quantitative Analysis

We utilized a one tailed t-test analysis to determine areas in the college choice process where Native students are similar and different relative to their white peers. We applied the Bonferroni correction method because we were conducting multiple comparisons on a single data set, which may lead to a greater likelihood of data appearing significant when it is not. The correction offers a modified P value to determine the significance and reduces the chance of a false positive (Agresti & Finlay, 2009).

To begin the analysis, we outlined which survey constructs fit within traditional college choice models (see table 10.1). They were embedded in the instrument before our analysis as part of a campus-wide survey meant to understand the college choice process and first year experiences of all UA students. Thus, the constructs were not specific to Native populations, but they still did highlight some important differences. The qualitative component more specifically defined the contours of what an Indigenous college choice model would look like.

Qualitative Analysis

An advisory team made of university administrators and faculty in key departments (i.e., admissions, outreach, Native American center, academic transitions, American Indian studies, and higher education) provided feedback in the development of the sharing circle interview protocol. Each sharing circle was transcribed verbatim and thematically coded. In the analytical process, there is no specific Indigenous term (that we know of) for data analysis, yet that does not mean Indigenous peoples did not organize information, analyze, and make informed decisions for phenomena occurring in life. "Coming to know" is the best English translation for the analytical process in meaning-making and understanding (Cajete, 1999, p. 80). With that teaching, specific to the research team, we met regularly to discuss potential patterns that emerged in the transcripts within the context of Brayboy et al.'s (2012) Native Nation Building and Peters' (2018) Native American Student College Choice model as they pertained to the college choice process. Using a holistic, interpretive analysis of "coming to know" (Cajete, 1999), patterns were compared to other patterns within and across stories to see how they were similar or different in relation to the context of college choice and Native Nation Building.

Family and Home: Native College Choice

Consistent with the Native American Student College Choice model, students for the current study shared stories where family and home influences were central and powerful drivers in the college choice process. Family influenced and informed college-going ideologies and served as powerful college recruiters. Home and cultural ties were also emphasized as critical factors in shaping decisions on which college to attend. Woven throughout the findings are the quantitative results that highlight the significance of family responsibilities and home, while the students' stories elaborate on and amplify the depth of the college choice process for Native students.

FAMILY-FORMED COLLEGE IDEOLOGIES

In line with Peters' (2018) model, family was a significant influence on the students' college choice process. The significance of family was reflected in the sharing circles when students discussed that their family first planted a seed that college was a viable option in various ways, such as witnessing a family member attend college. For Brian, growing up on the Navajo reservation, in a rural community located approximately 150 miles from the nearest college, seeing a family member attend college was very powerful. While sharing his story, Brian stated:

> One significant thing that made me have a better idea of college was when my mom attended college classes through a remote campus. . . . She would always go to college classes. She would be gone for about three or four hours and she would always go over there. . . . My mom wanted us to go to college too so maybe my mom is primarily the influence. Since I've described that college was sort of my everyday life or it was in my everyday life. Well not that we really lived in any place where colleges exist, we live in a pretty remote location.

The lack of proximity to college meant that Brian primarily had to rely on his mother's experiences as motivation to pursue higher education. Witnessing his mom attend classes through a remote campus opened Brian's understanding of college. He even mentioned that college was part of his *everyday life*, despite living in a location far from a campus.

Shane first became aware of college at the early age of 6 years old through his family. He shared memories of traveling with family to drop off a cousin at Fort Lewis College that ultimately sparked his awareness of attending college. Shane stated, "I was thinking that it was pretty far away from school. Well because she lived in [state's town] so it was mysterious to me about the very different geographical location of where she was going to school. I think it was my mom that told me that she was going to college." Shane was also raised on the Navajo reservation, far from Fort Lewis College. For Shane, these trips offered insight into the family commitment and travel time it took to go to college. He saw that his cousin was not close to home, which impacted his own thoughts of where he could go in the future.

Another way family influenced college ideologies (Kiyama, 2010; Peters, 2018) among students was through messages regarding the importance of education. Since she was a young girl, Cynthia, a first-generation college student, heard from family the importance of education. At the young age of 6 years old, Cynthia also formed ideas of being a role model to her younger sibling:

> My family instilled the whole education thing on us since very young, since I could remember, because they would always say that education is the key to our success. . . . And it didn't really hit me until my mom had my little brother and I was about 6, and that's when I realized that I have to be a role model, because he needs someone to look up to, and I'm the first person in our family to go to college.

Cynthia illustrates an example of a reciprocal exchange, a value common among Indigenous communities and Native Nation Building (Brayboy et al., 2012). Fulfilling her family's values by being first in her family to attend college while giving back by serving as a role model was a reciprocal exchange that Cynthia honored.

Family as Powerful College Recruiters

Family helped in searching for college in different ways depending upon whether family had experience in attending college. For those students who had a family member who attended college, they had a more traditional and direct approach. Clarissa's parents both attended college, but they did not acquire a degree, and she also had older siblings who were in college. Having family members familiar with the college application process was foundational for Clarissa as she navigated. Clarissa elaborated: "[My family members] were telling me what forms I needed to send in, what I needed to do to submit certain things and what to fill out and all of that. Yeah, since they had been through it, they already knew what the process was and they were kind of helping me along the way." Clarissa attended a large-urban high school with college resources available, but she relied on her family and shared that she did not utilize her high school's college resources.

For some students, researching colleges can be a difficult undertaking as they determine which college to apply to. However, for Sheila, Melissa, and Tisha this process was simple because they had family members who were college alumni of their desired college. Sheila shared, "The reason why I applied was, it was family tradition, and my family went to University of Arizona so it was kind of expected. But I really wanted to go to UA too because I grew up nearby, and UA is in my blood." Sheila attended high school in Tucson where UA is located. Having family members attend UA, Sheila formed ambitions to attend that same school. Therefore, Sheila's process was streamlined as she aspired to follow her family's college pathway.

First-generation Native college students had a different experience when compared to those students who had a family member who had previously applied to college. First-generation college students felt alone but they still were supported by family. Sophia explained her experience, "I was just kind of on my own and I'm the oldest. It was kind of hard. I didn't really explore college or get information or do research. . . . I was just like a guinea pig, we [Dad and Sophia] would do things wrong, we would miss deadlines, and we would have to do this and it was kind of tough." Sophia stated that the college choice process was tough and specified that while she was in this process her dad did his best to help her. Throughout the process, Sophia "pushed off" applying to college. But it was her dad and mom who intervened and guided her to complete applications. She shared, "My dad would be like, 'you better do that.' And then in one week I would send everything off. My mom drove me around to get papers and send them off." With parental support, Sophia narrowed down college options and applied. Family can be the students' first taste of college life and the best recruiters as students grow up; the students' home and cultural ties are also contributing factors to their college choice process.

HOME AND CULTURAL TIES

Similar to Peters' (2018) model where identity and community were significant, home and the cultural ties to home were important factors for students when deciding which college to attend. For both the quantitative findings and the sharing circles, the proximity to home was significant when considering which college to attend. Table 10.1 highlights the constructs that were relevant for the college choice process based on the survey results; specifically featuring the students' attitudes or experiences regarding their decision to go to college and what influenced that decision. We present findings that show Native students' hesitancy to leave home due to family responsibilities. For many Indigenous students they have important roles within their home that may tie them to helping their elders, watching over their siblings, or taking care of the land/home. In the sharing circles, we further understand their roles at home and the significance of being "close to home" as a powerful connection for Indigenous students and their college decision-making (Tachine, 2022; Tachine et al., 2017; Waterman, 2012).

Participants applied and gained acceptance to various colleges, including prestigious, elite colleges, across the nation. As students approached

Table 10.1. Results of t-test for Native American and white students on family and college choice processes. *Source*: Created by the author.

	Native American (n = 43)	white (n = 1,830)
Attitudes and experiences about college		
I have been planning to attend college since elementary school	3.51* (.810)	3.83* (.519)
At least one of my parents played an active role in helping me plan for college	3.34 (.762)	3.37 (.841)
I was hesitant to leave home to attend college due to family responsibilities	2.27* (1.162)	1.54* (.826)
Influences on attending University of Arizona		
I received scholarship(s) from the University of Arizona	.43* (.501)	.68* (.467)
I wanted to be near home	2.17* (.834)	1.78* (.792)

Note: * p < .003. Bonferroni corrected alpha based on original alpha of .05. Standard deviations appear in parentheses below means.

making a final choice on which college to attend, a powerful influence in this decision-making process was being close to home and family. Kaylene described, "Home is very important to me and I knew I was going to miss it so much so it [college] had to be somewhere close to home or the closest to home that I can get, so that I can go home every now and then." Kaylene applied to a handful of colleges and decided upon choosing a college that was about approximately 350 miles away—a day's drive. Sophia had a similar viewpoint as she shared: "I don't think like my family said like, 'You can't go far.' It was me starting to realize at the last minute that I was planning on going halfway on the other side of the United States. It kind of hit me that I didn't want to be that far. . . . I started realizing how homesick I would get or how alone I would be because I'm really close to my family and so I just kind of had to choose [state's college]." Sophia aspired to attend college far from home, and then she had an opportunity to go to school far from home. However, as she stated, she eventually chose to attend college closer to home and go to the University of Arizona, even though at first UA was a backup choice.

When students were probed about why they chose to attend college close to home, deeper understanding of how family shaped this decision emerged, as Clarissa shared: "For me, they [my family] didn't like the idea that their child being so far away from home because they always had the idea that when you leave, that you're not going to come back. That's what happened to my mom because she left the rez and she stayed in [state's city], but she still goes back but yeah she didn't like the idea that one of us is going to leave and not come back home." Clarissa's mom moved away from the reservation after she graduated from high school and did not return to live on the reservation. Because of her mom's past experience with leaving home, Clarissa felt like her mother believed that a similar experience could occur for Clarissa.

Tammy gave another perspective on why she chose to attend college close to home. Tammy considers herself to be closely tied to her Navajo traditional ceremonies as that is a way of life that she was raised in. Tammy shared: "I ended up changing my mind knowing that there is a really long distance between home and where I would be going to school. For me, I've been really tied to my traditional part of my life and that's a really big part of me and I wasn't exactly ready to go that far and just let go of all of the ceremonies and not to be able to go home to those kinds of things." Ceremonies are conducted within the ancestral lands of her people, predominately located within her tribal reservation boundaries. Therefore, she selected a college that was close by so that she could travel home for ceremony purposes, which points to the significance of the student's connection to their ways of knowing, the land, and their family. Tammy's story is consistent with the student experiences in Peters' college choice model, where cultural ties and connection to home kept students from looking at schools out of state so they could easily return when needed.

Discussion and Conclusion

Much of the college choice literature is normed around the experiences of middle-class, white students with college-educated parents in which college choice is frequently seen as an individual process (Iloh, 2019). Missing from traditional conceptions is the collective, interdependent, family-based dimension of college choice or how Native American students engage in this process. While we analyzed our work through Native Nation Building and Peters' Native American Student College Choice model, we found that students were not articulating college choice using Native Nation Building terminology such as to strengthen sovereignty or assert self-determination. However, they conceptualized college going from a *Family Building* framework to strengthen family and be a role model for future family members, which is ultimately a precursor to Native Nation Building.

Through both the survey and sharing circle analyses, there were substantial areas of departure and overlap for Native students. In the survey, Native students tended to consider college significantly later in their educational careers than their peers. This was not, however, a prescription for failure but highlighted that more of the story was missing. Within the sharing circles students shared how they were more proactive in receiving college knowledge from their family. These sentiments were rooted in family building and in seeking out their family and community for resources and support. This builds from previous studies that have found family to be a significant source of knowledge and support within the college choice process for Latina/o/x and Black students (see George Mwangi chapter 11 in this volume; George Mwangi et al., 2020; Knight et al., 2004; Luedke, 2020). Furthermore, we found that having a family member who has attended college, specifically the University of Arizona, to be significant for the sharing circles. The college ideologies (Kiyama, 2010) described within the sharing circle stories formed as early as 6 years of age. Students told stories of when they first visited college campuses with family that sparked college as a viable pathway and created in a sense a college-going culture within the home. Moreover, familial tradition at the UA also played a role for some of the students in the sharing circles as a brother, sister, or parent previously attending helped the participants solidify their plans to follow suit. The impact of seeing their family member attend college made it a possibility, and in some circumstances an expectation for them in the future. With this knowledge and concept of family building, it would be interesting to see how leveraging Native alumni and current Native college students might be able to perform a similar function for first-generation Native students.

Consistent with the idea of higher education as Native Nation Building (Brayboy et al., 2012) and Peters' college choice model, the decision to attend college tended to be made collectively between Native students and their families. The need to be close to home was important for Native students relative to their white peers. The desire to be close to home was frequently driven by the need to maintain ties with family and Native culture, and this was particularly important for students who frequently returned home to participate in traditional ceremonies (Waterman, 2012). As seen within the survey the students would weigh their options, considering their responsibilities at home, making proximity to home an essential part of their decision-making process because of their role within the family system.

This study has a number of implications for research and practice. The survey was designed based on non-Native conceptions of college choice that frequently did not capture important parts of the process that the qualitative component was able to reveal. The constructs assessed the students' success through an independent lens based on the individual and not a communal interdependent framework of family. Future quantitative work needs to be more intentionally rooted in Indigenous methodologies, following tribal protocols in the way that the sharing circles were developed (Kovach, 2021; Lopez, 2018, 2020; Lopez & Tachine, 2021; Nelson, 2015; Reyes & Lopez, 2024; Smith, 2019, Tachine, 2022).

The results also highlight the diversity within Native American students. There were different needs for students based upon first-generation status. Those who were first-generation required more support in the application process as they often felt alone. This is critically important because Native students began the college choice process significantly later than their non-Native peers and, therefore, have less time to negotiate the complexities of college going. For those students who were the first in their family to attend, their family's support and encouragement can be key in their success (Yellow Bird, 2020). These students were also motivated to pursue higher education to help better their family's circumstances, thus starting the family building path of others to follow. Additionally, there were differences that existed between students who lived on reservations versus those who did not. For those who lived on the reservation, being close to home to attend traditional ceremonies was important in their decision-making process. This is not to say culture and tradition was unimportant to those not living on the reservation, but rather reservation students distinctly desired to attend college closer to home.

In terms of institutional practice, these analyses highlight the importance of university outreach, but administrators need to be keenly aware of the cultural norms of the community. Just as traditional (white) approaches to scholarship would not have been effective for the current analysis, outreach efforts that neglect to take into account Native ways of knowing will also be ineffective. For example, college is traditionally viewed as a time when students forge a new identity separate from their parents (e.g., Tinto, 1993). Instead, these students' stories highlight the need to maintain strong ties with their families and communities—and an understanding that going away to college can weaken these bonds. Thus, outreach needs to be sensitive to these issues, and some approaches can include highlighting Native-specific support services, Native alumni, and programs that create a Native community within a predominantly white campus.

Too often university programming shies away from trying to increase parental involvement in their "child's" education, and this largely derives from the fear of "helicopter parents" (Shoup et al., 2009) or the worldview that, at the age of 18, students are now adults who have the right to make autonomous life decisions. This, again, is an area where some careful navigation and understanding of whiteness is required. Native student academic identity is forged around their familial and cultural connections, which should not be viewed as a deficit but as a worldview to be embraced and valued. The success of these students largely depends on how they can continue to honor their Indigenous ways of being, and this means that the university needs to be seen as a welcoming environment to families.

What this study has shed light on is the significance of family and their influence on their child's life. Through the sharing circles we saw the strength that family has in supporting their students on their path into higher education; regardless of whether their family had attended college, they continued to support and push them. The implication for families and their children is to continue to love and support your students. We encourage all the parents, families, and loved ones to keep asking those questions and advocating for your students; if you do not know the answers, ask around until you are able to find someone who does—this is the power of family and community.

While the work in this chapter is specific to one institution, there are implications well beyond this locale. We have identified a distinct collective college choice process or Family Building framework for Native American students that has the potential to enhance our understanding of college choice. Additionally, knowing what factors influence college choice may offer innovative ways institutional programs (such as access, outreach, and first-year transition), as well as areas within recruitment and admissions, can improve programming development and partnerships that would incorporate family in the college choice process. Recognizing family building during the college choice process can result in a smoother college transition, better situating a student for success and essentially resulting in greater Native Nation Building long-term.

Critical Reflection

1. What are ways that institutions and higher education initiatives could utilize and implement family building for Native students and their families?

2. How does family building resonate with your college choice process?

3. What institutional policies limit the ability for family building (as a college choice pathway) to flourish for Native students and their families?

Notes

1. Native, Native American, and Indigenous are used interchangeably throughout the chapter. Native peoples have the complexities of not only the ethnic identity label, but more importantly identity is rooted in sovereign nations, thus the unique dynamic of being both a racial and political identity.

2. Dr. Michelle Espino is a scholar in higher education. Dr. Espino's contributions to the field of student affairs administration and higher education focus on understanding how institutional cultures, policies, and practices as well as community contexts affect and inform educational achievement, outcomes, and experiences along the P-20 pipeline for POC, particularly for Latinx.

3. Systemic monsters are "the interlocking structures of power rooted in White supremacy, settler colonialism, racism, erasure, heteropatriarchy, and capitalism that disrupt sovereignty and belonging" (Tachine, 2022, p. 7).

References

Adams, D. W. (1995). *Education for extinction*. University Press of Kansas.

Agresti, A., & Finlay, B. (2009). *Statistical methods for the social sciences* (4th ed). Pearson Prentice Hall.

Brayboy, B., Fann, A., Castagno, A., Solyom, J. (2012). Postsecondary education for American Indian and Alaska Natives: Higher education for nation building and self-determination. *ASHE Higher Education Report 37*(5). Wiley Periodicals.

Burkhart, B. Y. (2004). What Coyote and Thales can teach us: An outline of American Indian epistemology. In Anne Waters (Ed.), *American Indian thought: Philosophical essays* (pp. 15–26). Blackwell.

Cabrera, N. L. (2019). *White guys on campus: Racism, white immunity, and the myth of "post-racial" higher education*. Rutgers University Press.

Cajete, G. A. (1999). *Igniting the sparkle: An Indigenous science education model*. Kivaki Press.

Dillman, M. L. (2002). *The college experience of Native American students: Factors associated with their choice of major, performance and persistence*. [Doctoral dissertation, University of Central Florida]. ProQuest.

Fann, A. J. (2005). *Forgotten students: American Indian high school student narratives on college access* [Doctoral dissertation, University of California, Los Angeles]. ProQuest.

Ford, K.S., Patterson, A. N., & Johnston-Guerrero, M. P. (2021). Monoracial normativity in university websites: Systematic erasure and selective reclassification of multiracial students. *Journal of Diversity in Higher Education, 14*(2), 252–263. https://doi.org/10.1037/dhe0000154

Fryberg, S., & Markus, H. R. (2007). Cultural models of education in American Indian, Asian American, and European American contexts. *Social Psychology of Education, 10*, 213–246. https://doi.org/10.1007/s11218-007-9017-z

George Mwangi, C. A. (2015). (Re)Examining the role of family and community in college access and choice: A metasynthesis. *Review of Higher Education, 39*(1), 123–151. https://doi.org/10.1353/rhe.2015.0046

George Mwangi, C. A., Malcolm, M., & Thelamour, B. (2023). Our college degree: Familial engagement in the lives of diverse Black collegians. *Race Ethnicity and Education, 26*(7), 872–891. https://doi.org/10.1080/13613324.2020.184 2347

Grande, S. (2004). *Red pedagogy: Native American social and political thought.* Rowman & Littlefield.

Grinde, D., Jr. (2004). Taking the Indian out of the Indian: US policies of ethnocide through education. *Wicazo Sa Review, 19*(2), 25–32. https://doi.org/10.1353/wic.2004.0018

Hossler, D., & Gallagher, K. S. (1987). Studying student college choice: A three-phase model and the implications for policymakers. *College and University 2,* 207–221.

Hurtado, S., Inkelas, K. K., Briggs, C., & Rhee, B. (1997). Differences in college access and choice among racial/ethnic groups: Identifying continuing barriers. *Research in Higher Education, 38*(1) 43–76. https://doi.org/10.1023/A:1024948728792

Iloh, C. (2018). Neighborhood cultural heterogeneity and the college aspirations of low-income students of color. *Children, Youth and Environments, 28*(1), 9–29.

Iloh, C. (2019). An alternative to college "choice" models and frameworks: The Iloh model of college-going decisions and trajectories. *College and University, 94*(4), 2–9.

Jackson, A. P., Smith, S. A., & Hill, C. L. (2003). Academic persistence among Native American college students. *Journal of College Student Development, 44*(4), 548–565. https://doi.org/10.1353/csd.2003.0039

Kiyama, J. M. (2010). College aspirations and limitations: The role of educational ideologies and funds of knowledge in Mexican American families. *American Educational Research Journal, 47*(2), 330–356. https://doi.org/10.3102/0002831209357468

Knight, M. G., Norton, N. E., Bentley, C. C., & Dixon, I. R. (2004). The power of Black and Latina/o counterstories: Urban families and college-going processes. *Anthropology & Education Quarterly, 35*(1), 99–120. https://doi.org/10.1525/aeq.2004.35.1.99

Kovach, M. (2009). *Indigenous methodologies: Characteristics, conversations, and contexts.* University of Toronto Press.

Kovach, M. (2021). *Indigenous methodologies: Characteristics, conversations, and contexts* (2nd ed). University of Toronto Press.

Lomawaima, K. T. (1995). *They called it prairie light: The story of Chilocco Indian School.* University of Nebraska Press.

Lomawaima, K. T. (2004). American Indian education: By Indians versus for Indians. *A companion to American Indian history,* 422–440. https://doi.org/10.1002/9780470996461.ch24

Lopez, J. D. (2018). *To help others like me Quechan and Cocopah postsecondary persistence for nation-building.* Arizona State University Press.

Lopez, J. D. (2020). Indigenous data collection: Addressing limitations in Native American samples. *Journal of College Student Development, 61*(6), 750–764. https://doi.org/10.1353/csd.2020.0073.

Lopez, J. D., & Tachine, A. R. (2021). Giving back: Deconstructing persistence for Indigenous students. *Journal of College Student Development, 62*(5), 613–618. https://doi.org/10.1353/csd.2021.0060.

Luedke, C. L. (2020). Developing a college-going habitus: How first-generation Latina/o/x students bi-directionally exchange familial funds of knowledge and capital within their familias. *Journal of Higher Education, 91*(7), 1028–1052. https://doi.org/10.1080/00221546.2020.1726702

National Center for Education Statistics. (2022). *Total fall enrollment in degree-granting postsecondary institutions, by level of enrollment, sex, attendance status, and race/ethnicity or nonresident status of student: Selected years, 1976 through 2022.* US Department of Education. https://nces.ed.gov/programs/digest/d23/tables/dt23_306.10.asp

Nelson, C. A. (2015). *American Indian college students as Native nation builders: Tribal financial aid as a lens for understanding college-going paradoxes* [Doctoral dissertation, University of Arizona]. https://repository.arizona.edu/handle/10150/556872

Nelson, C. A., Tachine, A. R., & Lopez, J. D. (2021). Recognize it's our land, and honor the treaties. In *Changing the Narrative, 15.* Lumina Foundation.

Pérez, P. A., & McDonough, P. M. (2008). Understanding Latina and Latino college choice: A social capital and chain migration analysis. *Journal of Hispanic Higher Education, 7*(3), 249–265. https://doi.org/10.1177/1538192708317620

Perna, L. W. (2000). Differences in the decision to attend college among African Americans, Hispanics, and whites. *Journal of Higher Education, 71*(2), 117–141. http://dx.doi.org/10.2307/2649245

Perna, L. W. (2006). Studying college access and choice: A proposed conceptual model. In J.C. Smart (Eds.), *Higher Education: Handbook of Theory and Research* (pp. 99–157). Springer.

Peters, B. A. (2018). *"My education, not only for me and my family but my people": Storied experiences of Native American students' college choice at four-year institutions in North Carolina* (Publication No:10970037) [Doctoral dissertation, North Carolina State University]. ProQuest.

Plano Clark, V. L., & Creswell, J. W. (2008). *The mixed methods reader.* Sage.

Reyes, N. A. (2016). *"What am I doing to be a good ancestor?" An Indigenized phenomenology of giving back among Native college graduates.* University of Texas at San Antonio.

Reyes, N. A. S., & Lopez, J. D. (2024). Ripples on the water: Understanding giving back among Native college students. In H. J. Shotton, S. J. Waterman, N. R. Youngbull, & S. C. Lowe (Eds.), *Developments beyond the Asterisk* (pp. 104–118). Routledge.

Sax, L. J., Gilmartin, S. K., & Bryant, A. N. (2003). Assessing response rates and nonresponse bias in web and paper surveys. *Research in Higher Education, 44*(4), 409–432. https://doi.org/10.1023/A:1024232915870

Shotton, H. J., Lowe, S. C., Waterman, S. J. (Eds.). (2013). *Beyond the asterisk: Understanding Native students in higher education*. Stylus.

Shoup, R., Gonyea, R. M., & Kuh, G. D. (2009). Helicopter parents: Examining the impact of highly involved parents on student engagement and educational outcomes. In *49th Annual Forum of the Association for Institutional Research, Atlanta, Georgia* (vol. 202009). http://cpr.iub.edu/uploads/AIR

Smith, L. T. (1999). *Decolonizing methodologies: Research and Indigenous peoples*. Zed Books.

Smith, L. T. (2019). *Decolonizing research: Indigenous storywork as methodology*. Bloomsbury.

Starks, J. E. (2010). *Factors influencing the decisions of Native Americans to attend or not attend college or vocational school* (Publication No. 3433010) [Doctoral dissertation, College of Saint Mary]. ProQuest.

St. John, E. P., Paulsen, M. B., & Carter, D. F. (2005). Diversity, college costs, and postsecondary opportunity: An examination of the financial nexus between college choice and persistence for African Americans and whites. *Journal of Higher Education, 76*(5), 545–569. https://doi.org/10.1080/0022 1546.2005.11772298

Tachine, A. R. (2017). Grandmothers' pedagogy: Lessons for supporting Native students' attendance at universities. In J. Frawley, S. Larkin, & J. A. Smith (Eds.), *Indigenous pathways, transitions and participation in higher education* (pp. 151–167). Springer.

Tachine, A. R. (2022). *Native presence and sovereignty in college: Sustaining Indigenous weapons to defeat systemic monsters*. Teachers College Press.

Tachine, A. R., Yellow Bird, E., & Cabrera, N. L. (2016). Sharing circles: An Indigenous methodology approach for working with Indigenous peoples. *International Review of Qualitative Research, 9*(3), 277–295.

Tinto, V. (1993). *Leaving college: Rethinking the causes and cures of student attrition* (2nd ed.). University of Chicago Press.

United States Department of Education. (2010). Tribal leaders speak: The state of Indian education, 2010 (Report of the consultations with tribal leaders in Indian Country). Retrieved from: http://www2.ed.gov/about/inits/ed/indianed/consultations.report.pdf

Walter, M., Kukutai, T., Carroll, S. R., & Rodriguez-Lonebear, D. (2020). *Indigenous data sovereignty and policy*. Taylor & Francis. https://doi.org/10.4324/9780429273957

Waterman, S. J. (2012). Home-going as a strategy for success among Haudenosaunee college and university students. *Journal of Student Affairs Research and Practice, 49*(2), 193–209. https://doi.org/10.1515/jsarp-2012-6378

Waterman, S. J., Lowe, S. C., & Shotton, H. J. (Eds.). (2018). *Beyond access: Indigenizing programs for Native American student success.* Taylor & Francis.

Yellow Bird, E. (2020). Settler colonial institutions of higher education: Indigenizations, generations & warriors (Chasing Butterflies). [Unpublished doctoral dissertation]. University of Arizona.

Chapter 11

Under the Baobab Tree

Developing a Family-Centered Framework for
College Choice with Black African Immigrant Families

Chrystal A. George Mwangi

❧

*On the front door of the Enemari house is a sign that states, "All
are welcome in our home," and the members of this household
truly live up to that statement. Each time I arrived to interview
the family there was always a meal prepared that I was obliged
to eat, at least a half hour of conversation expected before the
formal interviews began, and many other family friends in the
home that provided a lively environment. At the end of each
interview session, which was always held on Sunday evenings,
the father, Adakole, or one of the older children would get in
their car and lead me out of their neighborhood to ensure that
I safely got back to the highway and asked that I call when I
arrived home to make sure that I reached my house safely as
well. The Enemari family—Adakole (father); Owole (mother);
the four eldest children, Simon, David, Nehemiah, and Helen;
and the youngest child Agaba (who was engaging in the college
choice process)—welcomed me into their lives, providing personal*

narratives of their immigration history, educational achievements, college-going experiences, and family life.

☙

"Karibu sana!" Atieno Amolo expressed as I walked in the door of her Maryland townhome for the first time. This Swahili word literally means "draw close," but in this context Atieno was expressing to me "you are very welcome my home." Atieno is a 44-year-old Kenyan mother of three and has lived in the United States for 14 years. When I arrived her oldest children—daughter Sara, age 18, and daughter Hannah, age 17—were sitting in the living room watching TV while their younger brother Kimani, age 7, played with his toys in a corner of the dining room. When Atieno announced my presence, all of the children came to the front door to greet me and Sara began to make me a cup of Kenyan chai [tea]. Atieno's husband, Kenneth, is also a part of the Amolo household; however, he is pursuing business ventures in Kenya and thus participated in the interviews via the phone and video chat. Although their immediate family is separated by thousands of miles while Kenneth is abroad, I still saw a strong sense of togetherness among the family as Kimani sat on his mother's lap at the dining room table along with his sisters and his father [who was on a tablet on video chat] as I spoke to Atieno, Hannah, Sara, and Kenneth about their lives and educational experiences.

☙

One in four youth growing up in the United States have parents who emigrated from other countries (Batalova, 2024). These children are contributing to the increased diversification of American schools due to the massive influx of immigrants of non-European descent to the United States since the passage of the Hart-Celler Act of 1965 (Bolter, 2022; Chishti et al., 2015). The presence of immigrant children, particularly from nonwhite, nondominant cultures within US schools reinforces the critical need for culturally sustaining education practices and scholarship (George Mwangi & English, 2017).

To support this call, my chapter focuses on the role of culture and worldviews in the college preparation of Black African immigrants. African immigrants are one of the fastest growing immigrant populations in the United States, increasing by nearly 160% between 2010 and 2019 (Lorenzi & Batalova, 2022). There is a strong and consistent African immigrant presence in U.S. higher education and over 40% percent of this population holds a college degree (Lorenzi & Batalova, 2022). This chapter emphasizes Black African immigrant families' use of family heritage, culture, and immigrant identity in the development of educational aspirations and college-going strategies in the United States. The two vignettes at the beginning of this chapter are an illustration of the journey that I took with these families in developing a new family-centered frame for understanding college going: Under the Baobab Tree.

Engaging in Inquiry with Families

Each family participating in the study was comprised of (a) Black African immigrants from an Anglophone country and voluntary immigrants (not refugees or asylees); (b) parent(s) who were first-generation (immigrants to the United States who were born abroad) and at least one of their children being 1.5 or second-generation (child of first-generation immigrants who immigrated to the United States before age 12 or a US-born child of first-generation immigrants); and (c) a child being in grades 7–12 with the intent of college enrollment. Nine families participated, inclusive of 30 individuals. Families originated from Nigeria, Kenya, Liberia, and Ghana and the college-going children within these families represented the 7th, 9th, 10th, 11th, and 12th grades. All participant names used in this chapter are pseudonyms.

Participatory methodologies emphasize relational processes and relationship building (Kesby, 2000). As the introductory vignettes illustrated, I met with each family on three occasions in their home over three months, which allowed us to get to know one another in their space and co-construct the research. Although I conducted interviews during these sessions, we also ate meals together, shared stories, and engaged in conversation. Because of my research and professional experience with college access, parents expressed an interest in me speaking with them and their children about potential college-going strategies. This expectation made me more aware of my positionality and the power dynamic between the participants and myself. In response, I sought to provide the families with the knowledge I had as a means of reciprocity for their engagement in this project and to further empower their ability to navigate US educational systems. Therefore, we also spent time engaging in informal discussions about these topics and together considered various strategies that could help them to navigate college preparation.

During each session, interviews were conducted with the family together as a group (family interview) and then with individual family members. The first session focused on the family, such as family history, dynamics, and educational experiences. The second and third sessions focused on the families' college-going process. During the family interviews, we would often sit down together in their living room or around a dining room table. I used a semistructured interview protocol that provided initial guiding questions, one that deemphasized my role as directive and instead emphasized communication among the family (Beitin, 2007). After the group interview, I met one-on-one with family members, so that they would have the opportunity to describe their experiences privately and in more detail to me.

African indigenous knowledge systems indicate that the use of words alone may not be the most effective or appropriate type of communication to share lived experiences, emotions, and perspectives (Owusu-Ansah & Miji, 2013). Thus, I also used participatory diagramming during family interviews, which is a visual and oral method that shifts the interpretive focus away from the researcher to the participants (Alexander et al., 2007; Kesby, 2000). During group interviews I asked the participants to develop a diagram together and then encouraged them to discuss and analyze the diagram among themselves rather than solely describe it to me as the researcher (Kesby, 2000). In this way, participants learn from, act on, and extend the research findings that they have created through the diagram (Kesby, 2000).

Each family worked together to draw two diagrams with large poster paper and markers. During the first session, the family drew their familial network—specifically, which individuals in the network were involved in the college choice process and how the individuals were involved. Each household constructed the boundaries of their distinct family by diagramming their familial network and analyzing whom and how members of their network were involved in the college choice process. I worked with the immediate households to invite these additional individuals whom they identified as family and as involved in the college choice process to participate in the study. This helped to extend the notion of family beyond the "nuclear family" definition used in traditional college choice literature to include a broader kinship network (e.g., both immediate and extended family as well as fictive kin) (George Mwangi, 2015).

During the second family interview, families diagrammed their conceptualization of the steps or components of the college choice process. Families were asked in their group interview to discuss among themselves the diagram they created, express concerns regarding barriers to the college choice process that they perceived, engage in discussion about resources needed to successfully navigate the process, and develop strategies for navigating the process. Participatory diagramming helped provide a rich and more relevant portrayal of the college choice process for the families in the study, illustrating both their familial dynamics and communication as well as their understanding of the college choice process in ways that may have been missed without ensuring their ownership of interpretation and analysis.

During analysis, participants reviewed their interview transcripts and other data to work with me to develop an initial coding scheme. I asked participants to read through the documents and comment upon codes and preliminary findings. I also provided families with a document listing themes and patterns identified in their family dialogue data to gain their feedback and clarification. I used participants' reactions and suggestions to refine the coding system before moving into further analysis. Finally, I sent at least one member of each of the families a description of the larger storyline that was developed to confirm their satisfaction with it.

Constructing a New Frame

I began my research framed by a stage-based college choice model because it was what I was taught as the way to understand college choice. Yet, I also remained open to how families defined the college choice process for themselves. For example, through participatory diagramming, families drew what they perceived to be the steps or components of the college choice process without prior exposure to a college choice theory or model.

While I found some similarities between existing theories and the ways that families diagrammed and described their college choice process, the narratives families provided were richer and more multifaceted. Families described the college choice process being situated within and impacted by the college choice processes of parents, siblings, and other family members. Families were also projecting past the selection of an undergraduate institution by also discussing the graduate school choice process, career choice process, and the choice process involved in transferring from a 2- to 4-year institution. Additionally, college choice was often not limited by spatial or time boundaries. They utilized family and community networks both locally and across continents to navigate college choice and often conceptualized the process as part of the family's immigration history. Families described the process as being more of a reflection of developing and sustaining family belief systems and culture around college going and academic success than it was about specific milestones or stages.

Existing college choice frameworks were too restrictive because they described the process of a student, not of a family. Instead, my data revealed the importance of understanding how the families experienced college choice together, which is reflective of a family- and community-centric worldview found in African worldview and indigenous knowledge systems (Arthur, 2008, 2010; Nyang, 2018; Swigart, 2001). African worldview and indigenous knowledge are systems of thought grounded in African cultures and traditions (Belgrave & Allison, 2006). While these diverse cultures and traditions exhibit uniqueness and nuance, there is also similarity in the African worldview, for example, knowledge and ways of living focused on interdependence, spirituality, harmony, time orientation, sensitivity to affect, collectivism, balance, and oral tradition (Belgrave & Allision, 2006; Kambon, 1992). African indigenous knowledge reflects a relational worldview characterized by being collective, practical, social, and interpersonal (Mpofu, 2002; Nsamenang, 2006). Many African societies prioritize the needs of the family and community, along with collective growth and survival, above the individual (Kambon, 1992; Myers, 1988; Swigart, 2001), highlighting similarities to the Native Nation Building and Family Building frameworks applied by Yellow Bird and colleagues in chapter 10.

The African worldview system is "characteristically oral and passed on from generation to generation in the context of community living and activities" (Owusu-Ansah & Miji, 2013, para. 7; Kamya, 2005). This oral tradition is often communicated through proverbs, call and response, metaphors, storytelling, songs, and riddles (Knowles-Borishade, 1991; Ngara, 2007). The families in my study used metaphors to describe their college choice process as well. Ruth Obi described college choice as similar to baking a cake and Olaf Magimbi explained his family's academic expectations and support as comparable to putting a poster on a wall. Thus, I began to consider how a metaphor could describe the college choice process of the families. As I engaged in the data, I began to see the families as a living, breathing organism that grows and adapts together. I found the baobab tree to reflect many similar characteristics to the families in this study and in sharing this metaphor with them, they agreed. Thus, rather than conforming or limiting the findings to extant theories and frameworks, I proposed the baobab tree to be a more relevant metaphor for describing how the families engaged in college choice together.

THE BAOBAB TREE

The African baobab tree is found in over 31 countries throughout Africa, primarily in hot, dry savannahs (Sidibe & Williams, 2002). It is known for its massive height and girth, growing up to 60 feet tall and 115 feet wide (Sidibe & Williams, 2002). Baobab branches are typically located at the top of the tree growing upward toward the sky (National Research Council, 2008). This resembles a root system, which explains the baobab's nickname as the "upside-down tree" (National Research Council, 2008). Its scientific name, *Adansonia digitata*, refers to fingers, and each leaf of the tree has five leaflets resembling an outstretched hand (Sidibe & Williams, 2002).

This species is found to be among the most effective trees at preventing water loss, having root systems that spread further than the height of the tree (Sidibe & Williams, 2002). This root system contributes to baobabs' ability to survive in dry climates, making maximum use of the scarce resources around it. The baobab trunk can swell to store thousands of gallons of water within its wood's spongy tissue (Sidibe & Williams, 2002).

Baobab trees are a provider within their community, having many uses, including medicinal, sustenance, and bark fibers utilized for a variety of purposes. A baobab tree can create its own ecosystem (National Research Council, 2008) and communities use the hollowed trunks to make water reservoirs (Sidibe & Williams, 2002). Many of the plant parts are edible, including the leaves, flowers, fruit, and seeds (National Research Council, 2008). The large trees' trunks are naturally hollow and thus can provide shelter and storage spaces (Sidibe & Williams, 2002). The tree has exceptional vitality, and even after an entire tree is cut down or is blown over in a storm it regenerates from the root and continues to grow (Sidibe & Williams, 2002).

There are many African myths and legends about the baobab tree. It is a symbol of the strength of Africa and is referred to as the "tree of life" (National Research Council, 2008). Baobabs can experience drought, burning, and other harsh elements but continue to endure, heal, and thrive (Sidibe & Williams, 2002). The baobab's large stature and ability to give shelter provide a human meeting place for dialogue, sharing stories, and debate (Pakenham, 2004). Thus, these giant trees are a symbol of community and a gathering place (Pakenham, 2004).

The baobab tree represents endurance, conservation, creativity, ingenuity, and dialogue (Sidibe & Williams, 2002). The longevity of the baobab defines it as a living elder "on a continent, which reveres elders" (Pakenham, 2004, p. 102). In some African countries, community members give a funeral for a baobab when it dies, playing drums typically reserved for revered leaders; it "is one of the only trees in Africa preserved as repositories for the ancestors; hence it is believed to have spiritual power over its community's welfare" (Sidibe & Williams, 2002, p. 23). The baobab's branches, which grow straight up, have been said to reflect arms stretching upward in desire to reach heaven, in friendship, for hope, and for ambition (Pakenham, 2004).

Baobab Families

> Eventually, the rain stopped, and we found ourselves looking on a barren landscape of gravel and shrub and the occasional baobab tree, its naked, searching branches decorated with the weaverbird's spherical nests. I remembered reading somewhere that the baobab could go for years without flowering, surviving on the sparsest of rainfall; and seeing the trees there in the hazy afternoon light, I understood why men believed they possessed a special power—that they housed ancestral spirits and demons, that humankind first appeared under such a tree. It wasn't merely the oddness of their shape, their almost prehistoric outline against the stripped down sky. "They look as if each one could tell a story . . ."
>
> —Barack Obama, *Dreams from My Father*

As the child of an African father, President Obama's quote about his encounter with baobab trees in Kenya provides a fitting introduction to understanding the cases within this study as Baobab Families. Like the baobab trees in his quote that "look as if each one could tell a story" (Obama, 2004, p. 437), the families in my study each have a rich story to tell as well. Compiled together, their narratives parallel the wise and enduring nature of the baobab by reflecting families' intentional use of family and community networks, culture, strategies, and other resources to develop their own college-going culture and engage in the college choice process.

I view each of the families in this study as a baobab tree and every tree is unique. Thus, the families each have their own distinct structure and characteristics, including single- and two-parent households, families with multiple or single children, various household incomes, and differing nationalities. Yet, while differences exist, there are also similarities. Baobab Families possess diverse resources that they used to navigate college choice, which included those brought from Africa, those learned through life in US society, and those gained during the college choice process itself. Baobab Families each stored their resources within their tree's hollow trunk, utilizing them throughout the college choice process. While each family possessed its own set of unique resources, there were three types present across families: college-going legacies, cultural and familial identity, and family and community networks.

College-Going Legacies

Baobab Families described the goal of going to college as part of a larger family effort toward upward mobility and success that is rooted firmly in education. Each has an immigration history that initiated with a family member coming to the United States for an undergraduate or graduate degree. This was not surprising as one of the most common reasons for African immigration to the United States is for higher education (Arthur, 2010; George Mwangi et al., 2019). Adakole Enemari lived apart from his wife and children for nine years while he attained two master's degrees in the United States. Gatwiri Magimbi completed a college degree as a single mother with no other family in the United States. Both Ruth Obi and Atieno Amolo also immigrated to the United States to pursue college. These efforts required several sacrifices, including leaving one's home country, financial instability, and years spent away from loved ones. As these first-generation immigrants attained college degrees, they handed down their family's value of education and "college-going legacy" to their own children.

College going in Baobab Families was not based on a desire for individual success but instead was part of a plan to provide a better life for one's family and particularly for one's children. Even when their endeavors became challenging, parents found ways to achieve their goal. For example, Ruth Obi changed her career path after giving birth to her daughter, Priscilla: "[I could] either neglect my studies or neglect my child. But I knew my education could provide the best life for my child, so instead of quitting school, I switched to a more flexible major. I gave up my dream of being a pharmacist." Atieno Amolo's professional skills as a Kenyan journalist did not transfer to the United States, so she gave up that career, which she loved, to pursue a master's degree in education: "My focus was that I wanted my kids to grow up here [in the United States] and have the opportunities that are in this country . . . Maybe I won't ever be able to go back to journalism, but I still accomplished something in my life because my kids are in America."

First-generation immigrant parents pursued higher education in the United States for the benefit of their families. Therefore, it was natural for parents to view this achievement as a resource or value that they could provide to their children as a legacy. Adakole Enemari explained, "Education is our legacy. It is what my parents provided for me, and it is what we as parents provide for the children. It is why we [the Enemari family] are here [in the United States] and it is how we will succeed here."

Funds of knowledge provide an additional lens for understanding Baobab Families' college-going legacies. Although *funds of knowledge* is typically used to describe the adaptive strategies of rural and/or working-class immigrant populations who do not have a family history of (US) college education (Kiyama, 2010; Kiyama & Rios-Aguilar, 2018; Moll et al., 1992), for Baobab Families, going to college in the United States reflected a survival strategy and adaptive response because it was a means of entering the United States, remaining in the United States, and providing future well-being and economic stability for the family (George Mwangi, 2018a). These college-going legacies are deeply rooted within the families' immigration histories and identity, offering influential messages to 1.5- and second-generation children about the importance of going to college as representative of their familial and cultural self.

Further, some parents described acting as a role model for college because their children grew up seeing them attend college in the United States. While having parents who are college educated puts students at an advantage in achieving access to college (Almeida, 2015; Cabrera & La Nasa, 2000), going to college while raising their children gave parents in

Baobab families the opportunity to talk about college, expose their children to the process of pursuing a college degree, and often gave children the opportunity to be on a college campus at a young age. Parents' possession of a college degree creates exposure to opportunities for the family in the college choice process, while their stories of "back home" and narratives of struggle to achieve a college degree were cultural practices of communication and parenting that socialized their children toward college.

CULTURAL AND FAMILIAL IDENTITY

Families also reinforced college-going legacies to their children by stressing that education was a part of their family, culture, and heritage. Ruth Obi expressed that she often tells her daughter, Priscilla: "Nigerians as a whole love to go to school, they love education, no matter what it takes for them." Atieno Amolo's view of Kenyans and education was similar: "People, parents believe that children must be educated . . . so I just knew that it is me, it is my culture to go to college. It's like a culture." These examples illustrate how Baobab Families described college going as part of cultural identity. Portes and Fernandez-Kelly (2008) cite that immigrants often use family stories of "a respectable past, real or imaginary, in the country of origin" (p. 29) to instill high aspirations and motivation toward upward mobility.

Baobab Families attributing the value of education to culture served to link children to their family and African heritage. In defining academic success or going to college as a part of one's cultural identity, parents could engage children with their own African values, traditions, and upbringing. For example, getting an education and going to college was something that children in Baobab Families could do that was representative of their cultural self, even if they were unable to connect to their African heritage in other ways, such as speaking their parents' native languages or visiting their parents' country of origin regularly.

While literature on the educational experiences of children of immigrants cite that they often feel a responsibility toward performing well in school as repayment for sacrifices their parents have made (Cuevas, 2019; Guarnaccia, 2019), the children in this study also viewed performing well in school as a way to connect to their family. Even when students appeared pressured by or tired of education-based messages, they often showed a sense of pride in knowing their family legacy and being a part of it. For example, Agaba Enemari, Priscilla Obi, and Olaf Magimbi all expressed a desire to achieve academically as a part of what it meant to them to be a member of their family or ethnic group. For Baobab Families, the value of education became centered on the view that it was not only important to achieve academically, but that it was a value important to one's culture and family.

As with college-going legacies, messages regarding education as part of cultural and familial identity were often communicated through lessons, storytelling, and advice. This form of communication can help build a sense of identity that may have been lost or weakened through the process of immigrating and adapting to life in US society. Parents told stories to their children about their childhood in Africa, such as being at the top of their class in school, or how getting in trouble at school meant getting in worse trouble at home because the parents and the teachers work together in their home countries. Atieno Amolo explained, "Every time I remind them [her children]. I tell my story of how I would walk so many miles to go to school and how my wish was to go to college, but you had to be the best because . . . as I always tell them there are fewer opportunities in Kenya." Delgado Bernal's (2001) work with Latinx immigrant families and education led him to suggest that stories and lessons provide families with strategies for success. Olaf Magimbi illustrates the importance of these cultural ways of teaching and learning as he describes the importance of hearing stories about his family's heritage: "My grandpa was the first person in his tribe to go to college and to get out of the village." When Olaf goes to Kenya he also explained: "They [the men in his family] give me advice and talk to me about life and give me guidance. The values that I get when I go back, the values that my grandpa and other people tell me help me and I keep them in mind for myself when I'm back in the US." The stories about Olaf's family and the advice he was given made an impact on his values and how he led his life. Although the adult family members' messages and stories about education were not always congruent with 1.5- and second-generation children's frame of reference or experiences because they were being raised in the United States, they still served as a resource in guiding how the children viewed the role of education in their lives as part of their identity.

FAMILY AND COMMUNITY NETWORKS

Baobab Families defined themselves beyond the nuclear family, emphasizing extended family and community networks that were diverse, including siblings, extended family, other immigrants, church members, parents' former professors and co-workers, children's teachers and coaches, peers, and peers' families. They often included individuals of different educational attainment and individuals who lived in the United States or who lived in the home country.

All of the Baobab Families emphasized the importance of maintaining a close-knit family, as Gatwiri Magimbi explained: "I've had a lot of support from my family even when they're not here [in the United States]. And because we [she and Olaf] stay connected we're never that far away from them." Similarly, Ruth Obi discussed that her family is like insurance because, "in case of emergency, everyone would pool their last resource." Baobab Families also expressed the importance of family working together as a cohesive group for the betterment of the whole family. Gatwiri Magimbi described her family as a single unit, although many of her family members live in Kenya. Kenneth Amolo explains that, in Kenya, "you are part of the whole group, you are not an individual," and similarly Simon Enemari expressed: "In Nigeria, community is part of the system, the tradition, the way people do it."

Additionally, creating social networks in the United States was particularly critical when Baobab Families first arrived. For example, Adakole Enemari depended heavily upon his church in the United States while he was away from his family for nine years. Atieno Amolo participates in a Kenyan immigrant women's group (*Akiba*) that provides financial guidance, and Gatwiri received free babysitting from other Kenyan immigrants as she raised her son as a single mother. Immigrant social networks are important for helping individuals gain access to resources (Vélez-Ibáñez & Greenberg, 1992). Baobab Families also engaged in reciprocity, helping and supporting other immigrant families and international students as well.

Findings revealed that Baobab Families generally viewed child-rearing as a family and community effort. Olaf Magimbi explained this as follows: "In the African family when something happens with one person, the entire family will know about it. Like whenever I do something bad, my whole family will know about it within minutes. But it's good because the family can keep tabs on whatever I'm doing." Ruth Obi suggested that every child in the Obi family is connected to every Obi adult because they "belong to everyone and are the responsibility of everyone [in the family]."

This responsibility among adults in Baobab Families also included ensuring that children were achieving academically and on a college pathway. For Baobab Families, college choice was not solely experienced between parents and children but instead reflected involvement from their larger social networks. Twenty-first-century college choice research also expanded the concept of *parental involvement* to include *family and community involvement* as a means of understanding the academic aspirations of POC and immigrant students (see George Mwangi, 2015; Knight et al., 2004; Tierney & Auerbach, 2005).

"Growing" through the College Choice Process

The narratives of participants parallel the wise and enduring nature of the baobab by reflecting families' use of networks, culture, strategies, and other resources to develop their own college-going culture and engage in the college choice process. The findings demonstrate participants "growing" through college choice because as immigrants the Baobab Families were learning and navigating the US educational system and college choice process together. Four themes reflect how Baobab Families grew through college choice: (a) remaining rooted, (b) reaching toward the sky, (c) experiencing drought, and (d) regenerating from the root.

Remaining Rooted

Baobabs are among the most effective trees at preventing water loss, having root systems that spread further than the height of the tree (Sidibe & Williams, 2002). This root system contributes to baobabs' ability to survive in dry climates, making maximum use of the scarce resources around them (Sidibe & Williams, 2002). Similarly, despite scarce resources, Baobab Families described going to college as part of a larger family effort toward upward mobility and success that is rooted in education. For example, each family had an immigration history that began with a family member coming to the United States to pursue an undergraduate or graduate degree. Adakole Enemari lived away from his wife and children for nine years while he attained two college degrees in the United States:

> Once I started at [college in the United States] I couldn't go back home [to Nigeria] anymore because I was working to pay my tuition and had a family of four at home to send money back to, so it was not easy. [It took nine years] so that I could go to school here and then be able to have a job so that I could find a place for them to stay and to support them when they came here [to the United States].

Ruth Obi came from Nigeria through the Diversity Visa Lottery to attend college and become a pharmacist. She began at community college, but after finishing her associate's degree and transferring to a 4-year college Ruth unexpectedly became pregnant. Ruth changed her major after giving birth as she could not manage the demands of her biochemistry program, but she was steadfast in completing her bachelor's degree in information systems and later a master's degree in information systems. Similarly, after becoming pregnant while an international student, Gatwiri Magimbi withdrew from her US university and went back to Kenya, but she returned with her son years later as a single mother to complete her bachelor's degree.

Children heard stories of and experienced family members coming to the United States to pursue college and to provide their children with opportunities for education. The consistent message was that college is compulsory and they should go to college to contribute to their family's educational legacy. Expressions such as "there is no alternative to college," "college is very vital to us," "it's something we're expected to do," and "there's no other option" were commonly used by parents, college-going children, and other family members to illustrate the messages used in Baobab Families. Thus, remaining rooted in college going is communicated within the Baobab Families as an obligation and responsibility to preserve the college-going family legacy, to provide family and community uplift, and to be celebrated as a family success.

The exposure that children had to their families' struggles to adjust to life in the United States and pursue college had a major impact on them. Priscilla Obi expressed that she respected her mother, "Because she was a full-time student and a full-time mom, and she was still able to get us a house and all this stuff . . . and it gave me the motivation to try in school." In talking about her stepfather's stories of struggle in Kenya, Sara Amolo, expressed: "It motivated me definitely. To hear how they [Kenneth's parents in Kenya] struggled to pay for his schooling, something that is free over here [United States] and over there you have to pay for it. So that motivated me to do well and not take school for granted." Children described the value of seeing family go to college and it encouraged them to pursue the same goals. In defining academic success or going to college as a part of one's cultural identity, parents could engage children with their own African values, traditions, and upbringing. This was important given that the transmission of culture can otherwise be difficult in African immigrant families due to children growing up in a different country context from their parents, which can create "gaps in shared family history" (Kamya, 2005, p. 103).

Baobab Families also generally viewed child-rearing as a community effort, in which all were responsible. This responsibility also included ensuring children were achieving academically and on a college pathway. For example, the familial expectations and college process of older siblings triggered children to feel an "automatic" or unspoken expectation to go to college as well, such as for Agaba Enemari, who at age 5 decided he wanted to go to college and become a doctor because it was what his older brother Simon was aspiring to do. For families, academic and college preparation was not solely experienced between parents and children, but instead reflected involvement from their larger social networks who helped to normalize college going. As Andi Nyom stated, "It was from all angles, my mom and different people around me telling me about college." Even family members who did not go to college participated in reinforcing the importance of education.

Messages about college were not just transmitted from networks in the United States, but also from the home country. Because some children described parental messages about college as "repetitive" or "redundant," other individuals gave further perspective. Olaf Magimbi shared, "Like my mom tells me . . . 'the opportunity you have to go to school, a lot of kids don't have that in Kenya.' I hear that constantly and so sometimes I feel like, 'I really don't care at this point' . . . But when we go back to Kenya and I see kids my age in the village or hear my grandpa's stories about his struggles, it's like, 'okay, yeah I get it.'" Children expressed respecting and trusting these messages they heard from grandparents, siblings, aunts, uncles, cousins, family friends, and other individuals in their network.

REACHING TOWARD THE SKY

Baobabs are known as the "upside-down tree" because their branches reach toward the sky. Baobab Families wanted their children rooted in college-going culture, but also emphasized high academic striving and expectations, which align with baobab branches reaching upwards. Nehemiah Enemari summed this, "academic success for us is being able to put in your best efforts at whatever you do. Like when you shoot for the moon you can at least get to the stars."

Families expressed the importance of education, particularly attaining a college degree, as a fundamental family value. Children reacted differently to these academic expectations even within the same family. The children described being motivated by these expectations, but also feeling pressure or obligation to achieve academically or choose a certain college or career to please their families and represent their culture. Their reactions are similar to findings in immigrant education literature, in which some immigrant children pursued academic achievement to fulfill desires of the family rather than themselves (Nicholas et al., 2008). Although some children chose to eventually pursue their own passions instead of those of their families, they either kept their pursuits a secret or found a compromise.

Still, even when children appeared pressured or tired of education-based messages, they often expressed pride in being a part of their family's educational legacy. Agaba Enemari, Priscilla Obi, Andi Nyom, and Olaf Magimbi all expressed a desire to achieve academically as a part of what it meant to them to be a member of their family or ethnic group. Nehemiah explained that his siblings have a saying that in terms of their grades they are "no less than all A's and one B kind of Africans," which connects their grades to their African identity. For these families, the value of education became centered on the view that it was not only important to achieve academically, but that it was a value important to one's culture and family. When Olaf Magimbi's academic performance was not satisfactory, his family in Kenya told him that he is not living up to his responsibilities as a first-born child. Poor academic performance was perceived as the child not fulfilling family obligations or hurting the family's reputation.

While many parents discussed the benefits of their children growing up in the United States, they also saw advantages in maintaining African value systems to encourage academic success. For example, families described their home environments as stricter and more disciplined regarding academic performance, while US schools were seen as more permissive and praiseful. Many of these narratives resembled findings from education research on African immigrants' experiences, which describe their parenting as more authoritative than American parenting (Arthur, 2008; George Mwangi, 2018b; Obeng, 2008). Priscilla Obi explained, "I have two American friends that when they get a bunch of Bs their parents think it's fine. So when I get a bunch of Bs, they say, 'Oh that's really good [Priscilla]!' and I'm like, 'Really? My mom won't see it that way.'" When children performed poorly academically or were not showing academic discipline, they were chided by family members for being "too American." Children were socialized to believe that being African meant attaining above-average grades and going to college.

Families emphasized active home-based practices that were meant to reflect values of discipline and focus, while reinforcing academic expectations. This included rules like limited TV watching, going to the library, dedicated space for quiet time in the home, and regular dialogue about future planning and goal setting. Chelsea Fatoki explained that growing up, she and her siblings were restricted on how much TV they could watch because of the distraction it could bring to homework or studying: "Even though I lived on campus in college, I rarely watched TV during the week because it's just so ingrained in me not to do it." Agaba explained that at the Enemari house, there is space in the basement with desks to read the Bible or do homework, which his siblings nicknamed "the dungeon," so "when I come home from school or soccer practice, I change clothes, eat a snack and then get started on my assignments in the dungeon." The value of education is reflected in some of the "house rules" the Amolo family engaged in: "We have a rule that if it's Monday through Thursday, when we have school, we're not allowed to watch TV. On Saturdays, we take [Kimani] to the library and we all check out books," explained Sara. Across families, participants described the important role of family in ensuring children received high academic expectations, encouragement, and support in the home. Therefore, adults worked to create an environment that stressed educational achievement to ensure the children put forth their best potential academically.

EXPERIENCING DROUGHT

Baobab Families also experience challenges or "drought" in college choice. For example, while they trusted schools to provide resources for college, they did not trust schools to be invested in their children's success. Some expressed that teachers did not challenge their children or encourage their best performance. Victor Osei explained that teachers told him it is okay to get a lower grade in a college-preparatory class because they are more rigorous, while his family feels getting less than an "A" is unacceptable regardless. Parents were raised in different educational systems and struggled with some messages children received. Adakole Enemari expressed, "One of the problems we have raising children here [in the United States] is that in your home you have your own set of values and norms and principles that you want your children to go by. But when they go to school, the school has their own way that is different. Mixed messages." These mixed messages created confusion and frustration for children, and they questioned whether their families were correct regarding college going. While all families experience generation gaps between parents and children, in immigrant families this generational dissonance is further compounded by the fact that parents and children were socialized in different countries (Rumbaut, 2005). This can result in parents struggling to help their children navigate the US education system and cause intergenerational tension (Dennis et al., 2009; Rumbaut, 2005). In Baobab Families, when children saw parents lacking knowledge about college admissions, entrance exams, or cost, they began to generally question their parents' advice and decision-making, which created tension in the parent-child relationship. Gatwiri Magimbi explained, "I think he [Olaf] thinks I'm dumb. So, he says things like, 'No. That's okay. I'll ask my teacher.'"

While families had high expectations, they often found these expectations exceeded those of the school. This was incongruous for some parents, who had a different experience within the schools in their home countries. For Atieno Amolo, her experience in Kenya was that "teachers took my success personally and they took my participation seriously. But in the US, it's your responsibility, it's your problem." Minnie Fatoki shared her experience in Nigeria: "The parents give their children over to the teachers to teach, to discipline, to mold, to build them up. But in America, you don't feel that community investment. The parents blame the teachers, and the teachers blame the parents." Due to the lack of partnership with schools, families engaged in active home-based academic practices to augment the lack of attention or expectations they perceived from schools.

Parents also expressed being made to feel "different" by school staff. Ruth Obi was embarrassed at her child's school: "One of the teachers asked me in front of other parents, 'Do you speak English at home?' I guess with my accent they're questioning my English fluency. I try to correct people that in Nigeria, English is not our second language. It is actually the primary language. It's frustrating. That's why with the parent-teacher meetings I just try to get in and get out as quick as I can." Owole Enemari, Adakole Enemari, and Gatwiri Magimbi all cited similar experiences with teachers not understanding their accent or having negative stereotypes about African countries. These experiences made parents feel less motivated to get involved in their child's school or build relationships with school staff. Some researchers have suggested that parents of Color and low-income parents also experience stereotyping in the school setting (Cabrera & La Nasa, 2000; Marchand et al., 2019; Welton & Martinez, 2014). These studies concluded that teachers and other school staff often wrongly perceived these parents' limited participation in activities at their children's school as disinterest in their children's education.

Children also were teased regarding their cultural heritage in school. Agaba Enemari explained that classmates ask him questions, "Did you live in a hut?" and "Why don't you guys [Africans] wear more clothes?" Agaba explained the comments do not bother him because he feels there are many benefits to being Nigerian. However, Zeleza (2009) explains, "In addition to a racial tax, African immigrants pay a cultural tax, the devaluation of their human capital in a society where things African are routinely negatively stereotyped and despised" (p. 41). In the US context, the portrayal of Africa as a homogenous and primitive continent lends to African immigrants experiencing stereotyping and ignorant statements made toward their culture, accent, ideologies, and homeland (Zeleza, 2009).

Regenerating from the Root

Although Baobab Families experienced challenges in the college-going process, they remained steadfast in pursuing college enrollment. This behavior is similar to the baobab tree, which can survive harsh environments by regenerating from the root even if knocked down or damaged. To regenerate from the root, Baobab Families approached college choice as a family process with their engagement reflecting behaviors and decisions that best sustain the family.

Families discussed the college enrollment of one family member as a family investment and success. While the individual child would apply to college, decisions of where to go were ultimately family decisions, based on what was the best decision for the family as a whole as well as the best option for the college-going child. Adakole Enemari explained:

> We have five children, so they have to make sacrifices too. Otherwise, it will be, "Who do you send to college and who do you leave behind?" If you are going to give each one an equal opportunity and shot at the university, you tell them, "Okay, even though you want to go to MIT, what will doing that take away from your siblings? What money will be left to give for their college education?" We all have to work together as a team.

Even in single-child homes, families often discussed the importance of "putting family first" in decision-making about academics and college. As

Olaf Magimbi described, "I know my success isn't all about me, I want it, but I want to do it for them [the family] too." College enrollment was a family achievement adding to families' college-going legacies.

Children learned that college degrees mean success to the family and contribute to the family unit. As Esther Obi, a grandmother, explains, "[Education] was valuable to us [the Obi family] when we were in Nigeria. So we cannot come to this country and let it go. Education is something that is who we are and it will make our family successful." The children are now the first generation within their families to be raised in the United States and to be afforded the educational access for which the previous generation sacrificed. Olaf Magimbi, Agaba Enemari, and Simon Enemari spoke of wanting to get a college education in part to have a career that allows them to "give back" to their families for their sacrifices in the United States and Africa. These children are aware that their educational achievements are not only for individual gain but are goals that are also linked to a familial legacy.

Baobab Families experienced challenges such as a lack of US-based college knowledge (see George Mwangi, 2018b), tensions with schools, and intergenerational strain within families. Yet, this chapter demonstrates that the families' understanding of and engagement in college choice is situated within a college-going culture developed in the family and community environment that works to navigate their challenges. Baobab Families conceptualize college choice as a family process and therefore I used the baobab tree to represent the family as a single entity engaging in the process of college choice. They conceptualize the college choice process as an opportunity for family uplift and one in which the needs of the family unit are prioritized above the individual. Although the individual college-going student will eventually enroll in college, families perceived this milestone as a family decision, pathway, and success.

Critical Reflection

1. During the college-going process, how can schools balance tapping into the knowledge and expertise of families, while also serving as a resource and source of support to families?

2. What are the ways in which your culture or family framed the way you understood education and going to college? Reflect on whether this was in alignment with the ways the K–12 school(s) you attended framed education and college.

3. In this chapter, collectivism and familism were two pre-dominant values held by participants in the college-going process. What are other ways in which these values may show up for these participants as they continue to navigate the US K–12 and higher education system? How might these values work to strengthen and improve their educational experience, and in what ways might these values clash with dominant white norms in US P-20 schools?

References

Alexander, C., Beale, N., Kesby, M., Kindon, S., McMillan, J., Pain, R., & Ziegler, F. (2007). Participatory diagramming: A critical view from North East England. In S. Kindon, R. Pain, & M. Kesby (Eds.), *Participatory action research approaches and methods: Connecting people, participation, and place* (pp. 112–121). Routledge.

Almeida, D. J. (2015). College readiness and low-income youth: The role of social capital in acquiring college knowledge. In W. G. Tierney & J. C. Duncheon (Eds.), *The problem of college readiness* (pp. 89–113). State University of New York Press.

Arthur, J. A. (2008). *The African diaspora in the United States and Europe: The Ghanaian experience.* Ashgate.

Arthur, J. A. (2010). *African diaspora identities: Negotiating culture in transnational migration.* Lexington Books.

Batalova, J. (2024, March 13). *Frequently requested statistics on immigrants and immigration in the United States.* Migration Policy Institute. https://www.migrationpolicy.org/article/frequently-requested-statistics-immigrants-and-immigration-united-states-2024#children-immigrants

Beitin, B. K. (2007). Qualitative research in marriage and family therapy: Who is in the interview? *Contemporary Family Therapy, 30,* 48–58. https://doi.org/10.1007/s10591-007-9054-y

Belgrave, F. Z., & Allison, K. W. (2006). *African American psychology.* Sage.

Bolter, J. (2022, January 6). *Immigration has been a defining, often contentious, element throughout U.S. history.* Migration Policy Institute. https://www.migrationpolicy.org/article/immigration-shaped-united-states

Cabrera, A. F., & La Nasa, S. M. (2000). *Understanding the college choice of disadvantaged students: New directions for institutional research, number 107.* Jossey-Bass.

Chishti, M., Hipsman, F., & Ball, I. (2015). *Fifty years on: The 1965 Immigration and Nationality Act continues to reshape the United States.* Migration

Policy Institute. https://www.migrationpolicy.org/article/fifty-years-1965-immigration-and-nationality-act-continues-reshape-united-states

Cuevas, S. (2019). "Con mucho sacrificio, we give them everything we can": The strategic day-to-day sacrifices of undocumented Latina/o parents. *Harvard Educational Review, 89*(3), 473–496.

Delgado Bernal, D. (2001). Learning and living pedagogies of the home: The mestiza consciousness of Chicana students. *Qualitative Studies in Education, 14*(5), 623–639. https://doi.org/10.1080/09518390110059838

Dennis, J., Basanez, T., & Farahmand, A. (2009). Intergenerational conflicts among Latinos in early adulthood: Separating values conflicts with parents from acculturation conflicts. *Hispanic Journal of Behavioral Sciences, 32*(1), 118–135. https://doi-org.mutex.gmu.edu/10.1177/073998630935298

George Mwangi, C. A. (2015). (Re)Examining the role of family and community in college access and choice: A metasynthesis. *Review of Higher Education, 39*(1), 123–151. https://doi.org/10.1353/rhe.2015.0046

George Mwangi, C. A. (2018a). A family affair: Examining the college-going strategies of sub-Saharan African immigrants in the U.S. through funds of knowledge. In J. Kiyama & C. Rios-Aguilar (Eds.), *Funds of knowledge in higher education: Honoring students' cultural experiences and resources as strength* (pp. 106–124). Routledge.

George Mwangi, C. A. (2018b). "It's different here": Complicating concepts of college knowledge and first generation through an immigrant lens. *Teachers College Record, 120*(11), 1–36.

George Mwangi, C. A. (2019). Navigating two worlds: Exploring home-school dissonance in the college-going process of immigrant families. *Harvard Educational Review, 89*(3), 448–472. https://doi.org/10.17763/1943-5045-89.3.448

George Mwangi, C. A., & English, S. (2017). Being Black (and) immigrant students: When race, ethnicity, and nativity collide. *International Journal of Multicultural Education, 19*(2), 100–130. https://doi.org/10.18251/ijme.v19i2.1317

Guarnaccia, P. J. (2019). *Immigration, diversity and student journeys to higher education*. Peter Lang.

Kambon, K. (1992). *The African personality in America: An African-centered framework*. Nubian Nation.

Kamya, H. (2005). African immigrant families. In M. McGoldrick, J. Giordano, & N. Garcia-Preto (Eds.), *Ethnicity and family therapy* (3rd ed., pp.101–116). Guilford.

Kesby, M. (2000). Participatory diagramming: Deploying qualitative methods through an action research epistemology. *Area, 32*(4), 423–435. https://doi.org/10.1111/j.1475-4762.2000.tb00158.x

Kiyama, J. M. (2010). College aspirations and limitations: The role of educational ideologies and funds of knowledge in Mexican American families.

American Educational Research Journal, 47(2), 330–356. https://doi.org/10.3102/0002831209357468

Kiyama, J., & Rios-Aguilar, C. (Eds.). (2018). *Funds of knowledge in higher education: Honoring students' cultural experiences and resources as strength*. Routledge.

Knight, M. G., Norton, N. E., Bentley, C. C., & Dixon, I. R. (2004). The power of Black and Latina/o counterstories: Urban families and college-going processes. *Anthropology & Education Quarterly, 35*(1), 99–120. https://doi.org/10.1525/aeq.2004.35.1.99

Knowles-Borishade, A. F. (1991). Paradigm for classical African orature: Instrument for a scientific revolution. *Journal of Black Studies, 21*(4), 488–500. https://doi-org.mutex.gmu.edu/10.1177/00219347910210040

Lorenzi, J., & Batalova, J. (2022). *Sub-Saharan African immigrants in the United States*. Migration Policy Institute. https://www.migrationpolicy.org/article/sub-saharan-african-immigrants-united-states-2019#pathways

Marchand, A. D., Vassar, R. R., Diemer, M. A., & Rowley, S. J. (2019). Integrating race, racism, and critical consciousness in Black parents' engagement with schools. *Journal of Family Theory & Review, 11*(3), 367–384. https://doi.org/10.1111/jftr.12344

Moll, L. C., Amanti, C., Neff, D., & Gonzalez, N. (1992). Funds of knowledge for teaching: Using a qualitative approach to connect homes and classrooms. *Theory into Practice, 31*(2), 132–141. https://doi.org/10.1080/00405849209543534

Mpofu, E. (2002). Psychology in sub-Saharan Africa: Challenges, prospects and promises. *International Journal of Psychology, 37*(3), 179–186. https://doi.org/10.1080/00207590244000061

Myers, L. J. (1988). *Understanding an Afrocentric worldview: Introduction to an optimal psychology*. Kendall Hunt.

National Research Council. (2008). *Lost crops of Africa volume III: Fruits*. National Academies Press.

Ngara, C. (2007). African ways of knowing and pedagogy revisited. *Journal of Contemporary Issues in Education, 2*(2), 7–20. https://doi.org/10.20355/C5301M

Nicholas, T., Stepick, A., & Dutton Stepick, C. (2008). "Here's your diploma, mom!" Family obligation and multiple pathways to success. *Annals of the American Academy of Political and Social Science, 620*(1), 237–252.

Nsamenang, A. B. (2006). Human ontogenesis: An indigenous African view on development and intelligence. *International Journal of Psychology, 41*(4), 293–297. https://doi.org/10.1080/00207590544000077

Nyang, S. S. (2018). The African immigrant family in the United States of America: Challenges and opportunities. In B. I. Gill & S. O. Abidde (Eds.), *Africans and the exiled life: Migration, culture, and globalization* (pp. 161–175). Lexington Books.

Obama, B. (2004). *Dreams from my father: A story of race and inheritance*. Three Rivers Press.

Obeng, C. S. (2008). African immigrants' families and the American educational system. In T. Falola and N. Afolabi (Eds.), *African minorities in the new world* (pp. 247–260). Routledge.

Owusu-Ansah, F. E., & Miji, G. (2013). African indigenous knowledge and research. *African Journal of Disability, 2*(1), 1–5. https://doi.org/10.4102/ajod.v2i1.30

Pakenham, T. (2004). *The remarkable baobab.* Weidenfeld & Nicolson.

Portes, A., & Fernandez-Kelly, P. (2008). No margin for error: Educational and occupational achievement among disadvantaged children of immigrants. *Annals of the American Academy of Political and Social Science, 620*(1), 12–36. http://doi.org/ 10.1177/0002716208322577

Rumbaut, R. G. (2005). Children of immigrants and their achievement: The role of family, acculturation, social class, gender, ethnicity, and school contexts. In R. D. Taylor (Ed.), *Addressing the achievement gap: Theory informing practice* (pp. 23–59). Information Age.

Sidibe, M., & Williams, J. T. (2002). *Baobab: Adansonia digitata.* International Centre for Underutilized Crops.

Swigart, L. (2001). *Extended lives: The African immigrant experience in Philadelphia.* Historical Society of Pennsylvania.

Tierney, W. G., & Auerbach, S. (2005). Toward developing an untapped resource: The role of families in college preparation. In W. G. Tierney, Z. B. Corwin, & J. E. Colyar (Eds.), *Preparing for college: Nine elements of effective outreach* (pp. 29–48). State University of New York Press.

Vélez-Ibáñez, C., & Greenberg, J. (1992). Formation and transformation of funds of knowledge among U.S.-Mexican households. *Anthropology & Education Quarterly, 23*(4), 313–335. https://doi.org/10.1525/aeq.1992.23.4.05x1582v

Welton, A. D., & Martinez, M. A. (2014). Coloring the college pathway: A more culturally responsive approach to college readiness and access for students of color in secondary schools. *Urban Review, 46*, 197–223. https://doi.org/10.1007/s11256-013-0252-7

Zeleza, P. T. (2009). Diaspora dialogues: Engagements between Africa and its diasporas. In N. Nzegwu & I. Okpweho (Eds.), *The new African diaspora* (pp. 31–58). Indiana University Press.

Conclusion

YEDALIS RUÍZ SANTANA AND
CHRYSTAL A. GEORGE MWANGI

This chapter will use key themes highlighted across the volume to propose three forms of praxis and action regarding access to college for people of Color. Building on the scholarship and practice of an entirely POC authorship, this book addresses a range of college choice and access disparities, needs, milestones, and innovations centering the diverse and sophisticated voices of academic and community change agents dedicated to educational equity. The first is a set of strategies for applying the frameworks and concepts discussed throughout the book to educational practices that more effectively reflect the college-going processes and pathways of POC. We offer these strategies knowing that efforts to expand or revise long-standing frameworks should not be the goal. Instead, we are spotlighting POC-led college choice and access strategies. The second goal of this chapter is to propose a future agenda for researching college access and choice among communities of Color. By seeking POC scholars and practitioners as contributors of this book, the network among us continues to grow. With a critical mass of POC scholar-practitioners, future research questions will be asked and designed using culturally sustaining methods and the findings translated into strategies for additional POC engagement and representation in college access and choice scholarship.

Finally, the third is a "love letter" to POC college aspirants that provides possibilities for using the frameworks and concepts described in this book to support their college-going journeys. At the start of the book, we framed the literature review as an expression of our collective gratitude for the scholarly and practice-based contributions from among a wide range of POC authors. This approach is a divergence from traditionally structured literature reviews. Intentionally so, we actively acknowledge both the scholarship—as is common to any literature review—*and* the scholars as people who have likely faced additional hurdles in order to advance the literature and practice that center POC. Similarly, we conclude with a letter to future scholars as a message of care and hope for the reciprocation of steadfast commitment and admiration. We take this opportunity to be this voice to the reader, knowing that, while perhaps a less common approach, it is one that we believe will resonate with our future colleagues.

Strategies for Application to Practice

For decades, there have been numerous promising practices recommended to K–12 teachers, counselors, and other staff to help support the college access and choice processes of youth of Color. Instead of repeating each of those here, we focus our recommendations to K–12 practitioners on partnering with students, families, and communities of Color with three specific actions at the center. The first is learning from, valuing, and integrating the knowledge of students of Color and their families and communities into schools' college-going practices. Many students of Color are receiving active home-based and community-based information to access college. For example, in her chapter, George Mwangi illustrated how Baobab Families use their own strategies to supplement or overcome what they perceived as schools' low academic expectations and to ensure that their children were competitive college applicants. Yet schools were often not aware of nor did they acknowledge these practices. Schools can learn from families of Color regarding how they are developing college-going practices and cultures in their homes and communities to acknowledge and align them with school practices so that children are receiving consistent messages and expectations from multiple trusted individuals in their lives. Youth of Color should also be an integral part of the process in determining how to navigate college access and choice. For example, as discussed in chapter 2 by Arce and Carpenter, through youth participatory action research (YPAR) students can investigate challenges and assets related to college going within their communities and develop action-oriented responses that can be applied to their own process and those of their peers.

Second, there should be opportunities for students, families, and communities of Color to partner with K–12 schools through targeted and collaborative initiatives that meet culturally sustaining needs and logistical considerations (e.g., language interpreters). For example, school learning communities can be established to provide opportunities for schools, parents, and community members to come together as allies to assist students as they prepare for college. These efforts would allow K–12 practitioners to build relationships with families and their preexisting social networks and resources, which is critical in support of college preparation and college-going cultural capital (George Mwangi et al., 2018). As Yellow Bird and colleagues demonstrated in their chapter, family and community networks have a wide-ranging level of involvement in students' lives that can help to open or close doors to college options and pathways. Engaging as thought partners together through learning communities can provide a targeted space to learn from and with one another. Furthermore, using an "each one, teach one" approach, members of these learning communities can share college access information and resources with their wider networks, having an impactful ripple effect.

Yet, in order to build these partnerships, it will be important for K–12 practitioners to use culturally inclusive and responsive practices. Throughout many of the chapters in this book, students and their families stated feeling unwelcome by school staff because of racial stereotypes and assumptions. We recommend professional development and training for teachers and school staff to help them challenge their own biases, understand the systemic racism and other inequities present in their school spaces, and seek to take action to address the needs of students of Color in culturally sustaining and antiracist ways. As illustrated by Ruíz Santana in a *re*framework of the concept of resilience, while students of Color have the capacity to persevere and withstand obstacles, it must be acknowledged that despite support, students will continue to confront barriers to college access and there is a cost to that process. As K–12 teachers and counselors become critically conscious in their praxis, we recommend applying Arce and Carpenter's critically conscious college knowledge (C^3K) approach to working with students of Color in college access and choice as well. That model brings awareness to students about the racism present within predominantly white campus spaces and a strategy to navigate if they choose to attend those institutions, connecting them with alumni of Color who have gone to college and can speak about their experiences, connecting them to college students of Color and college outreach practitioners who bring a consciousness lens (see Correa & Ruiz in chapter 8 of this volume for the Student Bridges example), and sharing with them minority-serving institution (MSI) options as part of the college choice process.

It is also important that higher education institutions are involved in not just ensuring racially just access and enrollment of students of Color, but also their success and well-being through college. Again, there are numerous promising practices that speak to this recommendation, but we focus on two that are most in alignment with the ethos of this book. The first is to ensure the multiple assets that students bring to their college-going journey, as outlined in Luu's chapter 3, are valued in both the admissions process and through students' college experience. For example, we have seen admissions offices engage in practices like valuing students' work experience, babysitting younger siblings, or being a translator for their parents just as much as extracurricular involvement during the application process. Yet, this valuing becomes only performative if, once a student is enrolled, there are no supports and accommodations for these responsibilities.

Additionally, as Carey demonstrated in chapter 6, families' involvement in their children's lives does not end once they go to college. There is importance in remaining connected once in college and the children in these families will bring their familial and community values, experiences, and responsibilities to college as well. Instead of expecting students to sever ties with their families and communities, colleges and universities should play an active role in strengthening familial bonds for the betterment of students, families, local communities, and college campuses. Some universities are creating opportunities for greater family engagement; yet colleges should make it a priority to integrate and embrace families as well as strengthen ties between students and their families/communities. As this book illustrates, students' of Color families and communities are often their first teachers, providing some of the most important life lessons, which should be integrated beyond the K–12 experience and into the college experience to better support college student achievement and persistence.

Those that are directly looking to bridge college access resources for students and communities of Color are often themselves of Color and have experienced resource deficits like the students they are trying to support. College access programs within communities of Color can be found within schools, community-based nonprofit organizations, religious and faith-based organizations, and in programs focused on youth and workforce development. Some college outreach programs are supported by university initiatives with scholars who, like us, focus their research on access and choice as well as community learning and engagement. These programs provide strong partnerships with communities that support student populations who have college-going aspirations, especially when the support is responsive to the actual need of the community it is serving. As scholar-practitioners of Color who have been focusing our work on bridging resources, we believe that it is important to consider that these college access programs also are challenged by barriers and gaps. In our work, we have collaborated with practitioners who run the programs and whose motivation and commitment to the work is activated because they want to make change within the community, as demonstrated in Barber's chapter 5 and Morton's chapter 7. We must take a step back when doing college access work with communities of Color to honor the complexity of this work. The administrators and directors of college access programs and community outreach programs dedicate a substantial amount of time and resources to the sustainability of their programs by securing funding through grants and endorsement by boards of education, if the program is within the public school system. They are similarly navigating against systemic barriers. The uncertainty year by year is felt deeply not just by administrators but also by the participants of college access programs.

When higher education partners with community access and outreach programs, the partnership is touted as a positive initiative focused on increasing diversity in the university. However, too often there is a disconnection in understanding the holistic experiences of those who are engaged in the program. There is a day-to-day effort being made that goes unacknowledged and the resources being offered, despite the tireless commitment of outreach program staff, are limited and cannot reach every potential interested college aspirant. College outreach programs face serious challenges because many times, those who are the focus of the programs are in environments where resources are limited over a lifetime, impacting multiple generations' college access. There are finite resources that are inequitably distributed and communities of Color are forced to compete to be one of a select few who actually achieve access. At each step of the process, the milestones achieved are against the odds and upheld as evidence of resilience, as if resilience were akin to achieving a badge of honor or an award. But resilience is not like an award. Resilience is having to work harder to achieve less, and it comes at a substantial cost to our communities of Color as illustrated in Ruíz Santana's chapter. Therefore, as scholars and practitioners of Color, we emphasize that these college access and choice programs must also consider the multiple generations of aspirants previously overlooked if there is to be a model shift and a plan for sustainability.

Beyond the gates of a university or college are community-based organizations that are doing much to bridge resources. As stated by Barber in her chapter, as the CEO and president of a federally qualified health center, she is dedicated to "lift others up." Despite the initiatives that colleges and universities are enacting to integrate college student participation in community-based projects, there still needs to be improved learning and collaboration between both worlds. Community-based organizations are at the pulse of what is happening day-to-day in the communities they serve. As we learn from the Arce and Carpenter, Barber, and Correa and Ruiz chapters, there is a responsibility to our communities because they have experienced a constant cycle of closed doors in attempting to secure access to academic, training, and workforce opportunities. Our communities of Color have built opportunities for support and growth and are advocating tirelessly to respond to their own needs. There is rich knowledge and wisdom in these communities, but too frequently, from an academic perspective, efforts to engage with the community stem from a deficit perspective. We advise scholars and practitioners to be critical in their approach to partnership work, to engage with cultural humility in order to invite opportunities to learn from and work with the community as equal partners, and to also be open to guidance by their frameworks and practices. Consider that community work never ceases to ensure sustainability and bridging of resources amid the episodic engagement (limited by semester schedules and transient student participation) that academic partnership offers.

Beyond our academic and professional responsibilities within the university, we (Chrystal and Yedalis) partnered in leading college access programs as discussed in the introduction. We co-created curriculum, we purchased snacks, and we traveled twice weekly on a yellow school bus with undergraduate and graduate students 45 minutes both ways to a local high school where we engaged with a classroom full of college aspirants of Color who had, up to this point, received little to no college counseling despite their interest and high academic performance. For an academic year, we took on all aspects of developing and integrating the program. We did this as women of Color having lived experience navigating and negotiating college access and having to work harder compared to our white counterparts in order to achieve. Why is it that, decades ago, many of the contributors to this book experienced these same barriers in our higher education access and choice journey, as highlighted by Acevedo in chapter 9? As we know, systemic barriers continue to remain for communities of Color.

We offer our words as *consejos* (advice) and *un cariño* (a sign of affection) as many of you readers venture into college access, choice, and equity work. We ask that you take time to tune into yourself with love and affection and consider where you are headed in your educational and/ or professional path. To ground this process, we turn to the quote, "It is possible to speak with our heart directly. Most ancient cultures know this. We can converse with our heart as if it were a good friend. In modern life we have become so busy with our daily affairs and thoughts that we have lost this essential art of taking time to converse with our heart" (Kornfield cited in hooks, 2018, p. xii). We situate this reflexive process using three words from bell hooks that provide guidance for developing an intentional academic and professional journey: grace, commitment, and justice.

Grace centers the act of honoring who we are and where we want to go (hooks, 2018). Yedalis remembers walking into one of the library's carrels in the spring semester of her junior year in college. She was working on an application for a summer internship and the prompt asked her to describe who she was and what she aspired to achieve. As she contemplated the question, she realized that she had been so focused on her academic work that she had lost touch with the core of who she was. She sought to reconnect to the deep and rich texture of the many dimensions of her intersectional identities. We advise you to examine your positionality and interrogate your privilege(s) that has influenced your journey thus far. Take time to reflect on your family history by tracing back several generations if possible and consider your family's relationship to education and to your educational trajectory. Ask yourself, how did their history inform your ideas about and access to education? How do these things relate and have an impact on your life story? Then turn to your life and consider your own education.

Underscore some of the key events in your life that reveal something about your educational development. Examine your social identities, both privileged and marginalized. As you reflect on these notions and experiences, honor your multiple dimensions, your experiences, your uniqueness, your history, your gut feelings, your thoughts, your questions, your reactions. Also give credit to your accomplishments, your talents, and your skills. And truly embrace the time to learn and accept the opportunities to move from *not knowing to discovery*.

In addition to honoring who you are, consider and interact with the concept of commitment (hooks, 2018) and ask yourself, How do I want to show up? Be open to opportunities to immerse yourself in environments that are different from your own, that are critical of dominant narratives and that embrace diverse sources of knowledge. Develop deep and lasting commitments and ties to community-engaged work and education. Show up to learn, listen, and use humility to engage with communities that are different from your own. While it can seem that there are an infinite number of paths one can take, the ways in which you choose to show up and continue showing up can be a good way to map the path that aligns with your strengths and passions. Remember to show up and truly be present while critically examining and challenging your thoughts and actions along the way.

Finally, accept that scholars, practitioners, and students of Color frequently ground their academic and professional paths in their life's efforts to uphold and advocate for justice (hooks, 2018). This is especially true when their voices have not been invited or have had to be raised to succeed against a dominant understanding that would otherwise have excluded them. In these moments words need to be accompanied by action. Join them in the work!

Consider that many of us who are POC learned at a very early age that our survival depends on action. Many of us have never had the privilege to reflect on or be nostalgic for a time of lesser responsibility or a time of being or feeling carefree. For Yedalis, some of her earliest memories as a child were wrapped in the complexities of language justice. When her family moved from Puerto Rico to the states, her parents had their own definitions of grace, commitment, and justice as they sought opportunities for her to flourish. And while they sacrificed for her care, it also became clear to her that her work as a child was to be their advocate via her linguistic capital (by being bilingual). Her love of books developed out of her crusade to dominate the English language—a crusade of survival that drove her commitment to justice. To "know" and to have knowledge requires understanding your own positionality and your lived experiences. As Luu's chapter highlights, these early and sophisticated skills should be recognized as contributions to an academic resume for college—but they were not. A grounding source of knowledge is deepened within the reciprocity of learning and teaching. We can find a profound sense of belonging and strength by spending time with people who, first and foremost, treat communities with respect and offer spaces for reciprocal learning. In this way, mentorship becomes an opportunity to seek mutual learning and to share what has been learned so that a cycle of reciprocity is sustained. This, to us, is justice.

Take a moment to consider the following actions and find a peer and a mentor with whom you can reflect as part of your reciprocal learning and ongoing reflection. Engage in communities critically and with humility. Be willing to be vulnerable, open to learning, and to help shake and dismantle structures that marginalize and oppress in our society. Be ready to question and to speak up when you see inequity. Be prepared to interrogate your own position and your own privilege and take risks to reveal the privilege of others around you. Be prepared to challenge power and dominance in order to see and hear the voices of the true leaders within communities and join them in the work. Engage in humanizing work. Be challenged to act. Have compassion and love for yourself and others. Seek mentorship. Be a peer mentor. Join others in creating spaces in which individuals and communities can work collaboratively. Be open to dialogue as the process that involves active listening with empathy, searching for common ground, exploring new ideas and perspectives, and bringing unexamined assumptions into the open. Have the strength to *not* give up, even when you get disillusioned along the way. Here's to a great journey ahead. We hope to get to work with you as co-conspirators. And "Fuerza!" (Strength!).

Thank You to Our Colleagues of Color

We also speak directly to POC who are working in research, practice, and policy spaces to improve college access for communities of Color. We appreciate and respect the work that you do, and we encourage you to remember that your knowledge and skills matter and are valuable. As you know and as highlighted by Morton and Barber, the challenges we face in a white supremacist system do not disappear once we complete higher education and enter the workforce. We can be made to doubt ourselves and our knowledge in the work that we do and can become siloed and isolated in neoliberal work environments that want to see quick fixes to college access challenges that are steeped in systemic and institutionalized racial oppression. So, as you engage in your praxis, we remind you to develop and nurture professional communities of support, validation, and uplift that can keep you grounded and connected. This may also require you to build networks outside of your organization, but those networks can often be some of your biggest supporters, accountability partners, and advocates needed to make our work sustainable.

And please take care of yourselves and each other. There are many who will see your knowledge and your commitment and seek to constrain it with "opportunities" that will use you at your own expense because those opportunities presented to you are underresourced, not supported, and ultimately are setting you up to fail and become burned out. In building our communities of support, it is critical that we have individuals at multiple levels and in multiple spaces who can do the student/community-facing work, the policy/organizational work, the work in K–12, higher education, in between, and so forth, to create the kind of transformation needed to sustain our efforts and ourselves.

We also remind you not to let your knowledge be monopolized or commodified by majority colleagues who struggle to connect with our communities and are seeking to bottle and sell what we bring to our work. Even in writing this book, we struggled with knowing that while our targeted audience are POC invested in equitable college access for communities of Color, that anyone could (mis)read and (mis)use what is within these pages. However, we recognized that while this is always possible, we are writing with intentionality and awareness that we wish for you in your work as well.

Proposed Future Agenda for Research

We propose that the knowledge and models developed by scholars of Color and community-based leaders that are directly responsive to the lived experiences of communities of Color be acknowledged as instrumental sources of knowledge to guide future efforts in dismantling higher education disparities in college access. It is no longer the time to state that these models are needed. They exist. They are part of community initiatives and there are critical scholars of Color contributing to a growing body of literature who posit framings grounded in the lived truths of communities of Color. We cannot be satisfied with only a few scholars of Color being successful based on our resilience. We must be willing to engage in a radical and collective shift in how we approach college access and choice among communities of Color.

As we highlighted in chapter 1, scholars of Color have often drawn from diverse disciplines and knowledge systems to inform their research given the complex challenges and opportunities that exist in schools, colleges, and universities for communities of Color. The chapters in this book are also clear illustrations of this approach with research informed by areas and contexts such as ethnic studies, public health, sociology, student knowledge, pop culture, hip hop, and community and family knowledge. Acevedo highlighted in her chapter the challenges of having her transdisciplinary scholarship and framing accepted within education research outlets, and we appreciate her steadfastness and the steadfastness of others to disrupt status quo thinking. Similarly, we encourage the next generation of college access and choice researchers to read widely, reflect deeply, develop communities with common goals and diversity of thought, and engage the wisdom of communities of Color all to create space for the possibilities of future research.

As we have discussed throughout this book, knowledge exists both within and beyond the walls of the Ivory Tower. We do not suggest that one form of knowledge is better than another, but instead we have used this book to center the knowledges, voices, and experiences of POC both within and beyond academia to ground how we continue to know and understand college access and choice. We call for future research that continues this ethos with even more intentionality by being transdisciplinary in nature—working in collaboration between academic disciplines as well as with community-based knowledge bearers to transcend the boundaries of any one perspective in pursuit of research with the common goal of keeping the assets, challenges, needs, and desires of POC at the center in college access and choice.

While our book centers the experiences of students of Color within the United States, many of these students (as well as our book contributors) lead transnational lives, meaning they have lived in other countries or have parents who did and are now raising them in homes heavily influenced by those countries' contexts and cultures. This is reflected in the African students in George Mwangi's chapter and the refugee students in Luu's chapter for example. Students of Color are also not bound to a US-centric worldview that is white- and western-dominated by concepts such as adolescent autonomy and individualism as highlighted by Yellow Bird et al. and Carey. The chapters presented demonstrate the imperative of continuing to decenter this worldview in how we understand college-going identity, access, and choice for students of Color, and instead develop and engage frameworks that integrate the local and Indigenous with the global and transnational.

The next generation of scholarship should address college access inequities for individuals marginalized by race and ethnicity around the world. Efforts to reduce societal inequity via access to higher education are challenged worldwide by factors such as geopolitical tensions and the COVID-19 pandemic, which amplified education, health, and economic disparities. These impacts are not equitably distributed as women, racially and ethnically minoritized communities, Indigenous communities, people with disabilities, people with low incomes, immigrants, and other marginalized communities have and will continue to be disparately impacted (Goldin & Muggah, 2020; Santos, 2020).

Oppressions such as racism, anti-Blackness, and anti-indigeneity are not solely US phenomena, nor are they bound by geographic borders. Instead, they move beyond as well as through national boundaries situated within colonial and imperialist contexts. We need comparative and cross-nation studies emphasizing how countries are approaching inequity in higher education access to understand the global reproduction of inequity that both impacts and is reified by education systems worldwide. Research that works with communities of Color across national borders to understand their approaches, strategies, and knowledge for navigating college going can be used as a tool to build global solidarity and mobilization for improved access.

College access and choice scholarship can create clear bridges between K–12 and higher education within a single study; yet even this scholarship can fall short in engaging students' lived educational experiences beyond a snapshot in time. Being able to connect the educational experiences of students of Color across multiple years and moments is critical. We recognize that longitudinal studies can be costly and time-consuming for both researchers and participants. Yet, we offer the idea of building authentic and long-standing relationships with communities of Color so that "checking in" with these communities and being embedded within them becomes part of the relational process of being a researcher, similar to the work of the Caring Health Center described by Barber and the work of the Student Bridges Agency described by Correa and Ruiz. This approach would also allow for expanding the ways in which we consider how the choice process impacts students and how they think about themselves and engage into the future. Research should include examining not just future college GPA and retention but also the self-worth of students of Color, their well-being, and connection to family and community. These are factors that humanize these students and their families and communities as well as acknowledge and seek to mitigate the cost, described as *la cascara*, or the callus, by Ruíz Santana, of engaging the college-going process among students of Color.

We call for researchers to engage in scholarship that acknowledges the experiences of students of Color and their families and communities beyond a single college choice or access process. For example, as highlighted by Carey, George Mwangi, and Luu, the college choice process creates ripple effects in students' families and communities in diverse ways and future studies can examine the role of family across college access, transitions, and persistence for students of Color. It is important to understand how the college choice process impacts families as well as how family relationships impact or are impacted by a student who is enrolled in college. Understanding how families engage in college processes and how this engagement evolves over time can provide further insights into this important influence in students' lives.

A Letter to Students of Color

In chapter 1, we wrote a letter of gratitude to scholars of Color who laid the groundwork and foundation for this book and for research about college access and choice within communities of Color. Here, we write a letter to students of Color likened to James Baldwin's (1962) "A Letter to My Nephew." In his letter, Baldwin shares his perspective about the United States on the 100th anniversary of enslavement's end and provides his nephew words of affirmation, validation, and hope without sugarcoating the racist context that surrounds them. In one excerpt he states:

> You don't be afraid. I said it was intended that you should perish, in the ghetto, perish by never being allowed to go beyond and behind the white man's definition, by never being allowed to spell your proper name. You have, and many of us have, defeated this intention. . . . It will be hard, James, but you come from sturdy peasant stock, men who picked cotton, dammed rivers, built railroads, and in the teeth of the most terrifying odds, achieved an unassailable and monumental

dignity. You come from a long line of great poets, some of the greatest poets since Homer. One of them said, "The very time I thought I was lost, my dungeon shook and my chains fell off." (Baldwin, 1962, para. 5–6)

Baldwin's words continue to ring true today, and inspired by the ethos of his letter, we pen one to students of Color (SoC) across ages and stages:

Dear SoC,

We see you and your brilliance, and we want your light to shine forever brightly. Yet, writing this letter is difficult because we know that colleges and universities are a place that can often dim our light as they seek to "enlighten" us. Throughout the admissions process you are told that you have to make yourself worthy of acceptance into higher education and the importance of you being a "fit" in those spaces. Well, we're here to tell you that colleges and universities are fortunate to have your presence on their campuses, not the other way around. Many of these colleges and universities were built on the backs of our enslaved ancestors, on the land of our forcibly displaced ancestors, and cleaned and cared for by our underpaid and undervalued ancestors. Colleges and universities are reckoning with this history that has continued to impact our present. Higher education institutions need you because they will not survive without you in their classrooms and our society will not thrive without you attaining a college education. Just like the frameworks shared in this book, you bring innovation, diverse forms of thought, multiple cultures and identities, and the representation of our world to campus spaces. They know your worth, even if they will not say it, and so we say it to you. Remember that you choose them too and even if that choice is limited or is not your first preference, your power and value and brilliance remain with you.

Despite needing you, colleges and universities are not doing enough to change the barriers to make your access, your choice, and your college journey smooth. Keep in mind, not every journey into and through college is linear. A college degree for some represents years of commitment, one class at a time. For others it has meant starting and stopping multiple times to respond to other critical life events. Transfers from community college or between 4-year colleges are common college pathways. Each of us has college experiences that represent a journey reflective of the barriers—sometimes leading to a complete impasse—and as a result we want your journey to be impacted by your choices, your dreams, your inspirations, and real-life opportunities. It doesn't need to be linear, but we want it to be your choice, including the detours or redirects you take. To be clear though, for many of you, the detours you may have to face are a result of systematic barriers that keep us from moving forward. We can't stop making this known; when you recognize these barriers, speak on them; the barriers are not because of you but you may experience them. Be watchful of the small print; be mindful of putting your signature on any contracts, loans, or commitments; be curious and ask questions about how each course you take contributes to you reaching your goals of graduation. The truth is that some courses in 2-year colleges exist to cool your aspirations and keep you stagnant, while others will connect you with faculty, student peers, and staff that can be your biggest champions to ensure your success and to support transfer to 4-year colleges if you so choose. Being informed and persistent, asking questions, and seeking clear and transparent communication about college access is your right and power.

Both of us have been asked the question, "If college is such a damaging space for students of Color, should we still advocate that these students attend?" This is a question we constantly grapple with, but we always come to the same conclusion, which is "yes." While we don't suggest that college is the only way to have a "good" life, we know that it can lead to a number of benefits for you financially, professionally, intellectually, socially, and otherwise. We also know that in a society steeped in white supremacy, alternatives to college may not be any less challenging. Instead of limiting your future possibilities, we instead ask that you go into college aware of what it is and what it isn't. It is a place where you can learn, grow, develop amazing relationships and community, and be accepted. But it's also a place where you can feel lonely, invalidated, experience racism and other forms of prejudice, and be rejected. Unless you attend a historically Black college and university (HBCU) or tribal college and university (TCU), most of the college and university options were not created with you in mind and still are not doing enough to keep you in mind. It's important that you go to college with eyes wide open, knowing that campuses will not save or spare you from harm and may even perpetuate harm against you.

Despite the challenges, we both had transformative experiences as college students and wish the same for you. As you engage in the college choice process, we encourage you to start as early as possible and connect with programs and people that can share their knowledge about college with you. This could be your school counselor and teachers, but also consider others in your network—if you work, talk to your boss; if you play a sport, talk to your coach; if you are part of a religious organization, talk to the leadership; talk to your family members or people in their network who have gone to college—these individuals will likely have a sense of who you are and what you may need. The internet and social media also have lots of great information, but we know it can get overwhelming—federal and state government websites as well as college and university websites (those that end in .gov and .edu) are typically reliable in terms of timelines and requirements for applications and financial aid. And if there are programs available in your area about college and how to get accepted, look into them as long as they are affordable (or free)—having a support network is key to helping you stay on track with the college-going process.

As you seek out colleges and universities, check their websites not just for academics, cost, and admissions requirements (which are all important), but also look for the breakdown of their student demographics and for organizations that have students of Color who might be willing to speak to you about their experiences and how to navigate the institution (similar to the Student Bridges Agency organization that was discussed in chapter 8). They may be able to provide additional insight on the admissions process and can be a source of support if you end up attending their institution. Pay attention to the cost of college, but more so of what it will cost *you*—use the Free Application for Federal Student Aid (FAFSA) to determine what the total cost of each college or university you're looking at is going to ultimately be after financial aid is taken into consideration (net cost). And remember that no college or university is perfect—it is likely that your goals can be accomplished at lots of different institutions and so consider how this may be possible in order to widen your set of options for a college degree.

And when you get to college, we encourage you to find your people—those that affirm you and understand you and uplift you. They may be easy to find or they may be more challenging to find, but when you do, ensure that you support and take care of one another. Know that the talents, skills, culture, and knowledge you bring to your college experience have value whether or not you see them reflected in your textbooks or those that surround you. Finally, college is a path not easily traveled, so please be kind to yourself as you move through your experience. You are courageous and strong, but you also deserve grace and care.

Being in the university may disconnect you from your family, community, and connection to your cultural, spiritual, and ancestral supports. In fact, you may desire some distance at this stage for your own development, but always remember who you are and that you do not have to give up any of yourself to be successful in and get through college. At predominantly and historically white institutions, it may be difficult to find food, prayer, dialect, music, academic programs, salutations, or social practices that make you feel a sense of belonging. That can be difficult and can contribute to a real experience of isolation or weathering—a process by which accumulated stress can impact your well-being. Seeking out connections, friendships, social groups, and support is essential for maintaining wellness and balance throughout your college experience. You know what makes you flourish. Finding a way to connect with people who respect and value you for who you are is key. Many universities have community engagement and civic leadership programs that create opportunities for academic and community partnerships. Student-led unions, organizations, cultural groups, faith groups, arts, and wellness programs frequently include a wide range of interests and points of connection. These can be great ways to find peer groups and faculty committed to causes that connect to your life path.

Getting into college and finishing doesn't define your worth—there are so many structures at play that act as barriers to us that aren't there for others (the cost of college may be one; having family with experience in college may be another). You are a whole and beautiful person no matter your relationship with college. Your family is valuable beyond measure, whether or not they have experienced college. Your ancestors and their histories are sources of your incomparable narrative and unique story. Their contributions to society have often been invisible though pivotal to the success of the privileged minority in society. But know this: there is still far too much work to be done to honor and reflect the real experiences of college choice and access among POC. We wish to convey our deep and steadfast belief in you and want to hear directly from you about what you believe is important, what needs to change, and how changes should be made in order to hold the door open for your sisters, your brothers, your mothers and fathers, your children, and the members of your community.

In solidarity, Dr. Chrystal and Dr. Yedalis

Conclusion

As we stated at the onset of this book, broad gains have been made in college access. Yet, there are still major racial disparities in enrollment as well as racial stratification in where students attend college and in what capacity—both of which impact students' outcomes. While there are numerous existing strategies seeking to mitigate these inequities, our approach throughout this book is in starting from the standpoints, experiences, and knowledge of POC. Throughout each chapter we have offered diverse ways to frame access and complicate choice within the context of higher education and beyond as developed by POC with and for communities of Color. By sharing youth-centered, community-grown, and culture- and family-oriented frameworks, we do not provide all of the solutions. Instead, we have offered a volume that can serve in unsettling the boundaries of college access and choice scholarship by placing the knowledge, assets, and needs of POC at the center. This disruption to the status quo is necessary to awaken new approaches in pursuing racial equity in college access and to reinforce existing approaches that have centered and affirmed POC. Our final ask is that we move forward engaging two complicated tasks at once—continuing to fight against, dismantle, and resist racist structures that limit and prohibit the college access and choice of people of Color while also sustaining, reinforcing, and validating the knowledge, skills, and assets that people of Color bring to our process and our choice in college access.

Critical Reflection

1. How will you continue to fight against, dismantle, and resist racist structures that limit and prohibit the college access and choice of people of Color?

2. How will you sustain, reinforce, and validate the knowledge, skills, and assets of people of Color that are brought to the process of college access and choice?

3. Drawing from bell hooks and other POC scholars and practitioners, what tools and strategies will you add to your work to engage critically and reflexively to drive this work forward?

References

Baldwin, J. (1962). A letter to my nephew. *The Progressive, 1*, 160–164.

George Mwangi, C. A. (2018). "It's different here": Complicating concepts of college knowledge and first generation through an immigrant lens. *Teachers College Record, 120*(11), 1–36.

Goldin, I., & Muggah, R. (2020). *COVID-19 is increasing multiple kinds of inequality. Here's what we can do about it.* World Economic Forum. https://www.weforum.org/agenda/2020/10/covid-19-is-increasing-multiple-kinds-of-inequality-here-s-what-we-can-do-about-it/

hooks, bell. (2018). *All about love: New visions* (First William Morrow paperback edition). William Morrow, an imprint of HarperCollins.

Santos, B. S. (2020). *A cruel pedagogia do vírus.* Coimbra: Edições Almedina, S. A.

Contributors

Dr. Nancy Acevedo is Professor in Educational Leadership Doctoral Studies at California State University, San Bernardino (CSUSB). As an interdisciplinary scholar, she uses critical race theory and Chicana feminist theories to examine transitions along the higher education pipeline for Latina/o/x students. With her research, she advocates for equitable opportunities to college preparation and aligning college access with college completion. She was Inaugural Faculty Scholar in Residence at the UC Davis Wheelhouse Center for Community College Leadership and Research, Research Fellow for the Latinx Research Center at Santa Clara University, and Inaugural Diversity, Equity, and Inclusion Faculty Fellow for CSUSB. A first-generation college student from a low-income background, she earned her BA from the University of California, Berkeley; MA from San Jose State University; and her PhD in education with a focus on race and ethnic studies from the University of California, Los Angeles.

Joel A. Arce is a PhD candidate in the College of Education at the University of Massachusetts Amherst. His research examines the neoliberal and dehumanizing conditions that pervade the educational experiences of (racially) minoritized youth in the United States. He is particularly interested in the ways critical ethnic studies has and can be an avenue to transform public education and build power within and across intersectional social movements. Joel is in the process of completing his dissertation, which is an ethnographic case study that provides context-specific insights around the tensions, limitations, and possibilities of implementing ethnic studies in secondary public schools.

Tania M. Barber is President/CEO at Caring Health Center (CHC), a federally qualified health center (FQHC) in Springfield, Massachusetts.

She has been at CHC for 27 years and was steadily promoted, having begun as switchboard operator before stepping into her current role in 2013. She is the president/CEO and founder of the newly launched Tania M. Barber Learning Institute, a FQHC-led workforce equity and learning model with a mission to serve as a leader in access and equity in FQHCs through a "lifting others up" framework. Mrs. Barber holds a Bachelor of Administration degree in organization management and a Master of Business Administration degree in entrepreneurial thinking and innovative practices. Mrs. Barber serves and has served on boards at Massachusetts League of Community Health Centers, Mass-Hire, Health New England, Florence Bank, Bay Path University, and the Community Care Cooperative (C3). She believes in creating pathways of advancement for her employees and nurtures educational accomplishments and diversity within the organizations' workforce. She is the founder and pastor of Living Water Global Ministries and founder of EST.HER, LLC, and Touch Healing Encounter—TOUCH: Transformation Offers Undeniable Complete Healing. Mrs. Barber is a John Maxwell independent certified coach, speaker, and trainer.

Dr. Nolan Cabrera is Professor in the Center for the Study of Higher Education at the University of Arizona. He studies racial dynamics on college campuses, with a particular focus on whiteness. Dr. Cabrera is also involved in the controversy surrounding the Tucson Unified School District's former Mexican American Studies program. He is a recipient of the Spencer/National Academy of Education postdoctoral fellowship. Dr. Cabrera's publications have appeared in leading education and higher education journals such as *American Educational Research Journal, Review of Higher Education, Journal of College Student Development*, and *Research in Higher Education*, and his work has been used extensively in education, policy, and legal environments. Dr. Cabrera is a UA College of Education Erasmus Scholar, Emerging Scholar for the American College Personnel Association, Faculty Affiliate with UT Austin's Project M.A.L.E.S., and Faculty Fellow for the American Association for Hispanics in Higher Education. He completed his graduate work at UCLA in Higher Education & Organizational Change and earned his BA from Stanford University in Comparative Studies in Race and Ethnicity (education focus). He is a former director of a Boys & Girls Club in the San Francisco Bay Area and is originally from McMinnville, Oregon.

Dr. Roderick L. Carey is Associate Professor in the Department of Human Development and Family Sciences, in the College of Education and Human Development at the University of Delaware. His interdisciplinary research explores the school experiences of Black and Latino adolescent boys and young men in urban contexts, drawing from critical theories, sociology, and developmental psychology. He employs primarily qualitative approaches in researching and writing about Black boy "mattering" and the ways Black and Latino adolescent boys and young men conceptualize their postsecondary school futures and enact college-going processes. Prior to earning his PhD in curriculum and instruction with a concentration on minority and urban education from the University of Maryland College Park, he spent four years working in urban charter schools in Washington, DC, as a high school English teacher, coach, performing arts coordinator, and instructional leader. Roderick received his EdM in human development and psychology from the Harvard University Graduate School of Education and his BA in secondary education and English from the Lynch School of Education and Human Development of Boston College. His articles have been published in outlets like the *American Educational Research Journal, Journal of Adolescent Research, Harvard Educational Review, American Journal of Education, Race Ethnicity and Education, Educational Administration Quarterly*, and *Urban Education*, to name a few. He is Associate Editor for the *Journal of Adolescent Research* and serves on the editorial boards of *Urban Education* and *Equity & Excellence in Education*.

Dr. Ashley Carpenter is Assistant Professor in the Higher Education Program at Appalachian State University. She is an interdisciplinary scholar-practitioner working toward advancing equity and accessibility through K–12 and higher education pipeline pathways. As an arts-based methodologist, her work (re)humanizes education and challenges how academic socialization perpetuates neoliberalism and systemic marginalization, emphasizing participant action research. Prior to becoming a faculty member, she worked as a college administrator focused on recruiting and retaining minoritized graduate students—which now informs her teaching on higher education history, law, policy, and diversity topics. Her work has been published in the *Journal of College Student Development, Journal of Black Studies, Critical Studies in Education*, and the *Journal of Negro Education*. Ultimately, her mission is to pursue innovative, evidence-based practices to broaden participation and success in postsecondary education.

Olga M. Correa is a first-generation, Afro-Latina doctoral candidate in educational leadership at the University of Massachusetts Amherst. Her current research interest encompasses the influence that societal factors, namely race and class, have had on K–12 education policy and practice. In her dissertation, Olga uses qualitative methods to explore the multifaceted ways in which Black and Latino/a parents/guardians understand, participate in, or resist school choice in a medium-size affluent suburban community in the Northeast. Olga also serves as the director of the Cesar E. Chavez Multicultural Center at Lansing Community College where she oversees multifaceted comprehensive student support programs and implements strategies to promote a sense of belonging and inclusion for historically marginalized communities.

Dr. Chrystal A. George Mwangi is Associate Professor of Higher Education at George Mason University. As a transnational Black scholar, a central focus of her research examines access to educational opportunity for American and immigrant youth of Color. She draws from critical, participatory, and African-centered frameworks to understand the experiences of youth and their families navigating college access as well as the social-cultural-political-historical systems impacting this process. Her work has been published in journals including *Harvard Educational Review*, *Higher Education*, *Research in Higher Education*, *Review of Higher Education*, and *Teachers College Record*. She is Senior Associate Editor for the *Review of Higher Education*. Prior to becoming a faculty member, she worked for several years as a college administrator, including positions in undergraduate admissions, multicultural affairs, student conduct, and academic advising.

Dr. Diep H. Luu is Associate Dean in the Office of the Vice Chancellor and Director of the Undergraduate Advising Center at the Massachusetts Institute of Technology (MIT). Despite the odds of being a first-generation college student from low-income and refugee backgrounds, he earned his PhD in educational policy and leadership with a higher education concentration from the University of Massachusetts Amherst. His dissertation examined the role of community cultural wealth in college access and transition among students from refugee backgrounds, integrating an antideficit perspective, narrative inquiry research methods, and nearly two decades of experience helping college students succeed. His research focuses on college access, transition, and equity and student success among students from refugee backgrounds and other underserved student populations. His work has been published in the *Journal of Comparative and International Higher Education, Higher Education Policy, Comparative Education Review,* and *Studies in Higher Education.*

Dr. Judy Marquez Kiyama is Professor in the Center for the Study of Higher Education, Department of Educational Policy Studies and Practice, at the University of Arizona. Dr. Kiyama is a community-engaged scholar with nearly 25 years' experience in research, practice, and administration. Working alongside Latinx/o/a families and communities is at the core of Dr. Kiyama's research efforts. Her research is organized in three interconnected areas: the role of parents and families; equity and power in educational research; and minoritized groups as collective networks of change. It is through this collective work that Dr. Kiyama believes we can effect equitable change at organizational, local, state, and national levels.

Anastasia (Stasia) Morton, as a mother, New York City native, educator, creative director, facilitator, curriculum developer, fundraiser, event planner, an alumna of the Accelerated Studies in Associates Program at LaGuardia Community College, recipient of the Kaplan Educational Foundation scholarship and Passport to Leadership: Advanced Leadership Certificate receiver, Frances Perkins Scholar, Phi Theta Kappa member, and dynamic member of the Pioneer Valley community, wears many hats. She is passionate about education that empowers silenced youth by teaching them the importance of understanding and exploring internal and external identity, cultural capital, individual leadership style, the power of one's voice, and the individual narrative. Every day her enthusiasm and drive to see her students succeed creates a contagious atmosphere that propels them to see the best in themselves and excel in whatever future they choose. Since graduating in May of 2012 from Mount Holyoke College with a bachelor's degree in psychology and educational studies, she has worked as an AmeriCorps VISTA member, then as the Amherst Regional Public Schools' Family Center's youth leadership coordinator, overseeing programs such as Middle School Lunch Groups and Growing Up in Hip Hop workshops, Success after High School College Access Preparation, and the Look Forward/Look Back project with young men of Color. She moved from her coordinator position to a position co-teaching a Black Feminism class with Dr. Tammy Owens at Hampshire College, then teaching Social Justice Math to high school students from the High School of

Commerce through the UMass Upward Bound summer program to her current position as Upward Bound's assistant director of academic support. She continuously works to bridge the communication gap between families, schools, and government officials, ensuring the creation of youth services that encourage learners to break the chains of generational poverty and practice the skills necessary to increase their net worth through financial literacy, recognizing the importance of social awareness and confidence all throughout one's academic and life journey.

Kelsey Ruiz is a first-generation, Puerto Rican scholar-practitioner. Since her undergraduate career, Kelsey has invested in the practice of community engagement and preparatory mentorship to enhance pathways to higher education for first-generation, underrepresented, and BIPOC college aspirants. Kelsey is currently a doctoral student at Northeastern University concentrating on transformational school leadership. Her research examines systemic racial barriers and deconstructs college access models and frameworks that are associated with whiteness in higher education. Kelsey centers students' voices in service learning and community engagement on college campuses and local communities as counternarratives to whiteness and deficit perspectives.

Dr. Yedalis Ruíz Santana is a first-generation Puertorriqueña scholar-practitioner. She is the chief access and equity officer and executive director of the Tania M. Barber Learning Institute at Caring Health Center, a federally qualified community health center. Dr. Ruíz Santana leads the development of a workforce equity model that promotes advocacy, access, and equity through workforce development educational tools and programs designed to enhance the success, retention, and personal development of CHC's diverse employee community. Dr. Ruíz Santana earned her bachelor's degree in psychology and education from Mount Holyoke College and graduated with honors and Phi Beta Kappa. She holds a master's degree in policy studies, as well as a PhD in education, policy, research, and administration from the University of Massachusetts Amherst with a concentration in higher education focused on urban education, access, and equity with emphasis on first-generation students, BIPOC communities, and adult learners. She is a quantitative and qualitative researcher and is trained in educational program evaluation and assessment methodologies. Dr. Ruíz Santana is faculty affiliate at UMass Amherst's College of Education and teaches foundational courses on professional practice and career development, equity, justice, and antiracist frameworks. She has been Adjunct Professor for the American Women's College at Bay Path University since 2013.

Dr. Amanda R. Tachine is Navajo from Ganado, Arizona. She is Náneeshtʼézhí Táchiiʼnii (Zuni Red Running into Water) born for Tłʼízí łání (Many Goats). She is Assistant Professor in Educational Studies at University of Oregon. Amanda's research explores the relationship between systemic and structural histories of settler colonialism and the ongoing erasure of Indigenous presence and belonging in college settings using qualitative Indigenous methodologies. She is the author of the award-winning book *Native Presence and Sovereignty in College: Sustaining Indigenous Weapons to Defeat Systemic Monsters* and co-editor (alongside the lovely Z Nicolazzo) of *Weaving an Otherwise: In-relations Methodological Practice*. She has published in the *Journal of Higher Education*, *Qualitative Inquiry*, *International Review of Qualitative Research*, *International Journal of Qualitative Studies in Education*, and other scholarly outlets. She also has published thought pieces and essays in the *Huffington Post*, *Al Jazeera*, *The Hill*, *Teen Vogue*, *Indian Country Today*, *Inside Higher Ed*, *Navajo Times*, and *Marvel*, where she advances ideas regarding discriminatory actions, educational policies, and inspirational movements.

Dr. Eliza Yellow Bird is from Mandaree, North Dakota, and is an enrolled member of the Mandan, Hidatsa and Arikara Nation. She has over a decade of experience working in higher education advocating for marginalized students and challenging systemic barriers within academia. Her PhD is in educational policies and practice from the University of Arizona. Her dissertation explored settler colonial systems within higher education and how first-generation Native students navigate these spaces. Her research interests are access and retention of underrepresented students, specifically Indigenous students, in higher education. Overall, she is dedicated to supporting and advocating for all students on their path in academia and beyond.

Index

References to notes show the page number and the note number (153n2).

330 | Index

www.ingramcontent.com/pod-product-compliance
Lightning Source LLC
Chambersburg PA
CBHW021116270326
41929CB00009B/913